First Resorts

⇒ JON STERNGASS ⇒

FIRST RESORTS

Pursuing Pleasure at Saratoga Springs, Newport & Coney Island

The Johns Hopkins University Press

Baltimore & London

© 2001 The Johns Hopkins University Press
All rights reserved. Published 2001
Printed in the United States of America on acid-free paper
2 4 6 8 9 7 5 3 1

The Johns Hopkins University Press
2715 North Charles Street
Baltimore, Maryland 21218-4363
www.press.jhu.edu

Library of Congress Cataloging-in-Publication Data
Sterngass, Jon.
First resorts : pursuing pleasure at Saratoga Springs, Newport, and Coney Island /
Jon Sterngass.
p. cm.
Includes bibliographical references and index.
ISBN 0-8018-6586-7 (acid-free paper)
1. United States—Social life and customs—19th century.   2. United States—Social
conditions—19th century.   3. Tourism—Social aspects—United States—History—
19th century.   4. Resorts—East (U.S.)—History—19th century.   5. Saratoga
Springs (N.Y.)—Social life and customs—19th century.   6. Newport (R.I.)—Social
life and customs—19th century.   7. Coney Island (New York, N.Y.)—Social life
and customs—19th century.   I. Title.
E166 .S87 2001
973.5—dc21
00-011513

A catalog record for this book is available from the British Library.

Title page illustration: Courtesy of the Museum of the City of New York.

Contents

Acknowledgments

This book has had an unusually long gestation period. It dates as far back as the many wonderful summers I spent at Camp Boiberik outside of Rhinebeck, New York, where I learned the pleasures of unusual rituals enacted in a setting far from home. While I was working on my master's degree in medieval history at the University of Wisconsin at Milwaukee, Jack McGovern piqued my interest in social and cultural history. Over numerous games of pinball, he encouraged any harebrained idea that came to my mind by repeating his own personal mantra: "There's an article in that." I know he would have been pleased that I actually got a book out of it. Several years of entertaining visitors in Carson City, Nevada, aroused my curiosity about the role of gambling in American history and the idea of a vacation as a secular pilgrimage.

Richard Wade helped me through my examinations at the City University of New York and also suggested the topic of this book for my dissertation. My fellow graduate students insisted that multisite studies across an entire century were a dead paradigm and would never get published in an age of specialization. Professor Wade simply advised me, in his inimitable way, that "a paradigm is worth less than five nickels"; it gives me great satisfaction that he was at least partially correct. Thomas Kessner spent five years propping me up when I was depressed and bringing me back to earth when I thought I actually knew something. If I am still "circling the topic," I do so despite his best efforts. Josh Freeman, Gerald Markowitz, and Kathleen McCarthy all read early drafts and offered incisive and useful commentary. Katherine Kimball copyedited away hundreds of grammatical errors and awkward phrasings. Any and all errors in fact and interpretation in this book are strictly my own responsibility.

Two special friends generously gave their time to read and correct later drafts. Ed Wheeler offered numerous valuable comments on chapter organization and tried desperately to fix my shaky sense of where to put the commas. I could not quite work in Odysseus, but please note the presence of "eelgrass." Bill Lissak, *geist fun der Bronx* and my best friend, helped cut out innumerable superfluous digressions. He also possesses the rare perspicacity to realize that Nolan Ryan does not deserve to be in the Hall of Fame.

At Union College, Bob Wells has filled numerous roles for me, including boss, confidant, and purveyor of useful and practical advice. I owe the college itself a debt of gratitude for picking up the massive interlibrary loan bills, and kudos to Jane Earley for her help with all the copying. When the going got tough, Joyce Madancy and Andy Foroughi lent a ready ear, and Steve Berk and Steve Sargent chipped in with a kind word. Harriet Temps performed the same crucial functions with verve at the State University of New York at Albany.

A list of the numerous archives, libraries, and historical societies I have used would run into several pages, but I would like to single out some people who helped above and beyond the call of duty: Joan Youngken at the Newport Historical Society, Martha Stonequist at the Saratoga Springs City Historian's Office, Jean Stamm and Ellen deLalla at the Saratoga Springs Public Library, and Field Horne at the National Museum of Racing in Saratoga. Special thanks are also due to the hardworking librarians at the following archives (listed alphabetically): the Brooklyn Historical Society, the Brooklyn Public Library, the New York City Municipal Archives, the main branch of the New York City Public Library, the New York State Library in Albany, the New York State Historical Association at Cooperstown, the New York State Historical Society in Manhattan, the Saratoga County Clerk's Office in Ballston Spa, the Saratoga Springs Historical Museum, and the Skidmore College Library. Far from home, I received a friendly welcome at the Rhode Island Historical Society, the Southern History Collection at the University of North Carolina, and the Duke University Manuscripts Collection.

I would like to say thanks also to some people who have had little to do with the writing of this book but whose friendship has served me well over the years. Arthur Green, Elaine Goldberg, and Bev Jones all inspired me to become a better teacher, and Altina Waller gave me the opportunity to work at the college level. Dewar MacLeod always served as a benchmark, a sounding board, and a friend—I'll get to Montclair someday! Susan Daitch refused to read any drafts until it was too late, but I like her anyway. An old and special apartment mate, Mike "Mango" Mangasarian, provided endless Rhode Island color. Though he has been in Asia for many years now, rare is the week that I do not miss Marc Schiffman. May the age of laser printers never ruin the pleasure of receiving a handwritten letter from Jane Buder-Shapiro. Don Rubien does not need to read about an ideal fete, because for a brief moment, we (with Bill Lissak) were the carnival in Rio de Janeiro in 1985!

My sister, Amy Starr, inspired my love of leisure by taking me to Broadway shows when we were kids in Brooklyn; I am belatedly sorry I ate all the cheese off her slice of pizza. My parents, Jack and Adele Sterngass, continued to take me to Steeplechase Park and Coney Island over the years, despite my temper tantrum in front of Nathan's at the age of two.

One of the great pleasures of publishing a book is to be able to say in print how much I love my children, Eli ("Santy Anna"; Refrigerator Hockey League; "Little Pic"; Pat Day; marble mosaic races; Pup) and Aaron ("Sweet Thames, Flow Softly"; blankie-blankie; "This Old Man"; *Conga Crocodile;* "go that way"; Bunny). My life would be incomparably impoverished without them. This book is dedicated with all my love to my wife, Karen Weltman, whose support made it possible and without whom the sun would not rise and the moon would not shine.

≋ INTRODUCTION ≋

Transforming Resorts

AT THE DAWN of the nineteenth century, Saratoga Springs hosted no more than a thousand hardy travelers yearly, Newport floundered in the midst of a fifty-year commercial decline, and Coney Island's beach resembled a wind-swept wilderness. A hundred years later, the number of summer visitors to Saratoga had increased a hundredfold, the antics of high society at Newport transfixed America, and at least five million pleasure seekers visited Coney annually. "Those who talk of the mushroom growth of our Western cities," declared an astounded writer for *Harper's Weekly* in 1878, "might better spend their wonder and enthusiasm upon our Eastern watering-place."[1] Simply to speak the names of these resorts now evokes a host of images that help define the nineteenth and early twentieth centuries. Yet despite changes so dramatic in scope and scale, most studies of American resorts continue to concentrate on a single locale and are often limited to a specific time period. This book examines instead three quintessential American resorts across the sweep of an entire century. This approach allows the analysis to transcend local peculiarities or momentary aberrations and to highlight the general commodification of pleasure that occurred as capitalist values spread across the United States.

Although Saratoga, Newport, and Coney Island eventually offered distinct resort experiences, an onlooker who visited each site at the midpoint of their nineteenth-century development would be struck by the similarities more than the differences. At all three pleasure destinations, "grand" hotels dominated the scene, surrounded by vast public and semipublic spaces filled with gregarious and heterogeneous crowds. It is this similarity that makes their ultimate independent development all the more intriguing. By the first decade of the twentieth century, vacationers continued to swarm through busy Saratoga verandas, dining rooms, and parlors. In contrast, Newport's hotel industry, so prominent before 1860, had completely collapsed, replaced by the private "cottages" built by America's plutocrats. At Coney Island, three large amusement parks stole the spotlight from the island's hotels and became the focal point not only of many visitors' journeys but also of the periodical press.

Change is the stock-in-trade of the historian's craft, and the creation, subsequent popularity, and ultimate transformation of Saratoga, Newport, and Coney Island raise a host of questions about nineteenth-century American culture. Why did Americans begin to travel for pleasure in the first place? Did the attractions of each destination remain constant, or did they vary over time? Why did specific resorts develop divergent forms, often differentiated by social class? How unique was Coney Island, the realm of the day-tripper, compared with its higher-status competitors? To what extent were these watering places the forerunners of twentieth-century pleasure cities such as Las Vegas, Anaheim, Aspen, and Orlando?

The word *transforming* used in relation to these resorts implies several simultaneous meanings. On the most basic level, American resorts did not function in 1900 as they had in the middle of the nineteenth century. In their formative period, free mineral springs and beaches and enormous hotel verandas, parlors, and dining rooms perfectly accommodated promenading, flirting, and other noncommercial interactions. The social setting, as well as many of the amusements, allowed women more freedom than they enjoyed at home. Travelers could luxuriate in anonymity, alter their public personas, or search for ways to bond with strangers they otherwise would never have met. Both resort natives and sojourners perceived themselves as being on stage, performing before all the world in a vivacious culture of theatricality and masquerade. The experience encouraged a sort of voyeurism; participants attempted to decode the mystery of other people's social masks, all the while hiding behind disguises of their own. The first half of this book presents this quasi-democratic resort world in which all could "see and be seen."

Most of this playfulness disappeared, however, as commercialized leisure, souvenir hunting, and status seeking in restricted private settings undermined the social and personal possibilities of travel. The second half of this book chronicles changes at Saratoga, Newport, and Coney Island that mirrored the emerging belief that happiness could be achieved through consumption, an ideal based on immediate gratification and personal self-fulfillment often expressed through material possession. The increasing primacy of money can be glimpsed in the creation and popularity of Saratoga's nationally renowned gambling houses and horse-racing track. At Newport, the ultrarich converted their capital into the grandiose mansions that helped define the term *conspicuous consumption.* Coney Island's amusement park entrepreneurs marketed leisure experience by structuring it as a salable commodity, consolidating amusements, erecting fences, charging admission, and achieving an economy of scale similar to that of other industrial enterprises such as sugar and steel. More and more, American resorts subdivided the undifferentiated crowd into niche markets and promoted the idea that the pursuit of pleasure required the payment of money.

These resorts were transformed by, but also had a transforming effect on, American society. If the range of the visitor's experience narrowed as the century progressed, Saratoga, Newport, and Coney Island still reveal a nineteenth-century culture far less earnest and more pleasure loving than stereotypical portrayals. For every repressive etiquette manual, a tourist guidebook could be found promising mobility, pleasure, and freedom; for every Chautauqua lecture, there was a purposeless promenade down an airy veranda or beach. "The American people can no longer be reproached for not taking any summer recreation," noted the novelist, Charles Dudley Warner, in 1886 in an eight-part series on summer resorts aptly entitled "Their Pilgrimage." For in no other nation, he concluded, "is there such a general summer hegira, no other offers on such a vast scale such variety of entertainments. . . . There are resorts suited to all tastes and to the economical as well as to the extravagant."[2]

Some of the rhetoric, then and now, regarding the American penchant for work and self-improvement must be tempered by a midnight visit to John Morrissey's Club House in Saratoga, a morning on Easton's Beach in Newport, or an afternoon at the Coney Island Jockey Club. Many trends typically associated with twentieth-century America, such as the growth of commercial leisure industries and advertising, the creation of mass markets, and an increase in the proportion of income spent on consumption, have deep roots in the development of these resorts. Saratoga's track and casino both predate the Gilded Age, summer visitors built Newport cottages as early as the 1840s, and a hundred thousand people visited Coney Island on summer Sundays in the 1870s. When viewed from the beaches, racetracks, shops, or grand hotels of nineteenth-century resorts, the supposed turn-of-the-century transition from sterile "Victorian" values (e.g., gentility, production, and sexual separation) to a "modern" culture of vitality, consumption, and mixed-gender activities seems to be placed generations too late.[3]

A third sense of *transforming* is the effect that the first resorts had on the people who visited these places. The concept of ritual liminality yields a richer understanding of the attraction of these potentially magical places. According to this theoretical construct, society fits individuals into structures and defines their appropriate roles. People long for a deeper and less restrictive range of experience and participate in "liminoid rituals" whose symbols are in some way antithetical to the existing rules, hierarchies, and duties that usually govern social life. Certain intervals and actions acquire special meaning and become demarcated from the profane, and specific sites are associated with unusual experiences. This passage through a *limen* (Latin, "threshold") situates the participant in a period of transition and potentiality. In the twilight-zone world of liminality, the ritualist sheds customary responses; previous thoughts and behaviors can be subject to revision or criticism, and unprecedented modes of ordering relations between people and ideas become both desirable and possible.[4]

In the nineteenth century, Saratoga, Newport, and Coney Island served as liminal places, laboratories in which visitors could experiment with new or different ideas about the value of the work ethic, the significance of luxury in a democratic republic, the proper roles of men and women, and the relationship between community and privacy. American resorts offered a world in which participants could express themselves in ways that would normally have been proscribed by external judgments or internal censors. These public cities of play flowered in a society that supposedly revered the domestic hearth; they promoted a titillating culture of artificiality for people who claimed to detest hypocrisy, encouraged heterosocial leisure in an era dominated by the concept of a separate female sphere, and offered urbane pleasures for a nation with a strong antiurban streak.

By 1900, more Americans were traveling than ever before, but the market economy eroded the frisson so common in the antebellum watering place. A trip to the resort gradually lost its potential not only to reengineer society, undoubtedly a forlorn hope, but even to disturb the orderliness of social life. The quest for social status through spatial segregation made grand hotels, with their huge public spaces, seem anachronistic. Travelers ceased to think of themselves as pilgrims and tried to insulate themselves from a world of strangers. Preindustrial customs of hospitality prevailed only in commercialized form; the residents of resort cities feared and despised the tramp but revered the tourist as a (paying) guest and a source of potential prosperity for both individuals and communities.

Tourism has been a hallmark of modernity since the nineteenth century; while agglomerations of aristocratic villas by the sea predate Roman times, specialized mass resorts are among the most recent form of urban development. "The practice of summer travelling among the gentry and their imitators, is quite a modern affair," wrote John Watson in 1832. "Our forefathers, when our cities were small, found no place more healthy or attractive than their homes."[5] That, however, was before Americans began to flee the city, farm, or plantation for a day, week, or season, in search of some ineffable satisfaction. Less than sixty years later, *Century Magazine* reported that resort going had spread to every segment of the population:

> The rich and well-to-do middle classes appear most conspicuously, but the currents are swelled by small tradespeople, by pensioners on limited legacies. . . . Then come the work-people. . . . Your colored barber, when trade begins to slacken in the large town, informs you that he is thinking of taking a little vacation. The carpenter and joiner sends his wife and babies a hundred miles away to spend weeks or months on a farm that takes boarders. Factories frequently shut down for a week or more . . . professional men, college students, teachers, seamstresses, and fresh-air fund beneficiaries pour forth to the mountains, the seaside, the lakes.[6]

By 1998, 60 percent of American adults under the age of thirty rated "going away" as a "very important" feature of their lives; at the same time, approximately 7 percent of the world's workforce (more than 200 million people) were employed in tourism. The study of the origins and development of travel in the pursuit of pleasure is not mere nostalgic antiquarianism but is, rather, an examination of a leading world industry as well as a major component of American culture.[7]

For the most part, this pleasure travel was, and is, domestic in nature. In 1998, Americans made fewer than 60 million foreign journeys (including business trips) compared with more than 200 million visits to theme-type amusement parks and another 200 million summer trips to destinations a hundred miles or more away from home. Domestic tourist spending out-paced foreign expenditures by more than seven to one. The majority of Americans neither lust for adventure in Angkor Wat or Machu Picchu nor traipse through Europe or Mexico; even for visits of more than ten nights' duration, international trips constituted no more than 3 percent of the total. The typical American travelers who flood modern theme parks, casinos, and heritage sites are directly descended from the men and women who filled the spring, mountain, and seaside resorts of the nineteenth century.[8]

To visit is a transitive verb, and the act of traveling is a reciprocal activity. Any analysis of resort life needs to focus on both the visitor and the visited; the world created by their interaction reflects structures of meaning and dynamics of change in America. Cultural facts are often not expressed directly but reveal themselves in everyday acts, figures of speech, unconscious patterns of behavior, and the built environment. Latent social changes, repressed in more restrictive institutions or locations, can be studied at resorts, where people generally feel freer to challenge prevailing norms, exercise their fantasies, expand their horizons, and live their aspirations. Saratoga, Newport, and Coney Island served as American cultural symbols, no less than pilgrimage sites such as Jerusalem, Mecca, and Varanasi. Nineteenth-century American resorts embodied variations of the collective ideal and functioned as virtual holy centers for a secular society; the pursuit of pleasure at their springs, beaches, and hotels elucidates numerous aspects of American life.

The Creation of Saratoga Springs

Taking the City with Us

WHEN CONNECTICUT MIGRANT Gideon Putnam opened a three-story tavern adjacent to the springs at Saratoga, New York, in the first decade of the nineteenth century, the area's few residents mocked his optimism and ambition. Who, they wondered, would fill "Putnam's folly" in a rough frontier hamlet with a population of barely one thousand? Ignoring the conventional wisdom, Putnam laid out on paper a grandiose village around his tavern, with streets leading to free public fountains and an elm-bordered principal thoroughfare that measured an astonishing 120 feet in width. To attract visitors, he cleaned, tubed, and promoted several mineral water springs. To many, Putnam's effort seemed as productive as throwing money directly into the forest. But the Connecticut Yankee had the last laugh. By the end of the century, his tavern had become the Grand Union Hotel, among the most renowned hotels in the world, and hardly a single resort did not nourish ambitions of becoming another Saratoga Springs. Throughout the nineteenth century, Saratoga provided pleasure for visitors, profit for entrepreneurs, and a window to the values of the American people.[1]

Putnam certainly did not invent the concept of a mineral water spa. The ideology of the Reformation had suppressed pilgrimages to holy wells in England, a major form of the disguised recreational journey during the Middle Ages, but the English had simply created new excuses and new destinations. Resorts such as Bath, Buxton, and Tunbridge Wells served as secular alternatives in the seventeenth and eighteenth centuries, continuing the connection with holy water and bolstered by the justifications provided by Enlightenment science. These spas replaced the former pilgrimage centers, luring visitors who sought both hydrotherapy and entertainment.[2]

Several colonial American springs, borrowing the idea from the mother country, offered a setting in which planters and merchants could display their wealth on a grand scale. At the springs in western Virginia, the southern gentry took the waters, gambled on cards, drank corn whiskey, bet on horses, and flirted to an extent that astonished more sedate visitors. In the North, Boston merchants flocked to Stafford Springs in Connecticut in the 1760s, and urbane watering places outside Philadelphia, such as Yellow Springs and Bristol, also attracted sophisticated patrons. Although a relative Johnny-come-lately to this group of first resorts, Saratoga Springs initially enticed visitors with a similar program. Sojourners enjoyed the change in climate and scenery and ate and drank in vast quantities, hoping the healing waters would compensate for their indulgence.[3]

The springs of Saratoga owed some of their initial popularity to their medicinal utility. Many patients gladly chose to drink massive draughts of mineral water as an alternative to nineteenth-century treatments such as bloodletting, purgation, or opium-based painkillers. In an age of high mortality and puzzling epidemics, doctors emphasized hygiene as the key to their therapeutics, since most other treatments seemed futile. Theories of miasmatic contagion dominated antebellum medical science, and Americans who believed they had been infected breathing bad air searched desperately for climatic cures. City dwellers often chose flight as the best possible response to repeated cholera epidemics. Scoffers might decry the lack of scientific evidence favoring mineral water, but supporters claimed with equal validity that it was unscientific to deny the accumulated experience of millennia as to their efficacy. After all, doctors had administered remedies such as quinine, opium, mercury, and digitalis centuries before science could explain their action. Saratoga's springs reputedly cured everything from gastrointestinal complaints to gout, rheumatism to obesity. Each spring had its own devotees who argued endlessly over the abstruse advantages of various types of water. At Saratoga Springs, if the waters did not cure you, at least they did not kill you.[4]

Although located equidistant from New York, Boston, and Montreal, the springs of Saratoga did not boom overnight. The first European settlers appeared sporadically in the 1770s, but only Indians and local whites visited the hamlet until Philip Schuyler cut a path from his house on the Hudson to High Rock Spring in 1783. Six years later, Valentine Seaman's treatise on the mineral water drew attention to Saratoga. Dr. Benjamin Waterhouse, the physician who introduced Edward Jenner's method of inoculation into general practice in America, visited the area in the summer of 1794 and published a positive description in 1805. These accounts piqued the interest of the public, and people began to travel longer distances to examine the wondrous waters and upon their return home to describe what they had seen and experienced. Within a few years, Gideon Putnam's tavern had prospered sufficiently to add a parlor, a dining room, and a ballroom. Business was so good that, in 1811, Putnam began construction of another hotel, Congress Hall (figure 1).[5]

The success of Putnam's hotels drew several competitors. The Columbian Hotel, surrounded on three sides by gardens, opened in 1809, the Pavilion Hotel in 1819, and the original United States Hotel in 1823. A diarist in 1818 declared the town to be "one of the most unpleasant you ever saw" yet estimated the village's visitors at one thousand. Only four years later, Philip Stansbury, while on a two-thousand-mile walking tour, marveled that no place in America possessed "such magnificent boarding-houses, cupolas, and pavilions as Saratoga Springs." Even this building spree proved insufficient to house visitors in peak season. Jacques Milbert, a French traveler in the 1820s, was taken to a private home rented as an annex near one of the baths: "It was rather annoying to learn I was to share a room with three strangers, but I decided to accept the situation as Americans do."[6]

Many of the early visitors concocted tortured utilitarian, patriotic, moralistic, and aesthetic rationalizations to legitimate a stay at Saratoga. To pursue pleasure while meandering after health was one of the oldest subterfuges of the traveler, and the Romantics virtually perfected invalidism as a pretext for escaping mundane obligations. Rare was the antebellum guidebook that did not make reference to the necessity of evading the stifling summer heat of pestilential cities. Taking the waters at Saratoga, as in many cultures, combined sociability and therapeutics; the excursion not only alleviated suffering but also demonstrated possession of sufficient wealth to purchase leisure and travel time. Even at the popular water-cure establishments that so captured the antebellum American imagination, visitors eliminated the original austere treatment, based on five cold baths, and allowed billiard parlors, bowling alleys, and dance halls to infiltrate the sanitariums.

Figure 1. A greatly exaggerated depiction of the veranda of Congress Hall served as the cover illustration for "Saratoga-Galop," 1866. Note the black servant, or possibly slave, in the foreground. (Courtesy of the Saratoga Springs Public Library.)

Those travelers at Saratoga who claimed to visit for the sake of the waters were subjected to considerable teasing. Jacques Milbert noted that "time passes with a series of gay affairs; in the morning everyone drinks the water religiously; at night they make fun of it."[7]

As early as 1809, Valentine Seaman responded to the increasing popularity of Saratoga by producing a second edition of his mineral water analysis of 1793. Having never returned to the resort, he relied on reputation alone to announce that the celebrated medicated springs had become "the seat and empire of luxury and dissipation, the rallying point of parties and pleasure." Seaman complained that "where one person *now* applies there to repair a disordered constitution, twenty go, in the gaiety of health, to sport a sound one, against the enervating influence of revelry and riot." More reliable visitors of every persuasion echoed Seaman's judgment of Saratoga. Almira Read, the sick wife of a New Bedford whaling captain, journeyed eight days by sloop, steamer, and stage to reach the Springs in 1826. In her diary, she engaged in a constant battle with the imperfections of her soul, and she unfortunately found Saratoga to be a detrimental environment for personal piety. Read wrote that the nightly parties and balls "engross the attention of the old and young, sick and well, and this village place I fear will prepare more souls for destruction than these efficacious waters will ever heal infirm bodies." Elihu Hoyt of Deerfield, Massachusetts, also expressed surprise that Saratoga did not exhibit the zeal so common in many antebellum American health and reform movements. "One would suppose that we should find everybody here on the sick list—but it is far from being the case," he wrote in 1827. In fact, "many of the visitors come here probably in good sound health, for amusement, & for the sake of spending a week or two among the fashionable to see & to be seen."[8]

Whether pursuing pleasure or seeking better health, visitors promenaded to Congress Spring, the most popular of the myriad springs that dotted the village. William Meade's report of his 1817 chemical analysis of Congress Spring caught the entrepreneurial spirit of the age by speculating that Saratoga's waters could perhaps "become a lucrative article of commerce." This prediction was fulfilled when John Clarke came to Saratoga in 1822, fresh from economic success in New York City marketing carbonated beverages. Clarke purchased Congress Spring—now, contrary to Putnam's original scheme, a commodity whose waters could be privately bought and sold—and built a bottling plant next door. He used his business experience to promote the mineral waters, exported them as far away as Europe, and made a fortune. In some places, Saratoga waters sold for a higher price than wine, and scientists endeavored in vain to replicate their magical properties. By the 1830s, one guidebook bragged that scarcely a town in the United States of any magnitude lacked Saratoga water.[9]

Nowhere was Clarke's acumen better displayed than in his generous local embellishments, expenses he viewed as publicity for the village and his bottling enterprise. Although he owned the land, Clarke allowed visitors free access to his springs, and in 1826, he created bucolic Congress Park out of supposedly worthless swampland. The park soon filled with handsome Greek temple–like pavilions, fountains, benches, obelisks, and a bandstand, perfect for both public display and private flirtation (figure 2). Clarke also laid out Circular Street, the distinctive wide street circling the town, and in 1832 crowned the hill overlooking the park with his own immense Greek Revival mansion. His unflagging energy benefited both the city and himself; he invested heavily in local real estate, and by the time of his death in 1846, he owned almost a thousand valuable acres contiguous to Congress Park and Spring.[10]

Saratoga's rise to the position of "queen of spas" was not uncontested. Six miles to the south, the town of Ballston Spa competed vigorously, and several early prognosticators even predicted that Ballston would emerge triumphant from the rivalry. Benajah Douglas, the grandfather of the Illinois senator Stephen Douglas, built the first hotel in Ballston in 1792, and its immediate success encouraged further development. No expense was spared in building the Sans Souci Hotel (1804), a three-story high U-shaped behemoth boasting frontage and wings of 150 feet in length, gaming rooms, a tavern, and occupancy for 250 members of the cream of American society.[11] Elkanah Watson, commenting on an elegant ball he had attended at the Sans Souci in 1805, emphatically declared Ballston "the most splendid watering place in America and scarcely surpassed in Europe in its dimensions, and the taste and elegance of its arrangements." James Morrell of Pennsylvania thought the hotel exceeded "anything for gaiety and dissipation of any establishment or watering place I have visited," an opinion echoed by Jacob Cohen of Charleston, who resided there during the summers of the War of 1812. Ballston Spa proved a formidable competitor to Saratoga Springs.[12]

By the 1820s, the mineral waters alone no longer sufficed to attract

SARATOGA SCHOTTISCH.

NEW YORK.

38th nett.

PUBLISHED BY HORACE WATERS Nº 333 BROADWAY.

Figure 2. Congress Park, as depicted on the cover of "Saratoga Schottisch," 1851. Under John Clarke's patronage, the park acquired obelisks, benches, and pavilions, creating a perfect setting for public display and private flirtation. (Courtesy of the Saratoga Springs Public Library.)

sojourners. More than twenty important mineral spring sites dotted New York; a traveler in the Empire State could choose from iron springs in Columbia County, sulphur springs at Sharon or Richfield, and warm springs at New Lebanon, in addition to burning springs, oil springs, nitrogen springs, and salt springs in twenty other counties. Guests expected resorts to offer not only a bed and some form of mineral water but numerous amenities and a festive atmosphere as well. In Saratoga, tension had developed between more pious New England emigrants and those like John Clarke, who envisioned the commercial possibilities of the water. The behavior of many of the strangers dismayed local farmers and even village denizens, who thought the town had been "perverted into an unsunk Sodom." Northern Saratoga County claimed the distinction of forming New York's first temperance society in 1808, and some residents of Saratoga Springs supported this movement. Visitors who found mineralized spring water an acquired taste, or thought the libation more palatable if mixed with wine, began to patronize Ballston Spa, where the billiard rooms soon required repair from overuse. In the 1820s, Ballston and Saratoga possessed equal size and reputation, and the former even won the honor of hosting the county seat in 1819.[13]

Fearful that the resort would die, Saratoga's boosters maneuvered to ensure that provincialism and religious fervor would not doom the town's profit-making possibilities. The leaders of Saratoga Springs consciously pushed to separate the city from Saratoga County, and in 1819, New York State declared the village a special township possessing the right to govern itself without concern for neighboring sensibilities. Seven years later, the legislature incorporated the village of Saratoga Springs within the new township limits, specifically considering the promotion of mineral waters and the solicitation of tourists. The village charter urged the trustees to provide free access to the springs and erect buildings around private mineral springs for the convenience of visitors. The new village also retained the right to issue regulations for the cleanliness of the springs, control the hours during which spring water could be bottled, and "appoint proper persons to attend the spring, and draw the water . . . without demanding any compensation."[14]

Saratoga immediately made headway in the contest with Ballston. The Saratoga Springs Board of Trustees, in their role as excise commissioners, granted tavern licenses to ten individuals and permission to sell intoxicating liquors by the gallon jug to an even greater number of grocery stores. The village then waived several fines imposed on tavern owners for peddling liquor. The new proprietor of Congress Hall set aside rooms for billiards and in 1821 hired the African American master musician Francis Johnson and his Cotillion Band. Johnson performed his cheerful reels, marches, and quadrilles, with titles such as "Saratoga," and "Congress Hall," to the delight of visitors for every season except one until his death in 1844. Tipplers gradually returned to the Springs, enticed by the new Congress Park and the opportunity to drink and gamble.[15]

The county's culture wars subsided as local residents accommodated themselves to the tourist trade. The charismatic Christianity of the Second Great Awakening completely passed over Saratoga Springs, although revivals shook neighboring rural communities. The owner of the United

States Hotel bought the old Saratoga Baptist Church building and, in an act with unmistakable symbolic overtones, converted it to use as a clubhouse and billiard room. Almira Read lamented the profanation of the Sabbath at Saratoga, and Elizabeth Ruffin complained that she could see washing and ironing all day Sunday from her hotel window. When Union Hall, at the time the most conservative of Saratoga's hotels, engaged a band to play in its parlor, the music conflicted with the pious worship there. In the battle between dancing and praying, the devotees of Terpsichore outnumbered the worshippers of the Christian deity, and Union Hall consequently discontinued daily public prayers. Not long afterward, one man was heard to say, "If God made the country, and man made the town, the devil must have made Saratoga!"[16]

Doctors and hotel keepers now drifted out of Ballston Spa to set up practice at the Springs. In 1834, the Americanophile barrister Henry Tudor noted with surprise that the Springs exhibited "a very handsome and imposing appearance, . . . an air of importance, of gracefulness, and animation, that I found altogether wanting at Ballston. Here, I felt that a stranger might pass two or three weeks very agreeably." The 1838 edition of *The Tourist* notified travelers that "Ballston was formerly the most fashionable place of resort, but latterly, Saratoga has borne away the palm," a warning not present in an 1834 edition. Ballston Spa faded into obscurity, although occasionally visitors to Saratoga took the five-mile jaunt as a day trip. In the decade following 1830, Ballston's permanent population declined from 2,113 to 2,044, while Saratoga's increased 54 percent, to 3,384. The old Sans Souci was converted into a law school and later into a "ladies' seminary" and was finally torn down in 1887 to make room for business blocks bolstering Ballston Spa's new identity as a small industrial municipality. As the *New York Weekly Tribune* concluded in 1851, "Fifty years ago, 'everybody' went to Ballston Spa. . . . But the Saratoga belle of today scarcely knows the name of Ballston."[17]

In the period of Saratoga's triumph over Ballston Spa, approximately three hundred wooden dwellings clustered at the two extremes of the village, one near High Rock Spring and the other adjacent to Congress Spring. The three extensive hotels, the resort's most noteworthy feature, each accommodated nearly three hundred visitors, and all conveniently fronted Gideon Putnam's wide main thoroughfare, now named Broadway. Chattel mortgages on even small-scale hotels reveal extensive material holdings, yet fewer than a thousand visitors appeared in desultory seasons, and the entire length of Broadway contained only nine brick houses and many vacant lots. As late as 1835, some travelers complained that "though the place is the center of transatlantic fashion, it has the air of having been just redeemed from the forest." Regulations concerning animals in town and the maximum height of fences filled the minutes of the town board meetings of the 1820s, and one local diarist recorded in 1830 that a fat ox promenaded on the Union Hall piazza, to the annoyance and alarm of the guests.[18]

Some of Saratoga's underdevelopment could be attributed to the nature of preindustrial travel in America. Before the nineteenth century, a journey of any length was usually an arduous and time-consuming experience, indulged more from necessity than from choice. A round-trip sloop voyage on the Hudson River from New York to Albany consumed six days, at the mercy of wind, tide, weather, uncharted rocks, and uncertain seamanship. In the 1830s, stages from Boston and New York to Albany and Saratoga maintained service several times a week, but overland transportation moved at no better than seven miles an hour, even on so-called main highways, which were typically little more than packed dirt paths. One early guidebook to the area suggested stage travelers sit beside the driver, not only for more ample leg room but also to be "at liberty to take a *flying leap*" in case of accident.[19]

Saratoga might no longer be perched on the edge of the wilderness, but it still took Basil Hall, the splenetic English captain, "nine hours of jolty travelling" to cover the twenty-seven miles from Lake George to the Springs in 1827. The mother of the poet Margaret Davidson nearly fainted from "fatigue and debility" after taking the stage from Whitehall to the Springs. Elihu Hoyt found nothing unusual in allotting an entire day to travel the thirty-six miles from Albany to Saratoga, and Elizabeth Ruffin arrived "smothered with dust." The Fitch family meticulously chronicled their trip to the resort in 1820; they left Boston at 7:00 A.M. on July 22, 1820, and spent the first night in Worcester, the second in Belchertown, the third in Worthington, the fourth at New Lebanon, and the fifth at Albany. They did not reach Saratoga until 1:30 P.M. on July 28, and they stayed only two full days before making the arduous return; their sixteen-day excursion cost $186.[20]

The exhilarating breakup of age-old restraints on human movement in the early nineteenth century created the American resort as a mass destination. Each improvement in accessibility to a watering place led to more visitors from an ever wider market area. Robert Fulton's *Clermont* revolutionized Hudson River traffic on its maiden voyage in 1807 by steaming from New York to Albany and back in sixty-two hours. After the Supreme Court's *Gibbons v. Ogden* decision broke Fulton's monopoly on the Hudson in 1824, competition brought more customers and lower prices (seven dollars with meals one way in 1818; two dollars in 1840). With their relatively quiet low-pressure engines and elaborately furnished rooms, Hudson River steamers pleased passengers, but enough glitches remained to make traveling a dangerous adventure. The *Henry Clay*, filled with pleasure seekers from Saratoga, engaged in a race with another steamship in July 1852 and burst into flames just outside Manhattan. Lacking lifeboats or fire extinguishers, more than a hundred passengers perished; among the dead were Nathaniel Hawthorne's younger sister, returning from Saratoga, and the distinguished architect and landscape gardener Andrew Jackson Downing, en route to Newport to supervise the construction of one of his villas.[21]

Despite the perils, traveling became not only socially acceptable but desirable as an end in itself. The cultural achievements of James Fenimore Cooper, Thomas Cole, and Washington Irving created a vogue for the Catskills and made steamship travel up the Hudson corridor a common journey. The smashing success of the Catskill Mountain House (built in 1823) led promoters of the Northeast to replace inns with hotels and speculate in local improvements. A spate of commercially available guidebooks went through multiple editions, touting a "northern tour" with an itinerary encompassing the Hudson River and Catskills, the Erie Canal, Niagara Falls, and the White Mountains as well as exotic sites such as Auburn Prison, West Point, and the Watervliet Shaker settlement. Many noted antebellum writers emphasized the affinity between travel and interior exploration, including Washington Irving in *A Tour on the Prairies* (1832), Margaret Fuller in *Summer on the Lakes* (1843), and Henry David Thoreau in *A Week on the Concord and Merrimack Rivers* (1849). As early as the 1830s, in a story entitled "The Romance of Travelling," Sarah Joseph Hale remarked, "We must travel, if we would be in fashion."[22]

Even river travel seemed outdated after the English engineer George Stephenson demonstrated the practicality of the steam engine for commercial overland transportation. In the United States, railroad mileage leaped from 23 in 1830 to 30,000 in 1860 and 166,000 in 1890. Most railroad companies did not run first-class hotels in the United States before 1860, but the new transportation companies forged a symbiotic relationship with watering places. Railroads recognized the potential of resorts to build passenger traffic, and the tourist destinations avidly solicited their patronage. Watering places that failed to court railroads risked commercial failure. The difference between success (Atlantic City) and stagnation (Cape May) might depend on little more than a few minutes in railroad time, a few years in date of initial connection, and a few cents in ticket price.[23]

The railroad from Schenectady to Ballston Spa and Saratoga Springs was only the second railroad in all of New York state. Investors from New York City and Albany snapped up the company's stock, and workmen completed the entire route in July 1833, at a cost of $200,000. This twenty-five-mile railroad rewarded the faith of its backers, carrying 3,550 passengers between Schenectady and the Springs in its first month of operation and more than 4,000 in one week in August. A financial report of November 1833 revealed receipts of $42,000 with expenditures of only $16,000. By the railroad's third season, more than 30,000 passengers rode the new line.

Businessmen from neighboring Troy did not cede the tourist trade so easily to their rivals in Albany; when the state legislature chartered the Rensselaer and Saratoga Railroad in 1832, its entire stock issue also promptly sold out. Completed in 1835, the new line allowed the visitor from New York City to disembark from the steamboat in Troy and travel by rail to Saratoga. Troy-based investors eventually took over the Saratoga and Schenectady in 1851, and by the start of the Civil War, this enlarged Rensselaer and Saratoga carried 150,000 passengers a year on the one-hour trip to Saratoga, generating receipts of $192,000 on expenses of only $61,000. Simultaneously, the Utica and Schenectady's expansion to western New York, and the forty-mile Saratoga and Washington, which in 1848 connected the Springs with Whitehall on Lake Champlain and thence to Montreal, considerably expanded Saratoga's potential pool of visitors.[24]

Residents of Saratoga played a key role in boosting railroad construction; incorporators of the initial railroad included John Clarke, the physician John Steele, Rockwell Putnam (Gideon's son), and Gideon Davison. The latter, a local guidebook writer, publisher of the *Saratoga Sentinel*, and one-man tourism development agency, also served as commissioner of construction for the Saratoga and Schenectady. Not surprisingly, Davison rejoiced in an updated edition of his own guidebook that "a ride to the springs, which was formerly tardy and attended with clouds of dust and much fatigue and lassitude of body, now constitutes one of the greatest sources of novelty and pleasure." Arrival at Saratoga's railroad station symbolized the classic moment when the traveler fulfilled his long-dreamed-of journey from ordinary to magical ground, and the city obliged by rebuilding the station on an ever grander and more dramatic scale in 1843 and 1871.[25]

By 1840, the round-trip excursion from New York to Saratoga by steamboat and train took less than eighteen hours, astonishing diarist Philip Hone, who remembered "when a week was consumed in a voyage to Albany, and it was a day's journey (and a hard one, too) from thence to Saratoga. Now we dine at Saratoga and arrive at New York before people are stirring." When Charles Dickens had five extra days in New York City at the end of his American visit, he took a steamboat up the Hudson to investigate the Shakers and then spent two nights at West Point before returning to Manhattan, completing an excursion that would have been unimaginable to the previous generation. Clement Moore, author of the poem known as "The Night before Christmas," made several trips to the Springs in the 1830s. In his longest poem, "A Trip to Saratoga," he conjured up a daughter of marriageable age who whined to her snail-paced father, "We are sick to death of home, and almost wild of somewhat else on earth to get a sight. . . . Why should we dose [*sic*] at home, when all the world, with former times compar'd seems rous'd from sleep."[26]

The railroad and the steamboat completed the prerequisites for mass travel: a segment of the population with money and leisure time, an adequate transportation network, and conditions of reasonable safety and comfort at resort destinations. Domingo Sarmiento, the future president of Argentina, expressed amazement that he could board a Hudson River steamer in New York and travel to Albany for one dollar in 1847; George Temple had paid five dollars in 1812 for just the stage fare from Albany to the Springs. Now, Sarmiento's greatest expense was the three-dollar stagecoach fare from Lake Champlain to Troy. "The wonderful facilities for locomotion furnished by modern ingenuity," wrote James Kirke Paulding in 1828, even before the invention of the railroad, "have increased the number of travellers to such a degree, that they now constitute a large portion of the human family. All ages and sexes are now to be found on the wing, in perpetual motion." The journalist Francis Grund marveled that there was "scarcely an individual in so reduced circumstances as to be unable to afford his 'dollar or so,' to travel a couple of hundred miles from him, in order to see the country." Foreign visitors invariably saw geographical mobility as one of the defining traits of nineteenth-century Americans; they seemed "a restless, locomotive people: whether for business or for pleasure, they are ever on the move in their own country, and they move in masses."[27]

Visitor traffic to the Springs, sporadic at the beginning of the century, now became persistent. Saratoga's magnetism drew travelers from their usual orbits, forcing them to alter their itineraries. In 1816, young British lieutenant Francis Hall took the direct route from Troy to Quebec by way of Whitehall, ignoring Saratoga completely. He would be one of the last, for after 1820 few travelers through the region would bypass the Springs. An anonymous diary keeper who traveled from Boston to Canada in 1822 specifically returned to Saratoga from Albany after missing it on his journey southward. By 1845, even a guidebook dedicated specifically to Niagara Falls felt obligated to include sections on "the most celebrated watering place on the Globe." One traveler conceded he had never even seen Saratoga but nonetheless included in his account a cribbed synopsis from another source. No northern tour would now be considered complete without a visit to the Springs.[28]

Word of mouth remained one of the prime methods of popularizing Saratoga, despite the proliferation of travelers' accounts, resort advertisements, scientific treatises, newspaper articles, landscape paintings, and inexpensive prints advocating leisure travel. In a brief letter, Eleanor Grosvenor three times asked her cousins to visit her at the Springs in 1833. "Can you not come and spend some time with us here?" she asked, for "we have a pleasant room and what a visit we will have Such rides and rambles, and if we exhaust one spring, we can drain an other." Similarly, Saratoga so infatuated Mrs. Lucy Wooster and her husband that they insisted their daughter in Virginia join them and tried to procure an acceptable man to escort her: "Have you seen Mr. Rogers?—Does he not generally spend his vacation in travelling—perhaps he may be coming this way." When Elizabeth Ruffin arrived at Saratoga in 1827, she asked her diary, "Is this Elysium, my ears have so long heard?"[29]

Saratoga also profited from the well-publicized appearances of the political and social elite, whose testimony served as a form of public relations to build patronage at the spa. Local residents feted the Marquis de Lafayette on his American tour in 1825, and Joseph Bonaparte, brother of Napoleon and exiled king of Spain, spent five seasons there. The Springs attracted a

diverse "Who's Who" of antebellum society, as well as a constant parade of American dandies and European tourists who flaunted novel fopperies and earned the envy of the untraveled. So commonplace was the presence of American politicians that Vice President Martin Van Buren's appearance at a Saratoga ball received "no more homage than if he had been a shoemaker." By the end of the 1830s, John Calhoun, Henry Clay, Daniel Webster, and Van Buren had matched wits in social graces, poker games, and politics. James Buchanan, Millard Fillmore, and John Tyler all stayed in Saratoga during their administrations, and an honor roll of New York political lights included Aaron Burr, Thurlow Weed, Daniel Tompkins, Silas Wright, and William Marcy. Less-renowned letter writers invariably "dropped names" to reassure their correspondents that Saratoga was the place to be.[30]

The advent of railroad travel marked the greatest transformation of the Springs. Before its arrival, Saratoga had probably never hosted more than six thousand guests in any season, but in 1833, the number of visitors at the Springs jumped to eight thousand, and the *Saratoga Sentinel* informed villagers in 1835 that "the number of strangers arrived here last week cannot have been less than 2,000." The Panic of 1837, which threw the nation into prolonged depression, barely touched Saratoga. "The New York papers contain every day an account of increased commercial distress," reported Philip Hone in 1839, "affording a striking contrast to the gaiety and extravagance of this place." Taking note of the two thousand visitors, Hone concluded that "more money has been spent here than in any former season, some of which, I have no doubt, belongs more justly to the pockets of creditors at home than of the hotel-keepers here." A New York journalist reported in 1843 that the village was "crammed with people. The United States Hotel is literally bursting, every chink and cranny being stuffed, and every door and window forming an outlet merely for the mass pent up within."[31]

The largest Saratoga hotels covered immense spaces counted not by lots but by acres, and they kept expanding on a more luxurious scale. The assessed value of Union Hall, set at $40,000 in 1849, increased to $80,000 in 1854 and $200,000 in 1864. When local hotelier Henry Hathorn purchased rival Congress Hall in 1854, he immediately constructed an additional story and a ballroom. The United States Hotel, the largest of the Saratoga caravanserais, could accommodate more than 400 guests in 230 bedrooms and 20 private parlors. By 1860, its four-story main building and 800 feet of piazza gave it a commanding appearance in the city (figure 3). The *National Era* in 1850 estimated that Saratoga had entertained 35,000 summer visitors, including seasonal residents of boardinghouses; almost 14,000 of these guests had stayed at either Congress Hall, Union Hall, or the United States Hotel. Of an estimated 40,000 visitors to Saratoga in 1859, Congress Hall hosted 5,399, the United States 4,412, and Union Hall 3,995, representing 35 percent of the total. Despite their size, the "Big Three" overflowed so frequently that they had to "colonize" guests, that is, farm them out to private houses hired by hotels. In contrast, the entire village contained only 4,650 permanent residents, according to the 1850 census.[32]

The stupendous hotels constituted only part of the watering place's attraction. Saratoga consciously promoted itself as a city of play, and the resident population demonstrated considerable civic concern for its appearance and facilities. Leisured visitors in pursuit of pleasure demanded and received a level of municipal organization and social services in advance of the desires of the local population. An almost complete absence of industry in Saratoga eliminated any organized working class with interests at variance from those of the transient guests, so the tourist quarters generally possessed the best the city could offer in water or sanitation services. Saratoga quickly adopted technological breakthroughs such as the telegraph (1846) and gas street lighting (1853), but always at the hotels and on Broadway first. Local statutes tried to regulate markets and control peripatetic vendors, supposedly for the sake of public health but equally inspired by a yearning to keep the principal thoroughfares free for promenading.[33]

Saratoga's prosperity completely depended on its reputation as a healthful place. Some local residents even stooped so low as to circulate rumors that epidemics were ravaging this or that rival resort. The Springs did successfully avoid the scourges of typhoid and cholera, the terrors of nineteenth-century watering places, despite outbreaks in Newport (1854) and later at Bar Harbor (1873), the White Mountains (1875), and Nahant (1881). Saratoga possessed sophisticated water and sewer systems at a time when many major cities lacked even rudimentary infrastructure. The first serious fires in the early 1840s led the trustees to amend the village charter to permit taxation for the construction and then expansion of a reservoir and aqueduct specifically to provide a better water supply for fire fighting. "Scarcely too much can be appropriated in securing absolute cleanliness and consequent health," declared the president of the board of trustees. When some citizens

Figure 3. The United States Hotel, as depicted on the cover of "United States Quadrills," 1844. Resorts generated numerous dedicatory dance titles, and the sheet music doubled as a tangible souvenir. (Courtesy of the Yates Collection, Skidmore College.)

grumbled about the higher taxes required for the benefit of the health of strangers, the board reminded Saratogians that "the peculiar character of our village requires extraordinary care in this direction. . . . We have no excuse for inviting the stranger seeking health and pleasure, to a charnel house."[34]

Saratoga's fashionability also placed the city at the forefront of American urban landscape design. In 1827, the village trustees reduced each landholder's road tax sixty-two and a half cents for each tree planted along his or her property front. The hotels did their share by cultivating gardens and greenery; creepers carried in festoons from hotel pillar to pillar lent a languorous air to the resort (see figure 1). In 1800, Abigail May had not found "shade enough to shelter a Dog," and another early visitor from Virginia declared Saratoga "destitute of ornamental trees." By mid-century, however, elm- and maple-shaded streets and hotel courtyards were a hallmark of Saratoga's charm. Ellen Bond of Cincinnati, on the grand northern tour in 1850 with her parents and sisters, wrote in her diary that the grounds at Saratoga were "kept in such beautiful order, that it is a pleasure to walk thro' them. They are so finely shaded too." Visitors appreciated the complaisant efforts of the townspeople; Eleanor Grosvenor wrote her cousins that "the Inhabitants are out doing each other in makeing [sic] things attracting [sic] to company. With all the attractions of N.Y., the City people are marking 'not at home' on their doors and coming to this place."[35]

Saratogians promoted the city to appeal to the tourist trade, and as one writer observed, "even the most exclusive of the inhabitants are contented to pocket the humiliation during the few months of the great rush." By 1850, the city boasted forty-six hotels and boardinghouses, fifteen physicians, and forty-one merchants. The well-traveled Washington Irving declared that he had "never seen a watering place on either sid[e] of the Atlantic, where things were on a better footing and better arranged than in this." Prosperity engendered a building boom, especially in the area adjacent to the railroad depot and the United States Hotel known as Franklin Square. The Marvins, a prestigious local family of bankers, politicians, and, not coincidentally, owners of the United States Hotel, built several Greek Revival residences there indicative of their status as community leaders. In the census of 1850, in which the mean wealth of Americans was reported as $1,001, eighty-five Saratoga residents owned real estate valued at more than $5,000 and thirty-eight greater than $10,000, including three Putnam descendants, at least five other hotel keepers, printer Gideon Davison, railroad agent Joseph Wheeler, and jeweler Nicholas Young. Thomas Marvin possessed an estate worth more than $100,000. For some, it paid to encourage consumption, and Saratoga residents retained control of most of these touristic enterprises until the Civil War.[36]

When the Declaration of Independence was written, the village of Saratoga Springs did not exist; by the 1850s, the resort served as a metaphor for progress and seemed to epitomize the promise of America. Visitors stood openmouthed at the change from wilderness to resort, and the real estate market boomed as owners subdivided large pieces of land into building lots. "I can scarcely even imagine such a complete metamorphosis were possible," read one letter published in the *Sentinel* in the 1840s. After having enjoyed a stroll through the unsurpassed Congress Park, with its lakes, gushing fountains, and shady promenades, the writer recalled that only twenty-five years earlier, this park "was once a dark, dismal swamp, filled with huge treacherous bogs and quagmires."[37] The resort's popularity continued to skyrocket in the decade leading up to the Civil War. Between the censuses of 1850 and 1860, enumerators counted 55 percent more families in Saratoga Springs, and the number of dwellings in the city increased 66 percent. The 1860 census recorded 163 estates worth more than $5,000, 85 worth more than $10,000, and 7 worth more than $100,000, including those of three men who listed their occupations only as "Gentleman," two members of the Marvin family, and the owner of Congress Spring.[38]

Who were these votaries of fashion driving the expansion of the American resort? Tales of wealthy southern planters, emerging urban social-register types, and exotic foreigners filled the accounts of northern watering places. Yet while millionaires and planters gave the hotel trade its luster, guidebooks and visitors' accounts egregiously overstated this northern tour of the idle rich. A good deal of anecdotal evidence contradicts the assumption that only the crème de la crème visited the Springs. A *New York Herald* correspondent found "a greater diversity of character at the Springs than I was prepared to find. There are representatives of every grade in our society, except the lowest, and they are tolerably well apportioned." An anonymous British traveler projected his own fears when he noted that, "although the company consists of all classes, very few quarrels take place." John Godley's foray to the Episcopalian Church revealed almost no worshippers "of the higher classes," while Charles Latrobe, who passed two succeeding summers in Saratoga in the 1830s, discovered "a motley crew of men and women of all degrees;—patricians, plebeians, first-rates, second-rates, third-rates." Clement Moore's hero expressed disquietude about modern times, when even mechanics, milliners, and apprentices were running away to the thronged resorts. A sojourn at the Springs could involve moderate or extravagant sums; the forty thousand visitors to Saratoga in the summer of 1859 attest to prices within the reach of many Americans.[39]

Southern visitors, however, aroused the greatest amount of comment. The summer migrations of the planters had become a virtual ritual; future South Carolina governor Benjamin Franklin Perry believed in 1846 that "it was discreditable to me never to have been to the North." Although bogus Saratogas dotted the South, neither Harrodsburg (Kentucky), Limestone Springs (South Carolina), Madison Springs (Georgia), or even the venerable springs of Virginia could provide the same national exposure as a visit to Saratoga. One commentator claimed that "bad roads, almost impassable streams, and slovenly accommodations" would never deter southerners, for they regarded "the exhibition of themselves for such a brief time there [in the North] a full compensation for all the perils and privations encountered while outward and homeward bound." An informant told Frederick Law Olmsted on his southern journey that nouveau riche planters all "go North. To New York, and Newport, and Saratoga, and Cape May, and Seneca Lake. Somewhere they can display themselves more than they do here."[40]

As wealthy residents from south of the Mason-Dixon line flooded the North looking for health and pleasure, hotels responded by advertising southern cuisine and serving mint juleps. In 1822, Gideon Davison's guidebook, subtitled "A Trip to the Springs, Niagara, Quebeck, and Boston," included sketchy mileage figures from Charleston; ten years later, he published a book consisting solely of extensive tables of distances, from Charleston, Savannah, Norfolk, and Richmond. At the Springs, the southerner personified values that northerners both feared and cherished as the republic tried to adjust to increased leisure and luxury. Occasionally condemned and ridiculed for their extravagance, the members of the plantocracy also seemed to embody uniquely a lifestyle of courtliness, lassitude, and conspicuous extravagance. George Curtis, later a distinguished editor and reformer, discriminated at Saratoga between "the arctic and antarctic Bostonians, fair, still, and stately, with a vein of scorn in their Saratoga enjoyment, and the languid, cordial, and careless Southerners, far more precise in dress or style, but balmy in manner as a bland Southern morning."[41]

Southern visitors took a mixed view of the medicinal springs as the resort turned into a center of flirtation. North Carolinian William Lord wrote his wife back home on the plantation that she would be "amazed and disgusted to see the vast crowd at the Springs in the morning, among whom are the first Ladies of Company drinking this water, when the object is known by all the men." The wife of a Georgia planter implored him to think of her often among all the beautiful women. Charlestonian Christopher Jenkins spent the summer of 1826 playing billiards with southern friends, including members of almost a dozen South Carolina families. Jenkins drank six or seven tumblers of water in the morning but admitted in a letter to his wife that he spent evenings devoted "pretty much to the ladies, the last mentioned occupation I know you will be particularly pleased with for a man is always safe in the society of *ladies*."[42]

Few hotel registers survive from antebellum resorts, making the precise identification of tourists difficult. A careful examination of the 1853–54 register of the Tip Top House, located in the White Mountains of New Hampshire, reveals that this difficult-to-reach destination (only 566 names for two years) received significant patronage from urban dwellers of modest economic means and lower occupational rank. Foreigners (at 2 percent) and southerners (at 8 percent), often mentioned in contemporary accounts, were virtually unrepresented in the ledger. Similarly, northerners vastly outnumbered their counterparts from the South in the Saratoga Union Hall register from 1852 to 1856. For all dates sampled, residents of the slave states never constituted even 15 percent of new arrivals at Union Hall and totaled approximately 13 percent of the more than four thousand registrants in 1852. If this analysis undercounts southerners, because they generally stayed at Saratoga for longer lengths of time than their compatriots from the North, the discrepancy is offset by the fact that undoubtedly fewer southerners resided in the mass of subordinate boardinghouses and small hotels that dotted the city.[43]

Of course, the evidence of this sole surviving antebellum Saratoga hotel register might merely signify a reluctance on the part of slaveholders to visit the North during the turbulent 1850s. After the state legislature repealed the "nine months' law" in 1841, which had allowed limited residency to visitors accompanied by their slaves, southern planters with human chattel had good reason to be nervous visiting New York resorts. In 1852, a judge freed the slaves of Jonathan Lemmon on a stopover in New York, on the grounds that the state's constitutional right to emancipate applied as well to those in transit. This unprecedented decision provoked outrage in the South, and some made sporadic gestures toward boycotting northern resorts. Many southern intellectuals complained of the planters' propensity to "spend their time and money among their enemies and vilifiers"; the *Camden (S.C.) Journal* suggested in 1850 that anyone who visited Saratoga "ought to be drummed from the community when he returned." William Gilmore Simms grumbled in the *Southern Quarterly Review* that at Saratoga, southerners heard "themselves described as robbers and wretches by the very people whose thieving ancestors stole the negro with whom to swindle our forefathers." The *New York Daily Mirror* found southern sojourners in short supply in the summer of 1855. Planters feared interaction with free African Americans or worried their slaves would be "stolen" as a result of personal liberty laws.[44]

Ultimately, the southern stay-at-home movement failed miserably, for the fashionable planters had become addicted to their summer migrations. Wealthy southerners continued to visit northern hotels throughout the 1850s, and it seemed nothing short of war could affect their infatuation with Saratoga. The *New York Times* reported in 1856 that "the number of southern visitors at the Springs has never before been so large." In 1858, thirty-four Charlestonians simultaneously spent their holiday in Saratoga, and as late as September 1860, Henry Ravenal, the Charleston botanist, went on a three-day excursion from New York to Saratoga, where he met numerous southerners. The *Southern Literary Messenger* perhaps anticipated military strategy at Bull Run when, in the issue of November 1860, it urged its readers to journey north the following summer and spend the "six happiest weeks of your life."[45]

For southerners, Saratoga's atypicality was not restricted to its urban ambience or its emphasis on flirtation. At the Springs, dark-skinned people were perhaps more "visible" than anywhere else in the North. As early as 1820, a hand-drawn map displayed "a few houses of colored people" along Johnny Cake (later, Congress) Street near the hotels. The construction, operation, and maintenance of hotels and railroads provided opportunities for skilled and unskilled immigrants, minorities, and women alike: cooks, chauffeurs, entertainers, waiters, and servants. Solomon Northup, before being kidnapped and spending "twelve years a slave," worked as a hack driver and servant with his wife at various Saratoga hostelries from 1834 to 1841. In the winter, he played the violin and helped construct the Troy and Saratoga Railroad. According to the federal censuses, Saratoga's resident black population increased from 88 in 1830 to 239 in 1860, constituting 3 percent of the village population. These numbers are assuredly understated for the summer, since census takers were instructed to record people only at their permanent address. The 1850 census enumerated only seventeen black waiters (and only two white waiters) in all of Saratoga, and the 1860 census recorded but one waiter for the entire summer resort community.[46]

White servants might embarrass southerners, but the unabashed presence of free African Americans could also be upsetting. Some Saratoga hotels, such as the United States, prided themselves on having only black waiters, and others, such as the Windsor, on excluding them, while a few tried it both ways. Francis Johnson's African American band achieved a prominence that made many southern planters uncomfortable; in 1831, he wrote the music for the abolitionist standard "The Grave of the Slave," whose lyrics condemned the cruel demands of masters and preached "death to the captive, is freedom and rest." The hotel staff could be "uppity" as well. In 1855, twenty African Americans, mostly employees of hotels, almost precipitated a riot by attempting to use Congress Spring without regard to the "rules" of white folks. Jane Caroline North, a belle from South Carolina staying at the United States, confided uneasily to her diary in 1852: "The airs of the blacks are truly disagreeable, the first sight I saw on arriving was, a 'Nig' on a sofa lounging at his ease in the entry and gentlemen moving about without noticing him—to me how very strange it appeared. . . . No white waiter is permitted here, the blacks are supreme, we have found them very civil, but it is easy to see the least provocation would make them otherwise."[47]

Women and immigrants also found the resort community of Saratoga a particularly open job market. An Irish influx began with the building of the railroad through the west side of town, and in 1850, 11 percent of residents declared Ireland as their native birthplace (61 percent of these were women). Only ten years later, Saratoga's Irish population had increased to 1,180, 19 percent of total residents. The Irish built small homes on streets named for trees—Elm, Oak, Ash, Walnut, and Birch—and Saratogians soon referred to the area next to the rail yards simply as "Dublin." Abundant work for women at resorts sometimes meant considerable gender imbalances in the local population. In the censuses of 1840 and 1850, women outnumbered men in virtually every category between five and sixty years of age. By the census of 1860, 3,429 women but only 2,851 men lived in Saratoga; of those between the ages of fifteen and forty years, women outnumbered men 1,704 to 1,279. The majority of employed women clustered in service work, such as cooking, cleaning, washing clothes, and caring for children, although some filled positions in fashion and personal appearance, such as milliner, corset maker, lace maker, and seamstress. Saratoga was on the cutting edge for the employment of women, immigrants, and blacks in the market economy.[48]

Summer transients at Saratoga constituted the raw material for prosperity, and entire industries developed around them. The tourist market filled a crucial niche for declining Saratoga County farms faced with western competition. An 1872 ledger reveals that the Grand Union alone had to purchase more than twelve hundred quarts of milk, two hundred quarts of berries, eight hundred pounds of chickens, and fifteen hundred pounds of beef a day, as well as any other fish, vegetables, and fruits that could be procured in season. To prepare and serve the daily meals, the hotel required 30 cooks and 250 kitchen workers. Local farmers supplemented their family's earnings by supplying food for Saratoga's summer visitors. In another example of the prosperity engendered by the springs, Charles Granger moved his entire Mount Vernon Glass Works from Oneida County to the Saratoga vicinity in 1846 specifically to be adjacent to the ready-made demand for the off-site sale of mineral waters. The factory employed forty men and soon produced nearly a million bottles a year.[49]

Although, by definition, a tourist town turns leisure into a salable commodity, visitors to antebellum Saratoga generally overlooked the fact that a stay required hard currency and instead focused on the resort's distinctive dedication to pleasure through consumption. The French economist Michel Chevalier's observation that Americans "must be desperately listless at home to be willing to exchange its quaint comfort for the stupid bustle and dull wretchedness of such a resort" does not seem to be borne out by the majority of recitations of the daily rounds. More visitors shared the experience of an account in the *Plattsburgh Republican:* "This is the region of joy. Jest and song and revelry drive care away! Mirth winds her fairy dance till Reason reels, and folly hails her votaries as the sons and daughters of gladness." The sketch-writer George Morris complained that everything at the Springs beguiled one of pensive thoughts: "eating, drinking, walking and riding, gunning and fishing, dancing and flirting—balls, concerts, and parties—dressing for this, that, and the other. . . . Time is disposed of without the least difficulty."[50]

Between a visitor's initial arrival at Saratoga and the tallying of the final hotel bill, the nature of the amusements often seemed to exist outside the market economy. Arriving at Saratoga, the traveler entered a surreal environment in which few people seemed to do anything resembling work and beneficial waters flowed mysteriously and effusively out of the ground. Throughout the nineteenth century, the first order of business for cynic and believer alike was to parade to Congress Spring, where a "dipper boy" would ladle up a half-pint tumbler of mineral water. Elizabeth Ruffin admitted she walked to the springs not to imbibe but to "look about the difference in face, form, and manner of its frequenters." The voyeuristic nature of the morning promenade to Congress Park appeared in almost all visitors' accounts, for it was "a matter of pleasurable interest to see the faces of those who drink the water at this hour" (figure 4). A New York journalist clarified his own purpose: "Watching the ladies at the springs is one of the chief amusements of my leisure moments." Promenaders obsessively monitored the amount of mineral water they consumed, and guidebooks issued dire warnings against the widespread overdrinking of the water.[51]

In a society in which monetary transactions increasingly predominated, the mineral water springs of Saratoga offered a direct rebuke to the market economy. Antebellum visitors traditionally drank without charge from the springs, and many of those who gulped forty glasses before breakfast were simply reveling in their ability to exploit a free resource. Transgressors could pay a heavy price for tampering with the privilege of access without charge. When Daniel McLaren retubed Pavilion Spring and built the Pavilion House in 1841, he charged a small entry fee to cover the cost of his private improvements. An aroused citizenry called an "indignation meeting" and resolved that they would "under no circumstances visit the spring or drink the waters until the restrictions are removed; and the obnoxious regulations abandoned." They pledged to use their "utmost exertions to prevent this imposition from being inflicted on the public" and then proceeded to the Pavilion Spring, where they tore down part of his fountain. McLaren stigmatized the local citizens as a mob and offered a fifty-dollar

Figure 4. "Morning Scene at Congress Spring," *Frank Leslie's,* August 27, 1859. Almost all Saratoga visitors took a voyeuristic promenade to Congress Spring to gaze upon and evaluate the crowd. (Collection of the author.)

reward for information. That night, his bottling house, which had been producing as many as thirty thousand bottles a year, mysteriously caught fire. Ultimately, McLaren withdrew the "Saratoga Stamp Act," and people once again used the water without charge.[52]

The provision of meals also reflected tensions between preindustrial and commercialized forms of amusement. Hotels could not hope to make money on their food service, given the prodigality of the portions and the waste in the kitchen. The vast banquets served, instead, as marketing tools for both the hotel and the city (figure 5). For visitors, calculating the cost was irrelevant; because the room charge included hotel meals, the staggering plenitude of the dining room seemed virtually free. Some physicians advised habitual overeaters who wished to avoid gastronomic overindulgence to skip Saratoga completely. References to dyspepsia, the antebellum affliction of choice in the United States, peppered the accounts of visits to Saratoga. Americans viewed dyspepsia as a moral as well as a physical ailment, linked

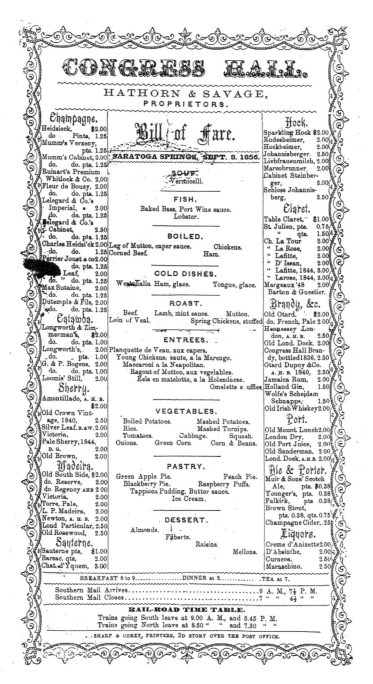

Figure 5. Congress Hall Bill of Fare, September 8, 1856. Printed daily menus, which also served as free souvenirs, became more common in the 1850s. The extensive wine list contrasts with Saratoga County's earlier fame as home to the nation's first temperance society. (Courtesy of the New York Public Library.)

to urban life and fashionable dissipations. At the resort, however, aspiring social climbers cultivated their rotundity in heavy, multicourse meals, all the while complaining of gastric distress.[53]

The simple pleasure of walking also played a major role in most visitors' experience of antebellum Saratoga. The visitor to the Springs constantly passed from one venue to another; movement without any specific object remained intrinsic to the resort experience. Even for those day-trippers who insisted on seeing the local sights, the presentation of one's self as an image for public consumption eventually became preeminent. Although few travelers left the Springs without a quick jaunt to either Glens Falls, Lake George, Watervliet (to see the Shakers), or the nearby Revolutionary War battlefield, these trips filled a mere day or two out of several weeks, and dusty summer roads made travel something of an ordeal. In the early years, a cavalcade of extravagant carriages carrying nattily attired gentlemen and ladies aimlessly paraded up and down the main thoroughfare every afternoon. When the mass of visitors began to arrive by train, however, promenaders simply ambled up and down Broadway, still having no real destination in mind.

Walking in town, visitors stumbled across all sorts of entertainments that offered an opportunity to combine popular interaction and display. For example, the Circular Railroad predated its offspring, the roller coaster, by half a century. Riders sitting in two airy cars that looked like horse gigs propelled themselves by pedal power in opposite directions around an eighth-of-a-mile track. Participants on this novel pleasure device included all combinations of ages and genders; Ellen Bond hinted at erotic possibilities when she recorded in her journal that her friend Luce had tried the circular railway with Thomas S., "working herself at a merry rate." This type of watering place machine, designed to cause laughter through unexpected physical movement and contact, belied the educative and healthful pretensions so common in the guidebooks of the day (figure 6).[54]

Many Saratoga amusements focused on novel ways of viewing the world. Panoramas were a staple of resorts, entrancing visitors by appealing to the new taste for travel. These paintings, which usually depicted an exotic locale, were mounted on the walls of a circular room around which the spectator walked. In 1835 and 1836, more than twenty-five hundred people viewed the *Panorama of the City and Lake of Geneva, Switzerland* at Saratoga, and the exhibit returned to the Springs in several subsequent sum-

Figure 6. "The Circular Railway," *Frank Leslie's*, August 27, 1859. This resort toy, a common heterosocial venue, predated the roller coaster by half a century, with no greater educative purpose. (Collection of the author.)

mers. In 1849, a panorama of Amsterdam, Holland, complete with a lecturing attendant, "was well patronized during the summer season." These resort entertainments ordered and beautified scenery and cities, converting them from unwieldy reality into transportable and desirable commodities for free-spending and relatively aimless guests.[55]

Saratoga's amusements reveal that the resort Saratoga was never a pastoral retreat for quiet self-evaluation but was, rather, a place of jostle, color, and activity. Visitors pilgrimaged to the Springs not in flight from urban life but on a journey to an intensified version of it; blather about nature served only as a rhetorical device to justify the voluntary and self-interested journey to the larger community. The residents, entrepreneurs, and village government of Saratoga explicitly rejected industrial development, declaring, "Nature did not intend Saratoga to be a manufacturing town." They put their faith instead in tourism and concentrated on manufacturing only a pleasant atmosphere. The resort suggested a civility associated with idealized cities; the spectacle of the promenade, so common everywhere in Saratoga's public spaces, virtually defined nineteenth-century urbanism. As economic inequality widened in the Jacksonian age, the Springs presented a sanitized rusticity without muck or smells, a metropolis without ethnic, racial, or religious riots. The resort's scanty country benefits did not threaten its urban identity, for most tourists to Saratoga admitted their indifference to "nature" and rapidly tired of the rural scenery so praised by the virtuous (figure 7). "The poetry of country life exists, indeed, chiefly in the imagination," conceded *Harper's Weekly,* "except where there is sufficient wealth to ingraft city conveniences upon the rural retreat."[56]

Saratoga Springs, like most northern resorts, attracted a predominantly urban clientele. In 1850, the populations of only nine American cities exceeded fifty thousand people, making up less than 7 percent of the population of the United States. Yet of the more than four thousand people who registered at Union Hall in 1852, at least 49 percent came from these cities, and many of the remainder resided in burgeoning towns such as Troy, Providence, Montreal, Rochester, and Syracuse. Saratoga presented a distinctly urban ambience, and even those who did not approve of the resort, such as George Templeton Strong, perceived it as "ambitious of looking as much like a city as it can, with its brick houses and paved sidewalks and immense wilderness of hotels." In 1857, the *New York Herald* complained that American watering places had been converted from "charming retreats into miniature and disjointed copies of city life, with a confusion of the ranks and ideas that prevail there." Whether viewed positively or negatively, public life at the Springs was as much a part of urban culture as the coffeehouse, town square, or public park.[57]

Saratoga's popularity flew directly in the face of transcendentalism and other nature-centered movements. Although the expansion of summer travel coincided with the popularity of landscape art and a nostalgic affection for the wilderness, American watering places stalwartly resisted the tendency to deify either unsullied nature or the historic past. Visitors generally ignored the romantic, patriotic, or even therapeutic allusions at Saratoga, giving precedence to socialization. The vast majority of visitors perceived Saratoga to be located "in a barren district" devoid of interesting features, whose paltry scenery was "surpassed by almost any resort of our

Figure 7. "Afternoon Lounge in the Gardens of Union Hall," *Frank Leslie's*, August 27, 1859. *Our Summer Retreats* (New York, 1858) simply concluded, "Life at the springs is a perpetual festival" (32). (Collection of the author.)

land." Yet it did not stop their arrival by the tens of thousands. Lamentations for a lost era of bucolic innocence merely served as an excuse to attend Saratoga's large resort hotels. Saratoga Springs was one of the first American locales to create and promote itself exclusively as a resort city.[58]

Antebellum Americans did not voyage to resorts to search for exotic host cultures, vicariously participate in recondite native rites, or lust after authentic experiences. At Saratoga, the visitors to resorts were themselves the exotics they wished to view. Perhaps some citizens of the newly urbanizing republic longed to commune with nature, but Saratoga held more visitors on any given summer day than places such as Mammoth Cave or Yellowstone received in a year. The prestige acquired by visiting remote and pristine locations could hardly compare with the feelings of the typical young woman who declared upon arrival at Saratoga, "Here I am at last!

The consummation of all my hopes has been attained and I have made my first appearance at the Springs!"[59]

Numerous nineteenth-century witnesses castigated Americans, especially those living in the Northeast, for their inability to relax and pass the time with no recognizably productive purpose in mind. The huge gulf between these descriptions and the glut of summer resorts calls into question the accuracy of these perceptions. An 1855 American guidebook that tabulated 103 mineral springs, 40 mountain resorts, 69 waterfalls, and 81 other watering places for those in pursuit of pleasure provided the evidence for Alexis de Tocqueville's claim that the "love of well-being is now become the predominant taste of the nation." Francis Grund's accusation that "such a thing as rest or quiescence does not even enter the mind of an American" must be discarded as unsupported by the evidence.[60]

Early-nineteenth-century Americans did express a rhetorical disdain for leisure, and their widely publicized moral directives advocating sobriety, discipline, and thrift survive by the volume. Examination of urban space, material culture, and everyday routine, however, tells a different story. For example, Henry Ward Beecher's early work, *Lectures to Young Men* (1844), considered wildly popular, sold sixty thousand copies in thirty years. This Calvinist tract warned against all amusements, including the circus, dancing, cockfighting, pugilism, gambling, the theater, and bacchanalian feasts. Yet total sales would not equal even two summers' worth of acolytes at antebellum Saratoga Springs alone. Although Beecher never abjured the *Lectures*, and in fact released several new editions, almost everything he subsequently wrote effectively repudiated these beliefs. Within the decade, Beecher decided personal enjoyment aided the public good, wrote a novel, and published his letters written on a sight-seeing trip to Europe. His sensational trial for adultery barely dented his popularity, and by the time of his death, Beecher personified a typical American attitude: he took a two-month summer vacation every year, although he remained on record as opposed to amusements.[61]

Washington Irving, who had brutally satirized the follies of fashion at Ballston Spa in 1807, was more honest. The "excitement of gay scenes, gay company, and the continual stimulus of varied and animated conversation" so exhilarated him in 1852 that he exulted, "I really think that for part of the time I was in a state of mental intoxication." Irving wrote his niece that he could not predict when he would return home: "I have found some old friends and made new acquaintances here, all very cordial and agreeable. There is no ceremonious restraint. . . . Every one seems disposed for social enjoyment." George Curtis, no friend of the resort, concluded, "while we laugh at Saratoga, its dancing, dressing, and flirtation . . . life is leisurely there, and business is amusement. It is a perpetual festival."[62]

The Revival of Newport

The Pilgrimage of Fashion

NO CITY SEEMED less likely to prosper in the first third of the nineteenth century than Newport, Rhode Island. While the reputation of Saratoga Springs ascended, the sun appeared to be setting on the city by Narragansett Bay. James Fenimore Cooper observed in 1828, "There are few towns of any magnitude, within our broad territories, in which so little change has been effected in half a century as in Newport." Adam Hodgson, who had visited from England at the same time, reported that he had seldom seen "a more desolate place . . . or one which exhibited more evident symptoms of decay. The wooden houses had either never been painted, or had lost their paint, and were going to ruin." The close habitations and the narrow, dirty, and irregular streets exhibited no trace of the attractions that had once rendered Newport a popular summer resort for the planters from the South. By 1830, when Rhode Island boasted 126 cotton mills, Newport could muster only a single cotton mill and a lace factory. The British actor Tyrone Power liked the city but observed that "trade, judging from the deserted state of the wharves, is now inconsiderable, although formerly of much importance." British travelers tended to visit Providence in the 1820s and often skipped Newport completely.[1]

It had not always been so. In 1774, Newport had actually been the fifth-largest city in the United States, with a population exceeding nine thousand. Seemingly advantageously located on the southwestern corner of Aquidneck Island, Newport's wharves boomed with commerce, legal and illegal. In its heyday before the Revolution, Newport served as home port to more than five hundred vessels, approximately two hundred in foreign commerce and about fifty of those employed as slavers. The city's twenty-two rum distilleries could not keep pace with the supply of molasses from the Caribbean. This combination of commercial success and accessibility by sea created a small colonial resort industry in Newport beginning in the 1720s. Less constrained by clerical control than many other colonial cities, Newport acquired a reputation as an enclave of varied entertainments and enlightened thought; its Redwood Library (founded 1747) was perhaps the most important cultural institution of colonial America. For those of high birth, accumulated wealth, or social accomplishment, Newport stood out as the leisure capital of mid-eighteenth-century America and the summer resort of wealthy inhabitants of the southern colonies and the West Indies.[2]

Numerous eighteenth-century visitors raved about Newport's weather, for the oppressive heat of summer rarely visited the city. The noted philosopher Bishop George Berkeley—who waited there, in vain, from 1728 to 1731 for support to finance a seminary in Bermuda to convert American Indians—compared Newport's climate to Italy's. Robert Melville, the governor of Grenada, gushed that "the climate is the most salubrious of any part of his Majesty's possessions in America." Newport "induced such numbers of wealthy persons from the southward to reside there in the summer," reminisced one visitor, "that it was ludicrously called the Carolina hospital." Dr. Alexander Hamilton, who had passed through Newport on an extended tour from Maryland in 1744, remarked, "I found it the most agreeable place I had been thro' in all my peregrinations." The *Newport Mercury* identified prominent colonial guests in America's first society column; in just the eight years before the Revolution, the newspaper individually listed more than four hundred visitors, and many others undoubtedly arrived without meriting special recognition. Ironically, not one New York name appeared in the *Mercury,* despite regular packet service.[3]

Both Newport's commercial prosperity and its reputation as a resort ended abruptly with the onset of the American Revolution. Newport's exposed location and its status as capital city and major port resulted in rapid British occupation in December 1776. The city's population dropped to half its prewar level, and many citizens failed to return after the cessation of hostilities. Brissot de Warville, who traveled the United States in 1788, wrote of Newport, "Since the peace, everything is changed. The reign of solitude is only interrupted by groups of idle men standing, with folded arms, at the corners of streets; houses falling to ruin."[4]

The devastation wreaked by the Revolution could hardly be overcome before the passage of the Embargo Act of 1807, the termination of the legal slave trade, and the War of 1812 decimated the remains of Newport's economic base. The new nation looked westward, and Newport, as a small part of Aquidneck Island, had no hinterland to tap nor readily available source of water power. As early as 1750, Dr. William Douglass had perceived that in reality, Newport was "not so well situated for inland Consumption; Providence is about thirty miles farther up Narragansett-Bay inland, therefore, in a few Years must be their principal Place of Trade." Providence's shipping first surpassed Newport's in 1790; thirty years later it had doubled that of its venerable rival. In 1824, the total value of property in Providence exceeded $9 million, while Newport's barely reached $2 million. No town in the United States, claimed a sympathetic gazetteer, "has experienced so many and so great vicissitudes as Newport."[5]

Newport residents congratulated themselves on the native-born Perry boys—Oliver, who triumphed on Lake Erie in 1813, and Matthew, later associated with the "opening" of Japan—but most visitors, if they stopped at all, agreed with one guidebook that the city presented an "aspect of decay as the commerce has been removed to Providence." Philip Stansbury, forced to take a one-day layover only because of a storm, observed in 1822 that "Newport is an ill-looking place, and almost devoid of the rural elegancies of surrounding trees or gardens," a far cry from the era when the city had earned accolades as the "Garden of America." The passionate Newport booster, George Mason, remembered that "the deadness was depressing. Grass was growing in the streets and there was one coach daily between Newport and Providence and one to Boston." The entire tax assessment of 1832 totaled only $6,834, and the tax book lists a mere 759 individuals, only 5 of whom were billed more than $100. By 1840, one pathetic distillery stood in Newport as a reminder of the rum industry, and the completion of a cemetery and a poorhouse represented major construction projects. According to legend, not a single house was built in Newport from 1815 to 1828.[6]

The failure of industry and commerce left Newport floundering. Between 1831 and 1860, people of wealth and enterprise incorporated several new businesses, including a small foundry and two midsize cotton mills. A delay in rail connections to Boston, however, had serious repercussions for the city's industrial base. A traveler from Newport to Boston needed to either take the New York boat to Fall River, Massachusetts, at an unreasonable hour or submit to a tedious ride in a lumbering stage, a journey that took most of the day. When the steamboats stopped running in the winter, businesses lacked even those alternatives. By the time workers completed the Old Colony Railroad link to Boston in 1863, Newport was an industrial backwater, most of whose mills were unprofitable or had burned to the ground. The city did experience a temporary shipbuilding boom in the 1830s and emerged as a minor whaling center, but only a paltry four whalers remained in the 1850s. The modern respect for clock and calendar time only slowly permeated the sleepy city on the Narragansett, where people still kept their hours by the sun and tradesmen sent out bills once every six months. The narrow streets and ancient buildings of the old town spoke of glories of a century past. From 1790 to 1840, during which time the population of the United States multiplied 334 percent, Newport's increased only 24 percent.[7]

Yet while the rest of Rhode Island hummed with the sound of mills and machine shops, Aquidneck Island pioneered a new tourist-based economy. Samuel Ward, son of Rhode Island's Revolutionary War governor, prophesied in 1793 that "there must be still a further decay till it [Newport] becomes a small neat summer residence for idle people of easy fortune only." The opening of the Francis Brinley House on Catherine Street in the early 1820s marked the beginning of this transformation. Renamed the Bellevue, this hotel accommodated eighty-five guests and served as the first regular domicile for a new generation of summer sojourners. Whitfield's, later renamed the Touro House, also advertised for strangers despite an external plainness that caused Tyrone Power to dub it "the Factory." "Newport is quite full, visitors flocking from every direction," wrote Samuel Ward's granddaughter, Julia Ward (Howe) in a letter of August 1836. "Houses swarm with straw hats and canes; the beach with nankeen tights, life preservers, oilcloth caps, bathing dresses. There are sailing parties, walking parties, fishing parties, riding parties, dancing parties, quiet parties—all kinds of parties." The presence of summer people spawned auxiliary businesses, bestirred the Newport real estate market, and began to form a dependable part of the local economy.[8]

The southern contingent had never entirely deserted Newport. In 1804, twenty-two-year-old John Calhoun, attending law school in Connecticut, reckoned "no part of New England more agreeable than the island of Rhode Island. . . . But it has rather an old appearance which gives somewhat a melancholy aspect." He professed to be "attached to N. Port on many accounts," not the least of which was his Newport cousin Floride, the daughter of a widowed Carolina low-country heiress, whom he eventually married. Other southern students also visited Newport while traveling to pass their summer vacations. Robert Habersham, a North Carolinian, recorded his experiences of his trip to Saratoga and Newport while attending Harvard in 1831 and 1832; a Georgian student discovered "an old fashioned town. . . . But the rides are handsome, the air pure and the girls *beautiful*."[9]

With peace, prosperity, and improvements in transportation, southerners appeared in greater numbers. In 1826, the *Mercury* reported that "the packet-ships which almost daily arrive at New York from Charleston, Savannah, &c are thronged with passengers. A greater number of strangers from the South, &c. are now residing in this Town and its vicinity, than has been known for several years past." South Carolinian Hugh Swinton Ball dropped out of Wesleyan in 1826 to study medicine in Vienna and requested funds from his older brother John. However, Hugh spent the summer in Saratoga and Newport, instead, and then demanded more money, since the previous draft was "not sufficient to answer my wants." His brother sent the money but caustically reminded Hugh he had given him $3,350 since the previous October. The next year, Hugh married Ann Channing, daughter of a prominent merchant with Newport roots. In July 1830, he wrote, "Newport is now quite crowded. I have never seen more or, even as many strangers here at one time. . . . This place is much more resorted to than formerly, but there is not sufficient accommodation, especially for transient boarders." The next year, Hugh reported "upwards of 1,000 strangers" in Newport.[10]

As at Saratoga, southern visitors to Newport literally rubbed shoulders with the free African American workers who could be seen everywhere. According to the 1860 census, Newport's 693 African Americans constituted 6 percent of the town's inhabitants, an unusually high number for a city north of the Mason-Dixon line. They played a major role as employees of hotels and boardinghouses and dominated the staff of the main steamboat line. African Africans in Newport built a vigorous internal institutional life complete with self-help and benevolent societies and churches. The community had sufficient numbers, organization, and confidence to protest public school segregation in 1857 and even unfair accusations by a southern visitor.[11]

But antebellum Newport would never be a reform-minded community in the Yankee tradition. The town's political conservatism was sufficiently well established by the 1840s that the prosecutors of Thomas Dorr, Rhode Island's populist leader, specifically chose Newport County as the most likely place to find a jury that would convict him. The city's residents often supported the antiabolition movement, appeasing southern visitors in the process. Newport's representatives to the state legislature, Benjamin Hazard and Richard Randolph (a Virginia native who married a local woman), vehemently defended a legislative attempt to prohibit the publication of abolitionist newspapers in Rhode Island in 1835. In turn, William Lloyd Garrison called Newport "the Charleston or New Orleans of New-England . . . that most defiled and obdurate town in New England, so far as slavery and the slave trade are concerned." Even in 1860, Abraham Lincoln carried Rhode Island by a large margin but defeated Stephen Douglas by only 32 votes (592 to 560) in Newport. George Curtis, reminiscing in 1880, actually blamed the miscalculations of southern political leadership and thus the entire secession crisis on the pleasure city by the Narragansett. "The misfortune," Curtis noted, "was that the Georgia or Carolina Senator or leader supposed that in the well-bred, easy, self-indulgent Newport world he saw was 'The North.' . . . Newport, with all its charms, was not a good place to study characteristic Northern sentiment and character."[12]

Newport's atypicality attracted more and more people eager to sample this new leisured environment. As the resort business grew, the city keenly felt the lack of a first-class hotel. The situation forced boosters to make a virtue out of a shortcoming by boasting that "living is cheaper here than at Nahant, Saratoga, or Ballston." In 1834, Newport's *Herald of the Times* complained that "not fewer than FIVE HUNDRED visitors were obliged, during the last fortnight, after arriving by the steamboats, to return or proceed elsewhere, from the want of accommodations." Anna Greenough Burgwyn enjoyed the good company and beautiful walks and drives of Newport in 1839, but with every hotel occupied, this Massachusetts girl, recently married to a North Carolina planter, could hardly find a place to stay. Thomas Hunter, returning to Newport in 1842 after a seven-year absence, discovered "new shops, new faces, new signs. . . . The strangers leave an abundance of money and a good portion of it goes into Dry Goods and shoe stores." Still, Hunter commented a few years later, "There have been upwards of three thousand strangers here this summer, and many more would come if there was accommodation." Americans perceived Newport to lack only Saratoga-style hotels in order to make it the premier resort in the United States.[13]

The opening of the Ocean House in 1844, with a capacity of three hundred guests, marked a milestone in Newport's history. The Greek Revival hotel, built at a cost of $22,000, stood four stories high on elevated ground (figure 8). Philadelphia diarist Sidney Fisher journeyed to Newport that year and found that "no other resort could exhibit a crowd so distinguished for refinement, wealth, & fashion." A sensational fire in August of 1845 destroyed this Ocean House, with several fatalities, but it was rebuilt in less than a year in an even more sumptuous style for a cost of $62,000. John Weaver, the proprietor, journeyed to Saratoga to examine the United States Hotel but did not like the layout. When the new Ocean House opened, with rooms for six hundred guests, it possessed not only a wide veranda but also a distinctive central corridor 250 feet long, 13 feet wide, and 14 feet high, parallel to the piazza in front and connected to it by wide passageways. On dance nights, the musicians played in the recesses of the corridors, while the guests formed files and sauntered around the two promenade spaces. Visitors bombastically described this second Ocean House as the "epitome of the luxury, beauty, elegance, and fashion of American summer society" (figure 9).[14]

The hotel mania continued in 1845, when the Atlantic House rose on the highest land in town facing Touro Park at Bellevue Avenue and Pelham Street. With its shining white Greek Revival portico and long porches across the length of its wings, the Atlantic House rivaled the grandeur of the new Ocean House. Word of Newport's resurrection spread, and in the cholera summer of 1849, an estimated four thousand strangers visited Newport without a single death attributed to the disease. The appearance of President Millard Fillmore and part of his cabinet at the Bellevue in September 1851 helped publicize the city, and Franklin Pierce plotted his 1852 candidacy from Newport's hotels. A rival three-story Fillmore House in the Italianate style soon rose alongside the Bellevue on Catherine Street; the older hotels rushed to spruce themselves up, and all competed to gain the most fashionable crowd. George Channing, a grandson of a signer

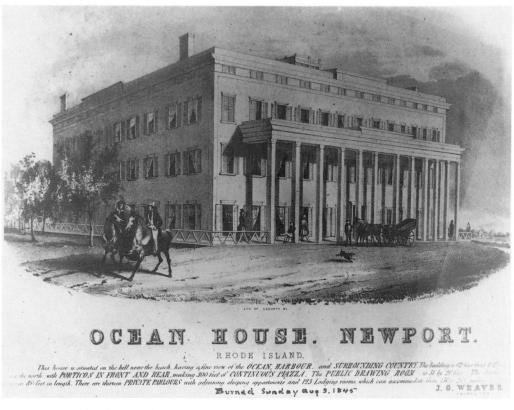

Figure 8. The First Ocean House, ca. 1844. In the description, the dimensions of the public rooms have priority, while the harbor is merely recommended as a subject to view. (Courtesy of the Newport Historical Society [P2341].)

of the Declaration of Independence, recollected returning to Newport in the 1850s to a rural area where he had played as a boy. To Channing's shock, not a vestige of the four-acre lot remained, now covered by a portion of the Fillmore House and other buildings. Even so, when James Harrison arrived in Newport in 1853 as part of a grand American tour, he still could not find any vacant hotel in Newport and apparently had to sleep on the steamboat.[15]

Newport's tourist boom reached an unprecedented magnitude in the 1850s. The first real guidebook appeared in 1852, listing six major hotels and announcing that since Newport had "become a favorite resort for rank, fashion, and beauty, from all parts of the Union, it has wonderfully smartened up. . . . New and handsome edifices arise—fresh streets are planned, and various improvements are made." George Downing, son of a famous and well-to-do African American caterer in New York City, opened a restaurant

Figure 9. The Second Ocean House, ca. 1890. Newport's new Ocean House, built in 1846, replaced the one destroyed by fire the previous year. The hotel's grandiose reconstruction included a greatly enlarged veranda. (Courtesy of the Newport Historical Society [P2339].)

in Newport in 1846 and then a luxury hotel in 1855 that attracted a distinguished white clientele until it mysteriously burned down in 1860. Visitors could also stay in old boardinghouses or new hydrotherapy resorts or even rent a furnished house for the season. Newspapers as far away as Charleston covered hotel openings for the convenience of the Carolina connection that lusted after cooling sea breezes. Southerners tended to patronize the Touro House, but the fashionability of the hotels varied from year to year. A temporary rivalry on Catherine Street developed between the Fillmore House, where Mrs. Pringle of South Carolina stopped, and the Bellevue, where Mrs. Pell of New York sojourned. Cabmen would call out to travelers drowsily stepping off the New York boat at three o'clock in the morning, "Are you for Pell or Pringle?"[16]

Just as the railroad transformed Saratoga, the replacement of sail ferries by regular steamship service set the stage for the return of Newport's halcyon days. In 1817, the *Firefly* initiated the new era by voyaging from Newport to Providence in twenty-eight hours. In 1822, the *Connecticut* made the initial steamboat run from New York to Providence through Newport in thirty hours, a time that, by 1829, was cut in half in boats now equipped with staterooms. The English novelist Frederick Marryat, on tour in America, specifically cited this route as an example of the impressive speed of American travel. Observers of American social mores commented that the ease and low cost of traveling meant it was more economical to keep moving than to stay home. "There never was known 'in the memory of the oldest inhabitant' so many strangers in town [Newport] as at this time," noted Thomas Hunter in 1842; "the hotels and boarding houses are stuffed to the roots, and hundreds come in the morning, who are obliged to leave in the afternoon for want of room."[17]

In 1847, the famed Fall River Line began what would be ninety years of daily service from New York through Newport to Fall River, the terminus for the Old Colony Railroad link with Boston (figure 10). The line's steamers covered the entire run in less than twelve hours (to Newport in ten) in grand style. By the end of the first year, the earnings paid for another boat, and in 1850, dividends paid 6 percent a month for ten consecutive months. The Fall River Line prided itself on its luxurious accoutrements and constructed steamers specifically to bedazzle passengers. The *Bay State*, the nation's largest ship in inland waters in the late 1840s, contained sumptuously furnished public rooms painted and gilded in the most splendid

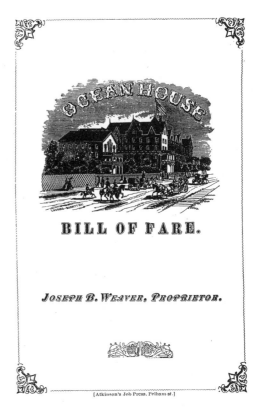

HOURS FOR MEALS.

Breakfast,.................. from 8 to 10 1-2 o'clock.
Dinner,...................... at 3 "
Tea,........................ from 6 1-2 to 9 "
Supper,..................... " 9 to 11 1-2 "

Early Breakfast and Dinner for Guests leaving by early Boats or Trains.

FOR CHILDREN AND SERVANTS.

Breakfast,............................. at 7 o'clock.
Dinner,............................... " 1 "
Tea,................................. " 6 "

Old Colony and Newport Railway.

DEPARTURE OF TRAINS.

For Boston, 3,00 a. m., Steamboat to Fall River.
" 7,20 and 10,30 a. m., and 3,10 p. m.
For Providence. 7,20 a. m., and 3.10 p. m.
For New Bedford, 7,20, 10,30 a. m., and 3,10 and 4 p. m.

DEPARTURE OF STEAMERS.

For New York, at 8,30 p. m.
For Boston, 5,30 p. m., via. Wickford.
For Providence, 7,00, 11,30 a. m, ,; 1,00 and 4,30 p. m. ; 5,30 p. m., via. Wickford.
For New York, via. Wickford, 7,00 and 11,45, a. m., and 5,30 p. m., connecting with Stonington Boats for New York.

BILL OF FARE.

JOSEPH B. WEAVER, PROPRIETOR.

[Atkinson's Job Press, Pelham-st.]

Figure 10. Ocean House Bill of Fare, August 23, 1871. The midday repast continued to be the major meal (as well as social event) at most resorts until the twentieth century. By 1871, one could travel from Boston to Newport by train, but New York remained conveniently accessible only by steamer. (Courtesy of the New York Public Library.)

style. The multitudes who thronged the New York–Newport–Fall River route sustained and justified this lavish expenditure while competition lowered the price, usually about one dollar without a stateroom and three dollars with one.[18]

The creation of a tourist industry in Newport provided real financial benefits for local citizens. The enlarged construction and domestic service industries contributed significantly to the economic revival of the city. Speculators and residents proposed roads, planted trees, and erected substantial buildings for the use of summer visitors. The mayor of Newport reported in 1854 that "hundreds of acres of land that a few years since were farms, are now town lots with costly mansions on them." As late as October 1851, land in the southern part of the city where Bellevue Avenue terminated sold for

$300 an acre; a few years later, speculators unloaded it for somewhere between $2,500 and $5,500 an acre. Newport property valued at $5.8 million in 1854 accrued another $2 million in fewer than ten years. Between 1849 and 1859, personal and real wealth in Newport increased spectacularly from $4.5 million to $10.5 million, mainly as a consequence of the presence of summer guests.[19]

The hotel industry generated money that substituted for the decline of commerce and the failure of industrial development. The leisured visitor to Newport required workers to perform the more utilitarian functions, and so tourism stimulated business and boosted the retail markets. The appearance of Newport's first directory in 1856 revealed a greater need by both visitors and locals for a listing of services. The first directory enumerated thirty-two carpenters and seventy-five grocers (eighty-five in 1858), and the number of clothiers, dry goods stores, confectioners, shoe and boot dealers, jewelers, and newspapers also multiplied dramatically. Newport tax records indicate that both retailers and wholesalers possessed much greater wealth in 1859 than in 1832 or 1841, their prosperity being directly linked to the development of the summer resort industry. Unlike the British resort at Bath, where conditions for laborers generally remained squalid throughout its glory years, the living standard of the average Newport resident improved from 1830 to 1860. The pattern of property ownership in Newport was not as sharply skewed as elsewhere in antebellum urban America, and a relatively larger proportion of the population shared in the watering place's newfound wealth. Far from destabilizing a mythical traditional structure, Newport's nascent service industry helped the previously stagnant economy to flourish.[20]

The influx of strangers to Newport also altered the built environment. The vast hostelries spawned a network of back streets (Liberty, Downing, and Fir Streets) and alleys (Fillmore Court, Bowler Lane) to accommodate ancillary services such as livery stables, storage barns, and housing for both hotel personnel and the servants of guests. Before the hotels were erected, one Newport resident reminisced that "not a pound of paint had been sold in the town since the Revolution, so dingy was the general hue of its antique tenements." Now, the white paint of the new Bellevue and the Fillmore House glared in the sunlight, and Newport resounded to the sound of carpenter's hammers. Building contractors thrived, while three Newport steam mills sawed and planed year-round turning out doors and windows.

Rapid growth after 1850 totally transformed the previously open land that had dominated the West Broadway area. Burnside and Callender Avenues, Davis Court, and Appleby, Covell, Edward, Feke, and White Streets were laid out. By 1870, more than two hundred structures had been built in this "New-town," twice the number that existed in 1850. On the other side of town, residential and commercial development along Thames and Spring Streets drifted southward, creating new neighborhoods and opportunities for employment.[21]

Collectively, the new visitors' preferences regarding health, comfort, housing, and entertainment exercised enormous influence over Newport's development. The local citizens and city government, recognizing on which side their bread was buttered, usually provided the amenities requested by strangers. For example, three windmills just beyond Broad Street were moved in 1849 so as not to frighten the horses of summer gentlemen. In response to complaints about dust, the *Newport Daily News* editorialized for the watering of Kay Street from Touro Street to Mann Avenue because it was "a very genteel thoroughfare." To deal with the growing responsibilities of Newport government, the town scrapped the town meeting system in 1853 and acquired a city charter; subsequent mayors encouraged by word and deed the metamorphosis of Newport into a fashionable resort.[22]

The citizens of Newport actively courted the tourist trade. Mayor George Calvert, of Maryland provenance, addressed the city council in 1854 on the importance of building roads for summer sojourners. "This is a new quarter pouring directly thousands annually into the treasury," Calvert stressed, "and by activity given to many kinds of business that supply the diversified wants of scores of wealthy new proprietors, contributing indirectly other thousands." The *Mercury* supported another new road on the grounds that "our capital is invested in hotels and cottages which are rented every season to those who expend large sums here. . . . They are now among our heaviest taxpayers." In fact, summer residents such as Ezra Bourne, Robert Ives, Daniel Parrish, and Charles H. Russell did pay higher taxes than most of the native wealthy families. The *Mercury* therefore concluded that the city government must supply the guests with the infrastructure necessary for their amusement, "seeing that we are to realize a substantial benefit by the carrying out of any such measure." The next year, the newspaper advocated easing the taxes on visitors for fear of driving this "wealth almost incalculable from our shore." Expenditures for repair and improvement of city streets in

1858 more than tripled the 1853 total, and money spent on fire protection doubled. Consequently, Newport's tax collection increased from $7,500 in 1841 to $15,000 in 1850 and then to $50,000 in 1855.[23]

Newport's economy depended almost entirely on seasonal cycles, and the schizophrenic resort city careened wildly between bustling activity and slothful lethargy. Hotel ownership rarely led to a fortune, given the fierce competition and the thin profit margins. Few could successfully combine the social and commercial aspects of the business, and street slang judged any man whose cleverness was doubted with the pronouncement, "He can't keep a hotel." Unlike the case of Saratoga, which had no commercial presence before becoming a watering place, some of Newport's wealthiest citizens had acquired their money in mercantile enterprises that predated the town's reincarnation as a tourist mecca. Yet gentleman farmers and representatives from some of Newport's oldest families operated or invested in many of the twenty-nine boardinghouses and eleven hotels listed in the 1858 directory.[24]

Newport's less exalted citizens entered into the developing service economy with varying degrees of enthusiasm, and conflicts sometimes emerged when wealthy cosmopolites came into contact with more conservative permanent residents. A character in Sarah Cohoone's novel on Newport conceded that the hotels had revived the town but felt they had planted the seeds of corruption by introducing "an expensive style of living, and a too great fondness for convivial entertainments." Natives occasionally drew the line when they felt the whims of wealthy visitors violated long-standing traditions. In 1835, William Beach Lawrence, the son-in-law of the New York merchant Archibald Gracie and later the lieutenant governor of Rhode Island, bought virtually all of Ochre Point (more than sixty acres) for $14,000. He made the farm there his summer residence and some years later sold a single acre for the amount of his entire previous purchase. He quickly regretted the transaction and built a stone wall on the boundary of his property across the three-mile Cliff Walk, long a favorite haunt of Newport residents. Local citizens turned out en masse to tear down Lawrence's wall and also dismantled a subsequent effort studded with glass. Lawrence sued, but the Supreme Court decided for the defendants on the basis of an old statute that gave fishermen access rights to the shore. From that day to this, strollers have been allowed to walk the Cliff Walk, alongside the floating loons and wild ducks on one side and the mansions of the great estates on the other.[25]

This type of incident, however, rarely disturbed for long the symbiotic relationship between hosts and guests. Difficult visitors may have paid the penalty in exorbitant bills, and sojourners often grumbled about being fleeced, but overt acts of disaffection remained considerably below the surface. The editors of the *Mercury* displayed a typical ambivalence regarding the transformation of Newport. While they advocated road building to keep tourist money flowing, they often railed against a nonproductive economy that encouraged loafing for nine months of the year and extortion the other three. Eventually, the newspaper despondently threw in the towel: "Newport has doubtless settled into a watering place and for the future must be known only as such. This we cannot but deplore . . . [but] we have grown dependent upon them [visitors]."[26]

If Saratoga promoted its natural springs, Newport lured visitors with its distinctive ocean beaches. Gulf Stream waters warmed Aquidneck Island, and many touted the bathing as the best on the seaboard. During the summer months, hundreds eagerly journeyed to the Newport beaches to plunge into the tumbling surf and make the air ring with laughter (figure 11). Easton's Beach, known as First Beach, stretched almost a mile from the northern edge of the Cliff Walk to the Middletown line; one correspondent called it "the finest strand I ever saw." Easton's had the additional recommendation of being the beach most proximate to the hotels, though still almost a mile away. Until the Jamaican planter and Newport entrepreneur Robert Johnston cut Bath Road (now Memorial Boulevard) through the old Easton farm in 1832, only two paths led down the steep hill to the water. Money raised by public subscription helped improve Bath Road in 1856 and allowed easier access to the invigorating saltwater bathing. From nine until noon, a white flag at Easton's Beach signaled that ladies and gentlemen could swim together as long as they wore bathing costumes.[27]

Across the Middletown line, Sachuest Beach (also known as Second Beach) contained a long expanse of dunes and unusual geological formations known variously as Hanging Rocks, Paradise Rocks, or Bishop's Seat. Here, Bishop Berkeley meditated on theological and philosophical subjects, thereby bestowing upon the site the romantic associations so dear to many antebellum travelers through constant repetition in guidebooks. William

Figure 11. "The Bathe at Newport," *Harper's Weekly*, September 4, 1858. Winslow Homer's etching depicts a group of rollicking young women and their male companions splashing in the waves at Easton's Beach without hats, gloves, or even wrist-length sleeves. (Collection of the author.)

Ellery Channing, a Unitarian minister, Newport native son, and a founder of American transcendentalism, also chose Sachuest Beach for formulating his thoughts on nature. In his dedication of the Unitarian Congregational Church at Newport in 1836, Channing confided that "no spot on earth has helped me to form so much as that beach." Consequently, Second Beach drew not only bathers but also pilgrims, sightseers, and painters such as John Kensett, John La Farge, and Thomas Worthington Whittredge (figure 12).[28]

Just as Saratoga looked to Bath in many ways, the nineteenth-century American seaside resort of Newport also had European predecessors. In the seventeenth and eighteenth centuries, French poets, Dutch seascape painters, and voyagers along the Bay of Naples celebrated the picturesque nature of the sea, beaches, cliffs, shipwrecks, and watery caves. By the early nineteenth century, the seaside resort had gradually supplanted the inland spa as the European travel destination of choice. *Sanditon,* Jane Austen's last and unfinished novel (1817), deals with rampant commercial speculation in a seaside town and the clash of so-called traditional values with consumer society. The new marine resorts consciously fashioned themselves in the physical and spiritual image of the mineral water spas. Doctors again provided the initial impetus by prescribing ocean air and saltwater bathing (simply another form of mineral water) as a panacea for virtually every disease. Swimming increased in popularity, publicized by events such as Lord Byron's foray across the Hellespont in 1810. Writers of the Romantic era constructed the seashore as a favorite spot for self-knowledge; even Nathaniel Hawthorne succumbed to the mood in his "Footprints on the Sea-shore," in *Twice-Told Tales* (1837). Respectable men and women, however, carried parasols when they strolled at the seaside, for only workers or hayseed farmers displayed a suntan.[29]

In the United States, the Napoleonic Wars delayed the emulation of English leisure models. Despite the vociferous arguments of bathing advocates, many Americans initially deemed the seacoast and riverside unwholesome in the summer. British travelers to inland Saratoga in 1835 commented that Americans "all run from the sea in the summer; while with us they are ready to run into it." Fashionable Americans loved the beach in the abstract but often shunned the disagreeable reality of swimming. "The pleasure of bathing may be great," wrote diarist Ellen Bond of bathing for the first time in her life at Newport, "but the discomfort afterwards can scarcely compensate." Few Newport residents built houses near the ocean, and no large field tent offered circulating books and chairs for those who wished to pass their morning on the sands, as was common on British beaches. The British consul accused American ladies of lacking any desire for "robust pleasures. When they reach the watering-places, they seem, many of them, to be victimized by inertia; they are loath to stir during the day." Sea bathing at Newport served primarily as a form of conspicuous leisure, not as an activity desirable in itself.[30]

Unlike the hotels of Cape May, New Jersey, located relatively close to the water, the most prestigious Newport hostelries resembled beached whales, stranded almost a mile from the ocean. When Anthony Trollope visited the United States in 1860, the famed British novelist complained that Newport's hotels were "built away from the sea; so that one cannot sit and watch the play of the waves from one's window." Even though the hotels provided

Figure 12. Thomas Worthington Whittredge, *Second Beach, Newport,* oil on canvas, ca. 1878–80. Whittredge was an avid peruser of guidebooks. Here, he cleverly combines the image of Newport's fashionable seashore with its layers of accrued historic associations with Bishop George Berkeley, William Ellery Channing, and transcendentalism. (© 2000 Sotheby's, Inc.)

omnibuses to carry bathers to the beach, the inconvenience still rankled. As George Curtis noted, "At Newport the Ocean is a luxury. You live away from it and drive to it as you drive to the Lake at Saratoga, and in the silence of midnight as you withdraw from the polking parlor, you hear it calling across the solitary fields." Ultimately, the benefits of air, water, and outdoor activity at Newport played second fiddle to the desire to socialize. Henry David Thoreau denounced the average Newport visitor who thought "more of the wine than the brine." To Thoreau's disgust, a "ten-pin alley, or a circular railway, or an ocean of mint julep" overwhelmed the experience of nature as the activity of choice of most vacationers. The creation of "bathing hours" in the morning at Easton's Beach, and the consequent parade of carriages to and from the beach, resulted from the desire of summer visitors not to swim but to see and be seen.[31]

The distance between the Newport hotels and the beach necessitated the creation of bathhouses, as no one could conceive of walking across the city or even a hotel in a bathing costume. Entrepreneurs erected the first rude stationary shacks on First Beach in the 1820s, a system somewhat different from the movable bathhouses in Europe. The American procedure meant the bather eventually had to leave the security of the enclosed bathhouse and enter the public sphere in a state of partial undress; no amount of disguise could hide one's "true appearance." This anxiety about exposure was particularly acute in the United States because men and women swam together, in contrast with European resorts, which often provided gender-separate bathing beaches. The popularity of mixed-gender bathing as a fashionable activity was a result primarily of the sponsorship of Newport's hotel dwellers, as well as those in Cape May and in Nahant, outside Boston.[32]

Before the nineteenth century, impromptu American arrangements for bathing meant participants more likely than not swam naked. An aged John Watson, looking back fifty years to before the Revolution, remembered when the activity was "too distant and rough for female participation." In antebellum Newport, however, the city oligarchs passed a bathing ordinance that restricted nude bathing in the summer. At noon, a blood-red banner replaced the white flag, and Easton's Beach filled with departing equipages. This red flag signaled that persons who preferred to swim without a bathing suit could now enjoy the privilege until three in the afternoon. The law stated that in order to bathe naked, one had to swim either in the unfashionable afternoon or at least seven hundred feet from the beach; violators risked a fine of one to five dollars. Ellen Bond's father complained he "could not take his dive '*au natural*'" in the morning and had to purchase a suit to escort his wife and daughters into the waves. As a result of the establishment of these sumptuary rules, however, Newport-style mixed bathing won many advocates in the United States. In 1846, *Orr's Book of Swimming* informed readers that in America, "ladies and gentlemen bathe in company, as is the fashion all along the Atlantic coast." By the Gilded Age, a guide to American seaside resorts declared that "a gentleman may escort a lady into the surf, at midday, with as much propriety and grace as he can display in leading her to a place in the ball-room in the evening."[33]

A beach and some waves would not suffice to create a resort; Americans had to be made aware of the charms of the Rhode Island coast. Books promoting Newport, such as Sarah Cohoone's *Visit To Grand-Papa; or, A Week at Newport* (1840), George Curtis's *Lotus-Eating* (1852), Edward Peterson's *History of Rhode Island and Newport* (1853), and Leila Lee's children's story, *The Dales in Newport* (1854), proliferated in the antebellum period. Articles on the city appeared with regularity in *Harper's Monthly*, *Frank Leslie's*, *Atlantic Monthly*, and the *Knickerbocker*. Ongoing controversy over the origins of the mysterious "Newport Tower," an old stone mill in the center of town believed by many to have been built by the Vikings, generated considerable interest in Newport's past. Henry Wadsworth Longfellow's "Saga of the Skeleton in Armor" (1841) and Harriet Beecher Stowe's *The Minister's Wooing* (1859) emphasized the city's connection to local legend and the American Revolution. Newport's many guidebooks, such as John Dix's *Handbook of Newport* (1852) and George Mason's *Newport Illustrated* (1854), promulgated the fanciful names, Indian legends, and sentimental poetry that appealed to antebellum America's romantic sensibility.[34]

Landscape painting especially helped publicize Newport to the patronage class. As rivers and harbors on the East Coast filled with mills and factories, Newport's relatively unspoiled countryside seemed an oasis of calm. Beginning in 1854, the Hudson River school luminist John Kensett turned out one or two Newport scenes yearly until his death in 1872. The noted painter William Morris Hunt settled in Newport in 1856 across from the old Jewish cemetery and later added a second-story studio to his rear carriage house. John La Farge worked at Hunt's studio in Newport in 1864 and also painted a series of Newport landscapes. The well-known American landscape artists Thomas Worthington Whittredge, William Trost Richards, John Twachtman, and Alfred Thompson Bricher all painted Newport's reinvigorated beaches and harbors throughout the 1880s. Their work found a ready market as souvenirs for upper-class tourists and initiated the packaging of the resort's natural attractions as purchasable commodities.[35]

Despite the beauties of the surrounding landscape, outdoor activities hardly engaged Newport visitors more than those at Saratoga. Guidebooks promoted the wild footpaths that rambled across Aquidneck Island, allowing sojourners the opportunity to wander and picnic on the cliffs overlooking the shore. The fact that the unconventional Henry James used and loved these natural areas when he lived in Newport from 1858 to 1864 perhaps provides the best evidence for their lack of popularity with the vast majority of Newport visitors. James swam at Second Beach, explored Paradise Rocks, Lily Pond, Cherry Grove, Purgatory, and Spouting Rock, and roamed the inland fields that lay untrodden and practically inviolate. The few other people who pursued these activities generally performed them not to commune with nature but to acquire social prestige. When less strenuous ways of achieving this goal became available, they quickly replaced any claptrap about the spiritual fulfillment of Newport's natural environment. "Most of us are really only shopkeepers," George Curtis perceptively noted, "and natural spectacles are but show-windows on a great scale. People love the country theoretically, as they do poetry."[36]

Although Newport seemed to be blessed with dramatic scenery, most visitors followed watering place tradition by paying lip service to "nature" while focusing the major portion of their energies on hotel life. According to a cynical report in *Harper's Monthly*, many of the couples who visited the seaside caves tarried so long "that they are presumed to be studying the natural geology, whose most grateful lessons are imparted by the lips." Hiram Fuller, owner of the *New York Daily Mirror*, delighted in assuming the persona of a southern girl and writing of her experiences in Newport. The fictitious Belle lived only for flirtation, which she believed "was the principal amusement of these watering places." The painter John La Farge fell in love with his future wife on a promenade to the Spouting Rock, and one journalist reported that "on moonlight summer evenings flirtation, simple, serious, and fatal, is so common on the Cliffs as to be endemic."[37]

The shift in the use of horses at Newport reflected the ascension of a public culture of gentility. In more innocent times, George Curtis had unconditionally proclaimed that "the great enjoyment at Newport is riding," and Sidney Fisher "rode every day" of his three-week stay in 1839. In the 1840s, though, more visitors enjoyed coaching than riding. The *Boston Transcript* reported that "the line of carriages to Bateman's, the Glen, and the Fort, lengthens perceptibly every afternoon," and devout congregants of Trinity Episcopal Church denounced the constant display of coaches on parade, which interfered with their prayers. Fort Adams, emplaced in a strategic position over the East Passage and Newport Harbor, made a convenient destination for the carriage enthusiasts. There, they could survey the harbor from the heights, a new maritime pastime that complemented the inherent voyeurism of bathing resorts. Construction of the fort began in 1814, but in 1850 it still stood incomplete, and tourists gradually displaced artillerists. When soldiers garrisoned the redoubt on Tuesday and Friday afternoons, the fashionable set drove there to hear the band play. "The friends who dined together an hour or two before now have the satisfaction of bowing to each other from carriages or from the saddle," related George Mason, describing the new Newport ritual.[38]

Life at the seashore consisted of an endless round of bathing, riding, dancing, and vegetating, with amusements adapted to every taste and every pocket. The routine of the day in Newport hardly differed from that of Saratoga, with the exception of the morning visit to the beach. In the 1850s, the major Newport hotels engaged the Germania Musical Society (about twenty musicians) to play daily while the guests promenaded and then again at night for dancing (figures 13 and 14). Ellen Bond praised the fine music in her journal, noting that "the afternoon passes away rapidly here."[39]

As at Saratoga, a ritualized schedule of activities developed. Each event had a loosely appointed time, place, and costume, ensuring the presence of sufficient numbers of participants and onlookers, often one and the same. Joseph Wharton described his typical Newport day in a letter:

> Our days here glide by in an easy manner, and I for one resign myself to indolence with scarce a struggle. We rise about 7 or 7:30, breakfast at the public table about 8, read the papers, and loaf around for an hour or two, and then either Anna or I go to walk or bathe, or a little later in the day, to visit—or else we part for our separate avocations. . . . In the afternoon . . . we answer letters, read or sleep until riding time comes at 5 o'clock, when we join the throng of equipages upon the Avenue, or some other of the pretty drives about the neighborhood. After tea, we stroll up and down the Hall, receive or

pay visits, and go to bed about 10:30, with the bustle and music in our ears, but powerless to keep us awake.[40]

Though not a "productive" day, this hardly represented a placid routine. One southern visitor attempted in vain to "rusticate" in Newport as early as the summer of 1842 but complained that his daughters refused to accept the quiet life. "In Newport, we are in a volcano of dissipating and I am completely tired of it, and [they] make me nearly regret to have left Charleston," he wrote to his son. Nonetheless, he continued to make the rounds of Sharon Springs, Saratoga, and Newport throughout the 1840s. In the 1850s, both Henry Ward Beecher and James Russell Lowell contrasted the serene life with the chaos and stimulation of Newport. "Pray tell me whether there is in Newport such a thing as *quiet?*" Beecher remonstrated. "How many people have you there, every one on the search for amusement? Do you ever get rid of the noise, or crowds, or excitements? You only exchange hot and dusty excitement, for excitements with sea-breezes. Can you find a place out of doors to be alone for half-an-hour? You cannot go out of doors without meeting somebody." Another journalist described an Atlantic House ball as a magical tableau of nonproductive activity:

> The great white pile was bursting with light and music. Every window and door was open. There were incessant flights of ladies across the hall. Carriages drove to the door, and dainty dames stepped out, rolled cloud-like up the broad steps, and disappeared in the house. Couples stepped through the windows upon the piazza. Dancers too tired to dance, and ladies whose mourning inhibited their feet, and not their eyes from pleasure, sat in large arm-chairs, and looked in upon the merry-making. . . . Enormous dowagers lined the great entry, a wonderful living tapestry, and before them fluttered the brilliant groups, idly chatting, idly listening, idly drifting down the summer.[41]

With images this appealing projected by the periodical press, no wonder American travelers raced from one destination to another. According to an article in the *Crayon*, the Islamic pilgrimage to Mecca paled before "the millions of human beings . . . moving relentlessly about from New York to Niagara, from Boston to the White Mountains, from Newport to Saratoga, from Philadelphia to Cape May." Fitz-Greene Halleck parodied this footloose attitude in an 1827 poem in which he observed that "the feet of you tourists have no resting-place." Nineteenth-century American elites imitated ancient pilgrimage circuits or, more closely, the ritual medieval

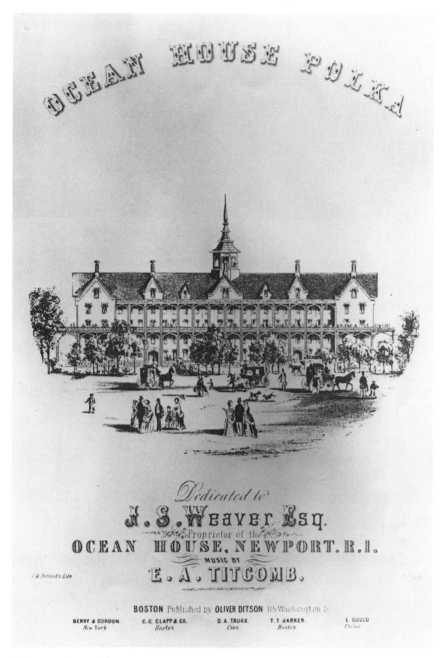

Figure 13. Second Ocean House, as depicted on the cover of "Ocean House Polka," ca. 1860. Newport served as one of the key points of entry into the United States for the scandalous polka. (Courtesy of the Newport Historical Society [P1884].)

PROGRAMME.

———————

1.—OVERTURE—Der Freischuetz,..............O. M. VonWeber.

2.—SOLO—For the Clarionetta,.......................Drewes.

MR. J. DREWES.

3.—POTPOURRY — From the new Opera of " The

Lilly of Killarney, " By Benedict, imported by

Mr. J. M. Waller, and arranged for Orchestra, by W. G. Dietrich.

(First time in America.)

4.—SCHLUMMER ARIA—Solo for French Horn.

MR. F. GEWALT.

5.—PHASES OF LIBERTY—Four Songs,

a. FREEDOM'S RALLY,   b. FREEDOM'S LAMENT,

c. FREEDOM'S REVIVAL,   d. FREEDOM'S JUBILEE.

Composed by Mr. A. D. LOGAN.

ORDER OF DANCING.

———————

1. LANCERS......................................

2. REDOWA......................................

3. GALOP..

4. LANCERS ....

5. POLKA..

6. QUADRILLE...................................

7. GALOP..

8. REDOWA ....

9. LANCERS ....

10. POLKA REDOWA..............................

11. GALOP. ....

12. LANCERS ....

———————

FLOOR COMMITTEE.:

WILLIAM WARDEN,   WILLIAM C. OTIS,

JOHN BARSTOW.

Figure 14. Benefit Concert and Ball at the Ocean House, August 14, 1862. The ritual of nightly dances helped create and sustain a sense of group solidarity. Most hotels hired their own dancing masters, who prepared participants for the hops. (Courtesy of the Rhode Island Historical Society.)

European social round of feasts and tournament. In the latter, the travels of the international knightly class took them from place to place but always among social equals and provided both host and guest an outlet to display social prestige. Medieval lords and ladies usually treated one another with courtesy based on the external signs that proved their status. Similarly, antebellum travelers flitted from resort to resort in a fashion so coordinated that one often saw the same faces from one place to another as one traveled the circuit. The watering place round helped create a sense of solidarity among those who journeyed in the summer season and enticingly beckoned all Americans to visit resorts.[42]

Pilgrimage, the religiously motivated desire to travel, is a form of sanctification common all over the world. Almost all people identify certain attributes of time and space, such as heights, water, or trees, as especially significant, if not sacred. Although Christianity did not require it, pilgrimage played a prominent role in the European tradition, particularly as a seasonal activity usually performed during warmer weather. People marked the year's progress with a series of alternations between the sacred and the profane that served as one way to rupture the sameness of commonplace existence; after all, Aristotle had speculated that no one could endure even the Absolute Good forever without becoming bored. The association of mobility with pleasure, autonomy, freedom, and an escape from necessity and purpose has been an element of modern Western culture since at least the Middle Ages. Some form of deliberate travel to a far place intimately associated with the deepest, most cherished axiomatic values of the traveler seems to be almost universal, both for individuals and groups.[43]

Most cultural traditions are familiar with the concept of humans as pilgrims, life as a journey, and death as a "passing," from which derives the image of travel as a metaphor for change. In nineteenth-century America, however, narrative sequences of voyaging were a pervasive thematic concern and recurrent symbolic action that linked works as diverse as Walt Whitman's "Song of the Open Road," Herman Melville's exotic travel narratives, and Mark Twain's *Huckleberry Finn,* and the influence of John Bunyan's *Pilgrim's Progress.* Images of mobility embodied in the concept of Manifest Destiny dominated American thought throughout the century, culminating in Frederick Jackson Turner's frontier thesis, which transformed the lowly migrant to the founder of American democracy. By tradition, American history began with journeys of exploration and escape, and mainstream culture elevated the voyages of the Puritans and the Pilgrims into national myth.[44]

Americans traveling abroad routinely envisioned their trips as pilgrimages to sacred shrines in quest of the ineffable distinction of the initiate. Guidebooks, with their quasi-religious imperatives about what sights to see and what responses to express, stressed the ritualistic aspects of traveling. Adventurers, missionaries, and tourists produced a flood of writings based on travels to Palestine; Mark Twain appended the subtitle, *The New Pilgrim's Progress,* to his travelogue, *The Innocents Abroad* (1869), and Herman Melville commemorated his spiritual journey in 1857 in *Clarel: A Poem and a Pilgrimage in the Holy Land* (1876). In nineteenth-century America, romantic quests, foreign sojourns, and especially the wanderings of fashionable travelers were all conflated with pilgrimage.[45]

In some cases, Americans conceived themselves as pilgrimaging to natural objects that revealed God's power and glory. Nathaniel Hawthorne opened "My Visit to Niagara" (1852) with the declaration, "Never did a pilgrim approach Niagara with deeper enthusiasm, than mine." Hawthorne bought a "pilgrim staff" from an Indian souvenir shop and, like so many others, approached the falls as if it were a religious shrine. Scenes from Thomas Cole's celebrated allegory of life as a river journey, *The Voyage of Life*, were the most frequently found engravings in American homes between 1850 and 1875. In the same way, visitors to Saratoga often expropriated pilgrimage terminology to describe their excursions, even though the resort lacked sublime natural sights. Thus, in 1825, Henry Gilpin wrote of Saratoga, "All parts of the country pour forth their children, on the pilgrimage of fashion, or perhaps of health." Jacob Delameter, writing on the efficacy of the Saratoga waters in 1844, discovered that "among the pilgrims to this shrine of health may be found a numerous and constantly increasing class of the wealth, the beauty, and the talent of the land." One guidebook envisioned Saratoga as "the great physical mecca. Hither come from near and far hundreds of pilgrims." This linkage between pilgrimage and Saratoga seems entirely logical because of the latter's origins as a health resort and its affiliation with healing water, an inherently sacred archetype.[46]

Pilgrimage, however, outgrew its relationship with the miraculous springs, as writers blatantly secularized the concept. "The infatuated Moslem who thinks so highly of his holy pilgrimages," observed one journalist in 1858, "needs only to watch the movements of our railways and steamboats during the sunny season to lose the last vestige of his conceit." Visitors constantly referred to both Newport and Saratoga as "the Mecca of Pilgrims from all parts of the country" and extended the metaphor as far as it could go. George Curtis ambled "down the street to Congress Hall, [where] we make a pilgrimage to the piazza. . . . For when Saratoga was first fashionable, Congress Hall was the temple of fashion." Even the aimless wandering at these two resorts echoed ancient pilgrimage practices with their emphasis on ritual circumambulation at the site. Migrations that in ancient times resulted from earthquakes, crusades, plagues, wars, or famines were now set in motion "by an irresistible craving for change, by worship of fashion, by hopes of improving health, by love of show and finery, and by love of the good things of life."[47]

This overt literary linkage of pilgrimage and tourism appealed to an American public that placed a high value on both religious sentiment and travel yet had become ever more worldly minded. As face-to-face culture disappeared in the United States under the onslaught of urbanization, new rites replaced the fading rituals of a more God-fearing society. Secularization, the process by which religious creeds, institutions, and symbols either dissolve or cease to dominate society and culture, made increasing inroads in nineteenth-century America. The expansion of capitalism transformed many religious festivals, such as Christmas and Easter, into profane celebrations of consecrated consumption. Obsessive rationalization led to, in sociologist Max Weber's famous phrase, "the disenchantment of the world."[48]

In response, even spiritual leaders attempted to harness the travel experience to reinvigorate Christianity. The Reverend B. Weed Gorham's well-known *Camp Meeting Manual* (1854) meditated on the wellspring of organizing a successful religious revival meeting: "The truth is, human life needs to be dotted over with occasions of stirring interest. The journey asks its milestones, or rather, if you please, its watering places along the way. Our nature requires the occurrence now and then of some event of special interest; something that shall peer up from the dead level of existence—an object for hope to rest upon in the future—an oasis in the desert of the remembered past." Yet the enthusiastic religious camp meeting disappeared as an institution of the rural backwoods, replaced by an entrepreneurial element that developed the site as a watering place. Covenant deeds at religious meeting grounds might require rigorous Sabbath observance and restrict unacceptable leisure activities, but eventually the town would allow dancing, and the meeting ground and tabernacle would slowly be supplanted by boardwalks and amusements.[49]

For Protestant America, which had officially rejected a pilgrimage tradition to areas of mystical significance, Saratoga and Newport served as disenchanted pilgrimage sites. A summer journey to these resorts allowed the visitor to demarcate time into mundane and sacred segments. Holidays—the very word derives from "holy day"—became disassociated from religion yet often retained a connection with travel to a distant place. Though moralists might label this travel frivolous, people utilized the choice of vacation destination as a means to define themselves in the modern world. Travelers often lived in remembrance of one vacation and in expectation of the next, and this anticipation helped make their lives tolerable. The goal of such journeys might have been secular, but antebellum resorts inherited from pilgrimage the concept of a hidden paradise, the hope of renewal, and the quest for strange knowledge in a communal setting. Travel, whether by tourists or pilgrims, generated an extraordinary drive to give personal testimony, and participants characteristically delighted in recounting details of their journeys long after the events had passed. Guidebooks, stories, testimonies, and travel accounts all worked to sacralize the site and accentuate its power.[50]

Nineteenth-century Americans eagerly grasped the potency of the travel experience. An 1841 travel guide asserted, "To give to home all its value and endearments, nothing can be better than travelling." As she approached Saratoga for the first time, young Eliza Thompson gushed, "We have been in such a continual state of excitement that I hardly know whether I am on my head or my heels." Edith Wharton lived in Newport as a young woman from June until February, yet for her, the famed city on the Narragansett held no charms. Her "travel fever" took her abroad for the other four months every year, and she later recalled that "it was then that I really felt alive." Joanna Anthon's diary recounted summer trips meticulously, but little else filled the journal except the death of acquaintances. For Anthon, the watering place not only offered an idealized vision of the possibilities of life, it was life itself.[51]

Like most sustained mass movements, accretions of legend, myth, and folklore attached themselves to both pilgrimage destinations and resorts. Visitors consumed stories about incidents at watering places, repeated ad infinitum in guidebooks, travelers' accounts, and word of mouth, incidents that would have been forgotten had they occurred anywhere else. Myths such as the invention of the potato chip at Saratoga or the origins of the Newport Tower grew ever more elaborate, and stories were often blatantly fabricated to add to the mystique of the vacation destination. For example, the legendary Saratoga tale of the espousal of William H. Vanderbilt's daughter to a poor Western Union clerk was totally fictitious; the groom was a proper Bostonian who had parlayed a modest inheritance into a fortune in railroad holdings. Anecdotes were recycled to whatever watering place celebrity was in vogue; the oft-repeated "don't let me detain you" anecdote about excessive consumption of the Saratoga waters, originally attributed to John Saxe, eventually transmigrated to the stuttering William Travers. Resort cities traced their "founding" back to events no more believable than the tale of Romulus and Remus. At Newport, the mysterious old stone mill took on iconic significance, while Saratogians propounded the story of Mohawk braves carrying Sir William Johnson in a litter to High Rock Spring for miraculous treatment of wounds received in the Battle of Lake George in

1767. That this unlikely story could not be corroborated had little effect on its popularity. Apocryphal or not, Johnson's arduous journey by litter supplied the perfect origin necessary for the city of play.[52]

By the time of the Civil War, the legendary cities of Newport and Saratoga divided America between them. The *New York Express* queried in 1848, "Newport or Saratoga?—That is the question now among the . . . fashionable *belles* and *beaux* of this city, and of Boston, Philadelphia, and Baltimore. Which is to be *the* fashionable place?" At these resorts, dreams of self-fulfillment, social advance, and erotic possibility seemed more real than at home. A pilgrimage to Newport or Saratoga counteracted to some degree the diminution of adventure Americans sensed in modern, urban, productive society. In response to the monotonous routine of life in a bureaucratic world, resorts created an opportunity for excitement and self-discovery and provided occasions to exercise personal autonomy. No wonder travelers who visited watering places reveled in their appellation as "pilgrims."[53]

Pilgrimage sites have a material as well as a spiritual side, and some Americans raised their voices against Newport's transformation from "a casual watering place" to "the haunt of the vicious, the frivolous, and the debauched." An increase in the number of saloons and brothels paralleled the growth in hotels, and a soup kitchen opened downtown near the wharves to serve the urban poor. The number of criminals swelled to such a degree that the city converted the Asylum for the Poor into a prison. As a result of the political upheavals in Rhode Island in 1842, collectively known as the Dorr Rebellion, the state legislature had expanded the powers of Newport's town marshal to allow the arrest of "suspicious, disorderly, or riotous persons." Unfortunately, the number of these undesirables seemed to multiply each summer; costs for police and night watchmen rose accordingly, and the city even authorized the town crier to purchase a bell in 1854. By that time, Newport mayors decried the "dens of iniquity" and "the slumbering spirit of rowdyism" in the community. "Look at the gathering at the United States, or Congress Hall, or the Fillmore, or the Ocean!" grumbled a New York newspaper. "A gathering full of the follies of fashion, the infatuation of wealth, above all, the pretensions of snobbism and absurd shabby genteelism."[54]

Of course, the history of tourism is replete with those who lament the popularization of heretofore undiscovered travel destinations. "The old Bellevue, and the present Touro House, then Whitfield's, sufficed for the strangers," reminisced George Curtis about the "old days" at Newport. "It was before the Polka—before the days of music after dinner—and when the word 'hop' was unknown even at Saratoga." Curtis contrasted this image of repose with the Newport of the 1850s dominated by hotel culture: "This amorphous 'Ocean'; this Grecian 'Atlantic'; this 'Bellevue' enlarged out of all recognizable proportions; this whirl of fashionable equipages, these hats and coats, this confused din of dancing music, scandal, flirtation, serenades, and supreme voice of the sea breaking through the fog and dust; this sing-ing, dancing, and dawdling incessantly; this crushing into a month in the country that which crowds six months in the town—these are the foot-prints of Fashion upon the sea-shore." The foundation of the Newport Histori-cal Society in 1853 reflected the fear that the more virtuous ways of the old Newport were rapidly disappearing. No less a Newport booster than George Mason plaintively asked in 1859, "Must our beloved city continue to bear the ignoble reputation of being nothing more than a fashionable watering place?"[55]

The failure of the temperance movement in Newport exemplified the moral decay seen by so many conservative commentators, who felt Newport prostituted civic virtue on the altar of commercial profit. The city did not have a reputation as a temperance town, just as it had not led the fight against the slave power. Even the smallest resort hotel furnished a place to drink alcohol in order to ease social intercourse, and all hoteliers felt threatened when the Rhode Island legislature passed a series of laws culminating with an 1852 act that stringently regulated the sale of liquors. The *Mercury* pleaded with locals to uphold the law, lest outsiders think of the city as a "community of rum suckers." Despite the presence of some pro-temperance Washingto-nians, however, most Newport residents viewed sumptuary legislation as a menace to the town's prosperity. The city quickly acquired a reputation in Rhode Island for its civil disobedience, and stubborn summer visitors, with the forbearance of hotel keepers, packed sherry and port in their luggage. A similar situation occurred again in 1886 after Rhode Island passed another prohibitionary law.[56]

Actions speak louder than words, and some of the criticism of Newport represented nothing more than antebellum uneasiness with leisure and lux-ury. Sidney Fisher journeyed to Newport in 1839 and, after staying three weeks, found it "very dull." He visited again in 1841, only to tire "of the lazy, useless, life I was leading" and return to Philadelphia. Yet in 1842, Fisher spent three more weeks in Newport ("not very agreeably") and concluded, "parties & balls in summer are in my opinion detestable. . . . There were no persons whom I cared for. . . . The accommodations were bad, much worse than heretofore. On the whole I was bored & think I shall not go again without a special object." Fisher must have found his object, for he stayed for three weeks the very next year. Of course, he "did not pass the time agreeably. . . . The place was crowded, the society was dull and commonplace . . . the balls I thought very stupid." He returned in 1844 ("There was nothing remarkable for beauty among the company"), again in 1846 ("less agreeable to me"), 1847 ("I suffered a good deal from ennui"), and 1848 ("the Ocean House was perfectly detestable, dirty, uncomfortable, ill-kept, and filled with hateful, vulgar people, chiefly New Yorkers"). Not until 1855, after as many as ten return trips, would Fisher momentarily admit that Newport could now be ranked as "a great place."[57]

Great or not, the city had fared well despite the collapse of its commercial economy. The saturnalia of fashion on the hill mocked the rotting wharves and old hulks that lay in the harbor. Promoters conceded that Newport's growth did not match that of industrializing northern Rhode Island; between 1830 and 1860, Newport's population jumped 32 percent (to 10,508), but the population of the state increased 80 percent, and that of Providence skyrocketed 201 percent (to 50,666). Nonetheless, Newport finally exceeded its population of a century earlier and in 1860 could claim to be the only city in the southern half of Rhode Island with more than five thousand inhabitants. In summer, of course, the number of people in town literally doubled. "Newport is pre-eminently our Watering-place, nor is there any in the world superior in variety or charm," declared *Harper's Monthly* in 1854; "Saratoga is a hotel, Newport is a realm."[58]

Newport's transformation from comatose seaport to summer haven had generally been a smashing success. It had become "the gayest of the gay," boasted the *Mercury*, "fashion thronging its streets." In 1859, local boosters organized a "re-union of the sons and daughters of Newport," a grand fete intended to advertise Newport ascendant for those who had missed the developments of the past twenty years. The resulting pageant drew more than "ten thousand strangers," according to front page headlines in the *New York Times*, whose correspondent complained, "Newport is always full—no way one could find a hotel even in normal conditions." The resort industry had enabled Newport to cast off the torpor in which it had been shrouded since the British occupation and to recreate itself as a pilgrimage center dedicated to pleasure and consumption. "We have the most absolute faith in steam factories," wrote one frightened letter writer from Providence, "[but] we do not wish to see any more built in Newport. . . . Let not the hum of spindles mock the music of the Sea." By this time, James Fenimore Cooper had completely reversed his three-decade-old judgment of Newport as an ancient town in repose. Returning from Providence to New York by steamer, Cooper noted, "Newport is breaking up for the season. Thousands have been there. It very fairly rivals Saratoga."[59]

THREE

The Rise of Coney Island

Strangers in the Land of the Perpetual Fete

AT CONEY ISLAND IN 1880, the air resounded with a cacophony of noise from twenty or thirty bands and carousel organs, the laughter of crowds, and the muffled roar of the surf. Donkey rides, fireworks, hot-air balloons, sea castles, hot dogs, and children all jumbled together in a chaotic mass. Dozens of hotels, including three immense grand hotels and another shaped like a giant elephant, shared the skyline with the tallest structure in the United States. Barkers cajoled, pleaded, and harassed strollers, while everywhere wafted smells of chowder and sausage. Saloons, bursting with people devouring clams and drinking beer, dotted the horizon, amid a bevy of peddlers with baskets selling all sorts of knickknacks. To an observer, the most astonishing thing was Coney's apparent permanence; José Martí noted, "This spending, this uproar, these crowds, the activity of this amazing ant hill never slackens from June to October, from morning 'til night, without pause, without interruption, without variation." Coney Island seemed to be a world's fair in continuous operation.[1]

Although superficially different, postbellum Coney Island shared many traits with its nineteenth-century predecessors. Like Saratoga and Newport, Coney initially offered people an opportunity to interact in a ritualistic setting beyond the ken of everyday life. Visitors enjoyed the seaside as a breezy place to see and be seen, a realm of pleasure and disorder, an experience tangential to economic calculation. Vast public spaces, and especially the three grand resort hotels that dominated the Coney Island scene in

1880, took their cues from models already in place at antebellum watering places.

It took Coney Island longer to develop as a pleasure destination, however, than almost all of its nineteenth-century rivals. The first Europeans to visit Coney probably sailed on Henry Hudson's *Half Moon,* which anchored west of the island in 1609. Deborah Moody, fleeing Puritan religious homogeneity in Massachusetts, received a charter from the Dutch in New Netherlands and founded the town of Gravesend in 1645. The town purchased "Conye Islant," at the southern edge of what is now Brooklyn, New York, from Native Americans in 1654, but Moody's plans to build a maritime city ran aground in the shallow bay waters. When Jaspar Dankers visited the area in 1679, he found the island deserted, except for some foraging livestock, the indigenous Canarsie and Nyack tribes having disappeared. The continuously changing topography of the marshlands discouraged easy development over the next two centuries; one phenomenal storm in 1839 came close to washing away the entire island. Gravesend's beach seemed little more than valueless scrubland until the popularity of sea bathing in the eighteenth century impelled a few peripatetic colonial aristocrats to visit. The diary of Elizabeth Drinker records an excursion one September morning in 1769 from New York to Brooklyn by ferry and then "to Graves end and down to the Beach or sea Shore. H.D. went into the Surf and then [we] Return'd and Dined at Garrett Williamson's."[2]

To reach Gravesend's beach at this time, excursionists had to ford the creek at low tide separating Coney from the rest of Kings County. "I have been to Coney Island several times this season," wrote David Tallman to longtime resident and town supervisor John Terhune in 1814. "If we had money sufficient to build good buildings & a Dock + bridge & get a steam boat to run down from New York in the morning & up towards evening it would exceed any place of resort in this Country." Tallman's prophetic vision, which also included a plan to construct "flo[a]ting Baths on the South Shore, & establish a race ground on the South Shor[e]s of the Island at low water," piqued the interest of John Terhune and his brother Abraham. They invested $6,000 to build a private toll road across the creek and then the Coney Island House, the first hotel on the island. The aptly named Shell Road (currently, McDonald Avenue), constructed of little more than thousands of seashells, connected the city of Brooklyn with the beach through regular stage service in the 1820s. The Terhunes stressed the restorative qualities of the seaside and the safety of the bathing, even for women and children, which supposedly gave "Coney Island advantages which are seldom equalled."[3]

Following the trail cut at Newport and Cape May, leisure entrepreneurs attempted to exploit Coney Island's seashore, although early plans rarely came to fruition. The beach remained deserted enough in August of 1827 for Captain Thomas Field to bring forty of his troops to the Coney Island House to practice their target shooting. In the memoirs of his youth, which he attached to his diaries of the Civil War, Walt Whitman fondly recalled visiting Coney regularly in the 1830s. After swimming, Whitman loved to race up and down the hard sand, with no other person in sight, "and declaim Homer and Shakespeare to the surf and sea gulls by the hour." Until the Civil War, empty beach littered with the decaying timbers of shipwrecks dominated many Coney Island vistas, and landscape artists flocked to the island to find richly evocative subject matter. Regis Gignoux inaugurated the trend when he presented *A Coney Island Beach* at the National Academy of Design in 1844. In John Falconer's *On Coney Island,* exhibited by the Brooklyn Art Association in 1864, no sign of the beach's incipient resort status could be ascertained. Painters continued to return to Coney Island and, as at Newport, stubbornly persisted in painting romantic patches of remote beach and windswept dunes even as these scenes disappeared under the impact of thousands of visitors.[4]

The slowly increasing desirability of the heretofore worthless salt marsh perplexed the conservative agricultural populace of the town of Gravesend, the titular owners of Coney Island. In laying out the town, each of the thirty-nine original Dutch settlers had received an equal share of land both in the town and on the beach. The descendants of these patentees were primarily farmers, and, as one gazetteer put it, "with the language, [they] preserve the industry and frugality of their ancestors." Until 1843, residents of this backwater had to journey to the town of Flatbush merely to use a post office, and they showed little inclination to profit from the beachfront property. From 1810 to 1830, Gravesend's population never exceeded seven hundred—a density of less than one person to every ten acres—and as late as 1860, only "about half a dozen families" wintered on Coney Island. Locals complained vociferously of wholesale breaking of the Sabbath when visitors began to arrive in ever greater numbers thanks to an omnibus line. A toll-booth keeper on Shell Road counted three hundred vehicles on July 4, 1844, drawn by new hotels and boardinghouses and the appeal of mixed bathing popularized by the wealthy at Newport.[5]

Just as Ballston Spa challenged Saratoga's dominance, any number of rivals to Coney Island arose within striking distance of New York. At least forty-eight American picnic groves and pleasure gardens, some of which lasted more than twenty years, operated in the metropolitan New York area between 1700 and 1865. Derived from European models, and ranging from minute beer gardens to the multiacre Elysian Fields outside Hoboken, these sites attracted individuals, social societies, and fraternal organizations. Hotel-oriented resorts also tried to attract Manhattan and Brooklyn clientele. In 1833, a company that included Governor John King and Mayor Philip Hone built the Marine Pavilion Hotel on the Rockaway peninsula (Queens County), where many wealthy New York families spent their summers. In the stiff competition for the moniker of New York's supreme watering place, Coney Island in the 1830s possessed no particular edge over the sea-bathing attractions of Long Branch (on the New Jersey shore), Rockaway, or Long Island. In fact, Coney Island lacked year-round inhabitants, and if the resort were to retain its reputation as "a place of great resort for strangers during the summer season," the impetus would have to come from somewhere else.[6]

Coney's surge began with better transportation connections from Brooklyn and Manhattan to the beach. The opening of the Coney Island Plank Road in 1850 eased access, and in 1860, the planks were removed so that horse cars could operate on the new Coney Island Avenue. In 1847, the year the Fall River Line from New York to Newport was established, regular steamboat service commenced from New York to Coney Island. A small side-wheel steamer charged fifty cents and took two hours to make the trip, enabling the visitor to leave New York on the 7:00 A.M. boat and return during the late afternoon with plenty of time to enjoy the surf. The immediate success of the steamboats resulted in a price reduction to twenty-five cents round trip. One visitor recalled a Sunday in the summer of 1850 when more than twenty-five hundred people visited the island: "The attractions of the place were the crowd, the trip, the cool-breezes, and the magnificent panorama of the Ocean" (figure 15). By this time, stages left Brooklyn for Coney Island several times a day during the summer, and hotels and boardinghouses were springing up like eelgrass.[7]

The Coney Island House remained the most prestigious hotel at the

Figure 15. "Scene at Coney Island—Sea Bathing Illustrated," *Frank Leslie's*, September 20, 1856. This early view reveals the resort's primitive state until the establishment of better transportation in the 1870s. (Collection of the author.)

shore, and the guest register from 1848 to 1852 was a veritable who's who of antebellum politics and culture, including P. T. Barnum, Jenny Lind (who visited on the day of her arrival to New York), Daniel Webster and Henry Clay (both on July 11, 1850), Washington Irving, Herman Melville, Sam Houston, James Gordon Bennett, Lyman Beecher, William Macready, William Gilmore Simms, Fitz-Greene Halleck, and Edgar Allan Poe. The hotel registered an average of fifteen arrivals daily during the summer, most of whom were from the North but some from as far away as Cuba, Mexico, and England. The unrestricted nature of the beach, however, did not please everyone; the "hordes of outside barbarians" so disturbed the *New York Herald* watering place correspondent in 1848 that he simply gave up and went to Saratoga in the middle of the summer.[8]

Until 1870, the western end of the island closest to Manhattan, known as Schreyer's Hook or Coney Island Point, generally dominated the entertainment scene. In 1844, a pair of speculators leased some land there and built the Coney Island Pavilion, actually little more than a large wooden platform covered with a tent. The Pavilion Hotel followed, and then a motley assortment of restaurants, bathhouses, saloons, and shacks. Each lot holder built to his or her own satisfaction, leading to a confusing array of structures, without first-class hotels or carriage drives. Well into the 1870s, only a wagon ride along the shore at low tide connected the Coney Island Point to the rest of the island. Mike Norton, a notorious local politician, and Mike Murray, a popular sporting man, owned Norton's Hotel and its accompanying seven hundred primitive bathhouses. The area earned a reputation among the more fastidious as a supposed haven for confidence men and a refuge for criminals. Popular opinion held that thieves and pimps pounced upon disembarking passengers at the landing, picking their pockets, tricking them at games of chance, and encouraging them to visit prostitutes. Rumors that Boss Tweed hid out at Norton's on his way to Spain after jumping bail in 1876 only enhanced the West End's notoriety as a place apart.[9]

To counteract this image, Coney Island's boosters touted its invigorating atmosphere and cool sea breezes, and urbanites began to flock there as a respite from the relentless summer heat of the metropolis. In 1863, Peter Ravenhall, a Brooklyn harness maker, leased land on the shorefront and built a bathing "palace" and restaurant noted for its champagne lunches. The island had still barely been touched by commercial development; a newspaper article in 1865 reported that the sensible public now visited Coney to fish, not like the ne'er-do-wells who gallivanted at Saratoga and Newport. That same year, Peter Tilyou opened the first of many beach establishments, renting out fancy flannel bathing suits and selling Bavarian lager beer for five cents a glass. "All day Saturday and Sunday," wrote a reporter in 1866, "while thousands of people swelter in our streets, the Coney Island cars from Brooklyn and the little steamer *Naushon*, from the City, were carrying hundreds to the island, where they enjoyed the luxury of a bath in the surf." Happy throngs gobbled down the local specialty of roasted clams; ten thousand a day were supposedly consumed at one hotel. An 1868 guidebook listed Coney Island unequivocally as the "best beach on the Atlantic coast," and the *New York Times* noted that Coney "has few attractions, but those few are supreme."[10]

Yet Gravesend's population density before the Civil War barely surpassed that of westernmost Suffolk County on Long Island. To visit Coney Island, Brooklynites had to ride incredibly slow fifteen-person omnibuses through the outer towns of Kings County, undoubtedly the reason that guidebooks sometimes listed Coney as a "minor resort." George Templeton Strong's visit to the island in October 1867 on a marine zoology expedition took almost three hours to cover the ten miles. The Brooklyn, Bath, and Coney Island Railroad (now the "B" train), owned by C. Godfrey Gunther, the former mayor of Brooklyn, had been set up primarily to connect Brooklyn and the country towns of Kings County, not to provide rapid transportation to the beach.[11]

This transportation bottleneck challenged the ingenuity of enterprising politicians, city planners, and speculators to devise new ways of satisfying the demand to visit the seashore. One distinguished attempt was Frederick Law Olmsted and Calvert Vaux's toll-supported Ocean Parkway, running from Brooklyn's version of the Arc de Triomphe at Grand Army Plaza to Coney Island's newly created Surf Avenue. Six miles long and two hundred feet wide, and built at a cost of a million dollars, the parkway, claimed Kings County boosters, represented a work of suburban embellishment without rival, "the finest drive in America," comparable, even, to the Champs Élysées. Still, it would take more than a wide boulevard, however beautiful, to lift Coney Island out of the pack to the forefront of beach resorts in the world.[12]

Steamboats provided an alternative to the difficulties of putting together a large-scale overland route to Coney across private property. By 1879, nine separate steamboat lines served the island from places as far away as Philadelphia, New Haven, Hartford, and Newark. Fraternal lodges, religious and social groups, and political organizations of every size sponsored outdoor gatherings at Coney, ranging from the Catholic Knights of America to the Sherman Park Association (real estate), from the Knights of Labor to Yale Lock Company, from the Odd Fellows to the Turnverein. The Iron Steamboat Company, which commenced regular service in 1881, invested $2 million in boats and piers and then tried to coordinate round-trip tickets with the railroads. Each of the company's seven vessels had a capacity of almost two thousand passengers, and the steamboat excursion to Coney Island quickly became an accepted special occasion in the Gilded Age.[13]

Steamboats needed to dock, and by 1880, no seaside resort worth its salt could be without an elaborate pier. This structure quickly acquired functions far beyond a mere landing dock and assumed the role of a meeting place, promenade, and amusement center. At Coney Island, the Ocean Pier and Navigation Company built the Iron Pier into the Atlantic in 1878. The even larger "New" Iron Pier on Surf Avenue near West Fifth Street, built for the Iron Steamboat Company in the same year, protruded a thousand feet into the ocean and contained a promenade deck, twelve hundred bath lockers, an elegant restaurant, a saloon, two barrooms, an oyster house, and an ice cream parlor (figure 16). By 1882, nearly two million people arrived yearly by steamboat at Coney Island, and the piers themselves became major attractions. They complemented the voyeurism of a stroll on the hotel veranda or the beach by providing additional possibilities for display, discussion, and flirtation. Tellingly, Coney Island's pier advertised itself as "first class . . . [with] all the accessories and conveniences of a hotel."[14]

Just as upstate railroads had initially developed as a way to connect visitors with the watering place of Saratoga, so the desire of urbanites to visit Coney Island instigated almost every Gilded Age railroad transportation project in Brooklyn. In an amazing burst of development between 1865 and 1878, entrepreneurs installed five major lines from Brooklyn to Coney Island and two more small cross-island spurs. An enormous amount of political manipulation, skullduggery, and outright bribery went into the acquisition of these franchises, and the competition generated incredible confusion as railroads changed names and owners and went in and out of service. By the summer of 1878, however, more than 250 trains daily transported visitors to and from Coney. These railroads provided only sporadic year-round service to Gravesend until the 1890s, because the needs of permanent residents paled before the possibilities of profit from travelers in pursuit of pleasure.[15]

The most prominent railroad was the double-tracked Prospect Park and Coney Island Railroad (now the "F" train), which could carry passengers from Park Slope in central Brooklyn to the ocean in thirty minutes. Business experts had jeered when Andrew Culver built the wide-gauge, but he aggressively promoted West Brighton and built a hotel known as "Cables" at the end of the line, surrounded by a broad plaza perfect for promenading (figure 17). The railroad produced immediate profits, carrying a million passengers the first year, two million the second, and almost four million by 1879.[16]

Fierce competition now ensued to win the patronage of visitors from Brooklyn and Manhattan, for Culver was not the only railroad man who sensed gold at the shore. According to legend, the grand Manhattan Beach Hotel owed its existence to the illness of the daughter of railroad financier

Austin Corbin, who deposited his family on salubrious Coney Island in 1874. Despite the "poor rooms, and poorer fare," Corbin's child recovered, and the banker realized that Coney "possessed all the requisites of a watering place—needing, to be appreciated and patronized, only *to be known.*" He quietly bought the leases and titles to the eastern end of the island for a ridiculously low sum and then gained control of the bankrupt New York, Bay Ridge, and Jamaica Railroad (parallel to the "D" train). Corbin combined the two enterprises, and voila, a new resort, Manhattan Beach, emerged on eastern Coney Island, where earlier maps reveal only a remote and inaccessible tidal swamp known as the Sedge Bank. Through skillful acquisitions, Corbin successfully converted his new railroad from a commercial freight carrier running east to west to a north-south road primarily hauling seasonal traffic to the beach.[17]

Corbin's machinations revealed that the title to the increasingly lucrative beachfront land remained notoriously vague. Did the original charter of 1645 grant the lands to the town as a corporation or to individuals as tenants in common? If the former, then the island belonged to the Town of Gravesend, but otherwise, the "common lands" belonged to the heirs of the original patentees, now in their eighth generation and scattered throughout the United States. In 1847, the commissioners of common lands had stopped dividing the rent money for the western half of the island with the descendants of the original patentees and began depositing it directly into the town's treasury. In 1860, the Town of Gravesend baldly declared itself de facto owner of this land. "In the absence of those having a better title," a journalist reported, "the Commissioners of Gravesend have arrogated to themselves the right to exercise jurisdiction in the premises which they do by charging a small amount of annual rent to those who have erected hotels and saloons." When Nicholas Johnson, a local resident and descendant of one of the original patentees, sued the town, the defendants successfully argued that the seventeenth-century patent awarded Coney Island to Gravesend, not to the thirty-nine individuals. Thus, the town acquired clear title to western Coney Island.[18]

Things were different on the eastern and central sections of the island, where Austin Corbin and William Engeman respectively had found purchasing the interests of the scattered heirs to be difficult and time consuming (Engeman located some heirs as far away as the Sandwich Islands). In 1873, Corbin's agents, including future Brooklyn mayor Alfred Chapin,

Figure 16. The New Iron Pier, Coney Island, ca. 1895. This pier, built in 1878, contained twelve hundred bath lockers, an elegant restaurant, a saloon, two barrooms, an oyster house, an ice cream parlor, and a promenade deck. Note the roller coaster in the corner. (Courtesy of the Brooklyn Historical Society [v1972.1.832].)

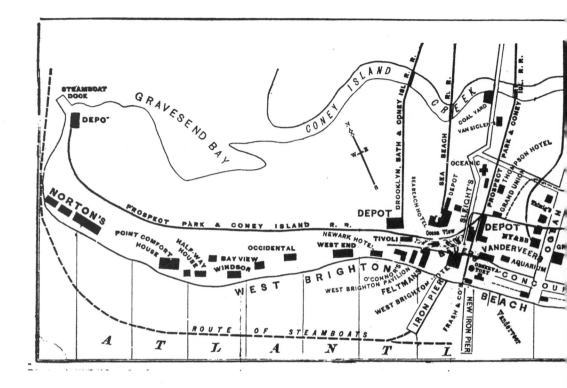

paid one dollar to each of 105 Gravesend residents for their claims to portions of land on the Sedge Bank. Corbin's representatives bought the titles in their own names and exchanged them among themselves to obscure ownership. By 1874, Corbin controlled two hundred acres, but he could not do much with the land because of the uncertainty surrounding the real estate. When he filed suit in New York Supreme Court in 1876 to establish title to his property, the court ruled that all contested property would be auctioned at a series of public hearings in the winter of 1876–77. Corbin's agents then proceeded to buy the lots for no more than $300 each. A raucous town meeting ensued in 1879, in which, according to the *New York Times*, "the old residents claim that a crowd of roughs, who were non-residents, were allowed to vote." Nonetheless, the commissioners of the common lands voted to abide by the decision of two assessors, one appointed by the Town of Gravesend and the other by Corbin, to set a price at which Corbin could purchase the town's claim to all of the land east of Engeman's prop-

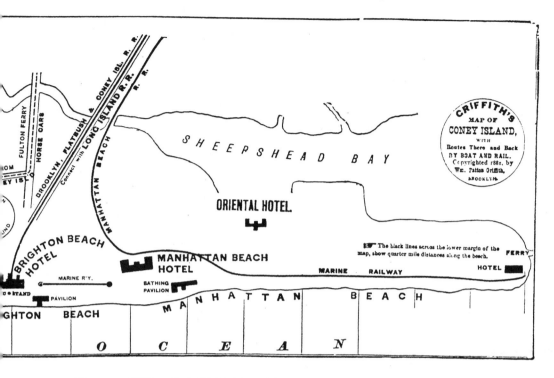

Figure 17. William P. Griffith's Map of Coney Island, 1881. The lines across the lower margins show quarter-mile distances; little more than a mile separated the steamboat piers from the Manhattan Beach Hotel. (Collection of the author.)

erty. Gravesend's assessor accepted the $1,500 assessment of Corbin's counsel without even determining the full extent of the property. Corbin therefore bought more than five hundred acres of shorefront land on eastern Coney Island for $16,500, which he immediately valued at $500,000 in a Manhattan Beach prospectus.[19]

On a site that the previous year had been the abode of wild duck, Corbin opened his Manhattan Beach Hotel in July of 1877. This lavish Queen Anne–style caravanserai, with a depth of 225 feet and ninety-one guest rooms, had ocean frontage of 475 feet. The hotel's first two seasons were so successful that visitors repeatedly had to be given beds in the dining room because of the extremely large crowds. Corbin expanded the hotel in 1879 by adding full third and fourth floors and raising the number of guest rooms to two hundred; he then proclaimed it "the largest sea-side structure in the world." Corbin followed this success with the Oriental Hotel in 1880, a quarter of a mile east and slightly larger than the Manhattan Beach Hotel.

At a cost of half a million dollars, the Oriental's architects integrated ornate Moorish characteristics into the hotel's details, resulting in a playful building replete with towers, pinnacles, minarets, and a mansard roof thrown in for good measure (figure 18).[20]

The Oriental and the Manhattan Beach hotels, separated from West Brighton by an unimproved expanse of sand, positioned themselves as "respectable" resorts. The two hotels, on a tract of five hundred acres with a two-mile sea frontage, each had room for more than four hundred overnight guests as well as restaurants, spacious piazzas, magnificent halls, and affiliated bands. According to the promotional material, Corbin's company possessed sole proprietorship of the land, "enabling it to control the character of its visitors; consequently, at no watering-place is the representation of the best social classes larger than at Manhattan Beach." Like all resort hotel owners, Corbin hired plainclothes police officers and security guards to patrol the area. "I never saw so many prosperous-looking people in one place, more with better and smarter clothes, even though they were a little showy," reminisced the novelist Theodore Dreiser of the Manhattan Beach Hotel. "What a cool, summery, airy-fairy realm!"[21]

The promotional material, however, clashed with reality, for the Manhattan Beach Hotel was decidedly not the place to go to escape the crush of the city. In the late 1870s, the *Brooklyn Eagle* often reported thirty thousand people or more at Manhattan Beach. Like most grand resort hotels, the Manhattan Beach existed to be filled by vast multitudes; more than four thousand people could dine simultaneously at the hotel's various dining rooms, and according to legend, thirty-two thousand had once been served within twenty hours. A huge pavilion near the hotel accommodated another fifteen hundred people at dinner. Like every major hotel on Coney Island, the Manhattan Beach reserved considerable space for brown baggers, with tables, seats, and waiters provided free of charge. The twenty-seven hundred bathhouses at Manhattan Beach obviously far exceeded the hotel's overnight capacity, and the enormous eighteen-foot-wide verandas could hold a thousand people, offering patrons wonderful views of the ocean, the beach, and more importantly, fellow promenaders. Like its counterparts in Saratoga and Newport, the Manhattan Beach thrived not on exclusivity but on an economy of scale (figure 19).[22]

Corbin's construction of the Marine Railway in 1878 indicates that he never took his claims to exclusivity too seriously. Rather than isolate his

Figure 18. The Oriental Hotel at Coney Island in 1915, shortly before its demolition. In listing sights to be seen, guidebooks often ranked hotels higher than monuments, ruins, battlefields, or natural attractions. (Courtesy of the Brian Merlis Collection.)

hotel, Corbin specifically built this railroad to connect the eastern tip of Manhattan Beach to his competitor, the Brighton Beach Hotel, and the crowds at West Brighton. By the 1880s, the double-tracked railroad had a seasonal ridership of eight hundred thousand passengers and turned a profit virtually every year, charging a nickel for a mere three-stop ride. Coney Island guidebooks urged visitors to West Brighton to travel to the Manhattan Beach and the Oriental, and Corbin encouraged the traffic, if only to further his real estate schemes. Although innumerable contemporaries commented on the linear social stratification of the island, from the wealthiest visitors in the far east by the Oriental Hotel to the dregs of the sporting life at Norton's Point, the boundaries were exceedingly permeable (see figure 17). Corbin and Engeman's control of large parcels of land expedited large-scale luxury development, but families landing in West Brighton still took the marine railways or trudged up the sandy beach for dinner at Manhattan Beach. The sheer size of the major hotels, direct imitations of those at Saratoga and Newport, implies that Coney Island was never developed to be a truly fashionable resort.[23]

The success of Corbin's railroad and hotels impelled some Brooklyn

Figure 19. Manhattan Beach Hotel, ca. 1895. The eighteen-foot-wide veranda indicates that railroad financier Austin Corbin anticipated large crowds when he built the hotel in 1876. (Courtesy of the Brooklyn Historical Society [v1972.2.23].)

merchants and politicians to organize the competing Brooklyn, Flatbush, and Coney Island Railroad. In its first full season in 1879, this railroad racked up large profits while transporting another million people to the shore. Corbin had demonstrated that a company-owned railway terminus could generate additional profits, and so the Brooklyn, Flatbush, and Coney Island built its own Brighton Beach Hotel at the end of the line. Not to be outdone by its two large rivals to the east, the hotel seemed to literally rise out of the sea, all quaint corners and gables and hooded shades and piazzas. The Brighton Beach presented five immense pyramid-capped towers set atop a building 460 by 200 feet, surrounded by beautiful grounds laid out with boardwalks and flower gardens. When eroding beach and encroaching waves threatened the Brighton Beach in 1888, its owners moved the six-thousand-ton hotel fully five hundred feet back from its previous position on one hundred specially built railroad cars. The Brighton Beach advertised two hundred rooms with gas and water in each, yet the downstairs restaurant could feed two thousand at a single sitting, and the hotel once served twenty-six thousand persons in one day. Coney's grand hotels all required vast patronage in order to succeed, and they remained popular and profitable through the nineteenth century, continuously enlarged or improved by management.[24]

Slightly farther to the west, the New York and Sea Beach Railroad (now the "N" train) serviced the area known as West Brighton. The town of Gravesend generally rented the common lands on the western half of the island rather than selling them, and these subdivided land holdings produced developers anxious for a quick profit. Leasing permitted builders with limited resources and pressing creditors to aim at the lower levels of the market. The New York and Sea Beach Railroad also divided its beachfront property into small plots and leased them to concessionaires who paid $25,000 annually in rent for the privilege. This created an amusement district of mechanical rides, shooting galleries, cycloramas, photo galleries, saloons, and other cheap amusements (figure 20). The continued presence of renters, small property owners, boardinghouse keepers, and purveyors of cheap amusements ensured that the island would not become a resort exclusively for the wealthy.[25]

Coney Island now filled with hotels both large and small. In 1873, William Vanderveer, a former bricklayer and plasterer, built an eponymous three-story hotel and bathing pavilion, later run by his wife, Lucy. Paul

Figure 20. West Brighton Concourse, ca. 1880. Andrew Culver's railroad culminated in a broad, grassy plaza, perfect for promenading and soon surrounded by hotels and filled by concessionaires. (Courtesy of the Brooklyn Historical Society [v.1973.6.666].)

Bauer, an Austrian immigrant, arrived on Coney in 1876 and leased twelve acres of oceanfront land the next day. His West Brighton Hotel, "the favorite of our Teutonic friends," offered rooms for 250 guests and a dining room capable of seating 6,000 as well as a pavilion across from the hotel, where live music could be heard. William Engeman, a former cook who became rich during the Civil War selling mules to the government, acquired an undervalued two hundred acres of seaside grazing land in the central part of the island at bargain prices (only $3,000) in 1868 and opened the Ocean Hotel, which he already valued at $5,000 in the federal census of 1870. "Within the memory of many of us, a complete change of residence during the hot months was a luxury confined to the comparatively few," noted *Century Magazine*. "Now the case is changed past recognition. Social conditions seem to be ordered to meet a general summer exodus. Summer hotels are everywhere."[26]

After the conclusion of the Philadelphia Centennial Exposition in 1876,

Engeman purchased the Japanese and Brazilian pavilions and the United States Government building and resurrected them in West Brighton as a beer hall, a dairy, and a three-thousand-seat restaurant and hotel, respectively. Andrew Culver also raided the Philadelphia Centennial, acquiring the priapic tower known as the Sawyer Observatory and reassembling it on Coney Island in 1878. In an age before skyscrapers, this forerunner of the Eiffel Tower seemed of truly stupendous height, taller than any building in the United States at the time. Two steam elevators hoisted spectators three hundred feet over the island to witness a twenty-mile view. Immigrants arriving from Europe saw the electrically lighted observatory at the city of play before they ever glimpsed the Statue of Liberty, until the amusement tower burned down in the great Dreamland fire of 1911. "Few, if any, visitors to the island will care about leaving it without ascending in the elevator to the top of the Observatory," noted the *Eagle*, "and many a pilgrim will go thither with that object in view." From the top of the observatory, visitors could possess the resort in their imagination, in a way similar to the bird's-eye cityscapes so popular at the time. The ascent allowed visitors to become temporarily godlike voyeurs, lifted far above the feverish motion of Coney Island, urban street life, and the anonymous crowd (figure 21).[27]

Nothing could be more logical than this reappearance on Coney Island of buildings from the Philadelphia Centennial, for the American exposition and the resort were first cousins. The managers of the Centennial had banned any on-grounds amusement area, featuring instead the new inventions by Thomas Edison, Alexander Graham Bell, and George Westinghouse. Across from the exposition's main building on Elm Avenue, however, a "Shantyville" offered restaurants, saloons, amusement booths, beer gardens, animal acts, balloonists, dioramas, an Indian encampment, and the Sawyer Observatory. Coney Island boasted essentially the same program, and the similarities were not lost on visitors. Coney was "a Centennial of pleasure, pure and simple, without any tiresome ulterior commercial purpose," noted William Bishop in 1880. "There is the same gay architecture, the same waving flags, the same delightful, distracting whirl, the same enormous masses of staring, good-natured, perpetually marching and counter-marching human beings. Its essential character is bound up with the crowd." Each successive exposition after the Philadelphia Centennial followed Coney Island's lead and more intimately integrated amusement and commercial areas into the fair. A dizzying round of grandiose world's fairs and expositions crisscrossed the United States, each encyclopedically instructive and morally improving but, concomitantly, fun fairs with cabarets, cafes, and commercial amusements.[28]

The Elephant Hotel, constructed in 1884, also projected Coney Island's architectural playfulness and strangeness (see figure 21). This metal behemoth housed a shopping mall and thirty-four guest rooms, while windows in the head allowed visitors panoramic views of the sea and beach. Crowds flocked to the tin-skinned elephant, climbing a spiral staircase up one hind leg and exiting down the other. They peered out windows on both sides of the body and trudged up to the howdah for a view encompassing the entire resort. So famous was this massive monument that for a generation, "seeing the elephant" signified a quest for satisfactions in disreputable quarters, perhaps because the rooms were later reputedly used for a brothel. Elephants in general, and the Elephant Hotel in particular, served as Coney Island's unofficial mascot for the rest of the Gilded Age.[29]

Within a decade, Coney Island seemed transformed, as if touched by a magic wand. "The run-up in the prices of Gravesend's Common Lands," reported the *Kings County Rural Gazette,* had no parallel, "unless it be in the mining regions of California." By any quantifiable standard, the changes were dramatic. In 1878, bathers found thirty-five hundred bathhouses for their convenience, and almost one hundred thousand visitors could dine at Coney at one sitting. Whereas before 1874 investors had staked barely $100,000 on Coney Island, by 1880 buildings, piers, improvements, and transportation probably represented the commitment of more than $10 million. Almost five thousand jobs existed where barely two hundred people had found employment in 1874. In 1859, Gravesend's entire tax rolls listed only 173 entries, and the town collected $3,600 on valuation of $33,000 aggregate real and personal property. In 1883, Gravesend collected total tax revenues of more than $23,000 on $2.2 million in real estate, and the value of any one of the major hotels exceeded the entire tax collection of 1859. "Surely watering place enterprise has reached its climax in Coney Island," commented one astounded visitor.[30]

Attendance skyrocketed as immense crowds ambled through a "veritable Vanity Fair of fun and enjoyment—a Babel of music and sound—fascinating to Youth and amusing to age." Imperfect estimates before the boom of the late 1870s range anywhere from 25,000 to 60,000 visitors daily on weekends

Figure 21. "Bird's-Eye View of Coney
Island," ca. 1880. To the right of the
Elephant Hotel is the Sea Beach Palace,
formerly the United States Government
Pavilion at the Philadelphia Centennial
and at Coney Island, the depot and hotel
of the New York and Sea Beach Railroad.
The rounded buildings on Surf Avenue
are merry-go-rounds. (Courtesy of the
Museum of the City of New York.)

J.S. JOHNSTON

VIEW OF CONEY ISLAND.

and 5,000 to 25,000 during the week. By 1880, daily summer ridership on the major railroads averaged 23,000, and estimates of Sunday crowds of more than 100,000 certainly were not unrealistic. The New York State Board of Railroad Commissioners reported in 1884 that the New York and Brighton Beach carried more than 4.5 million passengers at fifteen cents a head, the Prospect Park and Coney Island transported 3.5 million people the same year, and the New York and Sea Beach conducted 1.5 million to Gravesend's racetracks, saloons, shooting galleries, cheap restaurants, and beach. Even the Marine Railway and the Coney Island Elevated, the one-mile road that ran parallel to Surf Avenue from Brighton to Norton's Point, carried more than half a million passengers. In the 1880s, probably 6 million people visited in a summer, spending more than $10 million; the *Brooklyn Union* estimated Coney's crowd at a staggering 230,000 for the 1883 Fourth of July holiday. A cartoon from 1878 depicted "the three men who never saw Coney Island": a corpse, a blind man, and a cigar-store Indian.[31]

The massive capital investment needed to sustain huge hotels, display piers, and steamboat lines implied that Coney Island had now found a mass audience. The development of extensive railroad and steamboat connections allowed the pent-up workers from the cities of Brooklyn and New York to flood the island. In 1860, the combined population of Kings and New York Counties exceeded 1 million, an increase of 500 percent since 1830; in 1900 the two counties would total more than 3 million residents. A journalist for the *New York Evening Mail* noted, in 1879, that "Coney Island was simply New York moved down to the sea. Men, women, and children of all sorts, races, and conditions, mingle in the moving crowds as they would on Broadway, in perfect good order, with entire good nature." This reputation could cut both ways; those reviewers with aristocratic sympathies reviled the place. George Templeton Strong complained that the "civic scum" ebbed and flowed on Sundays and holidays, infesting Coney Island with "gent, snob, black-leg, fast-man, whore, and Bowery girl. . . . All conveniently accessible hotels and boarding houses are overrun by the vermin that hot weather roasts out of its homes in town." Charles Shanley wrote a disparaging review of "the vulgar associations and motley crowd" of Coney for the highbrow *Atlantic Monthly* in 1874.[32]

Yet the island in the 1870s and 1880s appealed to a broad range of urban citizenry as a place to go that was inexpensive and unreformed. With its concession stands, cool breezes, and relatively open spaces, the island successfully competed for patronage with Prospect Park and Central Park. Within the twin restrictions of time and wages, workers eagerly embraced leisure travel, just as they eventually emulated other trappings of middle-class lifestyle such as carpeting and wallpaper. Considerable evidence contradicts the myth that criminals and the bourgeoisie overran Gilded Age Coney Island, beginning with the fact that a hundred thousand people descended on the island each summer Sunday in the 1880s. Working people were a constant presence at Gravesend during the last three decades of the nineteenth century, their activities heavily reported in the daily press.

Workers often visited West Brighton in excursions sponsored by unions, businesses, and ethnic, religious, and political organizations. According to the *New York Herald* in 1884, Coney attracted "working men and their families, young clerks and saleswomen—the toiling dwellers in the crowded tenements." The island's expanding commercial amusement business depended on luring exactly this type of clientele. Several successful enterprises, such as Feltman's Ocean Pavilion, catered primarily to fraternal lodges and voluntary organizations. Paul Bauer, a leading Coney restaurateur, begged the transportation companies to hold down their fares to permit laborers to visit the seaside. When a five-cent railroad rate increase in 1886 threatened the well-being of Coney Island merchants, five hundred hotel keepers, music hall owners, brewery representatives, and local politicians signed a petition imploring the railroads to reduce their fares.[33]

These city dwellers benefited greatly from the Saturday half-holiday movement. Although usage of the word *weekend* barely predates 1879, the concept had been gaining ground since the 1850s. The practice of honoring St. Monday, a day taken off from work as a consequence of drunkenness on Sunday, gradually gave way to a segmented week that enabled capitalists to achieve increased efficiency by regularizing leisure hours. In 1890, more than ten thousand Brooklyn factories employed 110,000 workers producing goods valued at $269 million, securing the rank of fourth highest among American cities. The extension of the half-holiday to these workers—four of Brooklyn's five largest retail establishments closed at 1:00 P.M. on summer Saturdays in 1888—turned local urban attractions into commercial resorts. Laborers still worked eleven hours or more daily in 26 percent of all establishments in 1880, but work hours for most professions peaked around midcentury. The average nonagricultural workweek decreased almost 3 percent per decade between 1850 and 1900, freeing an additional fifteen hours every week for leisure activities. In "The Holiday Hallucination" (1888), Joel Benton complained bitterly that workers now had eighty-five days a year "consecrated to the surrender of toil. . . . A *full quarter of the year* is now practically made unproductive time."[34]

Almost every nineteenth-century commentator at Coney Island attested to the good humor and respectability of these hordes of working people. A Philadelphia newspaperman, Joel Cook, marveled at the evening rush for the steamboat and the railway: "The crowds who have been so good-humored all day are still well-behaved, and they stream through the ticket gates, a resistless tide." A feature article in the *Saratogian Almanac* in 1881 proclaimed that "nowhere else can be seen such a commingling of pleasure seekers of every class, differing in every characteristic except order and good behavior." Even a hostile witness such as William Bishop in 1880 conceded to the popular reputation of these crowds:

> Instead of a saturnalia of vulgarity and discomfort that may have been dreaded, it happily turns out that the people, arriving in such unique bulk and so splendidly received, constitute a most interesting distraction in themselves. Even those who do not like crowds may be reconciled to this one. It is excellently behaved. It scarcely seems to need the vigilant special police enlisted for the island. . . . This crowd is clean and neatly dressed, of very respectable social grade, of great good-humor, and on honest pleasure bent, and the spirits are insensibly raised in moving with it.[35]

But was a Sunday afternoon boat or train ride to Coney Island really equivalent to a journey to Saratoga or Newport? Although the experience of a day-tripper might differ from that of a hotel dweller, the essential motivation often remained the same. Like travelers to Saratoga and Newport, visitors to Coney Island desired a change, an activity outside normal routines of work and social commitments and outside the locations of these routines. The idea of a secular pilgrimage and "see-and-be-seen" culture remained intrinsic to the resort experience. Whether rich or poor, Jewish or Christian, black or white, male or female, Americans reoriented their sense of leisure in the nineteenth century, searching for something unique on hotel verandas and public beaches. All strata of people began to travel in pursuit of pleasure in the nineteenth century; Coney Island differed from Newport or Saratoga mainly in its accessibility, being only an hour in time and twenty-five cents in cost from two of the nation's largest cities. When William Bishop noted of Coney Island that "it is not a place to be permanent in," he merely repeated the standard interpretation of behavior at nineteenth-century resorts.[36]

Whether staying at a resort for a day, a night, a week, or a summer, visitors consciously and unconsciously responded to anxieties brought on by the great age of American urbanization. The number of Americans living in cities with populations greater than twenty-five hundred people had risen from 1 million (9 percent of the population) in 1830 to 6 million (20 percent) in 1860 and would eventually reach 22 million (35 percent) in 1890. This bustling city jumbled together heterogeneous classes, occupations, and peoples and severely restricted the open spaces familiar to many of its migrants. Cut loose from many of the homogenizing influences of their previous lives, the new urbanites experienced intensified anomie, a sense of normlessness, and daily confronted the diminution of an older sense of community as a personal experience. Cities were worlds of strangers, and gemeinschaft partially broke down when confronted with the new urban anonymity. For city dwellers, everything filtered through this lens of strangerhood. In the first half of the nineteenth century, parents even playfully referred to newborn children as "little strangers," and "Welcome, little stranger" could commonly be found printed or embroidered on articles for nursery use. The new urbanites may not have been completely uprooted from previous institutions and associations, but they commonly yearned for a means to bridge the chasm of strangerhood, as evidenced in the formation of social subgroups such as urban villages or immigrant benevolent societies based on place of origin.[37]

The sheer number of strange faces in the city could be unsettling. Henry Ward Beecher nostalgically lamented the passing of the compact New England town in which there were "no strangers." He contrasted this prelapsarian vision with the city in which thousands die "every month, and there is no void apparent. The vast population speedily closes over the empty space." The new mass society of the nineteenth century drew Americans' attention to the concept of the huge, inscrutable crowd. In Herman Melville's short story, "Bartleby the Scrivener," the title character, with a sketchy past and very little present, gradually performs a hermitlike withdrawal from all social encounters before dying alone in Tombs prison.

Despite its apparent vibrancy, Melville's city undermined community and shattered the human personality itself. "I always seem to suffer some loss of faith on entering cities," wrote Ralph Waldo Emerson to Thomas Carlyle in 1840. "They are great conspiracies; the parties are all maskers, who have taken mutual oaths of silence not to betray each other's secret and each to keep the other's madness in countenance." The American abolitionist and author Lydia Maria Child despaired of New York City life: "For eight weary months, I have met in the crowded streets but two faces I have ever seen before."[38]

The stranger, virtually by definition, was perceived not as a unique individual with a personal history and location in social space but rather as dangerous, difficult to predict or control. For better or for worse, codes of hospitality of the antebellum South usually excluded strangers; they received neither gifts nor dueling challenges, for they stood completely outside the social system. In 1868, the *New York Times* advised visitors to Coney Island to "mind their own business and . . . not seek to form acquaintants with strangers who may be wolves in sheeps' clothing," and a later guidebook warned readers not to "bet with gentlemanly strangers, as their game is apt to improve marvelously at critical moments." To escape one world of strangers (the city) only to enter another (the resort) represented a curious mode of movement. The traveler abandoned the safety and comforts of home, inevitably encountered toil and hardships, incurred at least some expenses, and had to establish if not new lodgings then new relationships.[39]

Yet visitors traveled to watering places like Saratoga, Newport, and Coney Island precisely in the expectation of meeting "strangers," an appellation commonly used by both resort-town residents and the visitors themselves. Before the eighteenth century, those who traveled were self-evidently "travelers," from the French *travail*, the very word retaining its sense of trouble, work, or ordeal associated with pilgrimage. The earliest record of the more specialized tourist (from the Latin *tornus*, which derived from a Greek word for a tool used to describe a circle) probably does not predate a reference around 1800, when someone commented, "A Traveller is now-a-days called a Tour-ist." That usage has been retained in twentieth-century speech, according to which travelers are either "tourists" or "visitors" (carrying the sense of a semiofficial journey of inspection). They are emphatically not "strangers." Yet this is the term that nineteenth-century Americans widely used as synonymous with *guest*. This usage reflected not only the novelty of leisure travel but also the perceived atomistic relationship of guests to one another at resorts.[40]

"Strangers" swarmed over all nineteenth-century resorts. For example, Francis Dallam, a cultured gentleman from Baltimore, traveled to Saratoga in 1827, where he found "the company is large about seven hundred but not such as are agreeable to me, all strangers and many of them foreigners [*sic*]." The hero of Sarah Joseph Hale's short story of the Saratoga scene was a businessman "in pursuit of that pleasure which has neither definite name nor aim, but must be found jostling among a crowd of strangers in a strange place."[41] At Newport, Mayor George Calvert proudly proclaimed that "hundreds of new buildings have been erected by our own people, or by strangers," while Cozzens Dry Goods store advertised to "customers at home, or strangers visiting this far-famed Eden of America." George Mason boasted that Newport engaged "the attention of strangers who would while away a few summer days by the sea shore."[42] Visitors to Coney Island easily adopted this way of looking at the leisured world, even as they traveled to a site that borrowed the culture of the promenade, veranda, beach, and grand hotel from established resorts. In 1840, one local historian described Coney as "a place of great resort for strangers during the summer season." The *New York Times* referred to Coney's visitors as "strangers," as did *Appleton's Guide to New York* and Townsend Percy's *Pocket Dictionary of Coney Island*.[43]

Yet despite the natural and romantic attractions of the seaside, the pilgrim to Coney Island did not embark on a Wordsworthian ramble to escape encroaching mass society. Like antebellum Saratoga and Newport, Coney offered an urban-style environment in which city people escaped crowds and nervous strain by courting even denser throngs and worse din. At Coney, the pleasurable excitement and disorder reminiscent of the city prevailed over the sanctifying backdrop and calm of the country. The majestic surges and timelessness of the sea, the untrodden shore, the ebb and flow of the tides, all served as nothing more than a stage set in which the multitudes could enjoy eating, promenading, dancing, bathing, and architectural excess. Efficient transportation tied all three resorts to great cities, and their principal amenities and attractions were urban: monumental public hotels and civic spaces, sophisticated communications, and city-style entertainments amid heterogeneous company. Ultimately, strangers came to Coney Island for reasons not appreciably different from those of sojourners to

Newport and Saratoga: to see other people and be seen by them, to share temporarily in a sense of interconnected, emotionally rewarding community in an unfamiliar and almost magical leisure setting.

The trip to Coney by crowded boat or train threw travelers together into an amorphous mass of cosmopolitan humanity. On arrival at the immense pier, visitors marveled at "people of both sexes, all ages, sizes, shapes, colors and nations; some seated, others moving with perfect freedom. . . . Jollity and good nature reigned supreme." Surrounded by sand and sea, the visitor viewed a surrealistic landscape with a skyline dominated by a 300-foot-high tower, a 120-foot-high elephant with legs 60 feet in circumference, and the great Iron Pier standing up on the sea like a broad palace of Aladdin. "No matter how much you travelled, sights you never saw before you'll see on Coney Island's shore," declared one poet, perhaps contemplating the landmark effigy of a large cow holding a reservoir of iced milk dispensed from the udders by costumed milk maids. Joel Cook gazed eastward down the shore toward the great hotels and bathing establishments at Manhattan and Brighton Beaches and tried to describe the scene: "As night comes the bright suns of the electric light blaze out to illuminate the pier, and myriads of lights are seen along the shore. . . . We are upon Coney Island on Saturday night, among probably fifty thousand visitors,—its illumination and fireworks trying to turn night into day,—while music fills the air and everything wears the aspect of a holiday."[44]

Coney Island, like other resorts, sanctioned the bending of social norms and the relaxation of the rigidities of life promulgated by the etiquette books. Its proximity to Manhattan and Brooklyn, however, cast the seaside's mockery of self-discipline and class hierarchies in a more provocative light than at Saratoga and Newport. One reporter viewed Coney's seashore as an egalitarian utopia: "Old Ocean is a grand old Democrat, and levels all petty distinctions. He buffets the rich and the poor alike, who, clad for bath, present very much the same appearance." The *New York Times* simply stated, "Coney Island is the true republic of watering places." Although this rhetoric belonged to the long tradition of describing the American resort as an inherently democratic locale, the image had some justification. The anonymity of the beach and the promenade cloaked fundamental conflicts and tensions and allowed people to believe that the seaside experience abolished boundaries of class identity, diminished economic tensions, and brought Americans together. Slumming fashionables who did not respond to Coney

Island's "frank assumption of equality" were assumed to be either hardened aristocrats or bigoted aesthetes. In 1878, *Harper's Weekly* declared Coney supreme among American seaside resorts, a "play-ground where rich and poor alike may take their pleasure."[45]

The diverse crowd fascinated Coney Island's visitors, and onlookers from every station of life came to mingle with it and make it their study. "Everything in the open air," gushed José Martí, commenting on the animated crowds, the immense dining rooms, and the flirtatious courtship behavior of North Americans. "The people come to see the people," declared Stephen Crane of seaside culture. In Crane's short story, "Coney Island's Failing Days," the main protagonist, who possesses no name beyond "the stranger," ambles about the resort, stopping "often to observe types which interested him with an unconscious calm insolence as if the people were bugs." Not surprisingly, the camera obscura often made itself at home at the nineteenth-century seashore. This enclosure magnified distant objects and projected them on darkened walls for the pleasure of furtive viewers. Theoretically, the camera obscura portrayed the beauty and majesty of the pounding surf, but spectators seemed more interested in couples making out on the beach, or at least so cartoons of the time implied.[46]

Writers may have rhapsodized about the equality that prevailed on the beach, but some groups manifestly attempted to deny the pleasures of Coney Island's "democracy" to others. Even in an age that venerated success, wealth alone did not guarantee security or respect. White Americans, made uneasy by the anonymous crowds of the city and the resort, wanted to make visual character distinctions to determine respectability. Race served as a handy segregating tool because it remained one of the last characteristics theoretically identifiable at a glance. African Americans at Coney were subjected to an unofficial color line, assigned Jim Crow bathhouses, and discouraged from bathing on certain sections of the beach. Hostility against dark-skinned peoples also took symbolic form. At Coney, any national prejudice could be gratified by knocking over Turks, Frenchmen, or Prussians in the shooting galleries and rifle ranges, but the various "Kill the Coon" (or "African Dodger") ball-throwing games remained the most popular aggressive amusements. A black man, or in "desperate times," a white man in blackface, thrust his head through an opening in a canvas screen while the public tried to hit him with baseballs, three throws for a nickel or a dime.[47]

Yet although African Americans who attempted to imitate white standards of gentility met mostly scorn, they often followed white patterns in leisure consumption. Many of Saratoga's hotels excluded black visitors, but the African American elite, including the Pinchbacks of New Orleans, the Churches of Memphis, the Pelhams of Detroit, and the Ruffins and Lewises of Boston, visited the Springs regularly anyway and stayed where they could. Another black vacationer journeyed to Newport and praised it as a watering place "where respectable, refined and well-bearing colored ladies and gentlemen have . . . little reason to feel their color." When New York City's beaches or pleasure gardens tried to exclude dark-skinned people, blacks created resorts, or "African groves," of their own. In the late nineteenth century, distinctly black resorts emerged, offering hassle-free retreats, amusement areas, and beaches for African Americans; the first black resort community in Florida took its name from Coney Island's Manhattan Beach. Photographs of a well-dressed black gentleman seated in the Congress Spring Pavilion in Saratoga and an impeccably attired black family vacationing at Coney Island, both circa 1880, reveal the lure of the secular pilgrimage to affect the leisure mores of some African Americans (figure 22).[48]

African Americans were not the only group who found themselves cast as "the indecent other" at resorts. In earlier decades, even tonier watering places seldom barred American Jews, and a sprinkling summered in Newport, in the Catskills, or on the Jersey shore.[49] In the late 1870s, however, several attempts were made to establish the watering place as a haunt of ethnic exclusivity, as Joseph Seligman discovered when he returned with his family to the Grand Union at Saratoga Springs in the summer of 1877. The clerk informed Seligman, a prominent New York City banker and financial advisor to Abraham Lincoln and Ulysses Grant, that Henry Hilton now owned the hotel and Israelites would no longer be accepted, because their vulgarity kept good Christian people away. Seligman wrote a furious letter to Hilton and sent copies to selected newspapers, which responded on cue with banner headlines. Hilton, whose chief notoriety to that date came from having bilked A. T. Stewart's widow out of his $35 million estate, also responded publicly: "The law yet merits a man to use his property as he pleases. . . . I believe we lose much more than we gain by [the Jews'] custom."[50]

Whether Hilton's actions inaugurated or simply confirmed a trend, a considerable number of New York hotels now advertised that "Hebrews need not apply." Although William Cullen Bryant, Henry Ward Beecher,

Figure 22. "Negro Family, Coney Island," ca. 1880. Although usually confined to Jim Crow sections of American beaches, many African Americans adopted the vacation patterns of white Americans. (Courtesy of the Brooklyn Museum of Art, X892.6; gift of the Brooklyn Museum Collection; photo by George B. Brainerd.)

Mark Twain, and Bret Harte all spoke out against anti-Semitism at resorts, an investigation of race prejudice at summer hotels in the *Forum* in July 1887 found the rejection of Jews in New York resorts so well established that it no longer aroused comment. In cheaper boardinghouses, hosts and boarders barred Jewish applicants, often associating them with African Americans and extending to them the nearly universal contempt in which the latter were held by white Americans. Late-nineteenth-century ethnological literature generally concluded that Jews were "black" or, at least, "swarthy." Austin Corbin later claimed that he "never knew but one 'white' Jew in my life." The identification of Jews, however, was not foolproof; an outraged Saratoga hotel clerk supposedly yanked the pen from the distinguished patrician (and non-Jew) Moses Thompson's hand after he wrote his first name on the register. Nonetheless, many New York hotels promulgated exclusionary policies until the state legislature declared them illegal in 1906, at which point hosts and guests unofficially boycotted undesirable groups. Yet despite the antipathy of the mainstream culture and harassment from hoteliers, Jewish vacationers continued to flood the Catskills, Saratoga, and Sharon Springs.[51]

The Hilton-Seligman affair reverberated at Coney Island in 1879, and with the same lack of success for those who practiced exclusion. At one meeting of Henry Hilton's short-lived American Society for the Suppression of the Jews, Austin Corbin entreated an enthusiastic audience of one hundred at the Grand Union in Saratoga, "If this is a free country, why can't we be free of Jews?" The very next month, Corbin acted on his principles by announcing he would not only bar Jews from his Manhattan Beach Hotel at Coney Island but would also banish them from the beach there as well. "Personally I am opposed to Jews," Corbin informed the *New York Herald* in 1879. "They are driving away the class of people who are beginning to make Coney Island the most fashionable and magnificent watering place in the world." Corbin's actions aroused so much controversy in New York City, home to the bulk of Jewish immigrants to the United States, that a compendium of responses published in book form as *Coney Island and the Jews* filled forty-two pages. On the island, the Brighton Beach Hotel specifically stated that it favored Jews, while Paul Bauer claimed Corbin's manifesto was merely "an advertising dodge." Like African Americans, Jews continued to visit Coney Island despite the expressed disapproval of some segments of the American population.[52]

Nor is there any evidence that women were in any way successfully excluded from Coney Island before 1900. The male sporting world of gambling houses, saloons, brothels, and racetracks played a major role at Gilded Age Gravesend, but as at Saratoga, amusements that actively sought members of both sexes more than compensated for the exclusion. In the nineteenth century, leisure opportunities were undoubtedly more restricted for women than for men, but a large number of women took advantage of the new diversity of commercialized activities at Coney, such as concert halls, dance pavilions, and variety shows. Visual evidence discloses a large number of women in virtually every venue, especially on the beach, and provides little indication that Coney Island was ever gender imbalanced. If anything, the island may have followed the resort tradition of Saratoga and Newport, where women often outnumbered men.[53]

Coney Island, like most nineteenth-century American resorts, presented a social paradox. It existed to provide a broad welcome to as diverse a population as possible; at the same time, participants desperately desired to exclude somebody to ensure sufficient status benefits. The ideal watering place promised accessibility to anyone "respectable," but respectability took on its most tangible form through reference to skin color. Racial distinctions muted social differences among whites and sanctified European Americans as respectable, permitting the perception of rough equality that served as the cornerstone of the "democratic" resort rhetoric. Yet whether because of emulation or simultaneous development, African Americans, Jews, and women all eventually followed their counterparts to the crowded beaches, springs, and hotels.[54]

Visitors often equated Coney Island with the ideal fete in terms borrowed from descriptions of Saratoga and Newport: a journey to a magical wonderland, shared public enjoyment in an urban world of strangers, and suppression of class distinctions. One astounded traveler to Coney Island exclaimed, "Were such spectacles arranged for a day and night only, on the occasion of some important fete, they would pass into history; but here they are for every day and every night the whole summer long." As early as the 1870s, Coney's mystique depended upon parallels it inspired with carnival, a feast of fools, a world turned upside down. Gilded Age Coney Island attracted crowds because of the way it temporarily allowed people to reject thrift, industry, and ambition for extravagance, revelry, and abandon. Joel Cook declared as much in 1880:

No French Sunday *fete* ever exceeded the jollity on Coney Island, as we saw it on a hot summer Sunday, when over a hundred thousand people went down there to have a good time. Think of a half dozen Atlantic Cities and Cape Mays concentrated along a four-mile strip of shore, with all the available bands of music in full blast; all the bars going; all the vehicles moving; all the minstrel shows, miniature theaters, Punch and Judy, fat woman, and big snake exhibitions that cluster around a mammoth circus, . . . all the flying-horses, swings, and velocipede machines in operation; and a dense but good-humored crowd everywhere, sight-seeing, drinking beer, and swallowing clam chowder; and you have a faint idea of a Coney Island midsummer Sunday.[55]

Intrinsic to this idea of a perpetual fete was the liberalized moral code of the beach, popular ever since Newport visitors pioneered heterosocial bathing. One pamphlet writer in 1883 complained that women at Coney seemed to magically toss aside their shore-bound bashfulness when they swam in the ocean, for "in the water they are ready for anything. They mount on men's shoulders and dive from them; they are ducked and floated and hugged by fellows of whom not infrequently they know nothing at all and to whom they are often introduced but ten minutes before." A journalist for the *Brooklyn Standard Union,* after witnessing a couple sprawled on the beach openly engaged in "shamefully licentious conduct," complained that the moment people arrived in Gravesend, they appeared to "abandon all the restraint imposed by the rules of decency and morality." A *New York Sun* reporter complained in 1877 of the promiscuous mingling of the sexes, "precisely as if the thing to do in the water was to behave exactly contrary to the manner of behaving anywhere else." Paintings and trade cards of the period, in which buxom bathing beauties bared milky limbs, interpreted the beach as one vast erotic theater.[56]

At Newport and Coney Island, the experience of sea bathing especially liberated women, propelling them beyond normal moral boundaries. In order to bathe, a woman discarded layers of corsets, petticoats, billowing blouses, mushrooming hats, and black parasols in exchange for ill-fitting pendulous flannel or woolen dresses, bloomers, long stockings, and floppy oilcloth caps. Yet when swimming at the seaside, a woman left the private realm and displayed herself in a public venue in essentially the attire reserved for her intimate life: barefoot, hair down, wearing a costume showing the shape of her hips. The seaside beckoned with the voluptuous potential of unexpected freedom and undreamed-of pleasures, and the mere contact of a bare foot on the sand could be a sensual invitation. In *The Awakening,* Kate Chopin uses Edna Pontellier's swimming lessons as a simile for social experimentation that ends in disaster; at the climax, Pontellier casts off her clothes and swims away. The erotic aura of the beach, thronged with strangers in a state of relative undress, the holiday atmosphere, and the suspension of everyday rules of sexual propriety set Newport and Coney Island apart from the mundane.[57]

No wonder the popularity of American resorts increased every year, for they provided a socially acceptable escape from some of the more irksome constraints on everyday behavior for all Americans. José Martí's ambivalence about the United States disintegrated when he journeyed to Coney Island in 1881; he described a numinous world filled with exotic fishes, bearded ladies, stunted elephants blatantly advertised as the biggest elephants in the world, hundreds of orchestras, endless rides for children, and innumerable lovers. The proliferation of this type of seaside resort undermines easy assumptions about the work ethic, social control, and the tyranny of respectability in the nineteenth century.[58]

By 1880, the name "Coney Island" served as a national metaphor for pleasure, and the spit of land at the southern tip of Brooklyn was already the most famous amusement center in the world. When new management converted Parker's Grove outside Cincinnati into an amusement area, they called it "Ohio Grove, the Coney Island of the West." The subtitle became the more popular designation, and before 1890 residents commonly called it Coney Island. In Rochester, patrons knew the park at Sea Breeze on Irondequoit Bay as "Rochester's Coney Island" as early as 1883; Charlotte, its rival, earned the appellation "the Coney Island of western New York" in 1891. Similarly, visitors in the 1880s referred to Revere Beach as "Boston's Coney Island." Even the *Saratogian Almanac* acknowledged that Coney Island was "*the* watering place of the country, at least so far as crowds and invested capital can go." Visitors to Newport who perused the first issue of the Fall River Line newspaper in 1879 found Coney Island described as "the greatest watering place in America. The best and worst of New York's population are emptied there on a hot afternoon, and virtue and vice rub elbows in harmony."[59]

In 1880, William Bishop called Coney "the greatest resort for a single day's pleasure in the world," and in the same year, Joel Cook christened it simply "the greatest watering place in the world." The noteworthy feature of these bombastic observations is that they describe a Coney Island anchored by three grand resort hotels: the Manhattan Beach, the Brighton Beach, and the Oriental. Although these hotels did not represent the totality of the Coney Island experience in the Gilded Age, their public nature and emphasis on gregarious interaction set the tone for the visit to the seaside resort, making it seem like a perpetual fete for anonymous strangers. As George Tilyou boasted—even in 1886, more than a decade before he founded Steeplechase Park, the first of the great Coney Island amusement parks—"If Paris is France, then Coney Island, between June and September, is the world."[60]

FOUR

The Public Resort

To See and Be Seen

NO SINGLE TOURIST'S ACCOUNT could elucidate the appeal of America's very public resorts. Instead, guidebooks reported a multiplicity of Saratogas, Newports, and Coney Islands, each attracting its own clientele: gamblers, immigrants, belles, millionaires, families, and invalids. A visit to a mid-nineteenth-century American watering place was truly a polysemic experience, that is, susceptible to multiple readings by a diverse audience. But even though resorts were created by thousands of independent decisions, these watering places represented the unconscious expression of particular social viewpoints. In theory, a resort destination could have evolved with an infinite number of contingent architectural configurations and modes of visitor behavior. Yet Saratoga, Newport, and Coney Island were characterized by large public spaces and grand hotels that encouraged gregariousness and a visitor's routine that threw men and women together in leisure activities. Chosen from limitless possibilities, this leisure setting reveals specific historical values. At mid-nineteenth-century resorts, Americans searched for a sense of community to overcome the nineteenth-century feeling of alienation, or strangerhood.

Noah Webster's first American dictionary, published in 1828, reported that the word *hotel* denoted a house for "genteel strangers or lodgers." The New York City Hotel, built with seventy-three rooms in 1794, was the first so-called hotel in the United States. The form replaced the old-fashioned inn, which rarely contained more than thirty rooms and often crammed as many guests as possible into a single room. Initially, many tavern keepers converted their establishments into "hotels" by simply rechristening them. But in the nineteenth century, the inn grew to grandiose size, following the trajectory of other semipublic spaces. Just as the innocuous wooden shed became the giant gateway rail terminal, the baseball park converted into the grand stadium, and the dry goods shop recreated as the department store, the rude inn was transformed into the magnificent grand hotel. Older establishments played down the original function of the inn as a mere shelter for travelers and added ballrooms and parlors to accommodate social activities.[1]

The building type achieved its modern form with the creation of the Boston Exchange Coffee House (1809), the City Hotel in Baltimore (1826), and the Tremont House in Boston (1829). At the Boston Exchange, the novel practice of putting numbers on rooms shocked visitors enough to appear in traveler's accounts, and the luxurious Tremont caused so great a sensation that a folio volume celebrated its architectural innovations. It was the Tremont's size that most impressed the Reverend George Lewis: "You live in a crowd—eat in a crowd, sitting down with fifty, a hundred, sometimes two hundred at table." State legislatures specifically chartered hotel companies to build "first-class houses," and boosters occasionally raised hotels in anticipation of railroad connections or even cities that never quite appeared. By the advent of the Civil War, life in America without the lavish hotel seemed unimaginable.[2]

With their festive human pageantry and architectural playfulness, hotels expressed ideal urbanity. Builders typically divided the ground floor into vast public rooms and placed guest quarters on both sides of upstairs corridors. Hotels in the shape of a U, a T, or an H provided the maximum amount of sunlight and air while allowing easy access from interior public spaces to porches and gardens. Foreign visitors, accustomed to a resort trade dominated by rented rooms appealing to elite patronage, invariably questioned the allure of a hotel, in which travelers lived surrounded by "some fifteen hundred eating, drinking, swearing, spitting, tobacco smoking and tobacco chewing citizens of the free and enlightened United States, for some four dollars per day." Visitors later in the century discerned that in Europe, the hotel was a means to an end, whereas in America, it was an end in itself. "People travel hundreds, nay, thousands of miles for the pleasure of putting up at certain hotels," reported two amazed European visitors. "Hotels are for [Americans] what cathedrals, monuments, ruins, and the beauties of Nature are for us."[3]

In the eyes of many European guests, the mass appeal of the American watering place tended to level the quality of the company downward. The scientist Charles Lyell grumbled about the way American hotels threw together people of diverse character, temperament, and background in the drawing room and at the dinner table. But this heterogeneity was a principal source of appeal for the socially ambitious, which included a sizable proportion of the population of the United States. "The absence of privileged classes, incites many people to elevate themselves in matters of appearance," explained the political philosopher Francis Lieber to his friends back in Germany, "[whereas] in Europe, they would be perfectly willing to keep a respectful distance." Traveling to resorts enabled Americans to purchase at least temporary social mobility by spending time in more affluent settings with prestigious people. James Buckingham, analyzing the popularity of antebellum Saratoga, concluded that

> the great charm to the vast majority is the gay and ever changing company that is found here from all parts of the Union, and especially the opulent classes, into which it is the constant aim and desire of those who are not opulent to get admitted. Hundreds who in their own towns could not find admission into the circles of fashionable society . . . come to Saratoga, where, at Congress Hall or the United States, by the moderate payment of two dollars a day, they may be seated at the same table, and often side by side, with the first families of the country; promenade in the same piazza, lounge on the sofas in the same drawing-room, and dance in the same quadrille with the most fashionable beaux and belles of the land.[4]

The grand hotels of Newport, Saratoga, and Coney Island systematically provided rooms, sumptuous meals, and efficient services on a colossal scale, all the while successfully disguising their role as profit-oriented businesses. Their larger-than-life size set them apart from everyday experience and linked visitors, both overnight guests and day-trippers, into a community of voluptuaries. Thomas Nichols marveled that Saratoga hotels numbered "bed-rooms for a thousand or twelve hundred guests, and dining-rooms, drawing-rooms, reading rooms, public parlors, bar-room, barber's shop, baths; everything on the same scale." In 1870, before it reached final apotheosis, a single Saratoga hotel employed thirty-five cooks and two hundred waiters to handle summer visitors who consumed 18,000 pounds of mutton, 7,000 pounds of veal, 27,000 chickens, 17,000 pounds of fish, 175,000 eggs, 35,000 quarts of milk, 13,000 pounds of butter, 9,000 pounds of ham and bacon, and 8,000 quarts of berries. Anyone who stopped in at the Ocean House or the Manhattan Beach ideally felt that the vast spaces and exotic setting existed for his or her own personal enjoyment. As Ellen Bond confided to her journal, the discomforts of the trip to Saratoga faded away in comparison with the experience of "inhaling the same atmosphere" as the counts and countesses: "Soon I will have an insight into high life!"[5]

This escape from ordinary preoccupations compensated for the dissatisfactions of watering place hotels, which guests accepted as a matter of course. Architects rarely concerned themselves with bedrooms, which were intended for sleeping only and whose diminutive size propelled visitors out into the public. James Buckingham grumbled that at Saratoga "the bedrooms are generally exceedingly small . . . scantily provided, and altogether inferior to what the scale and style of the house would warrant the visitor to expect." Magnificent piazzas, elegant drawing rooms, and elephantine dining rooms challenged description, but the average private room at even the most generous hotels rarely exceeded a hundred square feet and often housed entire families. In the early nineteenth century, large resort hotels contained several rooms of only thirty-six square feet, and "seven by nines" were remarkably common. All hotels sacrificed private comfort to public appearance.[6]

Visitors often excoriated the ill-cooked food, the impossibility of dining in private, and the scanty comforts at supposedly extortionate prices. The popular London journalist George Sala complained bitterly of his Saratoga stay and later wrote in italics, "*The Americans, so far as social grievances are concerned, are the most patient people in the world.*" Inadequate ventilation could leave visitors baking all night long or freezing in the late August nights. Antebellum hotel-room furniture usually comprised little more than a wooden bedstead, a table with two chairs, and a bureau with mirror, washbowl, and pitcher; closets and private baths were practically unknown. The state-of-the-art United States Hotel opened in Saratoga in 1874 by bragging that 65 of 768 lodging rooms included baths and water closets.[7]

Even as they flooded resorts, sojourners fulminated against the conditions. "What can be more comfortless," asked one magazine writer, "than to reach a huge hotel late at night and find all the best rooms occupied, with nothing left but dreary little stifling closets on the first story under the eaves?" At Newport, astonished inmates submitted to being "squeezed into an ill-ventilated little room, to which, in their own homes, they would not condemn a chambermaid, [and] endure[d], with a martyr-like fortitude . . . the Cabman's insolence, the Waiter's contumely, and the Landlord's un-blushing extortions." *Harper's Monthly* complained in 1857 that "about a million and a half of dollars . . . are left at Saratoga alone every season in exchange for the privilege of doing penance in the cells of its mammoth hotels during the hot weather, and grumbling about it during the cold weather." Visitors endured this discomfort, as one newspaper reported without any sense of irony, "for the sake of the pleasures and comforts and luxuries."[8]

For Americans, the resort hotel represented a virtual vision of heaven on earth. The main living quarters at the utopian community of Oneida, New York, resembled nothing if not a watering place hotel, with its emphasis on large communal spaces and pleasures in contrast with its hundreds of small private rooms. At Coney Island, half the rooms at the Brighton Beach Hotel surveyed the gravel-topped roofs of the kitchens, and one visitor could gain access to his room under the mansard roof only by crawling on his hands and knees. Yet the visitor concluded good-naturedly, "What was the difference? We were in our rooms as little as possible, and could go downstairs and hear Levy's five-hundred dollar cornet with as much satisfaction as the best of them." The veranda, the dining room, and the parlor of the hotel, as well as the beach, the springs, and the park, served as spacious stages for the pleasures of social interaction.[9]

The expansive veranda (interchangeably known as a piazza) defined the nineteenth-century resort hotel experience. The Congress Hotel in Cape May (1812) displayed one of the earliest examples, perhaps an imitation of the porch at Mount Vernon. Gideon Putnam took George Washington's seventy-foot piazza and expanded it to two hundred feet, raised it above street level, and placed it in an urban setting (see figure 1). The resort veranda lost its utilitarian aspect as an easy way to circulate around a build-ing and functioned instead as an active and permeable street wall, a space of its own mediating between the indoors and outdoors. Its betwixt-and-between condition framed the hotel and enabled guests to survey the social scene without totally participating in it (figure 23). A hotel like Newport's

Figure 23. Piazza of the United States Hotel, Saratoga Springs, *Frank Leslie's,* August 28, 1875. In *Harper's Monthly* (73 [1886]: 594), Charles Dudley Warner observed that "one might be amused at the Saratoga show without taking an active part in it, and indeed nobody did seem to be taking an active part in it. Everybody was looking on." (Collection of the author.)

Ocean House, destroyed by fire in 1845, announced its accession to the echelons of major destinations by grandiose reconstruction, including a greatly enlarged veranda (figure 24). Proprietors and guests typically discussed verandas in terms of length, for bigger was almost always better in the nineteenth century. The striking feature of Saratoga's United States Hotel was its continuous seven-hundred-foot veranda; Congress Hall responded by advertising its own immense colonnaded piazza, which ran the length of the building and extended two stories in height. Coney Island's Oriental Hotel even placed a seventeen-foot-wide promenade atop its main tower.[10]

The hotel veranda provided the perfect stage for the theater of resort life. Guests spent the afternoon or evening there, escaping the heat of their rooms or the crowded dance floor. Rocking chairs often lined these porches—the Union Hall inventory of 1848 already lists eighty-six—from

Figure 24. Grand Veranda of the Second Ocean House, ca. 1890. Idlers on verandas performed in the theater of resort life. (Courtesy of the Newport Historical Society [P23].)

which hotel guests could project an image of open amiability. The resort veranda tolerated a relaxation of disciplined middle-class posture usually reserved for private settings, all the while encouraging the visitor to play the role of public observer. *Harper's Monthly* editorialized in 1856 that "the rocking chair is an American invention, and is expressive of the physical inaction of the people." Charles Weld contrasted an afternoon at a German resort, where the company would stroll in the hills after lunch, with the Saratoga scene in 1855, "where to see each other and to be seen is evidently the main object. Accordingly, the ladies, in their gay attire, with their beautiful hair uncovered by bonnet or cap, promenade in the galleries and through the main street from hotel to hotel; some of the gentlemen, meantime, being seated in very remarkable attitudes in the verandas, from whence they enjoy commanding views of the ladies."[11]

A second semipublic space that defined the watering place was the cavernous hotel parlor, described by Anthony Trollope as large enough to substitute for the House of Commons. By 1850, no American home could claim to be refined without a parlor, a place that combined traditional communal visiting with the ceremonial display of aristocratic drawing rooms. By definition, residential parlors lacked beds or work equipment, thereby expressing the room's dedication to entertainment and the presentation of the family's most decorative possessions. In the same way, free-spending decorators filled hotel parlors with elaborate furniture, musical instruments, and dense foliage and encouraged an overstated theatricality of manner in an atmosphere of economically useless repose and beauty. These capacious rooms often exceeded two thousand square feet, and several hotels boasted more than one; the parlor of Coney Island's Oriental Hotel measured fifty by eighty-eight feet. The use of mirrors found a special niche in hotels, and especially hotel parlors; the Union Hall inventory of 1848 lists more than two hundred mirrors of every imaginable size. Glass reflected light and illuminated space but also played into the obsession with self and appearance at the resort. Margaret Davidson specifically called attention to the large mirror in the hotel parlor, which reflected "the splendor of every object."[12]

The parlor of the grand hotel offered a vantage point from which to view the rich, the famous, and the powerful in a neighborly fashion. The titanic parlor succeeded best when filled by hordes of garrulous visitors gathered round for idle chitchat or promenading to exhibit their graces. As on the veranda, anonymous onlookers cast a critical eye on every detail of behavior. One self-conscious woman noted that in the parlor, "heads appeared to turn on pivots in their zeal to recognize and be recognized," and Ellen Bond confessed that "to have someone point out the *Lions* as they enter [the parlor] adds greatly to our enjoyment." The ambience of voyeurism that permeated watering place consciousness could also make a hotel parlor an unsettling place. Abbey Goodwin preferred to stay home while her husband visited the Springs because "the gaiety and confusion in the parlors would almost make me dissy."[13]

The hotel dining room served as the third great semipublic space of the resort city (figure 25). Congress Hall advertised tables six hundred feet long, "daily spread with viands of ample variety and abundance." The traditional bountiful meals and extensive wine list at hotels continued throughout the century; a typical dinner could include more than fifty items on the bill of fare. Dinners remained a challenge to longevity and a celebration of profligacy precisely because resort visitors wished to discard the calculations of careful saving that marked everyday life. Yet this feast could also be

Figure 25. Dining room of Union Hall, *Frank Leslie's*, July 9, 1864. No support posts interrupted the view in the huge resort dining rooms, making it easy to examine fellow guests. At Saratoga's largest hotels, all the waiters were African American. (Collection of the author.)

a troubling experience. No visual devices broke down these prodigious refectories—the dining room of Newport's Ocean House measured 130 by 45 by 13 feet but contained no support posts—so visitors under the guise of eating were able to peruse, "with curious attention, the long line of faces on the opposite side of the table." The Manhattan Beach Hotel had two main dining rooms, of 3,200 and 6,800 square feet, respectively. The dining room, as the pseudonymous Samuel Sombre perceived, helped distinguish the resort destination, for "where people all convene, one best may see, and can be seen."[14]

The table d'hôte practice of the American hotel, according to which all ate together at set times regardless of station, particularly grated on foreigners. The unhappy wanderer who arrived at the resort after supper hour had to go to bed fasting. One innkeeper condemned Joseph Bonaparte, the former king of Spain, and his party for daring to eat privately at the United

States Hotel in Saratoga in 1825. Americans in the Jacksonian era considered exclusivity misanthropic or snobbish, an offense against the general happiness. The same attitude affected the judgment of American table manners, characterized as either nonexistent or egalitarian depending on the commentator's political philosophy. Few visitors to Saratoga or Newport before 1840 passed the opportunity to describe porcine Americans bolting down huge quantities of oleaginous foods at breakneck speed. Portrayals of the graceless resort hotel dining room often borrowed from the descriptions of urban environments: "Such a clatter of dishes and noise of knives and forks . . . mingled with a chorus of human voices, some commanding, some supplicating the waiters. . . . The din and confusion were so terrific as to utterly indispose me to dine." When the speed of meals began to slow in the 1840s and menus began to appear, the disappointment of foreigners was palpable.[15]

In quasi-public venues such as parlors, dining rooms, and verandas, resorts intermixed strangers, that is, people who did not know one another. A visit encompassed both the opportunity for friendship and the risk of exposure or shame. At its best, Alexander Mackay found, "the gaiety of the place is infectious, and we soon entered into it with the same eagerness as those around us." The dancing, dining, and promenading at the hotel necessarily required the guest to negotiate the awkwardness that came from public engagement with strangers. In theory, well-bred people did not intrude without official social introductions; Jacques Milbert reported that in the 1820s, it was "the custom [at Saratoga] to speak only to acquaintances or to those to whom one has been introduced." By the 1840s, however, most visitors to resorts had jettisoned formal presentation ceremonies. The pleasure of resort life lay precisely in its informality, the absence of the elaborate ritual of calling cards and returning visits. Since letters of introduction served little purpose in such an ephemeral environment, visitors were forced to rely on their wits.[16]

The resort titillated the visitor with its possibilities for unique social interaction, as southerner James Gilliam discovered on his trip to Saratoga in 1816. Gilliam divided his time among drinking the waters, riding, and spending time with "the ladies." At one dance, he met a jovial young woman whose name or standing in society he did not know. Because she came to the tavern "without the protection of a gentleman, or even a servant, I was surprised to learn that she was the sister of Judge Morris of Halifax, a man of great learning and respectability." Later, Gilliam enjoyed a ride with William Hall of Vermont only to discover, to his astonishment, that Hall had been a member of the notorious Hartford Convention during the War of 1812. "The prejudices of the Southern people have been strong against those gentleman," Gilliam reported, "that I should be anathematized for even speaking to one." Yet, the planter admitted, "I was vastly pleased with the gentleman." Gilliam later socialized with other members of the Hartford Convention and spent time with a Mr. Newbold, "a most pleasant companion for a Quaker—more so than I ever calculated on meeting with." At a resort, visitors had the liberty to converse with people who would have been deemed off limits elsewhere.[17]

This informality troubled many Americans, but all conceded it existed. The author of *The Two Brides* (1846) disparaged the low moral tone and class mixing at summer resorts; another newspaper correspondent fumed about the society at Newport, where one met "snobs, squirts, upstarts, fools and other nameless things, who are unfit to live on the earth, and too insignificant to live beneath it." The celebrated American author and man-about-town, Nathaniel Willis, complained in 1851 that a young lady might meet twelve gentlemen in a season at Saratoga, not one "presented by her father or mother, or by an elderly friend of her family," but entirely through the machinations of friends, peers, and random luck. Willis grumbled about excessively "promiscuous acquaintance" at resorts: "A game at billiards or a chance fraternization over juleps in the bar-room, is, in fact, the most frequent threshold of introduction to ladies at a watering place."[18]

The charms of summer resort life often correlated with the ability of the traveler to negotiate American social circles. To be unable to connect ensured that the hotel would be a dispiriting place with few attractions, even for the most prominent. Philip Hone, a former mayor of New York City, felt reassured that the arrival of "several of our clever New York lawyers" at Saratoga promised to infuse a little yeast to the unintellectual dough of "awkward women and stupid men," whose actual failure was that Hone had never seen them before. When the notorious iceberg John Quincy Adams visited Saratoga in July of 1843, he intentionally chose the hotel that had the fewest travelers at the moment. Nonetheless, he wrote in his diary, "I have got into a great crowd of Strangers; a position always painful to me, and for which from a perpetual want of presence of mind, I am not fitted." The former president fled to visit the battlefield as soon as possible and departed from Saratoga the very next morning.[19]

Although visitors to resorts dreaded a lapse in genteel performance and the commission of gaffes that would reveal their true nature as covert slobs, most remained more or less confident that the disquiet could be mastered and no lasting harm would be done. When Elizabeth Ruffin arrived at Saratoga on a Thursday in 1827, she wrote bitterly in her diary, "Out of a house full there is not an individual whom we've ever seen or to whom we can converse at all so the means of amusement and entertainment are very limited." Yet by the next day, she reported the experience was already "much more sufferable than was anticipated and can get along very well, true they are all strangers still but . . . I have made advances, they have met half way (some few) and between us have contrived to be tolerably sociable." By Saturday, "Better and better, I mean, as it regards my feeling of ease and independence." By the time she had to leave, the southern belle admitted, "Every day more and more reconciles me to my situation. . . . This place which at first was insupportable and the time to be spent here anticipated with horror, has become very agreeable to me and is to be attributed solely to the pleasant acquaintance formed."[20]

Without formal introductions, travelers needed some minimum loquacity to operate at resorts. Charles Weld thought it easy to make friends, but Charles Griffin (from Pennsylvania) searched Saratoga in vain for an acquaintance. He eventually boarded with Orrin Foot because Griffin thought he might be related to "the Foots in the section where I belonged." One New England youth, fresh from his valediction at a New England college, expressed dismay that no one even looked up as he registered at the hotel: "This is one of the humiliating aspects of Watering-Place life. You are one of the mass, and distinguished by your [room] number." He lamented, "I was lonely at first. Nothing is so solitary as a gay and crowded Watering-Place, where you have few friends. The excessive hilarity of others emphasizes your own quiet and solitude. And especially at Saratoga, where there is no recourse but the company. You must bowl, or promenade the piazza, or flirt, with the women. You must drink, smoke, chat, and game a little with the men. But if you know neither women nor men, and have no prospect of knowing them, then take the next train to Lake George." In William Dean Howells' *A Hazard of New Fortunes*, the nouveau riche Dryfoos sends his daughters to Saratoga, where "they felt that they were the best there. But they knew nobody. . . . They had all the privileges of a proud exclusivity without desiring them." The pathos of the situation so touched Howells that he made it the focal point of a later work, *An Open-Eyed Conspiracy: An Idyl of Saratoga*, in which the socially inept Deerings family has been at the Springs a week without speaking to anyone and lacks the "first idea how to amuse themselves here."[21]

For some, the watering place encouraged dissimulation; others interpreted it as a place where "the old restraints are thrown away, and . . . the inward nature peeps out and is caught in the fact." To view life as a performance is one of the oldest of human metaphors. Plato wrote of the stage of human life upon which people act out tragedy and comedy, and the *theatrum mundi* topos expressed in "All the world's a stage" was a commonplace in Elizabethan times. But with large-scale urbanization, the phrase took on extended meaning. Nineteenth-century urban Americans reveled in their ability to supersede the claustrophobic restrictions of preindustrial society, with its sense of personal obligation, propriety, and tradition. At the same time, they fretted over their inability to determine inward character by outward appearance and thrashed about for a key with which to discern the hypocritical from the sincere among strangers. "Every watering place has a character of its own," marveled Charles Dudley Warner. "But what is even more surprising is the influence that these places have upon the people that frequent them, who appear to change their characters with their surroundings." The life-as-theater metaphor enabled nineteenth-century Americans to endorse a multiplicity of codes of appropriate behavior simultaneously.[22]

Societies built on the promise of social mobility often can be spatially divided into front and back regions. The former, such as the hotel veranda, parlor, and dining room, encouraged a degree of social acting absent from the back regions, such as the tiny bedrooms. Superior private accommodations, a back-region function not generally open to evaluation by others, were superfluous at the public nineteenth-century resort. Even at the time, observers commented on "the evident regard for appearances with which everything is done in Saratoga—the houses and fences &c., all looking a great deal better in front than in the rear." The resort's physical organization also consciously minimized contact between workers and guests; the gargantuan hotels all maintained off-site laundry, livery, and service areas.

Performers, audiences, and stagehands all had an interest in maintaining the make-believe nature of watering place life.[23]

The resort's theatricality could be threatening; sojourners who expected a minimum standard of deportment from men and women found it increasingly difficult to judge respectability solely in terms of outward expressions of civility. Nineteenth-century domestic propaganda regarded the home as a morally pure safe haven inhabited by affectionate family members. This rhetoric gave a seditious tinge to any outward movement, whether to hunt, to go to town, or to visit a watering place. Away from home, visitors could act out roles they would otherwise hesitate to assume: married men became single, married women flirted, adventurers posed as aristocrats, and all could dance in the masquerade.

Critics singled out this stage motif in their assault on the effects of extravagance on the American character. At resorts, one disgruntled visitor observed, "all the pretty coteries of 'society' [are] brought together upon a theater disagreeably narrow, each striving to outshine the other in dress and display." Samuel Sombre, in his satirical attack on Newport, criticized visitors who treated life as a masquerade. A journey through the summer resort circuit served as an excuse to buy fancy clothes, grow a beard, journey in a new equipage, and pass among strangers for persons of wealth. "A watering place is a theater where the audience are also the actors," reported *Harper's Monthly* on Newport in 1854. "They play to themselves for their own amusement, and it sometimes happens that they do amuse themselves more than others."[24]

The resort opened up a new universe in the application of social masking. People live in society by using appearances and locations to decipher the identities of strangers and integrate them into a coherent worldview. When the Industrial Revolution broke down older norms and traditional patterns of deference, the problem of establishing an identity in a theoretically meritocratic republic of urban "strangers" became acute. The frisson of the American resort came from the sense that one's identity could float free. At beaches and springs, and in parlors and dining rooms, the nineteenth-century visitor could shed unwanted appearances and considered responses. Despite their numerous trunks, devotees necessarily left behind in the city some of their tangible social status along with the majority of their possessions. Posing gave the outward appearance of hypocrisy yet constituted a necessary skill in urban life in which the number of people one met and roles one played multiplied exponentially. "A good portion of the pleasure of travelling," reported James Kirke Paulding, "consists in passing for a person of consequence."[25]

If the resort permitted the assumption of new roles in a theatrical setting, the notion of role-playing found pretext and script in the larger trends of identity formation in America. The nineteenth-century emphasis on etiquette theoretically allowed social players to navigate the dangerous world of strangers. Widely promulgated norms attempted to stabilize identity amid the social confusion and ease the transition from a face-to-face society to the faceless metropolis. Advocates of manners claimed that outward appearance was at least a prerequisite, if not a reliable indicator, of breeding and status. The rituals of everyday life not only constituted ways to attain personal nobility but also separated the wheat from the chaff. An extensive lexicon developed around everything from dining room behavior and table settings to coaches and calling cards. Although the concept of courtesy emphasized dissimulation, many Americans accepted social graces as a legitimate form of disguise because, other than skin color, they were one of the last external indicators of character. One etiquette book reminded readers that "strangers, knowing you but slightly or not at all, will naturally draw their inferences for or against you from what they see before their eyes." Without the slightest sense of irony, advice manuals enjoined their readers to be genuine and constant, as opposed to artificial and hypocritical. "Usually, not to *seem* honest, is not to *be* so," declared Henry Ward Beecher in the 1840s. These believers in gentility, despite their protestations, consciously constructed a culture of artificiality, imitation, and pretension.[26]

Personal identity, that is, a "natural self," often seemed problematic in the nineteenth century, merely an outward and visible thing constructed out of the reflections of others. The Romantic movement's concern with the dichotomy between a meaningful inner life and inconsequential outer appearances fostered a fascination with multiple identity. The popularity of dramatic parlor games in the 1850s, the growing ceremoniousness of funeral ritual, the construction of parlor stages, and the fascination with makeup, special effects, and costume design revealed a recognition of the pleasures of social theatricality. The widespread notion that social conventions lead to a divided nature, part of which includes a pernicious hypocrisy, culminated in *The Strange Case of Dr. Jekyll and Mr. Hyde* (1886), a runaway best-seller in the United States. Participants in urbanizing American culture not only believed in numerous social identities but also perceived that they often conflicted.[27]

Although mistaken identity has always been a staple of comedy, resort fiction absolutely fixated on confidence and disguise. For example, one Massachusetts newspaper related the apocryphal story of the son of a U.S. senator who won the attentions of the Saratoga belles and the envy of the gentlemen until he was unmasked as the steamboat captain's steward. Bayard Taylor published a story in which the painfully shy hero tries to recreate his personality at watering places. "Now, here's a chance to turn over a new leaf. Nobody knows me," he thinks to himself. Unfortunately his love interest mistakenly identifies him as a lowly chiropodist. Innumerable cautionary tales hinged on the difference between virtuous and shallow Americans as they countered the wiles of devious foreigners, fashionable fops, and prehensile villains at resorts. At American watering places, claimed the British Consul George Towle, "spurious Italian counts and German music teachers with a spiritual air" lived in clover.[28]

In a commercial society, material symbols of rank can be purchased and manipulated in a "fraudulent" way. Vacationers empowered themselves by creating an appealing and prestigious cultural persona, casting themselves in the role of romantic hero or heroine of an adventure with infinite possibilities. In Nathaniel Willis's "Meena Dimity; or Why Mr. Brown Crash Took the Tour," the hero, a stagecoach clerk, travels to a resort in order to wreak vengeance on a local beauty in his hometown who has snubbed him. At Saratoga, everyone believes he belongs to high society simply because he has had experience helping ladies out of carriages. Through his new connections at the Springs, he returns home as Brown Crash, Esquire, and marries a woman even more desirable than his original choice. Similarly, in Lucy Comfort's *The Belle of Saratoga* (she also wrote *Love at Long Branch* and *The Newport Bride*), the heroine disguises herself as a maid at the Union Hotel, while one of the main male characters misrepresents himself as a "stranger" rather than reveal his true identity. When he later discovers the servant's "true" identity, he exultantly repeats over and over again, "I have found who they are!"[29]

This theme of tourist as imposter was not unique to American literature but reflected the broader impact of urbanization and the Industrial Revolution on perceptions of leisure travel. The English novelist Frances Trollope, most famous for her American travelogues, wrote *The Robertses on Their Travels* (1846) in which the entire three-volume joke entails the attempt by the bourgeois Roberts family to put on airs and deceive the natives on the Continent. The socially astute Mrs. Roberts assures her husband that if they travel with enough money to dress smartly and make a little show now and then, they will "very soon get jumbled together both with those above and those below them," because it is impossible "to find out (if people don't stay too long in one place) who *are* real people of fashion and who are not." In Charles Lever's *The Dodd Family Abroad* (1862), the family attempts to infiltrate the higher classes by masquerading in Europe as if they possess a fortune, but they are eventually done in by the devious intrigues of professional adventurers. Charles Dickens' "The Tuggses at Ramsgate" (1836) hinges on the exploitation of the newly rich Tuggs family by three designing impostors. When the Tuggses behave poorly at the seaside inn, they console themselves with the realization that "it didn't matter; who knew what they were, there? For all the people of the house knew, they might be common people."[30]

This ambiguity between fact and fiction particularly captivated antebellum Americans and permeated many areas of culture beyond the watering place. A fascination with the "unvarnished truth" helped propel the initial infatuation with photography; stereographs perplexingly presented a "true" photographic record magically reproduced in three dimensions. The claims of the newly ascendant penny press to objectivity did not prevent the *New York Sun* from breaking all circulation records in 1835 when it reported that the moon contained trees, pelicans, and winged men. Land speculation, the greatest American craze of the century, depended wholly on the popular belief in the veracity of promoters' claims. Probably half the paper "money" circulating in mid-century America was counterfeit, forcing merchants and customers alike to evaluate daily the legitimacy of the currency. Theodore Weld's *American Slavery as It Is* (1839) and Harriet Beecher Stowe's *Uncle Tom's Cabin* (1852), both huge best-sellers, claimed to present the "actual" truth.[31]

The United States at the time of the Civil War was a jamboree of exaggeration, chicanery, flimflam, and bunkum. Again and again, well-publicized hoaxes demonstrated an American fixation on illusion. The public delighted in challenges to its credulity, whether William Miller's scriptural exegesis predicting the end of the world in 1843 or the claim that the Vikings constructed the enigmatic Newport Tower. Thousands flocked to western New York to see the Cardiff Giant, purported to be a petrified man complete with neatly carved hair and beard. That master of ballyhoo, P. T. Barnum, gained fame and fortune exhibiting attractions to which large audiences, especially at watering places, were drawn simply to decide whether the show was genuine or contrived. Writers with an interest in history commonly fabricated documents, and the first significant American forger began his career in the 1850s. Pretenders to nobility roamed the continent, bamboozling investors and making a living on the lecture circuit. At least forty men vied for the distinction of the Lost Dauphin (Louis XVII), a situation hilariously parodied by Mark Twain in *Huckleberry Finn*. In fact, Twain began his career by perpetrating journalistic hoaxes in Nevada.[32]

Edgar Allan Poe returned numerous times to the idea that human destiny involves a freewheeling deceptiveness. In "Diddling Considered as One of the Exact Sciences," Poe detailed and glorified a host of confidence schemes. One of Poe's fixations was "The Automaton," a European machine that its promoters claimed could play chess without the aid of human agency. The Automaton first toured American cities in 1826; an imitation took up residence in Saratoga the very next year and soon became a watering place staple. When Elizabeth Ruffin saw it at the Springs, she typically tried to determine how it worked and whether there was trickery involved. Poe himself perpetrated several travel hoaxes, including a supposed three-day balloon crossing of the Atlantic and the *Narrative of A. Gordon Pym*, which played on the craze for accounts of voyages to the South Pole.[33]

Nineteenth-century Americans were voracious consumers of travel literature, and these narratives especially brought out creative fireside fabrications in which tales of lost continents competed with ancient maps of questionable veracity. The genre of travel writing was notorious for fraudulent or imaginary voyages, as if the act of traveling itself relaxed the traditional canons of truth and falsity. Hotel owners created Trumansburg giants or Nahant sea serpents to popularize their resorts. Anonymous and pseudonymous travelers, such as Mark Pencil, Thursty McQuill, Sophie Sparkle, and Samuel Sombre, wrote some of the most engaging accounts of the mineral springs and the seashore. Other visitors to resorts assumed a genteel voice in their accounts, adopting a tone that elevated them several rungs higher on the social ladder than their actual position.[34]

In the world of high geographical mobility that characterized American society, travelers were viewed as potential social counterfeits, tricksters, or "confidence men," a term newly coined in 1849. The confidence man, the ultimate "stranger," absolutely negated the belief that appearances reliably indicate social position. A master of disguise, he most commonly approached young people at the moment when familial and communal restraints fell away—that is, when they entered the city or the resort—and lured the unsuspecting to their doom. In vain, guidebooks warned visitors to the resort to be careful in forming acquaintances because one could never be certain as to the respectability of fellow guests.[35]

Herman Melville's novel, *The Confidence-Man* (1857), provided a benchmark by which this professional schemer could be defined. The action takes place on April Fools' Day on the ironically named steamboat *Fidèle,* "always full of strangers" coming and going. The *Fidèle* floats beyond the realm of any authority on a stately pilgrimage to New Orleans. The idea of impersonation dominates Melville's drama; each actor knows of fellow passengers only what they choose to present in dress, words, or actions about their past and present place in the world. Melville's ship of fools encompasses a multiplicity of mid-century Americans, similar to the typologies reported by numerous visitors to resorts. Not surprisingly, it is the world-traveling Cosmopolitan who propounds the belief that "life is a pic-nic; one must take a part, assume a character, stand ready in a sensible way to play the fool." The *National Era* reprised this motif in a series of articles in 1859 entitled "First Impressions of Saratoga," in which one acolyte took the steamer *New World* up the Hudson, surrounded by fashionable travelers.[36]

Like the watering place and the resort hotel, the confidence man had an ambiguous status with the American people. As a marginal figure without a fixed place in the social structure, he represented the threat of social disorder and served as a lightning rod for uneasiness about the increasingly changeable nature of personal character. Yet comic and satiric literature presented images of shrewd and roguish operators who delighted in entering a series of roles and making them work. On the frontier, backwoodsmen like hunter Davy Crockett or Mississippi boatman Mike Fink bragged of their deceptions, while in the East, the Yankee peddler, a peripatetic trickster, supposedly achieved his goals through constant theatricality. Southern humorist Johnson Hooper created the popular Simon Suggs, whose "whole ethical system lies snugly in his favorite aphorism—'IT IS GOOD TO BE SHIFTY IN A NEW COUNTRY.'" Charles Dickens decided that one of the chief distinguishing traits of Americans was "the love of 'smart' dealing, which gilds over many a swindle and gross breach of trust." After 1865, Horatio Alger personified this tradition in American success literature, encouraging readers to cultivate the art of the confidence man in order to seize the main chance. The American trickster, an exaggerated image of the traveler, became a covert cultural hero.[37]

The stranger, the confidence man, and the visitor to the resort all straddled the frontier between migratory and rooted communities. Confidence men especially loved watering places, and hotels responded by hiring detectives. Because guests and strangers looked alike, adventurers were often able to sneak in for a free meal or to secure a better hat upon leaving than the one with which they had entered. In Saratoga, local ordinance made it a misdemeanor to leave without paying the bills for room rent and board, and constables were invariably busy at the season's end. Accounts of Coney Island before 1880 absolutely obsessed over the presence of three-card-monte games and tried to expose the trickery of the card shark. "The parting of the fool from his money seems to be a law of nature," observed one visitor to Gravesend's beach.[38]

Of course, visiting a resort did not put one totally outside the social system. Many people came with friends or family and looked for and found familiar acquaintances. Brochures, word of mouth, and guidebooks constantly advised and set limits to tourist behavior. But an anticipation of continuity is basic to orderly social structure. In relationships without future expectations, the temptation to break rules was particularly strong; as Lydia Maria Child observed, "Where men are little known, they are imperfectly restrained." The crowds at the springs and the shore came and went so quickly that a stay seemed an allegory of life. "I have been here but a few weeks and have survived several generations," commented one visitor, "and the day after tomorrow shall pass off myself." Lucy Wooster wrote that "our meals are rendered interesting on account of the new faces that are always presenting themselves. . . . Since our arrival, the company has almost entirely changed." This rapid turnover meant friendships formed at watering places were often evanescent. As Timothy Flint coldly stated, "A painful appendage to most of these transient but pleasant intimacies is the reflection, that you met, are pleased with each other, part with regret, and can expect to meet no more on the earth." It also meant that visitors often "[threw] away everything like ridiculous etiquette, formality and ceremony."[39]

Merely checking into a hotel offered possibilities for humorous disguise. According to superstition, if a clerk were to close the old-style folio register, business would be bad for the rest of the day. Thus, the hotel register provided reading material open to the public, its perusal the daily pleasure of hundreds. Guests sometimes used the opportunity to express themselves in prose and poetry on politics, the hotel, the sights, or recommendations of wares. In the visitor books at Niagara Falls, Charles Dickens read "the vilest and the filthiest ribaldry that ever human hogs delighted in." The Coney Island House listed among its registrants in 1850 Samuel Niggerhead from Louse Point, Bill Blunderbuss from Shirt Tail Bend, and Julius Suqueezer, Esq., from Rome. Some entered themselves as governor of Coney Island or mayor of Hog Wallow, and many added "Cosmopolete" to their signatures as an honorific title. The noted architect Alexander Jackson Davis signed the guest register at the Tip-Top, in the White Mountains, "Architect by the Grace of God." Kangaroo, Whale, and Jumbo all signed into C. B. Moon's Lake House in Saratoga, as did John F. Bass, from China, and "A. Thompson & Lady," whose ultimate destination was "Heaven." One satirist claimed that falsely signing as "John Stubbs, of Stubbstown" would earn him not only a little dignity but perhaps, more important, a better hotel room.[40]

To revel in a vast and temporary gathering at the resort brought the excitement and uncertainty that something or someone exciting might be only an elbow away. Dialogues in leaflets distributed by tract societies often took the form of ephemeral encounters between traveling strangers, because the religious conversion experience seemed more credible in this abnormal environment. Visitors flocked together on the piazzas and in the parlors and often received surprising confidences that would probably have been carefully withheld from a more closely related person. Charles Dudley Warner's hero, after hearing one logorrheic outburst, remarked that "it is precisely in hotels and to entire strangers that some people are apt to talk with less reserve than to intimate friends."[41]

At the resort, romance could occur anywhere; in "Their Pilgrimage," Warner's hero and heroine first meet over breakfast in the dining room. Young people took advantage of the springs, beaches, verandas, dining rooms, and parlors to engage in widespread flirtation. Traveling relaxed traditional sexual discipline and transformed usual norms into a sort of temporary libertinism; after all, Casanova's amorous *Memoirs* were nothing more than a record of his journeys through the major cities of Europe. Charles Baldwin, residing near the Catskill Mountains and certainly no profligate, described a memorable ride to the tourist site of Kaaterskill Falls in this way:

> As my carriage was not wide enough for three on the seat, I sat on the laps of my two friends, and drove. They put their arms around me, which pleased me very much. At the several bridges I collected "toll" from each one of them in the shape of a kiss. Part of the time, friend Sarah sat on my lap and drove: while I put one arm around her waist *to steady her,* and the other arm around friend Lizzie. Lizzie also sat on my lap a short time. The whole party was in excellent spirits, and we had much fun during the whole drive.[42]

Flirtation was the ultimate social game, a play form of eroticism free from all immutable realities. For example, twenty-two-year-old Charles Griffin knew no one when he arrived at Saratoga in 1833, but within a week, his diary recorded numerous meetings, conversations, and evaluations of women. "There are so many misses," he despaired, "I can't remember them all." Another collegiate diarist at the Virginia springs began the summer by recording, "Times very dull—no dancing—women horribly ugly." By the end of the summer, he had fallen in love numerous times, and as for his diary, he was "too busy with the girls to write anything of consequence." Harvard student Robert Habersham's diary relating to his trips to Saratoga and Newport overflowed with references to women; he claimed never to have been "in a steamboat or a stage without dreaming of some pretty adventure I was to have with them." At Coney Island, one commentator noted, "beach flirtation is not only compatible with learning to swim, but indispensable."[43]

Resorts pioneered the rise of public heterosocial leisure and the devaluation of a strictly private female sphere. Nineteenth-century space may have been heavily gendered, but traveling exposed the most vulnerable points in this sexual division. To advocates of the ideology of separate spheres, the city represented the untamed male province of commerce and public life, while women dominated the refined sphere of the private home, the site of household and family. Rules of social behavior in the city, such as injunctions against making new acquaintances on the street, tended to restrict women's freedom. But women flocked to the exceedingly public beaches, springs, and water-cure resorts, where they took a prominent position.

Etiquette manuals may have cautioned women to remain at home and live vicariously through their husbands, but the ethos was only a code, not a description. Resorts weakened any attempt to divide American culture into two exclusive and antithetically gendered realms.[44]

Before 1800, more men traveled than women, and on the surface, the activity seemed to underline the difference between mobile males and home-bound females. Single males constituted the majority of guests at Ballston's Sans Souci in the 1820s, where men outnumbered women by a margin of two to one. Richard Cobden remarked on the small number of women on Hudson River steamers and in hotels in 1825. But by 1860, Lillian Foster noted that "the entire government of the affairs of the [watering place] community is in the hands of women." In many accounts, women planned and organized the summer trip over the objections of husbands or fathers. Chroniclers portrayed men as befuddled or uncomfortable amid the extended leisure of the resort. Urban hotels segregated the rare single lady traveler—as late as the 1890s, some hotels still built separate ladies' staircases—but at resorts, visitors more often commented on the scarcity of men.[45]

Women emerged from an idealized role as dependents and noncompetitors to organize and perpetuate the amusements at watering places. Depictions of resorts included stock characters such as the hotel belle and the female organizer who filled the role of master of ceremonies and controlled the tempo of group activities. On the beach, women assumed a freedom of movement and activity proscribed in etiquette books and suppressed in private parlors. In 1859, an English visitor, John MacGregor, singled out the informality of American women at the city of play: "I defy you to find such an upturning of all our conventional notions of woman's outdoor life." Many foreigners attributed the American mania for traveling solely to the desire of both sexes for flirtation. Salomon de Rothschild, who visited Newport in 1860, had a reputation for enjoying "lewd talk and nude photographs," but even he expressed shock that men and women, "married or not," visited the beach for mixed bathing or went off at night unchaperoned.[46]

For women, the resort offered the freedom to experiment with unusual styles of dress and behavior. *Godey's Magazine* explicitly compared Newport and Saratoga with Sodom and Gomorrah because women used "paint under their eye-lids to give a more brilliant effect to the eye." When Celia Wall wanted to introduce the so-called Grecian Bend, a Paris craze featuring an extreme S-shaped silhouette with bulging hips and buttocks, she chose Saratoga as the location most likely to grant acceptance. And no sooner did Amelia Bloomer introduce her eponymous outfit, in 1851, than it was sighted on the summer streets of Newport. *Harper's Weekly* reported women at resorts who "smoke, and drink sherry cobblers at night, and call gentlemen by their Christian names, and who are always very conspicuous." Eighty years after Marian Gouverneur vacationed at Newport in the 1830s, her most vivid memory was not the scenery, beach, or amusements but the dress and demeanor of a fellow guest at her boardinghouse. She recalled that Mrs. James Petigru of South Carolina wore the latest styles and "kept very late hours, often lingering in her room the next morning until midday." Elizabeth Cady Stanton singled out Saratoga and Newport as places where supporters of women's suffrage could receive a particularly "quiet and respectful hearing."[47]

Coquetry dominated Saratoga, Newport, and Coney Island virtually from their creation, just as feasts and fairs had always served as occasions for courtship and sexual encounters. As Thomas Grattan wrote, "It would be almost impossible to exaggerate, in describing the rage for flirtation which prevails among American females." Marriage was ostensibly the ultimate goal, for at resorts, parents could try to narrow the range of eligible partners. According to antebellum myth, watering places also mingled southerners and northerners and strengthened national harmony by fostering regional intermarriages. Most spectators took a more jaundiced view. The *Newport Daily News* witnessed "desperate damsels anxiously searching for rich husbands, and rakish men seeking for wealthy wives." In 1851, *Gleason's* reported parvenu belles and managing mothers congregating in Saratoga, "where ready exchange may be made of money and good looks for old family respectability and blood." George Towle noted that Newport and Saratoga had become "marriage bourses with their speculators and victims" and called the nightly balls "great matrimonial fairs, where the marriageable wares are shown off at their best." Only a year after his wife died, "Commodore" Cornelius Vanderbilt remarried an Alabama woman forty years his junior whom he had met at Saratoga.[48]

Yet overemphasis on this functional aspect of the resort masks the fact that the vast majority of single visitors never intended their summer flings to culminate in marriage. Achille Murat, son of the king of Naples, described resort ballrooms as a "field of battle" on which "a Thousand little coquetries are played off to draw a young man to declare himself, only to have the pleasure of refusing him afterwards." Eliza Thompson, the daughter of a North Carolina planter, came to Saratoga in 1834 and initially stayed at Union Hall. Eliza was disgusted: "As I did not come here to listen to lectures or prayers I proposed we move to Congress Hall, which is much the gayest and most fashionable house in the place." Her family immediately granted her wishes, viewing them as entirely reasonable. A writer for *Harper's Weekly* captured the sense of license and exhilaration of an unmarried woman at a seaside resort: "I came here this summer to enjoy myself, and Tom helps me do it. . . . It is a little game we are playing, and it is nobody's business but ours. People flirt at their own risk." Women at least partially responded to the erotic and judgmental gaze of the vast crowds through the spirited use of coquetry.[49]

Watering place flirtation hinged on the ability to disguise one's intentions and play fast and loose with "reality." In one story, the enraged narrator describes a woman at Saratoga who seduces men for her amusement: "She wears a variety of characters just as the whim takes her, and is 'everything by turns and nothing long.' . . . But Dick sees nothing behind the mask she wears." Men willingly participated in this most popular sport, fully cognizant of the fleeting nature of the vacation experience. One amorist rhapsodized to his beloved, "We should enjoy a week of supreme happiness—suffer in parting—and presently be solaced, and enjoy other weeks of supreme felicity with other Lulus." In another story, a youth at Saratoga jilts the object of his affections with a speech beginning, "The pleasure of a Watering-Place is a meeting with a thousand friends whom we never saw before, and shall never see again." Yet to his dismay, he falls in love, only to discover the object of his affections has actually been toying with him.[50]

To the horror of social conservatives, even married women flirted at resorts. Sidney Fisher visited Newport and confessed to his diary on 18 July 1841 that he had "had a flirtation with a married lady which afforded me some amusement, but no interest. We carried it pretty far." Financier August Belmont was shot in a duel after being accused of enjoying the illicit favors of Mrs. Oscar Coles of Saratoga Springs, famous for her romances as much as for her beauty. The content of numerous boasting letters attests that many young men journeyed to the resorts in the hopes of gaining sexual experience. The popular antebellum poet John Saxe, a regular visitor to the Springs, parodied the atmosphere in his poem "Song of Saratoga" (later put to music):

Now they stroll in the beautiful walks,
Or loll in the shade of the trees;
Where many a whisper is heard
That never is told by the breeze;
And hands are commingled with hands,
Regardless of conjugal rings;
And they flirt, and they flirt, and they flirt—
And that's what they do at the Springs![51]

The open spaces of the city of play assumed a special function in the theater of flirtation. Almost any reasonably attired person could freely walk in off the street, pass through the hotel lobby, and enjoy the courtyard park with its interior veranda (see figure 7). As one guidebook pointed out, the potential for amatory activity increased the attraction of these gardens, for their overgrown foliage made them "a perfect elysium for that large class of people who have 'something sweet to say' to each other, and perhaps, *perhaps*, a gentle caress to bestow if no one is peeping." Against the susurrus of the trees, prospective suitors examined the merchandise without any lasting commitment or fear of invasion of privacy. Evening dances intensified the salacious possibilities of a visit to a watering place, and hidden desires sought realization in a magical fantasy world.[52]

Of all locales for dalliance, the dance floor took pride of place. A New York newspaper referred to Newport's nightly hops as a "carnival" in which as many as six hundred guests danced until dawn. Dance crazes shook the antebellum fashionable world, and despite some disapproval, the hotel ball-rooms reverberated to the new steps. First, the waltz, with its "whirlings and lascivious windings" of couples at their own volition, displaced older dances. Then the mazurka, redow, and schottische followed in dizzying succession, often permitting intimate physical contact that had previously been unthinkable. The ballrooms of Newport's hotels were one of the first venues to host the scandalous polka when it arrived in America in 1844. The ritual of nightly dances and parties at resorts, with frequently changing partners and scanty introduction, often brought on a euphoric response.[53]

Masquerade balls especially added a provocative tension to the watering place experience. Nineteenth-century Americans, infatuated with making impressions, savored the thrill of manipulating the categories of class and gender. The *New York World* described the conclusion of one dance in sexual terms: "the panting women in the delirium of excitement; their eyes, flashing with the sudden abnormal light of physical elation, bound and lead like tigresses; they have lost their sense of prudence and safety." Salespeople appeared in resort towns with elaborate collections of costumes complete with wigs, swords, and other paraphernalia, while out-of-town newspapers reported breathlessly on the preparations—the Newport costume ball of 1848 filled the entire front page, seven columns wide, of the *New York Herald.* An eyewitness at one Newport masquerade noticed that while in Europe the majority of party goers dressed as peasants, democratic Americans frequently donned the trappings of royalty. Many resorts at the springs of Virginia made the connection more overt, staging mock medieval tournaments with jousting events. In playing the role of feudal lords and ladies, visitors linked themselves to Walter Scott's chivalric medieval past. Masquerade balls at resorts typically provided the climax to the season and further blurred the line between "true" and constructed identity.[54]

In general, women at resorts spent an inordinate amount of time changing their clothes; every time of day and each particular activity required a different outfit and personality to match. One female visitor to Saratoga observed that "men and women do things when stared at, they would never do alone by themselves. . . . Much of my pains-taking in dressing is to please a crowd of people, not one in a hundred of whom I know, or care to know." In *The Belle of Saratoga,* one girl declares that "there are so many people here and they stare so!" The unwieldy Saratoga trunk, so huge that Robert Louis Stevenson parodied it as fit only "to contain a human body," became a stock-in-trade of satirists. Iron bound and curved on top, to the despair of luggage haulers who could not stack them, Saratoga trunks stuffed with women's costumes spread the fame of the village around the world. Rumor had it that women based their departure date on the moment when they had completely exhibited their wardrobe, and William Butler's popular 1857 poem, "Nothing to Wear," parodied many a woman's putative plaint. The daughter of the British novelist William Thackeray visited Saratoga in the summer of 1868 and espied echoes of *Vanity Fair.* She wrote that visitors "overdress ridiculously. . . . I never saw such dressing in all my life— Generally in very bad taste." The temptation to wear flamboyant clothing, just as the temptation to overdrink and overeat, was an intrinsic part of the resort experience.[55]

Through public sociability, men and women at watering places conceptualized the world as a theater and themselves as both spectators and actors

rather than consumers. Obviously, not everyone could afford to fill fifteen Saratoga trunks with clothes, but the market economy exercised only
a covert presence on the antebellum resort experience. Once the visitor
checked into the hotel, there simply was not much to buy of a tangible
nature. The *Brooklyn Eagle* advised that any Coney Island visitor could read
the newspaper and learn "how to behave and how to see others behave."[56]

Those who creatively focused on this celebration of modern urbanity adopted the French tradition of the *flâneur,* literally, an "idler" or a
"lounger." This cosmopolitan, a person of leisure and a connoisseur of the
city's mundane delights, took pride in knowing and understanding others
not only personally but also categorically. The *flâneur* strolled the urban
scene without utilitarian purpose, free to follow any whim, savor the unexpected, or weave veils of fantasy around the multitude of passersby and pro-
saic urban realities. At the hotel, this visitor remained precariously poised in
a mysterious twilight zone between freedom and autonomy, on the one
hand, and estrangement and alienation, on the other. *Flânerie* on the veranda, the beach, the parlor, or the springs was public, other-directed, un-
disciplined, and most important, a free activity. To see and be seen defined
life at mid-nineteenth-century resorts.[57]

The urbanity of the resort reflected the attractions of the expanding city.
Despite the antiurban bias of many nineteenth-century intellectuals, several
noted authors allowed the vibrancy of the metropolis to momentarily allay
their anxiety. The narrator of Edgar Allan Poe's short story, "The Man of
the Crowd" (1840), delights in scrutinizing and describing the crowd passing by the window of a London coffeehouse until he impulsively follows one
"man of the crowd" for an entire day. In Nathaniel Hawthorne's *Blithedale
Romance,* the narrator concedes that "the thick, foggy, stifled element of
cities, the entangled life of many men together, sordid as it was, and empty
of the beautiful, took quite as strenuous a hold upon my mind. I felt as if
there could never be enough of it." In "Wakefield," Hawthorne's title character, under pretense of going on a journey, takes lodgings on the street next
to his house for no discernible reason and lives there anonymously for
twenty years, watching the world go by. Walt Whitman displayed a constant
enthusiasm for New York in poems such as "A Broadway Pageant" and
"Broadway." In "Crossing Brooklyn Ferry," Whitman turns his panoramic
gaze to "crowds of men and women attired in the usual costumes, how
curious you are to me!" If the city could be an infinitely entertaining spec-

tacle despite its size and all its problems, the resort, as a "purified" and magical city, promised even greater voyeuristic opportunities.[58]

Visitors to Saratoga, Newport, and Coney Island constantly demonstrated this new type of passionate urban spectatorship. Travelers both foreign and domestic considered themselves astute students of human nature and scoured resorts to construct the mythical "American character." If the myriad peoples and types that made up the United States could be known, it was at the resort where this seemed possible; Washington Irving satirized this commonplace as early as 1807 in *Salmagundi*. The scene, or the living actors who animated it, moved in endless succession; each day brought new faces and presented some new character to laugh at or admire. Urbanites visited resort cities not to probe the inner self but to indulge their fascination with the behavior of actors in a public place.[59]

Few writers described the resort world without conjuring up images of "all the world," usually in precisely those words. As early as 1820, a letter from a Virginian to the *Albany Statesman* expressed astonishment at the crowd at Congress Spring, "composed of all nations, sexes, ages, and complexions;—the American and the Europeans, the Asiatick and African—the brunette of the south, and the rosy-cheeked beauty of the north. . . . Such a diversified gallery of portraits I have never seen grouped together." By the 1830s this vision of "all the world" had become a cliché, but the heterogeneous nature of the setting itself had not lost its ability to astonish. Philip Hone declared in 1839 that "this is the meridian of the Saratoga season. All the world is here." Benjamin Franklin Perry wrote his wife in 1846, noting that "the world seems congregated here." "Everybody was there," George Templeton Strong concluded about Saratoga in 1841. At Newport, *Harper's Monthly* reminded readers that the discomfort of the inadequate hotel room was "the only tax he pays for the pleasure of being where the world is"; and rare was the Coney Island account that did not repeat the claim that it was the world's most democratic resort (figure 26).[60]

To witness the diverse and ever changing throng of humanity at the springs, on the beach, or in the street centered an otherwise diffuse and formless visit (figures 27 and 28). Herman Melville stayed at Saratoga only three hours but knew to take up "a commanding position on the piazza of the Grand Union, and surveyed at my leisure the moving spectacle of fashion and—in some instances—folly." The crowds drew the tourist gaze as if by magnetism. Southerner Caroline Gilman spent a week at Saratoga in

Figure 26. Bathing at Coney Island, ca. 1890. In an era before air conditioning, the breezy seaside naturally attracted urban dwellers. (Courtesy of the Brooklyn Historical Society.)

1838 attempting to write poetry but found it impossible because there was "something in the tone of things that prevents all fixedness of attention. It is enough to look at people all dressed up for show." The *Brooklyn Eagle* vicariously gave readers "glimpses from the piazza of the Brighton Hotel," at Coney Island, in which immense and happy crowds promenaded up and down the verandas and the beach. Henry Gilpin, author of the *Northern Tour,* concluded that "there are few who cannot, at least for a short time, extract some pleasure from such a scene."[61]

Resorts glorified nonproductive activity, and an atmosphere of *dolce far niente* permeated the air. To "kill time" or to be busy "doing nothing" brought prestige to the visitor. "If only the rich did this, all would be well," complained John Watson, "but are there not too many of those who aim to

imitate them who can ill sustain the loss of time and expense?" The correspondent for London's *Belgravia Magazine* blamed American summer prostration on the "sumptuous hotels. . . . Having everything at one's hands ready, without any personal exertion, superinduces indolence." African Americans voiced similar criticisms by reversing racial stereotypes: Solomon Northup commented that Saratoga encouraged "shiftlessness and extravagance," while James Thomas declared the Springs must have been "a charming place before fashion and folly got in."[62]

Antebellum visitors to resorts suffered not from boredom but from ennui, and therein lay a crucial distinction. Use of the words *to bore* in English has not been recorded before 1755; Samuel Johnson's famous dictionary of that year makes no note of the verb. *Ennui* implied a judgment on the universe by superior individuals, whereas *boredom* described a response to the immediate that bordered on moral failure. At hotel-oriented resorts,

Figure 27. "View of Saratoga Springs, from the Piazza of Union Hall," *Frank Leslie's,* September 3, 1859. By following a see-and-be-seen ethos, visitors conceptualized the world as a theater and themselves as simultaneously spectators and actors. (Courtesy of the Saratoga Springs Public Library.)

visitors constantly expostulated on the subject of ennui and wore their idleness like a badge of honor. The modern ethos—an appetite for the novel and for getting and spending money—had not yet conquered Saratoga Springs, Newport, or Coney Island. This watering place ennui served as the playful backdrop against which visitors created a common social world from a jumble of disparate strangers. Class conflict and latent violence tainted the public sphere in the metropolis, where the elite could use the parade and the promenade to project and legitimate their power on to the street. The resort, however, was a theoretically ideal world, the site of a secular pilgrimage, where all could participate in see-and-be-seen culture.[63]

Of course, performers in the hotel spotlight drew the praise and condemnation of a judgmental audience. Americans did use fashion as a way to exclude undesirables (such as African Americans and Jews) and to "cut" acquaintances; Mrs. DeWitt Clinton's scornful refusal to return President

Figure 28. "[Grand] Union Hotel," *Frank Leslie's*, May 28, 1870. Frank Leslie's newspaper often featured Saratoga Springs, partially because Leslie owned an estate outside the village. (Courtesy of the Saratoga Springs Public Library.)

Martin Van Buren's bow at a United States Hotel ball in Saratoga precipitated a huge scandal. Yet, living among strangers for a week or a summer, guests aspired to a state of amity, the friendly relations of a public character between individuals. In general, visitors to resorts amiably shared beaches and springs, walkways and stores, ballrooms and parlors.[64]

The threat to American society posed by affluence had been viewed with foreboding since the time of the Pilgrims, but the vehemence of antebellum condemnations gave the sense that the resort world seriously challenged dominant ethical standards. Popular moralists such as James Kirke Paulding and Sarah Joseph Hale castigated the parvenu for his coarseness, the dandy for his antirepublican ennui, and the belle for her narcissism and depicted the fashionable life as a first step on a slippery slope to debauchery and ruin. Anxious conservatives fretted that prosperity was transforming a republic of God-fearing freedom-loving idealists into a horde of mercenary egoists. Writers often associated social aggrandizement and leisurely dissolution with the women who were so visible at resorts. Saratoga (the "queen of spas") and Newport both acquired a stereotypical feminine image that was the very antithesis of republican simplicity: frivolous, expensive, over-dressed, displaced from the rhythms of commercial life.[65]

Nonetheless, the prescriptive literature of etiquette guides and success manuals, with their monotonous paeans to sincerity, were ineffectual at these first resorts. The resort, almost by definition, undermined moral self-improvement and genuine behavior by promoting the art of surface illusion. Determined to be happy, travelers underwent a sort of personality change upon crossing the magical borders and entering the realm of the springs or the shore. They followed minimal rules of etiquette while delighting in the ambience of hypocrisy and the sense that the strictures of everyday life did not necessarily apply.

The juxtaposition of the desire to experiment with boundaries of truth and falsity, the longing for a communal public life, and the yearning for a stable place in a free-floating social system created the piquant tension that was both the glory and the undoing of the nineteenth-century American resort. Saratoga, Newport, and Coney Island all teetered on the cusp between "all-the-world" democracy and exclusionary snobbery. Visitors heard languages of all nations and viewed persons of all degrees of character and intellect; and yet, reported one amazed magazine, "the conditions of accommodations do not vary materially. The order and propriety preserved in such strange co-minglings constitute one of the triumphs of American civilization."[66]

These "playgrounds" were places apart, isolated and virtually hallowed. The egalitarianism of the promenade, the emphasis on see-and-be-seen culture, the front-and-center presence of active women, the constant references to ennui, the lack of charge for the springs or the beach, all positioned Saratoga, Newport, and Coney Island as resorts within which special rules applied. Private country residences might carry with them blessings of their own, recorded the *Crayon* in 1858, but they could never possess the gypsy charm that hovered around the public resorts. Perhaps looking toward Gilded Age Newport, the magazine presciently concluded that "the wild romance of a locality containing hundreds of strangers thrown together indiscriminately, will in a great measure be broken as soon as we cross the threshold of a well-regulated single household."[67]

≋ FIVE ≋

The Commercialization of Saratoga Springs

Racetracks, Casinos, and Souvenirs

A MONTH AFTER the Battle of Gettysburg might not seem to have been a propitious time to launch a racetrack venture. Yet despite the dire need for mounts in the Union cavalry, promoters of Saratoga Springs managed to scrape together enough horses to fill four days of races in August of 1863. The blood had barely dried on the streets of New York City after the vicious draft riot when *Wilkes' Spirit of the Times,* the bible of the sporting world, reported, "It is now established that of the many thousands of people to be found at Saratoga at this season of the year, there are but few who will not eagerly avail themselves of the opportunity for such amusement and interest as the sports of the turf afford." The judgment proved to be exceedingly foresighted; the Saratoga track now stands as the oldest horse-racing venue in the United States still in operation.[1]

The touristic decline of the springs of Virginia after secession left Saratoga unrivaled as queen of spas, and by 1900, almost two hundred thousand visitors a year took advantage of the low rates, pleasant company, and myriad amusements. With the end of the internecine fighting, southerners gradually reappeared at the Springs; former governors of Maryland and Louisiana served as judges at the 1869 races, and the timer and starter both hailed from New Orleans. Nonetheless, by 1870, Saratoga had changed as radically as the nation. A smattering of visitors from Memphis, New Orleans, and Florida dotted the Union Hall register in 1869, but the South Carolina and Alabama planters were noteworthy in their absence. A series of fires in the

1860s cleared the way for the creation of the largest concentration of grand hotels the nation had ever seen, but they were usually filled by nouveau riche industrialists rather than southern gentry. The increasing numbers of visitors undermined any vestige of exclusivity attached to the Saratoga experience, and the resort added layer upon layer of possibilities for the purchase of pleasure.[2]

Saratoga's addition of the well-publicized horse-racing track and gambling facilities supplanted older styles of amusement. In the late nineteenth century, the exchange of money and goods within a secular market-oriented culture dominated American aesthetic life, moral sensibility, and leisure experience. Saratoga's transformation epitomized some of the cardinal features of this culture: the elevation of consumption as the means of achieving felicity, the democratization of desire, the acceptance of monetary value as the preeminent measure of value in society, and a cult of novelty and technology. Unlike New Hampshire or Niagara, which still depended to some degree on the sublimity of the mountains or the falls as a drawing card, Saratoga became a modern American resort precisely because the natural springs shrank to relative insignificance.[3]

The impetus for this change was provided by John Morrissey, in chronological order an undefeated boxing champion, the most famous gambler of his time, the first star athlete in Congress, and the initial impresario of American sports. Morrissey arrived in the United States in 1834, at the age of three, the son of penniless immigrants from Ireland, and before his eighteenth birthday, he had been indicted in several incidents for burglary, battery, and assault with intent to kill. The ambitious Morrissey parlayed this dubious fame into a career as a prize fighter, eventually claiming the title of heavyweight champion of the world by defeating James "Yankee" Sullivan in 1853. Morrissey's pugilistic skills attracted New York City mayor Fernando Wood's faction of Tammany Hall, and Morrissey triumphantly made the transition from brawler to politician and entrepreneur. His initial New York City gaming house opened in 1859 and quickly blossomed into sixteen faro establishments worth more than $500,000 only five years later.[4]

Morrissey's first Saratoga gaming house, built in 1862, stood only a few minutes' walk from the most fashionable hotels. Having already supplied gambling amusements for the evening, Morrissey reasoned that a racetrack would offer a focus that Saratoga's daytime routine had previously lacked.

"Old Smoke's" casino background prevented him from properly fronting the track, but he enlisted the support of three solid New York turfmen: wealthy sportsman John Hunter, lawyer Leonard Jerome, and stockbroker William Travers. In 1864, following the triumphant meeting the year before, these organizers purchased 125 acres, directly across Union Avenue from the old racecourse, for $12,500 and landscaped the new oval with a lavish hand. As General William Tecumseh Sherman closed in on Atlanta and just days after the carnage in the Crater at Petersburg, Saratoga offered four more days of racing in 1864, inaugurating the Travers Stakes, currently the oldest stakes race in the United States. A correspondent for the *Boston Journal*, although horrified by the revelry while "the country's heart was being torn asunder," admitted that "the races attracted nearly all the sporting community of the country."[5]

These horse races quickly became the focal point of Saratoga's summer. New Yorkers of high social standing dominated the Saratoga Association for the Improvement of the Breed (incorporated in 1865) and helped legitimate the racetrack. Hunter and Travers provided the panache, while rumors swirled that Jay Gould and "Commodore" Cornelius Vanderbilt had also invested. Although Morrissey's name was conspicuously absent from the list of incorporators, he retained a majority share of stock. The owners extended the schedule in 1865 to twelve races in six days; an estimated forty thousand visitors thronged Saratoga during race week alone, and dipper boys ladled nine thousand glasses of water from Congress Spring in a single morning (figure 29). A bound volume of vintage menus from Union Hall in 1865 contains daily notations of the number that feasted each night, beginning with 11 diners on 15 June and peaking at 1,477 on the final day of the races. Even the Saratoga County Fair now offered trotting races with cash stakes.[6]

With the Metairie Race Course in Louisiana ironically converted into a cemetery, Saratoga replaced New Orleans as the center of American turf sports. The Springs presented a neutral ground on which the western and southern stables could meet the best of the East for good purses. Sectional rivalries again piqued national interest, such as the famous clash between the northern thoroughbred Harry Bassett and the Kentucky-bred Longfellow in 1872. Despite competition from proliferating racetracks, Saratoga's average daily track attendance swelled to ten thousand. In 1877, Morrissey valued the Saratoga property at more than $250,000 and dramat-

Figure 29. "Horse-Racing at Saratoga," *Harper's Weekly*, August 26, 1865. Saratoga promoters consciously encouraged heterosocial crowds. The presence of women mitigated the outcast image of horse racing, a strategy imitated by vaudeville entrepreneurs later in the century. (Courtesy of the Yates Collection, Skidmore College.)

ically expanded the racing program to more than twenty days. Morrissey also acted as stakeholder for large bets and conducted auction pools, a role that contained no risk to the pool's manager. Since private bets could exceed $100,000, Morrissey's 5 to 15 percent commissions made his connection with the new track quite lucrative. He continued selling pools for several seasons even after the New York state legislature, of which he was a member, passed a law against them. By 1880, the track had acquired a national reputation as "the graveyard of favorites," an unsurprising moniker in a resort setting in which rational odds and decisions did not always seem to apply.[7]

The racetrack's thriving condition enabled Morrissey to augment his gambling operations at Saratoga; he bought thirty acres of swamp land contiguous to Congress Park and built a sumptuous red brick building for $200,000. Everything in Morrissey's Club House was first class, including gorgeously furnished toilet rooms and carpeted drawing rooms decorated with rich carvings and bronzes (figure 30). In private rooms upstairs, the biggest plungers of the day staked thousands of dollars, cash only, on the turn of a card. The Club House venture also proved extraordinarily profitable; Morrissey supposedly turned down an offer of half a million dollars for the establishment in 1872 while achieving net profits of at least that much from the first two years of brisk play. Success bred imitation, and by 1873, at least a dozen gambling houses operated openly at the Springs in defiance of the revised charter of 1866. "More like Baden-Baden every year, becomes Saratoga," reported one columnist.[8]

Neither horse racing nor gambling was new to Saratoga in the 1860s. In 1847, some local Saratoga tradesmen organized trotting races a couple of days a week throughout the summer for purses of up to $200. Similarly, one early guidebook warned that Saratoga contained "all the apparatus and paraphernalia of gambling and dissipation." Ben Scribner, a professional gambler, probably opened the first house devoted exclusively to wagering in 1842 in an alley conveniently near the United States Hotel and railroad terminal. "One of the first sights of passengers coming from one of the doors of the station," reminisced one resident, "was a room with windows open where a roulette wheel was in full operation and porters and others waiting for trains frequently gambled here." The *New York Herald* declared in 1847 that "every day at dinner the highest dignitaries of the church are to be found sitting side by side, in pleasant social communication with the gamblers of Park Row." Charles Gale owned two Saratoga facilities for public gaming in the 1850s, one so close to the office of the New York state chancellor that the clicking of the roulette wheel disturbed lawyers while they argued cases.[9]

The prominence of Morrissey's racetrack and Club House, however, gave them their significance. Events at the track now dominated the visitor's day, and any suspension of the races noticeably depressed the Saratoga scene. Horse racing and gambling as monetary transactions filled the space left by the declining value of reading, promenading, talking, listening to music, and even drinking. The track especially enshrined the new dominance of the clock by providing a workout time, opening time, post time, betting time, starting time, race time, and record time. Although there was no physical compulsion at Saratoga to wager, the visibility of gamblers and the fascination with instant profit seduced many visitors. Mildred Howells

Figure 30. "Morrissey's Gambling-House," *Every Saturday,* September 9, 1871. John Morrissey's Club House, a mecca for high rollers, was gorgeously furnished and exceedingly profitable. (Collection of the author.)

attended the races in secret so as not to offend the numerous clergymen staying at her boardinghouse, only to find most of her fellow guests there, too. The creation at Saratoga of the racetracks and gambling houses, in which monetary exchange predominated, weakened the aimless lounging and sense of ennui that characterized the antebellum period.[10]

Between the racetrack in the afternoon and the gambling houses after dark, the pace at the Springs was increasingly frenetic. The *New York Times* described a Saratoga summer as "a too prominent dazzle and dissipation, a weary round of heartless show, a fierce rivalry of dress and display, a succession of headaches and heartaches, and a *finale* of disgust and depletion. . . . It is hard to see how anyone comes here for relaxation." Critics intensified their long-standing condemnations of the Springs' moral tone; James Kirke Paulding's *New Mirror for Travellers* was republished in 1868, an astonishing revival for a parody that ridiculed the fashions and manners of a period forty years earlier. "You see men here, dressed in the loudest style of Franco-

Anglo-American fashion, driving four-in-hand drags filled with ladies of questionable virtue," wrote a disgruntled reporter, describing Saratoga for London readers of *Belgravia Magazine.* "The scenes in the gambling-houses at night and the language used would require the pencil of a Hogarth and the pen of a recording angel." Sidney Fisher visited the Grand Union in 1867 and seconded this view: "The men looked like thieves & the women like the whores many of them were." Yet Fisher concluded, "Probably, this will not be my last visit." He was not alone. James Blaine and Samuel Tilden visited Morrissey's Club House, joined by various generations of Vanderbilts, Belmonts, and Lorillards, and, so the gossips whispered, by Generals Ulysses Grant, William Tecumseh Sherman, and Philip Sheridan when they visited the Springs.[11]

Morrissey used several strategies to neutralize his critics. Unseemly behavior resulted in rapid ejection from the Club House; this so offended the irrepressible Jim Fisk and his ensemble that they cut short a Saratoga sojourn to take up residence at the less circumspect casino and racecourse at Long Branch. Morrissey also nurtured his revamped reputation as an honest gambler by hobnobbing with millionaires and politicians. By giving generously to local charities, playing the savior at mortgage sales, providing fireworks at the Fourth of July celebration, and, as a politician, presenting himself as a friend to the working man, he defused objections that professional gaming stole money from the community. To circumvent the possibility of local sore losers, Morrissey forbade any residents of Saratoga to gamble at his Club House; and in a bow to propriety, he barred women from the gaming rooms, although he welcomed them in the salon as sightseers, a privilege reputedly enjoyed by twenty-five thousand women in 1871 alone. Morrissey stalwartly defended these rules against gossip to the contrary: "I have lived in Saratoga nine years, and no lady has ever gambled, nor will ever gamble in my house. By request, ladies have been admitted to look at the house and furniture, but the comment it has occasioned both far and near prompts me to decline any further visits from them."[12]

Women did succeed in infiltrating the male world of the racetrack. A generation earlier, Americans had perceived unescorted females at the track as little better than prostitutes. Saratoga promoters, however, consciously fostered heterosocial crowds, sometimes charging women half price as an enticement. The presence of women mitigated the outcast image of horse racing, a strategy imitated by vaudeville entrepreneurs later in the century.

From the first Saratoga races in the 1860s, journalists sighted a considerable number of women, a finding confirmed by several illustrations for weekly magazines. In the 1890s, the Saratoga racetrack furnished a room in which women and children could bet on horses, the only such venue in the country. William Dean Howells reported that at Saratoga, "book-makers from the pool-rooms took the bets of the ladies, who formed by far the greater part of the grandstand." One newspaper, commenting on the multitude of women and children at the track, compared it with a Sunday School convention.[13]

Gambling particularly thrived at resorts, where communal controls were weaker, the desire to cross norms stronger, and a fluid sense of identity allowed wider leeway in social actions. Nineteenth-century sporting life, personified by John Morrissey, offered a twilight zone between the more clearly defined worlds of respectability and criminality. The sporting man had a dubious reputation: he frequented the saloon, gambled at the track, loitered in the poolroom, and proved his masculinity through fighting, womanizing, and drinking. Worse yet, the professional gambler seemed to pervert play by conducting games with "strangers" in an impersonal marketplace. Yet just as with the confidence man, many Americans viewed this resort sporting world with ambivalence. Professional gambling had been in official disrepute since colonial times, but no legislation could eliminate a cultural construct so in harmony with the American traits of competitiveness and materialism. By 1900, archetypes such as Bret Harte's western gamblers and Wall Street's risk-taking capitalists had become equivocally sanctioned cultural heroes. The Springs, with its widely publicized racetrack and gambling houses, celebrated this lifestyle.[14]

Morrissey's deft touch helped position Saratoga as the sporting resort par excellence as opposed to a mere gambler's haven. He never did win the recognition he craved from high society; Thomas Nast parodied him, and Sidney Fisher disparaged his "gross brutal countenance & most depraved & guilty look." But when he died of pneumonia in 1878 at the age of forty-seven, thousands lined the streets of Troy for his funeral, including most of the New York state legislature, which traveled there en masse from Albany. As a boxer, independent congressman, and, more famously, racetrack promoter and owner of the Saratoga Club House, John Morrissey became an American folk hero, romanticized in ballads and immortalized by Currier and Ives. For many, the sporting man's life, so closely tied to the resort experience, symbolized the very promise of America.[15]

Meanwhile, Saratoga's residents tried to appease competing constituencies by simultaneously supporting the business of pleasure, on the one hand, and the probity of moralists opposed to gambling, on the other. Although the city charter prohibited prostitution, gaming houses, and the breaking of the Sabbath, the board of trustees took their cues from the throngs of visitors who did not object to the city's mixture of virtue and vice. Neither host nor guest wanted to cleanse the municipality of the semilegitimate or outright illicit amusements. The village board tacitly accepted gambling houses for every class, although they occasionally tried to restrict their visibility or location on Broadway. A series of compromises eliminated the grosser manifestations of social disorder but allowed casinos, racetracks, and brothels to varying degrees. When authorities closed a gambling house on Washington Street in 1879, robbers brazenly "stole" the gambling machines right back out of the town hall. America's zealous protector of morals, Anthony Comstock, spent a week in Saratoga in 1886, launching raids and collecting evidence, and later published an unsympathetic report. Comstock even arrested "three peace officers of the county, who, with their badges concealed under their coats, were selling 'pools' in violation of the law." As a result, twenty gambling houses closed their doors, but they immediately reopened for business as soon as Comstock's agents left town.[16]

Other reformers also tried to refashion the Springs. Local resident Spencer Trask, a wealthy Wall Street banker, director of railroads, and president of Edison Electric Company, launched a fifty-thousand-dollar campaign against vice in Saratoga in 1890. Trask hired informants and published maps in his newspaper, the *Saratoga Union*, with the sites of gambling houses clearly marked. Not only did grand juries fail to issue indictments, but he angered large segments of the local population by threatening their livelihoods. Newsdealers refused to sell the *Union*, and one clergyman suggested that before Trask cast the first stone, he should first give up his brokerage office, since investment on Wall Street was no better than gambling. The internationally renowned columnist Nellie Bly also tried to expose Saratoga to the nation, a role she was particularly well suited to play, since much of her reportorial fame depended upon masquerade and disguise. "If one enjoys a democratic crowd, then one would love this women's poolroom," Bly informed readers in 1893. "Crime is holding a convention [at Saratoga]," she concluded, "and vice is enjoying a festival." Her attempt to discredit the resort may have sold copies of the *New York World,* but it merely cemented Saratoga's popularity as a morally ambiguous destination.[17]

Sometimes efforts to reform Saratoga could take a tragic turn. Cale Mitchell, intermittently president of the village from 1872 to 1892, owned a grocery, a real estate business, and a gambling house that rivaled the Club House in number of gamblers, if not nightly handle. Mitchell refused the requests of reformers to move his house off Broadway, and his intransigence led ambitious New York state senator Edmund Brackett to convince the state legislature to amend Saratoga's charter so the president would be chosen by trustees of the village rather than by direct election. Mitchell unsuccessfully fought the law through the court of appeals, and he eventually ended as a dramatic suicide on the doormat of Brackett's office in Saratoga's town hall in 1902. He had probably intended to murder Brackett, but the latter failed to stop at his office that day on his way to the train station. In this, as in most of the battles between Saratoga's gambling and reform factions, a majority of residents rejected the moral exhortations of Comstock, Trask, Bly, and Brackett, choosing instead to grope for a compromise position. Although individual owners might be harassed and morality occasionally restored, the racetrack and the gambling houses remained intrinsic to the Saratoga experience.[18]

In 1893, Richard Canfield, the celebrated "prince of gamblers," purchased Saratoga's Club House. A true rags-to-riches story, Canfield began his career as a night clerk at a New York hotel in the 1870s and ended as a millionaire art collector and sponsor of the artist James Whistler. Canfield's renamed Casino remained probably the only major summer-resort gambling house in the world that still barred women, and the sporting fraternity chafed on the Sabbath when its doors remained locked. Unlike his New York establishment, however, and in keeping with the spirit of the Springs, any male with the appearance of prosperity could enter the Saratoga Casino. Canfield also loosened Morrissey's credit restrictions and added luxuries such as a dining room with a gourmet French chef and a wine cellar filled with the rarest vintages. An estimated forty thousand people visited the Casino during the summer of 1894, even as the nation reeled in the midst of the worst depression in its history. The profits of that season alone equaled the purchase price, and in the twelve years of Canfield's operation, he accumulated $2.5 million in profit from a gambling house open only eight weeks a year. Like his predecessors, Canfield continued a policy of frequent largesse to the village, which kept him in good standing with townspeople and ensured him almost complete immunity from local interference.[19]

Saratoga's tinge of rakishness must have touched a popular chord, for the population of the town swelled 300 percent at the height of the August season. Seneca Ray Stoddard's guidebook declared that "Saratoga is one vast caravansary, every house a hotel, and every resident glad to see the summer's company, for it is meat, drink and clothing to them." The census of 1900 recorded the city's population as slightly more than thirteen thousand, but Saratoga's hotels could service twenty thousand visitors, and perhaps another twenty thousand rooms were rented out either in boarding-houses or by private families looking to make extra money. "There is nothing stranger than this apparently unlimited capacity of Saratoga to absorb people," commented one onlooker. Estimates of visitor expenditures ranged anywhere from $1 million to $20 million annually, depending on how high an analyst placed the multiplier effect of incidental expenditures by guests and the extravagances of the rich. Whatever the actual number, the city clearly demonstrated that an economy based on consumption could be just as profitable as one based on production.[20]

Saratoga's success did not come without its setbacks. A series of conflagrations in the 1860s and 1870s reduced accommodations to barely four thousand beds; the original United States Hotel, the Marvin House, Congress Hall, the Columbian Hotel, and Norman Bedortha's water-cure establishment all burned to the ground in a three-year period beginning in 1864. The ill-fated Grand Central Hotel, a five-story brick hotel on Broadway with 650 rooms, went up in flames in 1874, only its second year in operation (figure 31). Entrepreneurs responded to the calamitous fires not by building private residences but by rebuilding hotels on an even more extravagant scale. In 1870, George Towle had found the hotels at Niagara superior to those at Saratoga, but no one would dare make that claim twenty years later. A ramble through Saratoga's elephantine Gilded Age hotels covered miles of carpeting and acres of marble floors, presented views from thousands of windows, and revealed tons of comestibles stored in pantries.[21]

Saratoga's hotel renaissance, however, represented the triumph of outside capital over local entrepreneurship. Gideon Putnam and his family had owned Union Hall for sixty-two years, but in 1864 it passed to Charles and Warren Leland, members of a famous family of hotel keepers whose reputa-

Figure 31. "The Grand Hotel, Saratoga," *Daily Graphic,* October 27, 1873. This ill-fated hotel, a five-story brick hotel on Broadway with 650 rooms, burned to the ground in only its second year. The caption boasts that the rents of stores below was almost sufficient to pay the interest on the mortgage. (Courtesy of the Saratoga Springs Public Library.)

tion served as a national trademark. The Lelands purchased the hotel for $200,000, and then spent $3 million remodeling it into the most magnificent hotel in the world. "Nothing has been spared," *Frank Leslie's* claimed, "to make Union Hall a miniature paradise." The main dining room, probably the largest in America, stretched more than a city block in length, with twenty-foot ceilings and room for twelve hundred guests at a sitting, served by two hundred black waiters. The grounds of the Grand Union, as the hotel was now known, covered seven acres, including more than a mile of porch space (figure 32).[22]

The Lelands eventually ran out of money, and in 1872 department store magnate A. T. Stewart bought the Grand Union and four other Saratoga parcels for $532,000. Estimates on the cost of Stewart's additional improvements over the next four years range anywhere from $100,000 to $1.5 million. The merchant prince had the drawing room and parlor elaborately frescoed, installed crystal chandeliers, and completely rebuilt the north wing, with a five-thousand-square-foot ballroom sporting ceilings twenty-

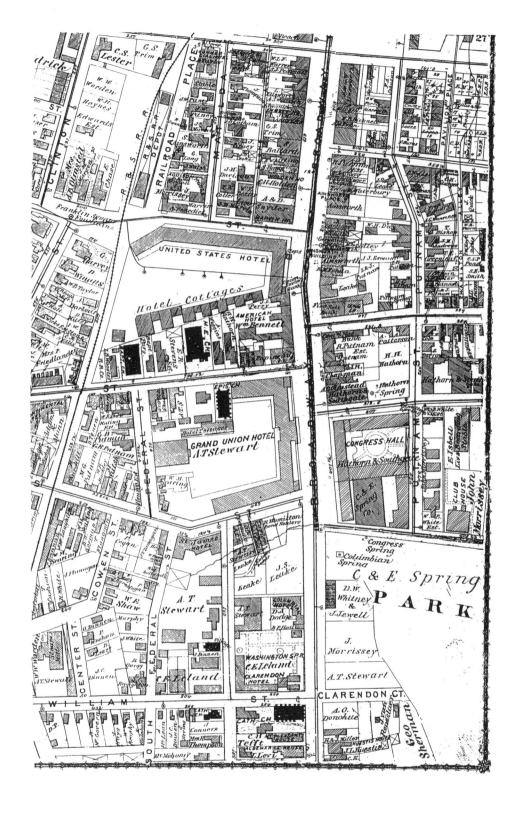

seven feet high. Adolph Yvon's allegory, *The Genius of America,* dominated the ballroom; this self-proclaimed "world's largest painting" totaled twenty-four hundred square feet, including the three-thousand-pound frame (figure 33). The hotel's eight hundred rooms could now house fifteen hundred guests on any given night.[23]

Alexander Turney Stewart, a Scottish immigrant, had acquired his fortune by essentially inventing the modern American department store. His "Cast-Iron Palace" opened in New York in 1862, and by mid-decade it had an estimated annual sales volume of nearly $100 million. Stewart introduced American shoppers to a fixed price policy, departmentalized stock, a liberal return policy, and bargain sales. His store transformed the drab, cluttered dry goods market into a sumptuous theatrical set in which women could participate in the public realm. In the process, he revolutionized retailing by carrying a greater variety of goods, encouraging inspection of merchandise, advertising on a massive scale, and centralizing management. Stewart's emporium played a crucial role in the democratization of luxury by entertaining shoppers while providing them with images of abundance to sell the idea of consumption. Like the hotel, the department store became a mecca for women, a home away from home, only better. Many Americans' first experience with mirrors, elevators, escalators, electric lights, and expanses of plate glass came either at the department store or the resort hotel.

Stewart's acquisition of the Grand Union, therefore, was a logical progression from his retail business. Both hotel and department store, filled with things to see and things to sell, symbolized modern urbanity. Their decorous exteriors, radiating tradition and order, contrasted with lively and diversified interiors. Patrons visited these businesses simply to gaze at the splendor and participate in the ambience of elegance; in both cases, functional public needs evolved into locations for consumer demands. The department store and the resort hotel, although technically private, offered the public staged antidotes to industrialized life—comfort, convenience, luxury, beauty, and entertainment—while concealing the bleaker "back regions" that would have reminded customers they were actually in a business enter-

(*Opposite*) Figure 32. Detail of Map Showing Broadway in Saratoga, *Combination Atlas of Saratoga and Ballston,* 1876. Saratoga's "Big Three" hotels—the United States, the Grand Union, and Congress Hall—all shared frontage on the same three-block section of Broadway and together could house five thousand overnight guests. (Courtesy of the Saratoga Springs Public Library.)

Figure 33. "A Hop in the New Ball-room of the Grand Union Hotel," *Frank Leslie's*, August 19, 1876. The department store mogul A. T. Stewart supposedly could not fit Adolph Yvon's allegory, *The Genius of America*, in his mansion. Instead, he stuck it in the Grand Union ballroom; the painting now resides in the auditorium of the New York State Education Building at Albany. (Collection of the author.)

prise dedicated to profit. Entrepreneurs enveloped consumer goods in an aura of magical self-realization; in 1868, Elizabeth Phelps's best-selling *The Gates Ajar* merged utopian aspirations and commercial processes by depicting one version of heaven as a consumer dream world. In the same way, a traveler could now unblushingly compare a sunrise at the Catskill Mountain House with a shop window, for window displays held crowds enthralled even when personal possession was beyond their reach.[24]

Since the beginning of regular railroad service, the Springs had trained people to become consumers; in 1848, the *New York Herald* reported that "every luxury that it is necessary to have outside heaven, can be bought at Saratoga." All the major New York jewelers, milliners, and haberdashers had opened thriving branches at the resort. When Ellen Bond visited Saratoga in 1850, she shopped almost every day and concluded that the city was "a good place to spend money." In 1854, the Saratoga Board of Trustees catalogued twelve "Fancy stores," three jewelry shops, and seven other specialty emporiums that displayed "the costly luxuries of fashionable life." Visitors to resorts appeared as if bewitched, willingly squandering carefully accumulated money that seemed conceptually different from "everyday" money.[25]

In the Gilded Age, however, the pace of Saratoga's commercialization increased by leaps and bounds. Hotels encouraged shopping by leasing their ground floor to retail tenants, and in this way, Saratoga's Broadway came to resemble the arcades of Paris as centers of the luxury trade. According to the 1894 Saratoga directory, the Grand Union leased space to at least nineteen stores, selling diamonds, flowers, dresses, gloves, art embroidery, millinery, confectionery, Indian and fancy goods, paintings, and art supplies. These stores participated in the veranda's sense of permeability, but their purpose was purely commercial. This resort trade offered vast opportunities for the enterprising salesman, as exemplified by the career of Benjamin Goldsmith, a poor Russian Jew who had come to Saratoga in 1865 peddling notions door to door. Twenty years later, Goldsmith owned a prosperous business on Broadway, selling fine wines and cigars and supplying luxury items to many of the hotels. "People visit Saratoga with money in their pockets," one observer blithely noted, "determined to enjoy themselves, and to spend their money freely, often extravagantly; and as a general rule they do so."[26]

Saratoga began to resemble local county and state fairs, which advertised their practical value while actually appealing to visitors' desire for diversion and material consumption. County and state fairs broke the monotony of farmwork but also introduced country folk to popular entertainment, urban mechanical amusements, and the exotic food concessions of the midway, as well as new consumer choices such as farm machinery. Ministers futilely protested against gambling at these celebrations, and the Saratoga County Fair tried unsuccessfully to restrict theatrical or mountebank exhibitions to two hundred yards from fairgrounds. Resorts and fairs led the way in the creation of a secular consumer culture.[27]

At Saratoga, visitors were encouraged to pass time in the most casual sort of shopping. Vacationers arriving by train expected to walk most of the time, and Saratoga had developed a dense pattern of land usage to facilitate the movement of pedestrians. In the Gilded Age, the city's layout still invited a leisurely stroll down Broadway, though one by now oriented mainly toward consumption. Seneca Ray Stoddard's guidebook of 1889 included a section on the stores of Saratoga not present in 1882, and a later directory unabashedly proclaimed that "the stores are many and varied . . . and voyages of discovery and shopping are among the amusements" (figures 34 and 35).[28]

Other Saratoga hotels followed the Grand Union's lead in grandiose remodeling, often building stores into their ground floors. The new all-brick Congress Hall, rebuilt in 1867 with help from the Delaware and Hudson Railroad, boasted eleven stores fronting Broadway. The hotel contained six hundred rooms, a promenade plaza 20 feet wide and 250 feet long, and an observatory on top, which allowed visitors to scan the scene. After personal inspection, the hotel connoisseur of the *New York Times* pronounced Congress Hall the "best built and most thoroughly equipped summer house in America." The United States Hotel, built at a cost of more than a million dollars in 1874, represented the pinnacle of Saratoga hotel construction. The hotel occupied the site of its predecessor, which had lain vacant since the fire of 1865, and was, of course, reputedly the largest hotel in the world, an astonishing accolade considering it catered to guests only in the summer. Visitors could promenade 233 feet of frontage on Broadway and 665 feet on Division Street, compared with the 125 and 60 feet, respectively, of the original United States Hotel. A half mile of verandas graced by a thousand rocking chairs surrounded six acres of grounds. Although small size still characterized many of the private rooms, the scale of the rest of the hotel was positively unearthly: 768 rooms, a parlor greater than four thousand square feet, and a dining room of more than ten thousand square feet (figure 36).[29]

No other American resort could present such a Brobdingnagian conglomeration of hostelries as Saratoga; the Grand Union, United States Hotel, and Congress Hall all shared frontage on the same three-block section of Broadway (see figure 32), and between them they could house five thousand guests overnight. Guidebooks touted these new or expanded hotels as major American tourist attractions. Baedeker's reported Saratoga's hotels to be "among the largest, if not the very largest, hotels in the world; and a visit to their enormous ball-rooms, dining-rooms, and piazzas should not be omitted." Observed one American in the 1870s, "Nowhere else in the world is the hotel so essentially a 'public' house as in the United States. . . .

Figure 34. "Afternoon Promenade, Broadway, in Front of the Grand Union Hotel,"
Frank Leslie's, August 21, 1875. Prentiss Ingraham's guidebook, *Saratoga: Winter and
Summer* (New York, 1885), commented that "Newport and Interlaken, Ems and Long
Branch have their special charms, but nowhere is so much of caravansary and general
splendor concentrated in so limited a space" than at Saratoga (27). (Collection of the
author.)

Publicity . . . in the halls, parlors, reading-rooms, dining-rooms is here
preferred to the comparative privacy which is sought in hotels abroad."[30]

Saratoga's grand hotels may have offered luxurious public rooms virtually unmatched in any private residence, but they also contained a major
concession to the privatization of leisure space, a trend that was gathering
momentum in the Gilded Age. In 1855, Disturnell's guidebook had advocated more isolated lodgings at Saratoga for those of "delicate instincts and
habits, who . . . shrink from ungenial society, crowd, and noise." Cottages
for the overflow of guests had been used since at least the 1820s, but the 566-
foot-long Cottage Wing of the new United States Hotel boldly sought to
capitalize on the growing American desire for privacy. Some of these cot-

Figure 35. "Summer Life at Saratoga," *Frank Leslie's,* August 30, 1879. At Gilded Age Saratoga, afternoon shopping and the nighttime display of novelties both complemented and competed with older forms of entertainment. (Collection of the author.)

tages were genuine two-story wooden buildings, but the bulk consisted of sixty-five suites with one to seven bedrooms and a parlor, bathroom, water closet, and private piazza (see figure 36). They were furnished more carefully and elaborately than rooms in the main hotel and attracted a more upscale clientele. The United States prominently advertised the new cottage wing as affording families "the same quiet and seclusion which a private cottage would afford, together with the attention and conveniences of a first-class hotel." Wealthy visitors such as the Goulds, the Vanderbilts, and the Wanamakers rejected private residences when they stayed at the Springs but compromised by sometimes paying up to a hundred dollars a night to stay in the cottage wing.[31]

The cottages served a second purpose related to the relative freedom of the resort; they ensured that Saratoga's extramarital dalliances could be

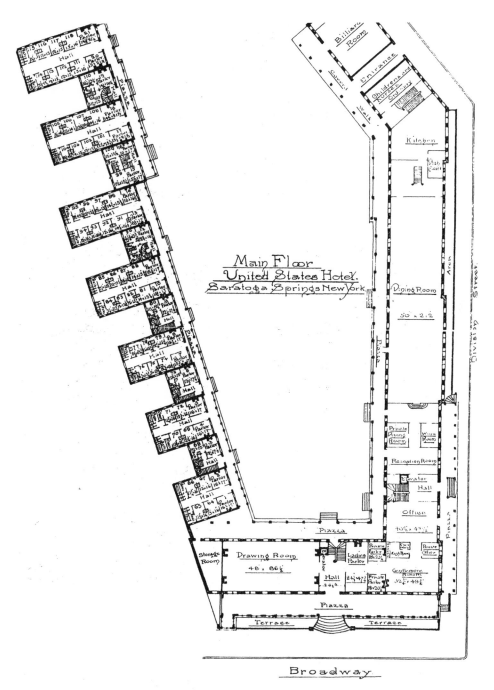

Figure 36. Blueprint of the Main Floor of United States Hotel, ca. 1880, showing the Cottage Wing to the left. The public rooms of the new United States Hotel were still immense, but the 566-foot-long Cottage Wing sought to capitalize on the growing desire for greater privacy. (Courtesy of the Saratoga Springs Historical Museum.)

handled circumspectly. Most hotels made such affairs difficult for unmarried couples and restricted access after eleven at night, but the cottages remained free from all surveillance. Many men were joined by their so-called nieces, fiancées, cousins, assistants, or secretaries, inspiring James Bennett to describe the suites as "the seraglio of prurient aristocracy." With extraordinary celerity, Alexander Stewart remodeled the Grand Union in order to match the United States, and the hotel cottage-system soon spread to hotels in Virginia, Sharon Springs, the Catskills, and across America.[32]

The sheer size of Saratoga's grand hotels allowed the resort to become a center of the Gilded Age convention trade, but this increased patronage came at a cost. Conventioneers represented the increasing intrusion of the mundane world on the once magical resort. Political parties often had their conventions at Saratoga, which benefited by its proximity to Albany. The American Bar Association (in 1878), the American Bankers Association, the American Historical Association (in 1884), and the American Economic Association (in 1885) all held their inaugural meetings in Saratoga (figure 37). In fact, the American Bar Association met at the Springs for nineteen of its first twenty-six years, for as one barrister exclaimed, "the meeting of the Association affords a very convenient excuse to come to Saratoga." Churchmen were also common conventioneers at the Springs, from the Salvation Army to the General Assembly of the Presbyterian Church. Visitors who brought their everyday work world with them evinced, by definition, a reluctance to jettison their professional identities, even in a leisure setting. Whereas vacationers strive for a sense of exhilaration, the desire of business travelers to maintain a certain level of continuity tended to result in a more emotionally disciplined resort world.[33]

The expansion of the hotels and the embrace of the market, however, spun off numerous opportunities in Saratoga for capitalists, entrepreneurs, and workers alike. In the New York State census of 1875, Saratoga Springs possessed 19 percent of the total number of dwellings in the county but 44 percent of the buildings valued at more than $10,000. From 1860 to 1900, the county's population grew 18 percent, while Saratoga Springs increased 90 percent (from 6,520 to 12,409). In 1869, there were 55 hotels and boardinghouses and 12 "Fancy Goods" establishments in a city of only 7,516. Thirty years later, Saratoga boasted an astonishing 128 hotels and boardinghouses and 17 "Fancy Goods" establishments. Quite simply, tourism paid.[34]

The increase in the number of tourists meant plentiful work in season.

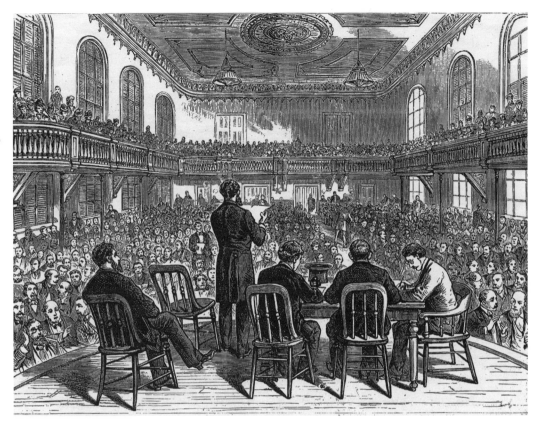

Figure 37. "Annual Convention of the American Bankers' Association in the Town Hall," *Frank Leslie's*, August 31, 1878. The mundane world increasingly intruded on the liminal resort. Conferences by professional organizations at Saratoga contrasted with Newport, where the social elite tried to project themselves as above profession. (Collection of the author.)

Every spring, the city required more carpentry and painting than a city of a hundred thousand inhabitants. Employment opportunities lured foreign-born residents, who consistently numbered between 15 and 20 percent of the city's population in the Gilded Age. The census of 1860 recorded only one Italian-born resident in all of Saratoga Springs, but the subsequent arrival of Italian immigrants metamorphosed "Dublin" into Little Italy. Italians gradually replaced the Irish as railroad workers; the *Saratogian Almanac*, in its list of noteworthy occurrences of 1880, marked May 20 as the "arrival of many Italian laborers." Labor troubles rarely interrupted Saratoga life for any length of time. Short-lived strikes by masons working on the Grand Union and laborers on the Saratoga Lake Railroad seem to have been ineffectual, and a national telegraphers' strike in large cities barely affected the Springs. The strikers in the railroad troubles of 1877 also seem to have found sympathy in short supply; there was no difficulty in finding people to work in and around Saratoga.[35]

Weak or nonexistent trade unions, the seasonal nature of the work, and a service-based rather than industrial economy all meant continued employment opportunities for African Americans as well. The black population expanded 37 percent in the postwar decade alone, mostly job seekers from the South. By 1875, one-third of Saratoga County's blacks had been born out of state; William Rogers wrote to the domestic of a local family, "Prehaps you know of some body els[e] that wants a waiter. . . . Thier is no place i want to go but saratoga." The black residential community averaged 4 percent of Saratoga's population between 1870 and 1900, but African American visibility was much greater in the summer, for as one visitor noted, "the vast hotel service is wholly in [their] hands." Cook and housekeeper Emma Waite worked at the Grand Union until she was laid off because, as she wrote in her diary, "of their getting white help." But within three days she acquired another job at the Continental Hotel and then switched to Congress Hall before the end of July. For several seasons, the racetrack assuaged Southern sensibilities by prominently posting signs barring blacks from the grounds, but the stables ignored the ban in practice. Until the twentieth century, African Americans constituted a noteworthy proportion of Saratoga's jockeys, grooms, and stable hands. A vibrant African American cultural life developed at the Springs, spiced by presentations by touring theater groups and well-known black lecturers and performers, as well as visits to some gambling houses, such as Cale Mitchell's, that accepted black clientele.[36]

Saratoga's residents, whether black or white, immigrant or native born, tried to create a pleasing environment for visitors, "without whose patronage," reminded a city commissioner, "this village would soon become a deserted, solitary place, and its inhabitants starve." All public works projects took the summer season into account, and utility companies consistently favored tourists over natives. The first electric lights in Saratoga illuminated the Grand Union's gardens, followed by lights on Broadway and then Congress Park, well before they lit any residential areas. In 1874, the Grand Union contained thirty-six bathtubs and ninety-nine water closets (for eight hundred guest rooms), whereas the remainder of Saratoga residences totaled only thirty-seven and fifty-one, respectively. The village sewage commissioners justified infrastructure expenses for visitors by reminding local residents that, "should an epidemic occur in our community at the very flood tide of one of our most prosperous seasons, every one of our boasted hotels and boarding houses would be vacated in a single week." The citizens of Saratoga viewed their guests as little more than potentially profitable commodities.[37]

The promotion of Saratoga Lake after the Civil War exemplified the city's conscious efforts to develop new touristic attractions. The lake had charmed patrons as early as the 1840s, but access was difficult. In 1865, a private group formed to create a grand four-mile boulevard from Saratoga to the lake past the racetrack, but they made little headway before dissolving in 1870. The city government promptly created an agency that eventually oversaw the creation of a road nationally renowned as one of the finest inland drives in the country. When visitors then complained of the dust, the city levied a sprinkling tax in 1874. The *New York Times* condescendingly reported that the Saratoga authorities had, "as a rule, shown a clear comprehension of the duties that devolve upon them." By 1886, Charles Dudley Warner declared the previously peripheral Saratoga Lake to be "the most picturesque feature of the region, and would alone make the fortune of any other watering place."[38]

Congress Park, redesigned in the 1870s by Frederick Law Olmsted's firm, represented another example of the convergence of the promenade and the market in the name of tourist development. While not nearly as large as Brooklyn's Prospect Park, a stereoscopic view bragged, "no park of equal size in the United States can be compared with it for beauty of natural scenery or elegance of architectural and artistic adornments." Visitors still used the park for display, and at night, the scene seemed the creation of a magician, with colored globes illuminating the enormous pines and green hillsides. The miniature lake in the center reflected the gilded kiosk, and a fairy bridge led to an island, where a band played. Tellingly, an entrance gate and admission charge now barred the random stroller from the revamped Congress Park and, therefore, from drinking at Congress Spring. While antebellum opinion had insisted that Saratoga water be freely available in the city, this antediluvian tradition did not survive. By 1880, the five springs closest to the major hotels all charged an admission fee to restrict access and recoup capital.[39]

The contrast between Saratoga Springs and its eighteenth-century European predecessors underscored the increasing penetration of the market economy in the United States. In England, masters of ceremonies dominated resort life by controlling the institutional apparatus that directed activities, introduced visitors, screened out undesirables, and arranged amusements. Under the long tenure (1705–61) of Richard "Beau" Nash as its master of ceremonies, the city of Bath developed into a tourist destination with projects financed by seasonal subscription. The customer paid for the use of the premises for a fixed price in advance, rather than at the point of consumption. Subscription anticipated revenue and underwrote improvements with little risk for the entrepreneur. The initial payment virtually guaranteed attendance, at which point the visitor might be lured into further incidental expenditure.[40] At the laissez-faire American resort, the absence of masters of ceremonies and seasonal subscription left visitors to their own devices. Entrepreneurs, conscious that there was no profit in promenading, began providing elaborate daily rounds of amusements and material goods to entice the free-spending, pleasure-loving crowd of visitors. A strange routine developed combining dawdling preindustrial inertia with the feverish activity associated with the new leisure culture and encroaching time discipline. The number of diversions at American resorts multiplied logarithmically into a dizzying round of social and recreational activities.

Saratoga acted as a magnet for wandering professional entertainers, part of the shift from more spontaneous and participatory forms of leisure to formally organized profit-oriented and spectator activities. A diverse selection of commercialized amusements—minstrels and theatricals, musicians and magicians, lyceums and lantern slide lectures, Swiss bell ringers and Siamese twins, panoramas and dioramas—stimulated the visitor's interest. Saratoga made it easy to maintain the magical vacation mood by providing a ceaseless round of evening concerts, traveling circuses, strolling carnival troupes, tableaux vivants, baffling ventriloquists, and amusing lectures (figure 38). P. T. Barnum so desperately desired to exhibit Tom Thumb at the Springs that he reluctantly paid a twenty-five-dollar licensing fee to the city even after publicly declaring he would never accede.[41]

The resort visitor's purchase of a guidebook also transformed the giddy pursuit of pleasure into a market commodity. With the possible exception of Niagara Falls, no resort inspired such a profusion of guidebooks as Saratoga Springs. Gideon Davison's *Fashionable Tour*, the book that touched off the

Figure 38. "Evening Concert on a Hotel Piazza," *Harper's Weekly*, August 1, 1896.
Victor Herbert regularly played at Saratoga between 1892 and 1910. He turned his
eavesdropping in the dimly lit hotel gardens into one of the nation's most popular songs
when he wrote "Kiss Me Again" in 1897. (Courtesy of the Yates Collection, Skidmore
College.)

travel craze in the United States, went through ten editions by 1840, including two translations into French. Other guides that featured Saratoga also flourished: *The Tourist* by Robert Vandewater went through nine editions, seven editions were published of Theodore Dwight's *Northern Traveller*, and resort goers could choose from six editions of Samuel De Veaux's *The Traveller's Own Book*. Seneca Ray Stoddard, the widely acclaimed photographer, guidebook writer, and mapmaker, began including Saratoga in his Lake George and Adirondack guides in the 1870s and continued the practice in his annual guides for the next forty years. Guidebooks doubled as tourist souvenirs and conditioned the traveler's experience by providing explicit commentary on the ultimate purpose of the trip; Herman Melville satirized their pompous and reverential style as early as *Redburn* in 1849. Whereas etiquette books modeled the new work and social worlds of the nineteenth century, guidebooks steered the visitor through the worlds of play and escape by providing a litany of travel.[42]

By the Gilded Age, no stay at a resort was complete without buying souvenirs, and few visitors came home from Saratoga without some token to show for it. Just as markets selling mementos invariably crowded the great medieval pilgrim sites, so shops and entertainment surrounded American tourist attractions. William Dean Howells wistfully reported on the end of his vacation, "I find myself wishing to imagine some form of words which shall keep a likeness of it at least through the winter; some shadowy semblance which I may turn to hereafter." As early as the 1840s, *Endicott's Pictures of Saratoga* offered a collection of thirteen lithographs for $2.50, but after the Civil War, viewbooks proliferated, and Saratoga scenes were embossed on a limitless variety of objects. In Marietta Holley's best-selling novel, *Samantha at Saratoga*, the malaprop-prone heroine returned home with a trunk so heavy her husband could not lift it, packed as it was with relics from various Saratoga sights. Visitors could also buy sheet music as a souvenir, complete with an engraving of the hotel, ocean, or park on the cover (see figures 1, 2, 3, 13). The desire to possess the liminal vacation experience forever must have been very strong, if the number of dedicatory dance titles is any indication; a nondescript piece like the "Saratoga Schottisch" (1851) went through several editions.[43]

Technically, a souvenir did not have to be purchased; resort goers liberated dinner menus, and Ellen Bond collected wild flowers from each site she visited and pasted them in her journal. By the end of the nineteenth century, however, many Americans climbed ladders of social mobility by purchasing appropriate material symbols. Physical property tended to take on the value of status markers when people removed themselves from traditional kinship groupings, whether temporarily at resorts or permanently through geographic mobility. Once purchased, the souvenir became the equivalent of a relic from a religious shrine. As a sort of Holy Grail, a keepsake of the trip consecrated the resort and spread its fame far and wide through mass-produced iconic reproductions.[44]

Since the invention of the daguerreotype in 1839, photographers had flocked to resorts. Men with cameras roamed the mountains, springs, and seaside in the summertime, photographing willing guests en bloc on hotel verandas. The three daguerreotype shops in Saratoga in 1841 multiplied to more than three dozen photography studios in the 1870s, many doing a brisk souvenir business producing stereographs for tourists. The widespread popularity of these twinned pictures illustrated more than just middle-class dedication to didactic self-improvement. No stereoscope topic was more popular than summer resorts and tourist attractions, specifically because they converted an ephemeral experience into a purchasable representation in a form of personal property. Photographers produced literally thousands of stereoscopic views of Saratoga for public consumption, often featuring the architectural grandiosity of the resort or displaying a superabundance of bodies filling the public spaces.[45]

Leisure entrepreneurs who attempted to create tangible profit out of symbolic capital now discovered that alternative imaginary landscapes could be as marketable as the real thing. Seymour Ainsworth, a dealer in Indian goods, set up an Indian encampment consisting of several empty lots containing tents and log houses where Indians, part-Indians, and gypsies from northern New York and Canada camped from late spring to early autumn. Although the Mohawks had enjoyed the Springs as a seasonal hunting ground, they never established any village on the site. The existence and disappearance of Indians, however, was essential to Saratoga's teleology, a stock-in-trade of authors of guidebooks and local history. Visitors vicariously appropriated images of Indians by reading novels such as *Saratoga. A Story of 1787* (1856), purported to be a thrilling Indian tale of frontier life and popular enough to be reprinted in 1866 as *Saratoga. The Famous*

Springs. Anxious to fulfill the customers' desires colored by *The Last of the Mohicans*, entrepreneurs endeavored to produce genuine Indians for tourist consumption.[46]

Saratoga's Indian encampment allowed visitors to experience American history closer to home instead of making the time-consuming and unpredictable journey to the Stillwater battlefield. The residents of the encampment attracted customers by selling beadwork, telling fortunes, and performing with the bow and arrow. When Marianne Finch visited from England, she was horrified to find that the Indians' "knowledge of English was confined to the subject of currency." Saratoga's Indian encampment prospered throughout the nineteenth century, resiliently incorporating the newest trends such as croquet courts, Punch-and-Judy shows, parades, merry-go-rounds, blown-glass souvenirs, rifle ranges, and medicine ceremonies. Stereographic views of this proto–amusement park displayed well-dressed visitors in an incongruous setting of cabins and tents, playing games and buying souvenirs at the stalls.[47]

Visitors to Saratoga increasingly demanded novel sites and spectacles, and the House of Pansa offered another commercialized fantasy, an exact replica of the home of a wealthy nobleman buried in the ruins of Pompeii. When the building opened in 1889, on Saratoga's Broadway adjacent to Congress Park and Spring, the *New York Herald* declared it "a monument that will take its place with the most impressive and unique contributions to the art of this country." Souvenir booklets (at fifty cents each) at the end of the fourth season bore the inscription "175th Thousand" (i.e., number sold). Baedeker's gave the Pompeia a hard-earned star, and it was the site of a large reception for President Benjamin Harrison in 1891. This type of fabricated site at Saratoga, recalling exotic and long-vanished eras, pioneered techniques used to great effect in later world's fairs and theme parks.[48]

Not all marketing ventures succeeded. Mount McGregor, an outlying spur of the Adirondacks only ten miles from the Springs, offered a wilderness setting and spectacular views. Neither a twisting railroad, built in only four months in 1882, nor the Hotel Balmoral, complete with large piazzas and room for three hundred boarders, caught the popular imagination. When Ulysses Grant was stricken with throat cancer, Mount McGregor promoter and Albany politician W. J. Arkell admitted, "I thought that if he should die there, it might make the place a national shrine—and incidentally a success." Grant did indeed die at Mount McGregor, but not before his struggle to complete his memoirs riveted the attention of the nation on the Saratoga suburb. For the next few years, one visitor claimed, "no traveller now goes to Saratoga without visiting the illustrious mountain." Yet Arkell's best efforts never quite bore fruit, perhaps because in his attempt to turn Mount McGregor into an American pilgrimage site, he had "banished from the premise everything that savors of money-making." Arkell claimed he lost a fortune in the attempt: "Instead of making the place, Grant's death killed it absolutely. After his death, as people came to the mountain, the moment they stepped off the train they took off their hats and walked around on tiptoes." The Hotel Balmoral burned in a suspicious fire in 1897 and was later replaced by a sanitarium and, eventually, a prison. Only four thousand visitors made the trek in 1908, and the railroad tracks were soon abandoned.[49]

Nor could Saratogians transform their city into an all-season resort, despite the new promotion of winter sports. A hotel, rifle range, trotting track, and three-chute toboggan slide occupied Cale Mitchell's land northeast of town. The slide especially attracted a great deal of attention—*Harper's Weekly* prominently featured tobogganing in Saratoga in 1885—but not enough to attract a cold-weather clientele. The Mitchell brothers sold the property in 1886, and the toboggan slide closed in 1890.[50] The city also tried to hold an annual Floral Fete, modeled after the efforts of the citizens of Nice, France, who had successfully used the idea to revive their moribund carnival and turn it into a tourist attraction. Saratoga's Floral Fetes may have attracted as many as fifty thousand spectators in the 1890s, but the novelty soon wore off, and the city held only one festival of flowers after 1902.[51]

In all these cases, whether successful or not, Saratoga's promoters specifically constructed a more commodity-oriented leisure strategy for the resort. Saratoga businessmen, led by John Morrissey, tapped into this potential source of profit when they organized the first in a series of boat races on Saratoga Lake in 1871. Morrissey realized these regattas would not only produce good public relations but would also attract visitors who would stay at the hotels and while away their evenings in the gambling casinos. Despite protestations by alarmed viewers about the immorality of permitting college students to gambol about the sinful spa in the summer, the city heavily promoted intercollegiate athletic competitions, offering attractive prizes as well as generous expense accounts for participants. For the regatta of

1874, the Rensselaer and Saratoga Railroad donated $1,500, and each large hotel chipped in $500; they were amply rewarded when *Harper's Weekly* featured the event on its cover, and thirty thousand spectators attended what amounted to a weeklong festival of sport. The next year's collegiate boat race at Saratoga was the most newsworthy event of its day, the subject of several pages of feature articles in newspapers for a week. A vast multitude overflowed the makeshift grandstand, with a seating capacity of twelve thousand, to watch Cornell defeat twelve other colleges while large sums of money changed hands.[52]

Finally, the springs of Saratoga themselves became commodities independent of their medical efficacy. Mineral water in the Gilded Age remained both an American fascination and an opportunity for profit, through either the water itself, a hotel next to the springs, or land speculation around the site. When scientists in the 1880s attempted to survey five hundred mineral springs on the efficacy of their cures, hotel proprietors wrote three-quarters of the responses, and most enclosed advertisements and tourist information with their limited scientific expertise. Yet the business continued to grow; in 1883, 189 springs produced 7 million gallons of water valued at $1 million, while in 1905, 732 springs produced 46 million gallons worth more than $6 million. As late as 1916, Arkansas Hot Springs attracted one third of the total visits to the United States National Park System and recorded more visitors (118,000) than Yellowstone, Sequoia, Yosemite, Mount Rainier, and Crater Lake combined; and no conglomeration of springs attracted more scientific or commercial activity than Saratoga. Guidebooks spread its fame internationally, scientists speculated on the nature and usefulness of its waters, and pathetic western resorts attempted to capitalize on its name.[53]

At Saratoga, joint-stock companies had gradually replaced local residents as the owners of most of the springs. They invested large sums, in some cases almost a million dollars, in retubing springs and erecting capacious pavilions. The Congress and Empire Spring Company, formed in 1869, became the largest mineral-water company in the world, producing a million bottles annually and maintaining agents in major European cities. Investment in mineral springs remained costly at Saratoga; the original High Rock Spring, initially underdeveloped by John Clarke so it would not rival Congress Spring, sold for $25,000 as late as 1904.[54]

Neither the state nor the village regulated or restrained the mineral-water industry, allowing hucksters to merrily separate vacationers from their money. Pamphlets, complete with testimonials by local doctors, advertised various springs and promised cures for any and all diseases. Saratoga's most reputable physicians, although not charlatans, often combined therapeutics with boosterism. Many were intimately connected with the promotion of the resort and the writing of guidebooks: John Steel's guidebook went through at least ten printings before 1860, Milo North's seven, and Richard Allen's four. Saratoga's two most famous hydrotherapists wrote pseudomedical treatises in which they claimed any number of diseases could be cured by a stay at their establishments.[55]

These valuable springs had originally been regarded as independent properties, each having no legal relationship to any other in the area. In the spirit of laissez-faire capitalism, the *Saratoga Sentinel* pronounced in 1883 that no one questioned the wisdom of privately owned springs. Yet methods had recently been devised to extract carbonic gas from the Saratoga waters to carbonate bottled beverages. Spring owners, seduced by the lure of greater profits, permitted deep well pumps operated by steam power to increase the yield of gas by increasing the flow of water. Gas companies pumped more than 150 million gallons of mineral water, and the aquifer's water level dropped almost a hundred feet. Saratoga residents, watching the corporate rapacity with increasing distress, finally jettisoned their belief in the unregulated market and appealed to the government of New York for rescue. In 1907, the state supreme court set a precedent when it ordered Sylvester Strong to cap his sanitarium's four-hundred-foot-deep spring (all but eighty-six feet laboriously drilled through rock) because it interfered with the more senior Hathorn Spring. The next year, the legislature passed an antipumping act; gas companies fought this bill tooth and nail all the way to the United States Supreme Court, which declared the act constitutional in 1911. By the time the state agreed to purchase the depleted springs, the gas companies had permanently exhausted the two most famous, High Rock Spring and Congress Spring.[56]

In case after case, a consumer ethic had infiltrated public life at the resort. Free entertainment, long the hallmark of a stay at Saratoga, now competed with the blatantly commercial locales of the stores, gambling houses, and racetrack. The United States Hotel began to restrict chairs on its piazzas and parlors for the exclusive use of guests, and the springs charged admission fees. In 1878, the Windsor became the first Saratoga hotel to challenge the common dining hour by offering the European plan. Guidebooks internalized the transformation with barely a whimper: "What is proper to do at Saratoga, and what is most enjoyable, is not a matter of collective experience," declared Seneca Ray Stoddard in 1882. Instead, "whatever one feels like enjoying, that comes under the head of purchasable pleasure, can generally be had at Saratoga." At the Springs in the Gilded Age, everything desirable, from sex to social status, could be commodified, that is, assigned a specific value and then exchanged or bought and sold.[57]

The Saratoga day, formerly filled with ennui, had now been segmented by entrepreneurs and turned into a showplace for novelties. The question "What shall we do?" constituted the basic premise of the guidebook industry. People craved action, and the old aimless wandering no longer satisfied. The word *vacation* had become a verb as well as a noun, signifying activity as well as a period of time. The *New York Times,* describing resorts in the 1870s, reported that "old hands generally do nothing. . . . But the young people—the inexperienced ones—are all in ferment. Instead of resting, they want to be up and doing." For this younger generation, the track, the gambling house, and the store gradually replaced the desire to lounge and promenade. Individual, not communal, experience now underlay most of Saratoga's activities. The resort visitor in these times not only accepted the commodification of leisure but gloried in it, as consumption became a major tenet in the formation of an American ethos.[58]

William Dean Howells described some of Saratoga's distractions for hapless visitors who did not know what to do: "a turn on the circular railway or the switchback; or we could take them to the Punch and Judy drama, or get their fortunes told in the seeress' tent, or let them fire in the shooting gallery, or buy some sweet-grass baskets of the Indians; and there is the popcorn and the lemonade." In each of these examples, Saratoga's amusements required cash for participation. Gilded Age visitors could choose from Barnum's mammoth circus show, Madame Carlotta's balloon ascension, lectures by Oscar Wilde, aquatic exhibitions by Captain Paul Boyton, vocal concerts, and human oddities; the range of activities boggled the mind but also drew out the wallet. Nor does this include the ever present enticements of the racetrack or the gambling house. Saratoga, which had once celebrated American idleness, now declared its obsolescence. The freedom of the aimless promenader to set playfully the aims and meanings of his or her nomadic adventures had been expropriated by the marketplace.[59]

This new resort style, unlike its antebellum predecessor, reveled in the equation of consumption and happiness, though remnants of the resort's see-and-be-seen culture survived in the ostentatious display at Gilded Age Saratoga. In contrast with the stereotype of staid, disciplined Victorians, the Springs served as the scene for exhibitionist contests and the creation of celebrities famous for being famous. Fearless plungers entranced the masses with their escapades involving fortunes wagered on the turn of a card or the length of a horse's nose. "Saratoga is the place in America to see diamonds," announced the *Times* of London; the enterprising if illiterate Joseph Dreicer opened a shop in the Grand Union and became one of the wealthiest jewelers in the United States. In more innocent times, numerous Saratoga stories made the moral point that true value hid beneath a modest exterior. Now, Diamond Jim Brady justified his moniker by parading at the Springs with some of his thirty sets of jewels consisting of more than twenty thousand diamonds. An anonymous letter captured some idea of the Saratoga scene in the writer's astonished description of a woman at Saratoga wearing "twelve diamond rings, diamond earrings, breastpin, watch chain pin, sleeve buttons, pin to hold up her eye glasses, all diamonds." This new cult of personality and spectacle, which would become characteristic of the twentieth century, greatly depended for its effectiveness on the public's acceptance of "what it cost" as the principal determinant of value in America.[60]

Overdressing had always been synonymous with a stay at the Springs, but Oscar Wilde's popular and profitable visit to Congress Hall in 1882 instigated a golden age of male dandyism at Saratoga. The Springs provided the perfect stage for this type of peacocking, allowing those so inclined to monopolize the public gaze. Abingdon Baird, Evander Berry Wall, and Robert Hilliard competed for the title "king of the dudes," the object and envy of all eyes. These apostles of aestheticism found a welcome at the relatively liberal postbellum resorts, where they confounded gender roles by applying rouge to their faces and wearing feminine attire around the Grand Union. In 1888, Wall temporarily vanquished his rivals by appearing in Saratoga in an astonishing forty complete changes of costume in one day. Yet even the dandies at Saratoga, all claiming to be aristocrats of élan and poise, depended to a large extent on the "vulgar" act of shopping.[61]

Of course, since the birth of resorts in the eighteenth century, radiant stars had entertained a public bored by the inertia of daily life. The very concept of a "celebrity" as the personal embodiment of fame dates from the first half of the nineteenth century, not coincidentally the onset of the

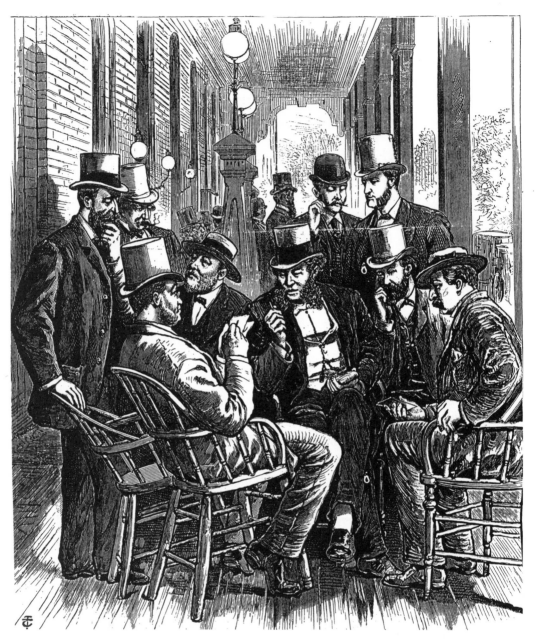

Figure 39. Railroad Barons on the Millionaires' Piazza of the United States Hotel, *Frank Leslie's*, August 30, 1879. The 1874 agreement to fix railroad prices was widely known as the Saratoga Compact. "Commodore" Cornelius Vanderbilt loved the Springs and met his second wife there, but although his grandchildren continued to visit, they chose to build their mansions in Newport. (Courtesy of the Yates Collection, Skidmore College.)

Industrial Revolution and the growth of resorts. As the century progressed, however, the distance between spectators and the object of their vision grew. Guests arriving at Saratoga after 1860 longed to see luminaries such as Vanderbilt, Morrissey, and Canfield, as if they were national monuments. Visitors could then purchase stereographic portraits of these worthies, or even use opera glasses to observe celebrities as they sat rocking on the north veranda of the United States Hotel, known to all as the Millionaires' Piazza (figure 39). In an article entitled "Don't's of Hotel Life," the *New York Recorder* issued a disheartening warning that would have been almost unthinkable before the Civil War: "Don't think because you're important in your own town, you're somebody in a hotel." Although superficially similar to antebellum see-and-be-seen voyeurism, the new cult of the celebrity undermined the older tenuous equality of voyeurs.[62]

A Saratoga visit at the turn of the century still entailed promiscuous mingling with strange faces and forced familiarity with strange customs. Journalists continued to praise democratic Saratoga, where "we all live in each other's presence, take our repasts in vast crowded halls and stare each other out of countenance." The legendary crassness of the Springs produced a distinctly American resort, for gambling attracted the raffish rather than the correct, and the racing crowd was inclusive to the extreme. Bookmakers, sporting men, profiteers, bonanza kings, and denizens of the demimonde rubbed elbows with politicians, health seekers, ministers, millionaire industrialists, and the turf aristocracy. When two hundred thousand people visited the Springs in a given summer, any claim to exclusivity disappeared. Visitors continued to view Saratoga as a place of "absolute freedom from restraint of any kind" or "a perpetual festival," concepts that would later be recycled and used to describe many leisure activities throughout the twentieth century. Yet the resort's popularity in the Gilded Age held within it the seeds of its own decline. The more the values associated with monetary exchange and commodification intruded after the Civil War, the less Saratoga seemed essentially unique, or even different. The once liminal experience became ever more mundane, as commercialism banished ennui in a world that increasingly devalued communal experience.[63]

SIX

The Privatization of Newport

"Coarseness and Vulgarity Are Never Seen Here"

IN THE SUMMER OF 1870, young Henry James wrote a series of travel sketches for the *Nation* on northeastern American resorts. In his description of Saratoga Springs, James criticized what he called the "momentous spectacle: the democratization of elegance." With a new racetrack and gambling casino and expanding hotels, the Springs seemed perfectly constructed to offend his finer instincts. "Substantial and civilized" Newport, at least for Henry James, shone in comparison; the difference, he declared of his old hometown, lay in the disparity between "a group of three or four hotels and a series of cottages and villas." At Saratoga after the Civil War, commercialization had undermined the public character of the resort. Now, privatization at Newport eroded the delicate sense of accessible community fostered by hotel culture. Saratoga, as James noted, retained a democratic element through the use of common tables, sitting rooms, and urban spaces. Newport's visitors, on the other hand, pioneered the privatization of leisure time through the privatization of resort space. They tried their best to eliminate the possibility of interaction with strangers and to sunder the "see" and the "be seen" halves of watering place life.[1]

Throughout the late nineteenth century, Americans viewed Saratoga and Newport as archetypes representing conflicting ideals of social life. Superficially, they were complementary, for as John Saxe noted, "At the one you go into the water, at the other it goes into you." Yet by 1900, both cities differed radically from their antebellum predecessors. American resorts had become battlefields upon which citizens fought for social supremacy, and Newport sojourners consciously tried to position themselves several rungs on the social ladder above visitors to Saratoga. The *Newport Daily News* asked pugnaciously, "What has Saratoga, but its hotels?" Newport's boosters bragged their watering place contained no "horse-jockeys, blacklegs, billiard-markers, nor cozeners masquerading in the ill fitting garments of gentlemen; no ballet dancers, clairvoyants, demireps, nor adventuresses flashing in jewels and jadery." Saratoga simply did not offer the specific cachet necessary to consolidate social position in America. If Newport people laid "a little too much stress upon family distinction and even upon wealth," one journalist asked rhetorically, "who that can does not take pride in these things?"[2]

One by one, Newport's hotels expired—the Bellevue and the Fillmore closed in the late 1860s, the Atlantic House in the 1870s—to be replaced by private residences. In the 1860s, George Towle still found the Newport hotels "on a scale of spaciousness and luxury which it would be hard to find even in New York," but a guidebook warned in 1874 that "the visitor who has not been in Newport in ten years, will be lost in wonder and astonishment" at the absence of hotel life. The number of private summer houses rented or built now defined a good season for Newport, not the occupancy rates at hotels. The *New York Times* in 1875 featured an article on Newport with the headline, "The City of Cottages: Decline of Newport Hotel Life," and the local newspaper reported in the same year that "Newport is not losing prestige—it is only going to be the China of watering places, built round with a great wall of exclusiveness."[3]

The fate of the Atlantic House symbolized this transformation. After the bombardment of Fort Sumter, the United States government transplanted the Naval Academy from exposed Annapolis, Maryland, to Newport. The Department of the Navy leased the Atlantic House for $5,500 a year and altered the hotel to serve as a winter-occupied educational establishment (figure 40). The academy remained in Newport for only four years, but the Navy subsequently played an integral role in the city's off-season stability. By establishing a torpedo station on Goat Island in 1869, and then the Naval War College in 1884 on the site of the old Newport Asylum, the navy's presence provided a steady source of income in the city. But the Atlantic House never recovered its former glory and gave up the ghost in 1876, having served less than thirty years. The next year, surprised visitors found

Figure 40. United States Naval Academy at the Atlantic House Hotel, ca. 1862. After the bombardment of Fort Sumter, the United States government transplanted the Naval Academy from exposed Annapolis, Maryland, to the Atlantic House in Newport, where it remained for the duration of the war. (Courtesy of the Newport Historical Society [P167].)

that Park Gate, a large private summer villa owned by a Philadelphia visitor, had displaced the hotel.[4]

The fashion for a country house by the sea had come back into vogue in eighteenth-century Europe. Cultivated men of the Enlightenment imitated the annual Roman *peregrinatio,* moving out of the city to make the rounds of their out-of-town villas. The European country house afforded an opportunity to demonstrate one's taste, a principal means of achieving social distinction. In Newport, visitors amalgamated this fashion with the doctrines propounded by a number of influential nineteenth-century antebellum architectural manuals. Alexander Jackson Davis's *Rural Residences* (1837) and Andrew Jackson Downing's *Architecture of Country Houses* (1850; reprinted nine times by 1866) widely popularized the solitude and freedom of the family home in the country, isolated from the world of business.[5]

There was no intrinsic reason that cottages should be more fashionable than hotels; in fact, one journalist complained that the idea that cottage living gave one "social advantages not possessed by hotel-boarders, is one of the wildest delusions that a real-estate man ever thrust into the head of silly people." Many travelers initially considered country villas dull, a stage unfit upon which to display leisured magnificence compared with the opulent grand hotel. For other Americans, however, permanent residency in a single-family dwelling embodied the platonic ideal of higher status and greater wealth. Walt Whitman wrote, "A man is not a whole and complete man unless he owns a house and the ground it stands on," and the Baptist minister Russell Conwell reiterated the same thought in his "Acres of Diamonds" lecture. "The absence of the stereotyped hotel life with all the cheapening influences which follow in its train," enthused one haughty Newport guidebook at the turn of the century, "gives to the Newport summer a certain individuality and refined restraint seldom found elsewhere. . . . Coarseness and vulgarity are never seen here."[6]

The cottage industry had deep roots in Newport, reaching back to colonial times, but Lieutenant Governor George Engs initiated a modern real estate boom when he bought the rural estate of the Kay family in 1835, subdivided it for seasonal residents, and laid out Kay Street on the site of an old ropewalk. These early cottages acted as a magnet, drawing other summer visitors to Newport. In 1839, George Noble Jones, a high-living Savannah planter who had married a Newport woman, bought a ridge-top lot on the dirt road that was to become Bellevue Avenue and built a cottage there for his summer use. Jones entertained in this summer house, later known as Kingscote, throughout the 1840s and 1850s until the Civil War made Newport an inhospitable resort for southern visitors. Kingscote's stick-style Gothic Revival architecture, by Richard Upjohn, and grounds laid out by Andrew Jackson Downing contrasted mightily with the first Greek Revival Ocean House across the street. The juxtaposition of the two epitomized the rivalry between Newport's cottage industry and hotel life.[7]

At the same time, Alfred Smith, a crafty speculator and high-powered salesman, played a key role in transforming Newport into one of the nation's premier residential watering spots. Smith, born in neighboring Middletown, was a frugal New York City tailor by trade. In this capacity, he met some of the richest men in the United States, and it was on Smith's advice that William Lawrence bought Ochre Point in 1835. Flushed by his initial success, Smith relinquished his sartorial career in 1839 to try his hand in real estate. He joined with Charles Russell, a Newport native who had made a fortune as a merchant in New York, to buy three hundred acres of land south and east of Touro Street in the 1840s for the specific purpose of building summer houses. The timing was propitious—the first Fall River steamer and the opening of the Atlantic House and the second Ocean House wildly increased the popularity of Newport—and they had no trouble disposing of the lots at a considerable profit.

Smith's next coup occurred in 1851. With Joseph Bailey, Smith purchased 140 acres of land from the old farms south of the town limits and adjacent to the hill behind the Redwood Library for only $27,000. The following year, they cajoled the Newport Town Council into lengthening Bellevue Avenue south to the beach, over the opposition of the Hazard family, through whose land the extension passed. The city awarded the Hazards $1,450 on appraisal and completed the new section in 1853 for less than $23,000, thereby creating large tracts of desirable land for subdivision and sale (figure 41). Sidney Fisher recorded his vision of the area in his diary in 1855: "Hundreds of beautiful cottages where I knew open fields. A large, refined & rich society living in elegant villas." Nathaniel Willis predicted that "the more sensible and luxurious" country seats would ultimately gain at the expense of the hotels, and he recommended that artists lose no time in "making sketches of the gregarious days of watering-places while they last."[8]

Sure enough, a cottage-building mania infected Newport in the 1850s. The Newport tax book from 1852 named twelve nonresidents (including four from Boston, four from New York) as owners of real estate, together assessed for more than $100,000 of real and personal property. Only two years later, sixty additional summer houses had been constructed, most spreading down Kay Street, Catherine Street, and Old Beach Road. More business activity took place in Newport during the next five years than in the previous fifty. Land near Bellevue Avenue skyrocketed in price, and once worthless property along the cliffs increased proportionately. Speculators subdivided whole sections of the city into building lots; from January 1851 to May 1853, Newport property worth more than $1.5 million changed hands, and the formerly sleepy town averaged more than three real estate transactions a week. "How fiercely the fever of land speculation rages in Newport," observed one journal in the 1850s. "How fathers dreaded to be drawn thither by their families lest they should be forced to buy a place. . . . How everybody had a secret about the land he was going to buy." Newport's reputation was such that Henry Cabot Lodge's father considered buying a house there in the 1850s, sight unseen.[9]

Alfred Smith justly earned his reputation as a high-pressure salesman; few prospective buyers who took a seat in his carriage emerged without a piece of Newport real estate. Julia Ward Howe, owner of an estate at Lawton's Valley, five miles outside of Newport, reminisced that Smith "managed to entrap strangers in his gig. . . . In the summer of 1852 my husband became one of his victims. I say this because Dr. Howe made the purchase without much deliberation. In fact, he could hardly have told anyone why he made it." The Newport tax book of 1853 listed the former tailor as the seventh-richest man in Newport. Everywhere on Aquidneck Island, visitors saw signs for cottages and lots for sale or let, urging them to "consult with A. Smith." His lifetime gross sales probably exceeded $20 million, although he continued to live on dowdy Mount Vernon Street, several blocks from the fashionable world he had helped to create. When Smith died in 1887, he left a multimillion-dollar estate, including several foreclosed houses on Bellevue Avenue. His lesser-known partner, Joseph Bailey, also did quite well. In 1849, the city assessed Bailey $10.20 on personal property of only $3,000; fifteen years later he paid $390 on an assessment of $65,000.[10]

The *Newport Daily News* marveled that "every year makes Newport more of a city and less of an ordinary watering place . . . and many, who formerly were guests at the *House,* now occupy their own mansions for the summer." Wealthy New York and Boston families paying higher taxes than many native families considered it a small price to pay to be in the select company. Disturnell's guidebook (1855) alerted readers that Newport cottagers were "the more stately, the more literary, [and] the more fastidious" compared with Saratoga's "shoals of fast young men, ambitious mammas, and eligible daughters, who will drink the waters out of custom and coquetry." Newport's inaugural directory in 1856–57 counted 174 summer sojourners, more than two-thirds of whom were from New York, Boston, or Philadelphia, with a sprinkling from the South. Even the city government joined the rampant speculation, suggesting in 1853 that the Newport Asylum for the Poor on Coasters Island be sold to wealthy buyers as a site for summer residences. When the painter John La Farge squandered his inheritance through immoderate living, he sold his house on Kay Street for $18,000 in 1864, more than twice what he had paid for it three years earlier, despite the uncertainties of the Civil War. "The whole Island is destined to cottages and gardens," the *Springfield (Ill.) Republican* exulted just after Gettysburg.[11]

The cottage boom affected even the undeveloped western section of Aquidneck Island. Until Edward King bought the Harrison farm for shore lots in 1857, that remote area was mostly rural marshland. In 1859, Alfred Smith launched a project to connect the new Harrison Avenue to an extended Bellevue Avenue by means of a scenic drive along the south shore, but landowner John Hazard objected, and then the Civil War intervened. In 1866, a petition of 125 people inspired the commissioner of highways to act, and Smith assured the completion of the drive by constructing at his own expense a stone bridge over the creek that ran from Almy Pond to the Atlantic (figure 41). This new road, lined with wild rugosa hedgerows and marshes filled with waving cattails set off by the sparkle of the sea, served as a wonderful backdrop not only for carriage rides but also for manor houses. George Frederic Jones, Edith Wharton's father, spent far more money on his Newport summer cottage, built in 1861, on Harrison Avenue than on his Manhattan townhouse.[12]

Although Newport County ranked as one of the wealthiest counties in the United States according to the 1860 census, the Newport of ostentatious plutocrats did not really exist before the Civil War. No estates exceeded a valuation of $500,000, and only Edward King's surpassed even $200,000. The socioeconomic elite consisted of fewer than three hundred families whose social influence gave tone to local society but who lived fairly unpretentiously. The households of the fifteen richest men in Newport County in 1860 averaged five servants apiece, and the two millionaires employed only nine servants between them.[13]

Then the glamorous Belmonts glided in. August Belmont—international banker, American agent for the Rothschilds, and rejuvenator of the Democratic Party—had married Newport native Caroline Perry, daughter of Admiral Matthew Perry, who had "opened" Japan. Belmont rented a villa on Bellevue Avenue for the summer of 1860 and enjoyed it so much he bought the fourteen-acre plot next door for $47,000 and built the magnificent if

Figure 41. Detail of Map of the City of Newport, 1859. Bailey's Beach, Newport's most select recreational enclave, barely existed in 1859 before the extension of Bellevue Avenue to the Atlantic and the creation of Ocean Drive. (Collection of the author.)

misnamed mansion Bythesea. Belmont's neighbors in the Bellevue Avenue vicinity soon included Hamilton Fish, James Lennox, Erastus Corning, William Schermerhorn, and Ward McAllister. The cost of erecting and laying out the grounds of an elegant villa now ranged from $50,000 to $200,000, while furnished cottages rented for as much as $8,000 a season. "The time when one could live economically [at Newport], unless in a boarding house, is not likely to return," *Harper's Monthly* mournfully noted. In his weighty 1875 tome, *Newport and Its Cottages*, George Mason described forty-five principal dwellings, including twenty-six owned by New Yorkers, six owned by residents of Newport, and six by Bostonians.

Anthony Trollope declared he had "no objection to become the possessor of one of those 'villa residences,' but I do not think that I should have 'gone in' for hotel life at Newport."[14]

A dance at a cottage might be little different from one at a hotel, but the former had a guest list that enabled the host to discriminate against those deemed undesirable. The symbolic importance of the Gilded Age ballroom is difficult to overestimate. The luxurious remodeling of the old Kingscote in 1881 entailed the addition of a spacious dining room large enough to hold extravagant dances. When Mrs. William (Caroline Schermerhorn) Astor purchased Beechwood in 1880, she added an even larger ballroom to accompany the wide and high-ceilinged piazzas on three sides of the old estate. As the reigning queen of society, Mrs. Astor's presence clinched Newport's rise to social dominance in the American social whirl. Ward McAllister, her New York friend and the self-appointed Petronius of the Gilded Age, had already sorted out the American social hierarchy by enumerating the elite Four Hundred, the number having supposedly been chosen as the capacity of Mrs. Astor's New York ballroom. "If you go outside that number," McAllister told the *New York Tribune,* "you strike people who are not at ease in a ballroom or else make other people not at ease." Notably absent from McAllister's 1892 list were some of America's greatest business leaders: J. P. Morgan, E. H. Harriman, John D. Rockefeller, and Jewish financiers such as Abraham Kuhn and Solomon Loeb.[15]

The city of Newport naturally received McAllister's seal of approval since he descended from the Ward family of Rhode Island and had come to Newport as a child with the migration from the South. McCallister eventually married a millionaire's daughter and in the real estate boom of the 1850s bought a farm north of Newport. He thereby followed his own deceptively simple advice on entering society: "If you want to be fashionable, be always in the company of fashionable people." Elizabeth Drexel Lehr remembered how this dictum resulted in a hermetically sealed Newport:

Dire indeed was the fate of those who were not "acceptable" if they had been unwise enough to take a villa for the whole season, for in so small a community there was no escape for them. Every week their humiliation was brought home to them more and more as one after another the all-powerful queens of Newport chose to ignore their existence. Splendid balls and dinners every night, but not for them. Bathing parties in Bailey's Beach, yachting at Hazard's, but both these sacred precincts were closed to them. Their men were not permitted to join the Reading Room or the Casino Club; their women had not the entree to a single drawing room. . . . They could only sit in the palatial villa they had so rashly acquired and accept their defeat with what grace they could. They seldom had the temerity to last out the season. A month of ostracism would usually send them over to the less aristocratic but more hospitable pastures of Narragansett, where they would try to console themselves with the big summer hotels on the water front, the smartly dressed crowds on the Pier, the friendly holiday atmosphere which they had sought in vain at "The Millionaires' Playground."[16]

The privatization of Newport space had dramatic repercussions on the resort experience, for the siphoning off of wealthy visitors affected the quality of the city's hotels. Newport hostelries had sometimes been compared to their detriment with those of Saratoga and Niagara, but after the Civil War, vituperative attacks became the norm. "Degenerated would be a clever word to apply to the hotels in this city," complained the *New York Times* in 1865. "Such things as first-class hotels have ceased to exist altogether in Newport. . . . There are no persons of note stopping at any of these houses, although the city is filled with the *creme de la creme.*" Three years later, the *Times* reprised the same theme regarding the Ocean House: "For a hotel of its size and tariff, it is about the poorest kept house we ever visited." Even locals noted a disturbing decrease in convention business. Travelers typically view innkeepers as indolent, rude, and rapacious, but the disparagement of Newport's hotels far surpassed the normal bounds of hostility.[17]

By the summer of 1874, barely a dozen families spent an entire summer at a Newport hotel, and the falling off in patronage bred a bitter cycle. In antebellum days, the major hotels had been constantly remodeled. Now they seemed antiquated next to their new residential competitors, yet their owners lacked the capital to make improvements, and so the buildings grew more vermiculous with each passing year. The unending litany of complaints about Newport hotels also weakened the trade. In the late 1870s, the city developed two distinct social circles following disparate orbits; the Ocean House rarely filled more than a third of its rooms, and its dreary hops failed because the cottagers resorted to private social gatherings instead. "The shadowy and meretricious hotel life at the spas and the sea-side is steadily growing into disfavor," reported *Harper's Monthly* approvingly.

"Sensible and self-contained persons have become weary for discomfort, dissipation, and heterogeneous crowds under the name of pleasure, preferring to choose their own society and to make their own domestic arrangements." In the controversy over Jewish patronage at Saratoga, the *New York Times* reported hotel business was so bad in Newport that they would let anyone lodge there, "from a blackamoor chief to an Irish king."[18]

By the time Mark Twain and Charles Dudley Warner caricatured the gradations of the American pseudoaristocracy in *The Gilded Age* (1873), Newport reigned supreme as the snob's destination of choice. When the novel's parvenu heroine dares to suggest to some antique Washington, D.C., society matrons that Long Branch and Cape May, despite being "low," might serve as an acceptable substitute for distant Newport, Twain's dowager instantly rebuffs her: "Nobody goes *there*, Miss Hawkins—at least only persons of no position in society. And the President." Her daughter adds, "Newport is damp, and cold, and windy, and excessively disagreeable but it is very select. One cannot be fastidious about minor matters when one has no choice." Even presidents did not always meet with a warm reception. An oft-repeated and perhaps apocryphal story insisted that Chester Arthur had been snubbed at a Newport ball for insufficient pedigree and wealth and was forced to whistle up his own carriage outside the Casino.[19]

Newport visitors in the Gilded Age specifically altered antebellum canons of fashionability in an attempt to create social distance. In "Our Pilgrimage," Charles Dudley Warner's hero commits several faux pas in his Newport visit of 1886. First he takes a stroll along the Cliff Walk on Sunday, only to find himself walking with butlers and maids on their day off. He then stays in a hotel, even though he knows "that in going to a hotel in Newport he was putting himself outside the pale of the best society." The next day he makes yet another mistake; he visits Easton's Beach and discovers to his surprise that "it had ceased to be fashionable to bathe at Newport. Strangers and servants may do so, but the cottagers have withdrawn their support from the ocean. . . . Bathing in the surf is vulgar."[20]

Warner's hero learned the hard way that nineteenth-century amusements became fashionable when the upper classes attended particular springs, entertainments, or sporting clubs and fell out of fashion when they withdrew their support. By the 1890s, a newspaper informed readers that "the idea that the Four Hundred go in bathing is an exploded one. The beach is now given over to excursionists and the humble class of cottagers." Socially dominant groups at Newport tried to outdistance the consumption patterns of their rivals by rejecting as banal activities they had previously considered exquisite. Once the mass of people could afford some luxury, such as sea bathing, the upper classes lost interest in it or declared it obsolete; *Scribner's* proclaimed, "Bathing at the beach as a feature of social summer life is over." The *Ladies Home Journal* summed up the trend:

> It is no longer fashionable to bathe in the surf at Newport. Madame Haut Ton discovered that it was possible to meet her neighbor's maid in the water . . . [or the] summer tourist, whom she regards as very undesirable to know. . . . The people in bathing are usually those who do not care for the opinion of the fashionable world, or those from the hotels. Hotel life is not interesting. Unlike some of the other summer places, life does not center in the great caravansaries; and so unless one has an extensive acquaintance among the Newport people, it is extremely stupid to be at a hotel.[21]

Although architects influenced by the Romantic tradition aligned Newport's cottages to the sea, the fashionable mansions typically rejected the water as anything beyond passive landscape. Their inhabitants, however, did not totally ignore the ocean. Bailey's Beach, Newport's most select recreational enclave at the junction of Bellevue and Ocean Avenues, drew the summer colony away from Easton's, now known to them as "the Common Beach" (figure 42). Entrance into its restricted club, later known as the Spouting Rock Beach Association, represented the acme of social success. Only the select few could bathe at Bailey's, and watchmen ejected anyone who was not accompanied by a member or without a note of introduction. At Bailey's, cottagers escaped from the voyeuristic loafers at Easton's who "make a practice of laughing and jeering at bathers, both ladies and gentlemen, while going out from the houses to the water." Public access differentiated the exclusive Bailey's from the public Easton's in the same way it distinguished the cottage from the hotel.[22]

When the cottagers chose to visit the beach, bathing dress could still magically dissolve constraint. At Bailey's, the Newport cottagers behaved playfully and informally while in no way discarding their class privileges. A photograph of Harry Lehr, William K. Vanderbilt, and Harold Vanderbilt at Bailey's Beach in the 1890s shows them enjoying the same kind of hijinks often attributed solely to the proletariat at Coney Island (figure 43). Similar freedom was enjoyed by the young men, coquettishly dressed

Figure 42. Easton's Beach, Newport, ca. 1890. First Beach looks somewhat forlorn in this photograph. By rejecting as banal pleasures they had previously considered exquisite, dominating groups continually outdistanced the consumption patterns of competitors. (Courtesy of the Newport Historical Society [P2340].)

as women, captured by a photographer in front of bathing booths around 1896 (figure 44). Americans of all classes enjoyed the liminality of the beach with an abandon at odds with their supposed concern for strict rules of conduct.[23]

Just as religious pilgrimage sites often developed social stratifications, a trip to Newport, the mecca of fashion, as opposed to Saratoga, the sporting resort, communicated cultural meanings. Newport's lack of grand hotel life resulted in the city's gradual disappearance from the pilgrimage round of watering places. Before the Civil War, the hotel belle flitted from the Catskills to Sharon to Niagara to Saratoga to Newport, causing a stir wherever she appeared. By the 1880s, the *Nation* viewed her as an object of "pity or contempt . . . for hotel life indicates both that she has no cottage, and no cottage friends to ask her to stay with them." An English magazine seconded this opinion: "The cottage residents of Newport, who remain long after the fashionable Hegira, bestow considerable compassion, and a good deal of disgust, on the inmates of these large hotels." Newport now resembled a distant shrine of supreme religious importance, promoting its own

Figure 43. Hijinks at Bailey's Beach, Newport, 1894. William K. Vanderbilt, Harold Vanderbilt, and Harry Lehr (l. to r.) seem to be enjoying the same kind of relaxed informality often attributed uniquely to the proletariat at seaside resorts such as Coney Island. (Courtesy of the Newport Historical Society [P1714].)

Figure 44. Cross-dressing millionaires at Bailey's Beach, Newport, ca. 1890. These five wealthy scions of the American plutocracy, three of whom are coquettishly dressed as women in front of the bathing booths, do not look particularly staid or repressed. (Courtesy of the Newport Historical Society [P2072].)

symbolic styles of veneration and drawing a national elite different from the clientele of local shrines of minor deities.[24]

Even for some of the so-called elite, simple monetary calculations precluded a trip to Newport now that it had become unfashionable to stay in a hotel. George Templeton Strong agonized in his diary over the opportunity to rent George F. Jones' cottage for the summer of 1858, wavering between "I know I'm a fool and can't afford the luxury" and "Ellie would be delighted . . . but the *Monish!!!*" Strong eventually declined and instead stayed in a boardinghouse in Brattleboro, but where Strong feared to tread, others eagerly rushed in. English author John Chadwick returned to Newport in 1881, after an absence of two decades, only to be shocked by the prevalence and expense of the houses. Chadwick found the city "almost exclusively occupied by rich visitors each holding or renting a villa. There are no piers, no bathing machines, no public bands or music, and no tourist visitors. To me it seemed a dull place." Henry Pierrepont, a Brooklyn millionaire, drove around Newport in 1883 "to see the new cottages, of which there are on the Gibb's + Lawrence + Sears Estates a great many—too crowded I think, + many of them too expensive."[25]

Periodicals of the day debated whether this Newport trend toward private cottage life at summer resorts constituted progress or tragedy. By and large, most agreed with *Century* that "the summer cottage has been elastic enough to meet the needs and purses of every grade: it ranges from that which is almost a palace . . . to the economical boarding-place or the Adirondack cabin." Edward Bok, writing in the *Ladies Home Journal,* issued a diatribe against summer hotels, claiming they forced women to overdress and sapped their strength through late social hours. The *Nation* viewed the trend less optimistically: "The rapid growth of cottage life . . . has killed the hotels in Newport, and is killing them in Bar Harbor and some other places. . . . To be in a place where there is a great deal of cottage life and not share in it is not pleasant."[26]

Some of the nation's brightest cultural stars found cottaging at Newport to be rather agreeable. Washington Irving declined an invitation to visit on the grounds that Newport was "too gay and fashionable," but the literati of Cambridge and Boston, such as Henry Wadsworth Longfellow, Henry James Sr., Thomas Wentworth Higginson, the historian George Bancroft, the actor Edwin Booth, and the artists John Sargent, John La Farge, and William Morris Hunt, gradually deserted Nahant for the city on the Narragansett. Bret Harte arrived in Newport in 1871 with ten thousand dollars' worth of magazine contracts to fill and spent the summer lounging on beaches and verandas, entertaining lavishly, and turning out little high-quality work. Julia Ward Howe's Town and Country Club, founded the same year to combat the possibility that "the Newport season should evaporate into the shallow pursuit of amusement," attracted the Shakespearean actress Charlotte Cushman, the biographer James Parton, Charles Brooks (translator of Schiller), Katherine Wormeley (translator of Balzac), Oliver Wendell Holmes, the author Helen Hunt (Jackson), and the indefatigable dilettante Thomas Appleton. Most decided against a stay in Newport's hotels for a residence in the suburban Kay Street–Catherine Street neighborhood, not quite as expensive as Bellevue Avenue or Ochre Point; from 1870 to 1873, builders constructed more than sixty new homes in this area.[27]

A private dwelling differed from a resort hotel in that the latter, with its vast semipublic spaces, required some sort of code for the interaction between random visitors. In theory, private vacation residences should have allowed for casual behavior with self-selected company. In practice, Newport's wealthier cottagers often intensified the rigid decorum of summer life, using ceremonial ritual as an expression of class position. They "do not bathe in the ocean. . . . They do not walk, they do not row, they seldom sail, and if they fish they hire men to bait their hooks for them," complained one journalist. "They strictly observe all the formalities of city life." New York millionaires like the Belmonts gave elaborate dances and thought "dinners niggardly without a dozen courses and as many kinds of wine." The private feasting retained the gluttony of the hotel dining room, only devoid of any public audience. Cottagers even privatized dancing; etiquette books now recommended that masquerades open to the general public "should be shunned as questionable amusements," but they remained perfectly acceptable within "the protection of home."[28]

Like the antebellum hotels, Newport's mansions provided ornate settings for the costume balls, private dinner parties, and entertainments of the summer season. The modifications of William Wetmore's Chateau-sur-Mer epitomized this transition to privatized extravagance. Wetmore, who had acquired a fortune in the China trade, bought land in Newport as early as 1840 but did not build on Bellevue Avenue until 1852. Five years later, at his rough-hewn granite retreat, Wetmore supposedly staged the most magnificent fete ever given in America to that time. After his death, his son commissioned the New York architect Richard Morris Hunt to produce large-scale renovations. Hunt so altered the appearance of the chateau in the 1870s that later observers believed the original house had been torn down. He transformed Wetmore's human-scale retreat into a palatial Newport mansion by adding a dramatic three-story-high entrance hall and imperial staircase, converting an old service wing to a thousand-square-foot billiard room, and raising the mansard roofs to towering heights. Estates such as this caused one English visitor to exclaim in 1880, "We know every sea-side resort in England and on the Continent, and nowhere is there anything comparable to Newport."[29]

Figure 45. Coaching on Bellevue Avenue opposite the Newport Casino, *Harper's Weekly*, September 18, 1886. Although the Ocean Drive coaching route took participants away from the hotel verandas and the town, it still began in front of the Casino, a vestigial remnant of the antebellum see-and-be-seen ethos. (Collection of the author.)

The opening of the Ocean Drive in 1867 further weakened any sense of common public space in Newport. Previously, the main venue for coaching display had been the afternoon drive on Bellevue Avenue, easily viewable by spectators on the veranda of the Ocean House. In the spirit of see-and-be-seen ennui, glittering carriages ambled down the avenue, without specific destination (figure 45). The *New York Times* reported in 1868 that "the turnouts at Newport are much handsomer and more numerous than those here [Saratoga], though the reverse is true of the hotel residents." Maud Elliott recalled, "Never have I seen in Hyde Park nor in the Champs Élysées, a finer display." But the new Ocean Drive circuit supplanted this aimless Bellevue Avenue parade as the main focal point of the afternoon. No less dazzling, it gave participants a specific purpose and destination, took them away from the hotel verandas and the town, and generally removed the drive from the realm of public spectacle. By the turn of the century, more private performances based on amusement rather than refinement replaced the carriage parade altogether.[30]

The decline of hotel life, the unfashionableness of bathing, and the construction of Ocean Drive allowed Newport's mansion dwellers to withdraw from public life. They resided away from the town and visited, ate, danced, gossiped, and went to church among themselves. Yet the cottagers, not far removed from hotel culture either spatially or temporally, never totally confused exclusivity with privacy. Most mansions remained a spectacle for profane contemplation, "about as secluded as the cups and saucers at an afternoon tea." The free access to the Cliff Walk, still protected by law, permitted the curious almost to stroll in the backyards of the great Bellevue Avenue houses. An occasional millionaire such as Mrs. William Waldorf Astor might build a brick wall between her cottage and the walk, but a reporter from the *Liverpool Evening Standard* noted that virtually nothing prevented spectators "from walking up the lawn and staring into Mr. Lorillard's, or any other cottager's lordly windows." Newport guidebooks routinely included lists of summer residents and villa owners, complete with maps for use in locating their residences. The cottagers did not mind; they longed to occupy center stage, as long as they could exercise some degree of control over their public images.[31]

This element of control was difficult to achieve. Gossip had always been a staple of hotel-oriented resorts, but a remnant of preindustrial deference tended to limit the damage. Visitors at hotels either reveled in the ticklish stares of "all the world" or at least tolerated them as the price to be paid for participation at the watering place. By the Civil War, however, many visitors feared the more modern type of public inquisitiveness, where personal stories could circulate totally outside an individual's control. One antebellum southern visitor to Saratoga, unfamiliar with the turn to commercial celebrity culture, threatened to use his horsewhip on impudent "Northern puppydom." He accused newspapers of feeding the prurient appetites of their readers by detailing "the way in which you eat, drink, sleep, sing, laugh, talk, walk, or ride,—perverting what you say or do, your most innocent performances, and discussing the merits of your wife and daughter as if they were bales of merchandize."[32]

Newport's cottagers attempted to use private accommodations to regulate the flow of personal information, but with uneven results. William Mann, who acquired Newport's *Town Topics* newspaper in 1885, successfully combined blackmail and journalism in his magazine for two decades. Mann terrorized the numerous guilty consciences of Newport, and incidentally made a lucrative living, by threatening to publish the "dirt," whether true or not, regarding the city's most esteemed visitors. Yet despite the lure of privacy and the drawbacks of publicity, Newport's elite visitors needed spectators. After all, a community of equals cannot provide an atmosphere of deference. George Curtis caught this peculiar relationship in his lament over the displacement of public life in Newport: "For fashion dwells in cottages now, and the hotel season is brief and not brilliant." The cottagers occasionally appeared at the hotels to hear concerts and dance, "but they come as from private palaces to a public hall, and disappear again into the magnificent mystery of 'cottage life.' "[33]

Newport's famous Casino perfectly captured the competing pull of public versus private display (figure 46). James Gordon Bennett, the irrepressible son of the publisher of the *New York Herald* and one of the most spectacular profligates of the Gilded Age, spent $100,000 building the Newport Casino in 1880 as a rival to the staid Reading Room. "The necessity of a place where citizens, hotel boarders, and others may rendezvous and give receptions, parties and balls," one correspondent wrote, "has long been felt in Newport," for few Newport ballrooms of the 1870s could house a large dancing party comfortably. "Newport did get along without the Casino but it would be difficult to tell just how it was done," declared a local newspaper.[34]

The Casino, on the same Bellevue Avenue block as the Ocean House, represented a final Newport attempt to salvage the more egalitarian experience of resort life. The building, the first major commission of the famed architectural trio of McKim, Mead, and White, provided a public rendezvous for all of summer society. Guests entered under a large central arch and wandered through a picturesque structure that contained a ballroom, a theater, numerous piazzas, restaurant rooms, and grass tennis courts. So striking was the Casino that its presence dominates George Lathrop's 1884 novel entitled, simply, *Newport*. Gentlemen stockholders paid annual club dues, but anyone could purchase membership for daily or weekly admission. "The poor mechanic or clerk can take his wife and children to the Casino every Sunday," the *New York Times* reported, "and listen to a capital concert for twenty-five cents per head and only twice that amount is charged for admission in the daytime." Biweekly dances at the theater supplanted the hops at the hotels; Maud Elliott reminisced, "Everybody attended them; the elders to watch, the youngsters to dance on that perfect parquet floor. What

Figure 46. The Earl and Friends at the Newport Casino, 1908. At its best, the Newport Casino provided a public rendezvous for all of summer society. Unlike the clannish Reading Room, the Casino willingly opened its doors to women. In this photograph, the Eighth Earl of Grenard courts American money in the form of Beatrice Mills, daughter of Ogden Mills; they married the following year. (Courtesy of the Newport Historical Society [P2083].)

an improvement it was over the old crash-covered carpet of the Ocean House!"[35]

Yet the popularity of the Casino waned rapidly. After 1885, Newport mansions positively swaggered with size and display and provided the pompous private stage sets for leisure-class interaction. Noted dandy Evander Berry Wall recalled, "In those days, we stuck to our friends, our own class, our own people." The nation's best-known architects vied to create the most prodigal summer palaces on Newport acreage smaller than a few city blocks. The theatrical ballrooms of Richard Hunt, the king of these monument builders, overwhelmed the playfulness of McKim, Mead, and White's more modest masterpiece. For sheer grandiosity, the Newport Casino could not compete with the Breakers.[36]

Hunt's Newport career began in 1862, when he rented the residence of his brother William, the noted painter. Like many architects working in Newport before 1880, Richard Hunt built asymmetrical domestic residences related to the natural setting, juxtaposing building materials of various textures to enhance the play of light. Although a few Beaux Arts mansions had been constructed in Newport in the 1870s, earlier cottages seemed virtual models of the American country house, with their broad wraparound porches, intricate woodwork, and multiple balconies. Hunt built his own Newport house on Greenough Place in a hodgepodge of styles without any of the daunting magnificence of his clients' mansions. In the 1880s, however, Newport patrons began to desire a grander and more overtly historical form rather than the eclectic novelties of the Queen Anne style. Hunt, sensing the insecurities of his clients, altered his style to match, and he soon filled Newport with bastardized neoclassical, Renaissance, and French designs.[37]

Wakehurst, built for James Van Alen in 1888 and surrounded by a high stone wall, initiated the change in Newport's architectural aspirations. The New York real estate developer Ogden Goelet occupied Hunt's French Renaissance Ochre Court (built in 1891 at a cost of $4 million) eight weeks a year. For Oliver Belmont's Belcourt Castle (built in 1893 for $3 million), Hunt lavished almost as much attention upon the horses' stables and carriage house as on the living quarters. In response to William K. Vanderbilt's request to develop "the very best living accommodations that money could buy," Hunt transformed half a million cubic feet of white marble into an $11 million cottage ($9 million for furniture and decoration). Modeled after the Petit Trianon at Versailles, this Marble House, completed in 1892, hosted

Figure 47. Postcard of "Marble Palace," ca. 1905. The Marble House's reign as the most expensive Newport "cottage" ($11 million) barely lasted five years before it was overtaken by the Breakers. Here, Richard Morris Hunt's palace is reduced to a postcard for possession by the masses. (Courtesy of the Newport Historical Society [P604].)

the Vanderbilts only seven weeks out of the year (figure 47). Throwing aside Andrew Jackson Downing's exhortations to republican simplicity, wealthy Americans joined this architectural battleground of competing egos.[38]

The Breakers, commissioned by Cornelius Vanderbilt II, marked the pinnacle of ostentatious cottage building at Newport. When the original Breakers burned to the ground in 1892, Hunt replaced it with a fireproof Italian Renaissance behemoth with seventy rooms, thirty-three for domestic staff. Hunt was particularly sensitive to the issue of flammability, since he occasionally vacationed in Saratoga and had supposedly helped rescue several women from the disastrous United States Hotel fire in 1868. For the Breakers, Hunt and Vanderbilt designed spaces such as the extravagant library, oversupplied with gold leaf, walnut *boiserie*, panels of gold-embossed green Spanish leather, and, apparently with no sense of irony, a large sixteenth-century French fireplace with the inscription, "Little do I care for riches, and do not miss them, since only cleverness prevails in the end." A comparison of the loggia (a covered outdoor sitting room) of the two

Breakers reveals the movement toward grandiose private theatricality. Peabody and Stearns' original (1879) timber and brick room was fairly dark and unassuming (figure 48), but in Hunt's building, the two projecting wings enclosed a grand, open, double-level space with a large tripartite arcade at ground level and a marble mosaic ceiling (figure 49). The glass wall between the Great Hall and the loggia enabled the viewer to look right through the sitting room to see not a crowded street or park but an expansive view of the ocean.[39]

By the time Hunt died in Newport in 1895, only days before the ball to celebrate the opening of the Breakers, Newport's nabobs had abandoned the anachronistic concept of a semipublic gathering place such as the Newport Casino. *Harper's Weekly* reported in 1893 that twice a week a crowd of spectators gathered in the gallery of the Casino ballroom, hoping to see "the elite of swelldom arrive [and] . . . twice a week the elite fail to arrive." Nor did the public Casino restaurant succeed, for as Maud Elliott noted, it was "out of the Newport tradition to eat or entertain away from home. Many other attempts have been made to establish a fashionable restaurant. It is of no use." Even the concept of a "casino" became privatized. When McKim, Mead, and White executed their next commission for a casino at Narragansett Pier in 1886, they jettisoned the more whimsical Newport features and instead moved toward a much greater monumentality. By 1902, their "casino" for John Jacob Astor's estate at Rhinebeck referred specifically to a private personal pavilion.[40]

The new private palaces subtly affected the psychology of the old hotel-oriented resorts. Because the plutocracy concentrated their immense summer residences in a few places such as Newport, Lenox, and Bar Harbor, "Society" could assemble and function without any assistance or interference from hotel keepers or unwanted guests. Of course, lesser visitors could still view the captains of American industry, and guidebooks titillated readers with information on "how fashionable people spend the day." One observer reverted to the older theatrical analogy: "To those who understand the subject, just to watch the passers-by on Bellevue Avenue is like watching a play; to read the names of new-comers on the real estate list like reading a romance." Only now the participant had been reduced to a window shopper; one could still watch the performance, but the gaze would not be returned. In comparison with Coney Island, one critic explained, Newport was "the only watering place in the world where there are no hotels and no hotel life,

Figure 48. Loggia of the First Breakers, Newport, ca. 1880. In Peabody and Stearns' original Breakers, built for Pierre Lorillard in 1879, the timber and brick loggia was fairly dark and informal. (Courtesy of the Newport Historical Society [P2338].)

no fashionable promenade, no scene of gaiety accessible to the stranger for an admission fee." At Newport, the concept of "see and be seen" had been broken into mutually distinct activities (figure 50).[41]

Cottage building might have been all the rage at Newport, but it never really caught on at Saratoga. In 1831, the notorious Madame Jumel, mistress of Aaron Burr, purchased several acres of land in Saratoga and built the city's earliest noteworthy summer home. Later visitors to Saratoga continually pointed out that a more "delightful spot for the creation of country residences could not well be found." Yet George Sheldon's compilation of ninety-seven noteworthy *Artistic Country Seats* (1887) enumerated thirteen in the Newport area (the largest grouping) and only two at the Springs. Other than Henry Hilton's three-hundred-acre private park and house (Woodlawn) and Spencer Trask's fifty-five-room Gothic mansion (Yaddoo), no Richard Hunt–scale monstrosities were built at hotel-oriented

Figure 49. Loggia of the Second Breakers, Newport, 1895. Richard Hunt's rebuilding of the Breakers revealed the movement toward grandiose private theatricality. In both loggias, the presence of a telescope reflects the desire to retain some vestige of the voyeuristic element so essential to nineteenth-century vacationing. (Courtesy of the Newport Historical Society [P2319].)

Figure 50. Lawn Fete at the Breakers, ca. 1915, rare photograph of a private Newport party. The mansions provided a breathtaking setting, but, of course, the guest list was extremely exclusive. (Courtesy of the Newport Historical Society [P1712].)

Saratoga. Not everyone was pleased. "The mistake we have made in Saratoga was putting up costly hotels instead of attracting rich people to build cottages," grumbled a Saratoga real estate dealer in the 1870s. "In the latter case we would have had strangers to pay the taxes now very onerous here."[42]

Newport as a resort best capitalized on the increasing desire of the wealthy to construct barricades of exclusivity. Before the Civil War, an Upper Ten Thousand, satirized by Charles Bristed and James Kirke Paulding, tried to organize themselves into a fashionable society, residing in a world of sumptuous town houses, fashionable cotillions, well-dressed servants, personal libraries, multiple carriages, and sojourns at watering places. The Industrial Revolution, however, increased the scale of what constituted wealth and added multiple levels to the American social hierarchy. New aspirants to New York and Boston society overwhelmed the old Knickerbocker-Brahmin cliques, and gradations began to appear even in the highest strata; by 1900, four thousand American millionaires, twenty of whom were worth more than $75 million, competed for status. Ward McAllister succinctly dismissed the old days of the 1860s in remarking that "bygones must be bygones. New York's ideas as to values when fortune was named, leaped boldly up to ten millions, fifty millions, some hundred millions, and the necessities and luxuries followed suit."[43]

In the compact preindustrial city, people defined their social position by dress, behavior, and the deference they demanded from and granted to others. By the Civil War, few of these constructions of social distinction retained their validity. Social inferiors in cities failed to doff their caps or avert their eyes before their superiors. Americans of all classes eagerly perused newspapers and magazines searching for clues as to how the Four Hundred dressed, entertained, and married. Etiquette books furnished readers with glosses on upper-class manners and delineated models of the fine points of behavior, which, if imitated, would assuage the collective uncertainty of individuals in mass society. When older conceptions of respect and honor broke down, self-declared financial, social, and intellectual elites searched for new ways to acquire recognition and organize society.[44]

As newcomers poured into American cities from the countryside and overseas, well-to-do residents departed by means of expanding transit systems. The horsecar, omnibus, steam ferry, and commuter railroad all worked to dismantle the physically contiguous walking city and inaugurated new aspirations. A move upward in income frequently meant a move outward toward the city limits and a greater degree of isolation. In William Dean Howells' *The Rise of Silas Lapham,* the social ambitions of the newly rich Laphams take on a geographical dimension when Silas seeks acceptance by constructing a lavish house in the prestigious Back Bay of Boston. The wealthy, and then the bourgeoisie, protected themselves from crime, begging, industrial ugliness, and undesirable strangers by establishing conditions of "invidious distinction" (the phrase is Thorstein Veblen's) in work and residential environments, cultural and leisure activities. To this day, the chief metaphor for alteration of status in America remains social "mobility." The proliferation of alarms, locks, lighted streets, and antitramp legislation all demonstrate a fairly new concern with protecting private spaces. In *Malbone* (1869), Newport resident Thomas Wentworth Higginson captures the growing mania for private entertaining when one character fantasizes secret underground passageways connecting all the best Newport houses, to which only a select few possess keys and outside of which "improper acquaintances in vain would howl for admission at the outer wall."[45]

Nineteenth-century Americans believed that everything had its proper and specific place: Indians on reservations, lions in zoos, the insane in asylums, athletes on sports fields, or the wealthy in class-based residence zones. Those with power and economic advantage strove to compensate for blurred social distinctions by rationalizing space to generate clear geographical distinctions. Well-to-do merchants, professionals, and manufacturers abandoned plebeian venues such as saloons, racetracks, theaters, parades, and volunteer fire companies, most of which consequently became rowdier and less attractive to social groups emphasizing self-discipline. The urban public realm broke apart into a world of clubs, lodges, parishes, and gangs. Recreational activity, which had the potential to bring people together to some degree, now sorted them out along lines of neighborhood, ethnicity, and economic class. Class-segregated theaters evolved in nineteenth-century America after audiences undermined the traditional spatial distinctions that delineated social classes in the pit, gallery, and boxes. Higher-status groups constantly tried to monopolize or create new categories of luxury goods, leisure opportunities, and cultural knowledge, for just as there could be no deference without spectators, there could be no distinction without levels of culture.[46]

The history of modern tourism is replete with examples of social segregation, infiltration by lower classes, and the subsequent search by elites for peripheral areas free from so-called contamination. In Europe, extreme class consciousness characterized travel after the Enlightenment, and successive class intrusion in the development of tourist destinations resulted in a chase-and-flight dynamic. The three pioneering English travel archetypes of the eighteenth century—the spa city of Bath, the seaside town of Brighton, and the continental grand tour—all shared an analogous fate; the bourgeoisie replaced the aristocracy and was, in turn, displaced by less privileged economic groups when inexpensive transportation permitted them to travel.[47]

Whatever else their sins, nineteenth-century American elites and bourgeoisie did not desire a world without leisure. Yet no matter how ornate the shipboard cabin or Pullman railroad car (invented in 1867), the high and the humble exited onto the dock or station simultaneously. When inexpensive access undercut the singularity of visits to eastern resorts, railroads advertised the American West by guaranteeing that the considerable expense ensured traveling with only well-bred and cultured people. Similarly, Raymond and Whitcomb, the first indigenous U.S. travel agency, founded in 1879, attempted to repeat the success of Thomas Cook's formula in England. Both offered the "exclusivity" of prepackaged tours to be purchased by like-minded travelers who could no longer find each other in depersonalized urban society. The tourist agency then isolated them from the outside world on their trip.[48]

It was far more difficult for subordinate groups to appropriate space than fashion, etiquette, or even culture. Women, blacks, immigrants, and members of the lower socioeconomic classes might adopt the concept of the vacation, but a specific place could be restricted. Carefully planned and privately financed cottage communities, such as Tuxedo Park in New York (1886), not only eliminated hotel proprietors but also segregated the owners from alien classes, races, or cultures. Jekyll Island (established in 1888), a mere twenty-four square miles off the coast of Georgia, acquired the reputation as the club of the "hundred millionaires" whose clientele supposedly controlled one-sixth of the world's wealth. "The cottage life here [Saratoga] hasn't killed the hotel life, as it has at Newport and Bar Harbor," remarked one of William Dean Howells' characters, "but the ideal of cottage life everywhere else has made hotel life at Saratoga ungenteel."[49]

Newport's shift to cottage-style exclusivity bred local competition, as shore resorts on both sides of Narragansett Bay tried to pick up Newport's discarded visitors. Between 1866 and 1871, entrepreneurs erected ten hotels across the bay at Narragansett Pier, enticing the multitudes with its gregarious public culture and encouragement of sea bathing, both activities out of fashion at Newport. Guidebooks positively contrasted the Pier, where one enjoyed "the traditional good fellowship of its society," with Newport and its "tedious and often cold and repelling formalities." Rocky Point, another Narragansett Bay resort located between Providence and Newport, attracted a more working-class clientele lured by mechanized amusements, cheap food, and the beach. By the 1890s, as many as fifty thousand pleasure seekers crowded the resort on Saturdays and Sundays.[50]

Newport occasionally tried to show another face, an alternative to the great mansions on the cliffs. To offset the competition from the Narragansett shore resorts, private citizens and city government combined to spruce up Easton's Beach in 1887, adding bathhouses and a six-hundred-foot-long pavilion complete with veranda, café, and two bandstands. Throngs of factory workers from the mill towns of Providence, Pawtucket, and Fall River flocked to these Coney Island–style improvements. By the 1880s, Newport had become a popular New England travel destination, one which, according to one guidebook, "well repays the tourist of more humble circumstances for his pilgrimage." This new wave of travelers, however, rarely stayed for more than a few days. Excursionists sampled the new facilities at Easton's and occasionally infiltrated the beautiful drives, curious to see the palaces they read about in the newspapers. They learned the names of the most prominent cottagers, gazed upon their mansions, speculated on their daily life, and bought view books, but they remained segregated in the postbellum city of play.[51]

Nevertheless, the success of the Newport resort industry, both high and low, could be glimpsed in the increasing prosperity of the city. Seventeenth-century Newport's development had converged around Washington Square, while maritime success in the eighteenth century led to development near the quays. In the 1830s, a visitor described Newport as "one long line of close-built, narrow streets, running parallel with the water about the base of a steep hill, with many others climbing its side." Then the city underwent a startling expansion. In 1872, the *Mercury* announced a "larger number of mechanics here than we ever recollect before, at least two thousand more than last year," all of whom needed a place to live. Thames Street expanded southward, a warren of wharves, warehouses, narrow alleys, and tenements. In the Broadway area, small businessmen converted older structures into stores and constructed new commercial buildings that vied with Thames Street as the center of retail activity (figure 51). As a seaport and a navy base, Newport possessed a more diversified economy than either Saratoga or Coney Island, but summer tourism, with its recycled dollars, took a back seat to no other industry in its importance. George Mason, who in 1859 had condemned Newport's ignoble reputation as a fashionable watering place, proclaimed in 1884, "Commerce we have little or none, and our manufacturers have nearly or quite died out, but we have not come to a stand." With the increased tourist trade, the city budget expanded from $48,000 in 1859 to $289,000 in 1884, and tax revenues rose accordingly. During the same period, expenditures for streets and highways rose from $10,000 to $76,000; for security watch and police, from $4,000 to $21,400; for the fire department, from $1,500 to $41,000; for street lights, from $2,300 to $24,000; for expenses for paupers and vagrants, from $800 to $6,000; and for municipal salaries, from $4,500 to $17,410. [52]

Despite possessing only two noteworthy textile mills, the city was never on firmer footing. From 1860 to 1880, Newport's population increased by more than half, the value of taxable property skyrocketed from $10.5 million to $27.5 million, and the valuation of personal estates almost doubled. Sumptuous summer residences stood on land that in 1859 was only fields, and pleasure craft and passenger ships had replaced China clippers and African slavers in Newport's reinvigorated harbor. In 1863, the Old Colony Railroad brought a spur line across the Sakonnet River and down Aquidneck Island, finally connecting Newport by rail with Boston. Several steamboat companies provided Newport with regular service to not only New York, Providence, Fall River, and the Connecticut coast but also satellite resort destinations such as Narragansett Pier, Wickford, and Block Island. For a six-month period in 1879, Fall River Line boats averaged five hundred passengers per trip, nearly four hundred thousand total, and the line re-

(*Opposite*) Figure 51. Detail of Map of Newport, R.I., *Newport Directory,* 1890. Newport underwent a startling expansion in all directions in the Gilded Age; the pursuit of pleasure by visitors led to a profitable service-based economy. (Courtesy of the Newport Historical Society.)

mained fully booked through the 1880s. The spectacular *Priscilla* (1894), the largest side-wheel steamer in the world, delighted passengers with its luxurious accommodations and enormous size.[53]

Residents understood that the city's economy depended to a great extent on pleasing its visitors, yet they sometimes found it difficult to reconcile the ideal of republican equality with the provision of services to a newly moneyed elite. A resort community ethos evolved whereby locals viewed service to intrusive vacationers as a burden to be tolerated but never enjoyed. Strangers and hosts began to commodify each other as objects, feeling free to act in the self-interested terms that characterized the marketplace. The Newport cottagers' economic domination translated into social distance rather than gregariousness; they referred to residents as "our footstools" or "our dear villagers" in the same way that medieval lords and pilgrims had typically held the locals in contempt. Summer visitors enhanced their status by constructing elaborate taboos against contact with members of the lower economic classes on privileged ground such as Bellevue Avenue or Ocean Drive. In response, many local merchants maintained a separate price scale for cottagers and saw little harm in charging wealthy visitors prohibitive prices. Consuelo Vanderbilt recalled a shopkeeper immediately adding 50 percent to the bill when the servant gave her address as "the Marble House."[54]

This is not to say there was not an occasionally overt conflict over certain issues, such as who would pay for the watering of the streets. A particularly contentious debate developed over trolley lines; year-round residents and a swelling tide of day-trippers wanted a trolley to replace the summer omnibuses that ran from the harbor to Easton's Beach. The summer colony, however, looked askance on the idea of a street railway crossing Bellevue Avenue or running on Bath Road, where it would terrorize horses and interfere with their coaching. Summer cottagers threatened to boycott local stores if the line went in, and a group calling itself the Newport Improvement Society spent large sums trying to secure an injunction against the road. In this case, the majority won out; in the summer of 1889, the first electric trolley carried passengers crosstown from Commercial Wharf to the beach for a nickel. A similar debate ensued over automobiles. Notwithstanding the Newport summer colony's infatuation with the horseless carriage, the cottagers successfully kept Bellevue Avenue an unpaved haven for carriages until a referendum in the 1920s replaced the dirt with hardtop.[55]

The cottagers more successfully prevented the establishment of a sporting culture or the resurrection of the grand hotel industry. Newport cottagers occasionally gambled, but Richard Canfield's Nautilus Club (1897–1904), located on Bath Road near Bellevue Avenue, barely turned a profit and never remotely rivaled its Saratoga cousin. No new hotel was ever built on the cliffs or near the ocean, according to insider Elizabeth Lehr, because "the elite of Newport despised such plebeian buildings. Whenever one threatened to make its appearance the kings of the trade, jealous of their privacy, banded together and nipped the project in the bud by buying out the interlopers." The fashionable colony looked with favor only upon hotels patronized by commercial travelers and representatives of the New York shops, such as the discreet little hotel owned by the Muenchingers at 32 Bellevue Avenue or the larger Perry House and Aquidneck House. Maud Elliott simply concluded that in Newport, "hotels are taboo."[56]

The old Ocean House, increasingly tawdry amid Richard Hunt's assemblage of Beaux Arts taste, responded to the transformation of Newport with changes that were merely cosmetic, at best. Management altered the address on the hotel's stationery from South Touro Street to Bellevue Avenue in hopes of garnering the prestige of the avenue, but despite the addition of some elevators and bathrooms, the Ocean House had become a Newport anachronism. Some held fast to the belief that Newport's cottages represented a temporary aberration and society would eventually "become more cosmopolitan—more like Saratoga and similar watering-places." An occasional star visitor, such as President Ulysses Grant in 1869 or Oscar Wilde in 1882, or a noteworthy ball, such as the 1875 affair in honor of the officers of the British frigate *Bellerophon*, raised hopes for a hotel revival. Some tour books vestigially declared that Ocean House hops were the most brilliant entertainments of American summer resorts, but more often, the dances received only dutiful notice, cast against the glare of the great mansions. The Ocean House survived mainly as a landmark and a reminiscence, and few were distraught when the once great caravanserai burned down in a spectacular blaze in September 1898, except that the blaze almost set fire to the Casino next door. No large hotel replaced the Ocean House in Newport until the Viking Hotel opened in 1926.[57]

Long before that point, visiting intellectuals and nostalgic locals were composing threnodies over the transformation of Newport, plaintively looking back to an era when they "did not realize that the old town was dull."

Osmond Tiffany, who emigrated from Baltimore before the Civil War, remembered "no gorgeous equipages, no liveries, no balls, no receptions, no clubs or casino, no palace cottages, no priceless tapestries, no bric-a-brac, and yet people enjoyed themselves quite as much if not more." The construction of the Newport Water Works and Hanging Rock Road in the 1880s radically altered the paradisiacal vistas that had so attracted the nation's foremost landscape artists; William Trost Richards now complained that the summer homes obscured his views. Gilded Age writers excoriated the cottagers' arrogance, vanity, and sloth, often in contrast to the lives of the "honest workingman," and used Newport mansions as a metaphor for un-American self-indulgence and incipient class conflict. Julia Howe's Town and Country Club gave up the ghost in 1905; "the old, friendly Newport gradually disappeared," she wistfully remarked, and "its exquisite social atmosphere, half rustic, half cosmopolitan, and wholly free, is no longer found."[58]

Despite the criticism, Gilded Age Newport continued to prosper. Land unsalable in the early part of the century, and commanding in 1880 "little more than the price of a Western homestead," was valued at $10,000 to $14,000 an acre in 1900. In 1893, Edith Wharton, who claimed she was "never very happy" at Newport, spent an extraordinary $80,000 for, in her own words, "an ugly wooden house with half an acre of rock." Every year added to the number of cottages and villas and to the provision made for the accommodation of visitors. Elizabeth Lehr and her husband went to Newport every summer, "for in those days so much prestige was attached to spending July and August at the most exclusive resort in America that to have neglected to do so would have exposed a definite gap in one's social armor." According to Lehr, "It was an accepted fact that only those whose position in society was unstable never went there. Let them vaunt the charm of a country holiday, of a summer spent in Europe as much as they would, they deceived no one. Their acquaintances knew they stayed away because they were afraid. For Newport was the very Holy of Holies, the playground of the great ones of the earth from which all intruders were ruthlessly excluded by a set of cast-iron rules."[59]

It was this Newport of conspicuous consumption, conspicuous leisure, and conspicuous waste that starred in Thorstein Veblen's *Theory of the Leisure Class* (1899). After pondering the significance of the mansions, Veblen concluded that competition put pressure from below on established families to express and validate their position by appropriate patterns of consumption. Material goods represented bridges to hopes and ideals; people asymptotically tried to realize fantasies through the accumulation of merchandise. Emulation replaced coercion in providing the glue that held the social structure together despite its inequalities. Veblen presciently placed no hope in the solidarity of the proletariat, whose values and potential for revolutionary activity he felt had been contaminated by the specious desires provoked by entrepreneurial marketing. Subordinate groups would emulate dominant ones as best they could, given unequal access to financial resources and free time. Certainly the evolution of resorts seemed to confirm much of Veblen's view; longtime travelers constantly complained of the increasing accessibility of watering places and the corresponding decrease in status one acquired by visiting. As early as 1807, Washington Irving had decided that "a spirit of noble emulation" drove people to resorts; Veblen simply added the theoretical props.[60]

The multimillionaires who created Newport as a bastion of American exclusivity were not exempt from the chase-and-flight dynamic. Obsessed with appearances, driven by a competitive spirit, and fearful of strangers, they erected private Newport palaces in hopes of achieving recognition. Unlike elites in a more traditional society, who do not need visible manifestations of their status because everyone already knows it, the Vanderbilts, Astors, and Belmonts lived in a country with no established class system and few national traditions or responsibilities to follow as precedents. As a consequence, they eagerly imported titles, artifacts, and styles to substitute for their own lack of rooted credentials and conventions. At Newport, they rejected hotels and desperately aped the hereditary aristocracies of Europe, hoping to bask in the reflected glory. Cultural advisors supplied Newport cottagers with the best international taste money could buy, filling European period-piece mansions with historical bric-a-brac and devising gardens with Japanese teahouses and Ottoman kiosks. This canon of expensiveness gradually affected the word *cottage* itself; the mass of lesser rural summer dwellings now came to be called "bungalows."[61]

Although the men paid the bills for Newport's conspicuous consumption, they often appeared drab and boorish in comparison with their more socially adept and cultured wives. Dronelike husbands, detained by business, often made only hurried trips on the steamers to join their families for the weekend. To escape the round of luncheons, teas, dinners, musicales, and picnics, they formed men's clubs (e.g., the Reading Room [1853], the Golf Club [1895]) or built huge yachts on which they disappeared with chorus girls. The double standard toward illicit affairs was alive and well at Newport, as long as they were conducted discreetly among the very best people, not like at Saratoga, where liaisons in hotels with bejeweled women from the demimonde were condoned. When Newport hostesses deemed extra men necessary for dances or bridge parties, they could always fill in with young officers from the War College and Torpedo Station. The novel "hen dinners," introduced in Newport about 1895, jettisoned the superfluous males altogether.[62]

Despite the shortage of men, Newport retained its antebellum reputation as a marriage bourse, though titled Europeans now replaced wealthy southerners as the quarry of choice. After the nuptials of Leonard Jerome's daughter Jennie and Lord Randolph Churchill in 1874, marriage to Europeans reached epidemic proportions, capped by Consuelo Vanderbilt's marriage (later annulled) to the Duke of Marlborough in 1895. At least nine women from Newport society married peers of the British realm, most of whom they had first met at Newport summer parties. When Gertrude Vanderbilt actually married the American-born Harry Whitney at the Breakers in 1896, the band excitedly struck up the "Star-Spangled Banner" after the usual compositions by Wagner and Mendelssohn.[63]

At Newport in its most memorable years around the turn of the century, talented, shrewd, and forceful women created and sustained the complex ceremonial life of the summer world. In the city, women might have to defer to their spouses' wishes and entertain business-connected undesirables, but at summer cottages, wives dominated every activity for the season. Women had long been the driving force in watering place social activities, even though men officially ran the hotels. Now women controlled most of the resources of the vast palaces as well, sometimes handling summer budgets as high as $300,000. They battled fiercely for social supremacy, using profligate spending and theatrical gestures for artillery in a round of endless festivities.[64]

Newport summer life in the Gilded Age gave the lie to Alexis de Tocqueville's prediction that an American aristocracy would "scarcely ever enjoy leisure as secure or complete" as its European counterpart. To be run in the grand style, the new cottages required even more service personnel than the older antebellum hotels. Already in 1866, Mrs. George Templeton Strong returned from a Newport visit vowing not to be envious of Mrs. Paran Stevens' fourteen servants. But the Belmonts hired sixteen house servants and ten yardmen for their mansion; the Marble House trumped them with nine French chefs, while the Breakers had accommodations for at least a dozen grooms. After Pierre Lorillard introduced livery in 1866, Newport cottagers attempted to acquire status confirmation through the presence of costumed servants of European descent. Black servants became déclassé at Newport, although they still dominated the service of the Fall River Line. The foreign born outnumbered native African Americans ten to one in Gilded Age Newport, each nationality specializing in a servile task for which they were reputedly especially well suited: the steady English butler, the skilled French chef, the difficult if indispensable Irish maid.[65]

The underlying competition between wealthy visitors lent a playful air to the resort, and Maud Elliott justifiably awarded Newport the appellation, "the cradle of American sports." One by one, European pastimes such as cricket, tennis, golf, foxhunting, polo, and yachting migrated to Newport social clubs and then proliferated throughout the United States to varying degrees. Newport's industrial capitalists did not object to sports per se, but they strove to isolate themselves from the popular games of the day and establish an aura of privilege in their favorite diversions. The arrival of the New York Yacht Club's annual regatta in 1883, and the addition of Newport as an official stop on the club's tour in 1890, confirmed Newport's status as the center of American yachting, featured even in children's board games. Newport held its first international polo match in 1886, and the Newport Country Club hosted the first National Open Golf Championship Tournament in 1894 (figure 52). These sports not only provided a degree of excitement and an element of chance to an increasingly routine life but also necessitated a large investment of capital and time.[66]

The city's relationship with tennis best personified the incessant drive to manufacture status out of leisure. Cottagers adopted tennis as a fashionable pastime in 1875, shortly after its laws had been codified in England. Dick Sears, from a reputable Boston family, won the first United States National Lawn Tennis singles championship at the Newport Casino in 1881 and repeated the feat for the next five years. Wealthy Newport visitors used the concept of amateurism in tennis to establish social distance, for the non-professional players initially belonged to the same class as the spectators. In the 1890s, Newport's tournament served as the de facto national champion-

Figure 52. Newport Country Club, 1908. The club hosted the first National Championship Golf Tournament in 1894, but Newport's athletic amusements tended to promote style as much as sport. The city's sports competitions might be national, but the scene was one of private privilege. (Courtesy of the Newport Historical Society.)

ship and attracted fanatical patronage from the cottage set. Support for tennis and golf stood as a visible rebuke to Saratoga's preoccupations with hosting business conventions and wagering on cards and horses. By the time the National Tennis Championship moved to New York in 1915, however, professionals had supplanted amateurs. The taint of money, as well as the competitive failure of the amateurs, meant the experience no longer mattered to Newport's elite.[67]

While men made Newport synonymous with polo, tennis, and yachting, their wives and sisters did not gather dust. It had not been long since Lydia Child, in *The Mother's Book*, had cautioned young women that skating and sliding should not take place in mixed company, but resorts helped break down these reputed canons of propriety. Female cottagers at Newport often presented themselves as self-assured, vigorous, and desirous of personal pleasure and self-expression. Women took advantage of the partial escape from mundane rules and expectations to bowl, swim, and roller-skate, to play croquet and badminton, and to shoot on the archery range. In the 1880s, some began to wear bloomer outfits and compete aggressively at tennis at the Casino; one wealthy resident claimed that both men and women at Newport virtually made a fetish out of physical exercise. This adoption by Newport women of greater physical activity helped popularize the women's fitness movement.[68]

Once a leisure class hierarchy had been consolidated, wealthy Newport visitors dropped much of the pretext of formality and again behaved in anarchical ways, although this time in a private setting. Under the energetic leadership of Alva Vanderbilt Belmont, Mamie Fish, and Tessie Oelrichs, Newport society demolished the impeccable public dignity of Ward McAllister's Four Hundred and achieved its most brilliant period from 1890 to 1914. This devil-may-care triumvirate utilized sarcasm, mimicry, and elaborate practical jokes to parody the entertainments of stuffier peers and engage in extravagant self-mockery. Their absurd prodigality became a staple of mass circulation newspapers, such as Newport's "dog dinner," at which the guests' canine companions dined on paté and chicken, or another dinner in which a fish-filled stream flowed languorously down the center of the table. Mrs. Fish once assembled a throng on the pretext of meeting a Spanish nobleman and brought in a monkey instead; on another occasion she had her male accomplice impersonate the czar of Russia. Private masquerade exhibitions such as the Servants' Ball, the Mother Goose Ball, and the Harvest Dance (in which millionaires dressed as French peasants) seemed to represent the apex of inbred self-deprecating decadence before World War I. These exclusive parties began to resemble the lavish Indian ritual of the potlatch, at which some tribes distributed or even destroyed goods on a grand scale to demonstrate the extent of their wealth. At both Newport dinners and potlatch ceremonies, mutual relations and obligations were expressed in haughty challenges of personal esteem and dramatic contests of conspicuous waste.[69]

The trends initiated in Newport at the turn of the century—conspicuous consumption, marriage with titled Europeans, lionization of athletes—made the city a transitional order between the haute monde of the Gilded Age and the twentieth-century cult of personality and spectacle. For example, Alva Vanderbilt Belmont, the first society woman to get divorced, played an active role in the woman suffrage movement. As a hostess, she limited the time spent dining, dispensed with the practice of separating men and women after dinner, and invited actors and actresses to her parties. When she replaced the graceful society ball with "coon breakdowns"—dancing parties with black bands playing ragtime where couples danced lasciviously—her action bestowed the official imprimatur of the ruling cultural powers of the time. Aspiring Americans gleefully emulated Newport cottagers, whether their fashion sense or their grassy front lawns. The latter, inspired by the prestige of the grandiose Newport mansions, typified this process. Carefully cropped lawns, in the absence of grazing sheep, required considerable expense, time, and labor to keep up and thus projected luxury, power, and distance for middle-class suburbanites.[70]

By 1900, Gilded Age Newport had completed the transition from an antebellum resort centered around hotels to a schizoid world of day-tripping factory workers who shared the city with august millionaires living in private mansions. The elite Newporters defended social station and privilege but also tried to develop their own sense of fellowship vaguely reminiscent of the old hotel-oriented first resorts. "The plutocrats have gradually more and more given up trying to pretend that they liked equality, and the give-and-take of democratic hotel life," concluded the *Newport Mercury* in 1889. Instead, they "have drawn off into their cottages—villas they call them now—and taken a good deal of satisfaction in the reserve and withdrawal from the vulgar herd of resorters." Newport's cottagers succeeded in isolating them-selves from the universe of strangers. Their retreat into a private world, without the social interaction created by the common verandas, dining rooms, parlors, and urban spaces that defined antebellum resorts, repre-sented one of the cutting-edge trends of twentieth-century leisure culture.[71]

≈ SEVEN ≋

"That Was Coney As We Loved It, and As the Hand of Satan Was upon It"

IN 1895, CAPTAIN PAUL BOYTON conceived of what might be considered the first true amusement park. Boyton, who had acquired an international reputation performing publicity stunts in a lifesaving buoyant rubber suit, opened his large water circus, Sea Lion Park, directly behind the Elephant Hotel at Coney Island. The concept quickly drew imitations. George Tilyou's Steeplechase Park, featuring a Ferris wheel festooned with incandescent lights and a horse-racing ride that capitalized on Coney's reputation as a racing center, began collecting admissions in 1897. In 1903, Frederic Thompson and Elmer Dundy opened Luna Park, with its stellar attraction, a ride called A Trip to the Moon. Dreamland appeared the following year, complete with white faux–Beaux Arts buildings and a 375-foot central tower, accompanied by a charming waltz to commemorate its opening. These amusement park owners invested heavily in land, buildings, and machinery, which gave them unprecedented control over the content and style of leisure within the park.[1]

These amusement parks captured the popular imagination and are now considered quintessential Coney Island, but the more vivacious, spontaneous, and unique aspects of Coney's history occurred decades earlier. Under the leadership of political boss John McKane, Gilded Age Coney Island offered a safe environment and attracted enormous and heterogeneous crowds of six million visitors a season as early as 1880. There was something for "all the world" at Coney: racetracks for the sporting crowd, the attractions of the beach for families, concerts for the artistically inclined, music and dance halls for those in search of romance or drink, mechanical rides to get the blood racing, and extravagant spectacles to eradicate ennui. It was the Gilded Age entrepreneurs at Coney who constructed the infrastructure, imaginatively experimented with commercialized leisure and technological novelty, and promoted the carnival-like experience in a resort setting.

No matter how much the popular press stressed the uniqueness of Steeplechase, Luna Park, and Dreamland, they clearly borrowed heavily from the nineteenth-century's see-and-be-seen public culture. The uniqueness of the Progressive Era amusement parks lay not in their ambience of license but in their very movement in the opposite direction. By installing fences and maintaining private police forces to patrol the grounds, the parks restricted access and replaced the anarchy outside the gates with an ordered environment conducive to profit making. For all their vitality, Coney Island's amusement parks represented not the rise of a new urban culture but rather its transformation under the impact of commercial values and a consumerist ethos.[2]

Horse racing, by combining spectacle with money, served as the perfect bridge between the older, communal entertainments and the more modern commercial ones; not surprisingly, three prominent racetracks opened on Coney Island in the 1880s, virtually within walking distance of one another. John Morrissey's success at Saratoga had inspired a revival of American thoroughbred racing, and a flood of new racetracks such as Jerome Park in Westchester, New York (1866), Long Branch, New Jersey (1869), Pimlico in Baltimore (1870), and the Fair Grounds in New Orleans (1873) arose to compete with the track at the Springs. At Coney Island, the enterprising William Engeman established the first racetrack at Brighton Beach in 1879. The curiosity of afternoon crowds at the seashore, combined with the novelty of multiple races and the sponsorship of the large hotels and railroads, made the institution a great success (figure 53).[3]

Encouraged by the popularity of horse racing at Brighton Beach, a group headed by Leonard Jerome, August Belmont, William K. Vanderbilt, William Travers, and Pierre Lorillard Jr. incorporated the more prestigious Coney Island Jockey Club (CIJC). The CIJC opened the Sheepshead Bay Racecourse on Ocean Avenue (less than a mile from the Manhattan Beach Hotel), complete with a grandstand seating five thousand, for a six-day meet in June 1880. The group plowed the profits back into the track, extending it

Figure 53. Brighton Beach Grandstands, 1905. Although the Brighton Beach facility could not compare with the Coney Island Jockey Club's ornate grandstand or judges' stand, the crowds here indicate that William Engeman's track possessed its own unique ambience that made it equally profitable. (Courtesy of the Keeneland Association Library [Keeneland-Cook 2250 (KL09307401)].)

to a mile and a furlong in 1884, adding a turf course in 1886, and carefully landscaping the grounds until critics rated the Sheepshead Bay racecourse as the most picturesque in America (figure 54). By the 1890s, the CIJC awarded $500,000 annually in purses; the Suburban, the Futurity, and the Realization Stakes became classics of American racing before the Kentucky Derby won national renown. The inaugural Futurity offered a $40,000 purse, which increased to $49,500 in 1893; in contrast, the Kentucky Derby purse did not even reach five figures until 1915. Sheepshead Bay real estate boomed, as speculators bought old farms by the water and brought in suburbanites grown familiar with the area because of the racetrack.[4]

The third Coney Island horse-racing venue was the inspiration of the Dwyer brothers, noted stable owners and plungers who had made their

Figure 54. Louis Maurer's painting *The First Futurity* (1888), at the Coney Island Jockey Club. The race paid an unheard of $40,900 purse; Proctor Knott held off Salvator, both ridden by African American jockeys. (Courtesy of the National Racing Museum.)

fortune as butchers. They bought the old trotting track on Gravesend (now McDonald) Avenue, erected a grandstand that held eight thousand spectators, and organized the Brooklyn Jockey Club in 1885. The Brooklyn Jockey Club prospered from the start; its property was small and inexpensive, its patronage heavy, and it paid dividends that soon made its stock impossible to acquire. Coney's visitors could now gamble on horses virtually every day in the summer, and with its trio of racetracks, Coney Island replaced Saratoga as the center of American thoroughbred racing until the New York State legislature criminalized bookmaking in 1908.[5]

The tracks at Gilded Age Coney Island pioneered significant alterations that were harbingers of a more commercial approach to leisure time. Until 1870, owners bred and trained horses to run distances of three or four miles several times an afternoon, distinctly limiting the possibilities for wagering. Coney's tracks led the way in discarding these match races in favor of sprints of less than a mile and a half. Shorter races meant younger horses did not wear out as quickly, and more races could be run daily—Brighton Beach proudly announced on its program, "five or more races each day." In response to widespread wagering on the Hayes-Tilden election, New York had banned the auction pool, but the "invention" of bookmaking enabled Coney's tracks to flourish even after the 1877 prohibition. Many bettors were not rich; petty entrepreneurs ran open book at twenty-five cents, and for some, a two-dollar bet constituted plunging. Nonetheless, an investigatory committee estimated that punters wagered more than $10 million each summer at Coney Island. Witnesses counted twenty-five gambling booths on the grounds of the CIJC in 1883, thirty in 1884, forty-five in 1885, and sixty in 1886. The *New York Herald* estimated that on a good day at the Sheepshead Bay track, more than $400,000 was wagered; promenading seemed very tame by comparison.[6]

Coney's racetracks retained an aura of preindustrial class mixing; they were places where the elite participated in, or at least passively acquiesced to, the recreational lives of common people. At almost no other venue, except perhaps at the brothel, did rich and poor intermingle so closely, and this quality made them a natural fit at the nineteenth-century resort. Unmarried and working-class men cavorted at Coney Island with a hedonistic fringe of the upper class in a subculture inimical to most dominant social mores. Even women joined in; a Chicago reporter visiting a Coney track in the 1880s could "hardly find a woman on the grand stand who is not openly and often excitedly risking her money."[7]

Boxing matches at Coney Island also drew a heterogeneous crowd to cheer and gamble. The State of New York technically banned the primal sport of prizefighting, but in this magical realm, the police rarely enforced the letter of the law. West Brighton occasionally hosted boxing matches in the late 1880s, but the resort came into its own as a prizefighting mecca with the organization of the Coney Island Athletic Club in 1892. The club featured sixteen fights in its first fifteen months of operation and generated a net profit of more than $100,000, not counting the money that changed hands on the side. Over the next few years, the Coney Island Athletic Club sponsored many American championship bouts in a cavernous arena with a seating capacity of ten thousand. Most famous was the twenty-five-round brouhaha between heavyweight champion Jim Jeffries and challenger Tom Sharkey in 1899, the first fight ever filmed. Shown in vaudeville theaters around the country within a week after the fight, the film projected Coney's image as a place apart to a national audience.[8]

The presence of the sporting life at Coney provided seasonal employment for many workers, beginning with the African American and Irish jockeys who dominated the island's famous races. Further down the pecking order, stable hands, farriers, blacksmiths, wheelwrights, and liquor dealers all thrived at the resort. African Americans, who at the time represented less than 2 percent of the population in Brooklyn and Manhattan, made up 8 percent of Gravesend's year-round population. Of the forty-five people, all males, residing at the Brighton Beach Racing Association in 1880, twenty-seven were black. Other workers lived in the huddle of wooden shanties in "the Gut," a ten-block area roughly between West First and West Fifth Streets. The *Brooklyn Union* identified the residents of this area as about half laundry women and racecourse helpers "and the rest German and Hebrew storekeepers, waiters and other boarders." Although some newspapers claimed the horrors of the Gut were vastly overrated, its shanties did offer a variety of entertainment ruses to lure visitors to saloons, gambling dens, and brothels. "There is scarcely any variety of human flotsam and jetsam," reported one visitor of Gravesend, "that is not represented in its permanent population." Both the federal census of 1870 and the state census of 1875 counted fewer than 2,200 residents of Gravesend, but the 1890 census enumerated 6,937 residents, an increase of 226 percent. Even Newport and Saratoga, with increases of 55 and 59 percent, respectively, could not match this pace.[9]

As at Saratoga, the protection of politicians exempted Coney's gray enterprises from the rigorous enforcement of Gilded Age penal codes. The town's judges, policemen (never more than thirty), and populace rarely showed any inclination to interfere with what they viewed as victimless "crimes." Local law enforcement agents either accepted bribes or acknowledged the futility of harassment, because gamblers, brothel owners, and Sunday businessmen usually practiced their trade with impunity, sometimes operating within shouting distance of police headquarters and the town hall. After one rare crackdown, a Republican district attorney in Kings County failed to obtain a single conviction out of fifty-seven indictments for gambling, and his Democratic successor intentionally shielded violators of the laws. Even token raids horrified small business owners who depended on visitors. After a raid in 1885, sixty-four West Brighton merchants signed a resolution imploring Gravesend authorities to allow gambling "as a means of livelihood and of amusement to thousands of outsiders." When Anthony

Comstock and forty-one special deputies raided Coney Island, a scornful crowd followed the officials and loudly jeered when nothing related to wagering could be found at any racetrack.[10]

Gravesend's much-maligned law enforcement was controlled by John Y. McKane, who for fifteen years held numerous positions simultaneously in the booming resort town and appointed many of the remaining members of the town boards. As health commissioner, McKane could decide on a certain policy, as chairman of the town board he could order it implemented, as chief contractor of the town he might profit from the construction, as chief of police he prevented any interference with his work, as town auditor he approved his own invoices, and as chairman pro tem of the Kings County Board of Supervisors he carefully paid those bills in full. No wonder McKane served as a lightning rod for both Gravesend's successes and its failures.[11]

Like Saratoga's John Morrissey, McKane had emigrated from Ireland, with his parents, as a child. McKane began his rise to one-man government as a carpenter in Gravesend, where by 1875, 18 percent of the residential population were Irish born. He parlayed his reputation for honest work and a private life above reproach into election as constable in 1867 and then a seven-year term as one of the three commissioners of common lands, reputedly the first non-Gravesend native ever elected to the post. He willingly worked with railroad magnates Austin Corbin and Andrew Culver but refused simply to lie down before their various development schemes, insisting that the local railroad and the hotel corporations should pay their fair share of taxes. As a town resident who had married a local girl, McKane enjoyed a reputation in Gravesend as a fighter for community interests.[12]

McKane derived his power from his influence over the ballot box and the real estate lease. As the supervisor who signed every municipal land transaction, McKane controlled much of the island's undivided land, some of it in huge lots three hundred feet wide and stretching almost two thousand feet from the Atlantic Ocean to Coney Island Creek. He gained business for his contracting firm in the 1870s by leasing land to friends at bargain prices: sixteen shorefront acres to Charles Feltman for $25 a year, two lots adjoining the railroad depot to Charles Gunther for $25 a year, and two lots adjacent to the horsecar terminal to William Vanderveer for $64 a year. Even so, the rental income from the common land paid to Gravesend continued to increase: from $728 in 1868 to $9,000 in 1873 and more than $17,500 in 1878.

If the subleases are taken into account, however, the land's value probably exceeded $200,000. A New York state senate investigation exposed considerable fraud in the management of the common lands, but McKane simply sold them in 1884 to their former leaseholders at discount prices.[13]

In 1887, Assemblyman Alexander Bacon launched a full-scale state investigation into corruption in Kings County and especially Gravesend. More than half of the twenty-three hundred pages of testimony concerned pool selling, gambling dens, and brothels in Coney Island and the public officials who protected them. The Bacon Committee recommended McKane's indictment as well as Gravesend's immediate incorporation into the City of Brooklyn, yet the succeeding grand jury took no action at all. Many residents (as well as the Democratic Party of New York) wrote the entire investigation off as a political vendetta, and McKane continued to wield power in an independent Gravesend.[14]

McKane's election day shenanigans also supported the idea that Coney Island was a world unto itself. In 1884, McKane endorsed the victorious Grover Cleveland for the presidency, and Gravesend voted Democratic by a margin of three to one. After quarreling with Hugh McLaughlin, Brooklyn's Democratic leader, McKane exacted his revenge by ensuring Benjamin Harrison a stunning majority against Cleveland in 1888. A happy McKane told the press, "I don't believe there is another community in the United States where a Democratic majority of 900 could be turned into a Republican vote of 800, as has been done in Gravesend, and as I honestly believe for my sake." When a court decision ruled that Gravesend's voters must vote in their precincts instead of going to the town hall, where the "monarch of the sands" supervised the election, McKane redrew the districts into six pie-shaped areas, with the town hall at the center. By cutting six doorways into the hall, his oversight of voters remained unchanged. Gravesend experienced the same electoral irregularities as most of urban America in the Gilded Age, but the scale seemed more dramatic. In 1893, the town registered more than six thousand voters out of a total resident population of only eight thousand.[15]

The McKane era ended that very year, when William Gaynor, running for the New York Supreme Court, twice attempted to copy the Gravesend registration lists to no avail. On election day, when a group of locals headed by McKane himself met good-government proponents armed with injunctions, he supposedly informed them that "injunctions don't go down here."

A tussle ensued, and McKane audaciously arrested Alexander Bacon on a charge of disorderly conduct. This time McKane had gone too far, and a Kings County grand jury indicted him, along with four Gravesend justices and eighteen police inspectors. In the notorious trial that followed, a jury deliberated only twenty hours before assessing McKane six years at hard labor. He was released, a broken man, in 1898 and died the next year.[16]

Under McKane's rule, however, Coney Island had moved to the forefront of American seaside resorts. He had facilitated its growth and prevented the privatization of the beach by sponsoring leaseholders who generally subdivided the land. When visitors arrived, they consequently found dozens of inexpensive amusements crowding the island, each owned as a private concession. If this system often led to the construction of ephemeral buildings of limited architectural pretension, it also produced intense competition, low prices, and novel entertainments. McKane's town government excelled in delivering basic services such as water and electricity to residents and businesses. For example, until the 1870s, Coney Island had dumped its sewage directly into the Atlantic Ocean or Sheepshead Bay without any regard for tide or bathers, littering the beach with old mattresses, decayed vegetables, and deceased animals. McKane instigated the construction of an up-to-date separation system that was the envy of other resorts; a Saratoga Springs committee journeyed downstate in 1884, specifically to view the sewage system, in search of solutions to their own disposal problems. Even Brooklyn mayor Charles Schieren conceded that McKane did deliver essential services to his constituents.[17]

The criticism of McKane's rule in the metropolitan press was often politically motivated or focused on issues barely tantamount to crimes by prevailing contemporary definitions: horse racing, three-card monte, and violations of Sunday closing laws. The last, in particular, embroiled Coney Island's merchants in a long war of attrition with proponents of Sabbatarianism. The island offered enticements that made it a logical destination in which to release the tensions created by the stress of weekly toil; as early as 1877 the *New York Times* claimed Coney was "an argument against a too strict Sabbatarianism." By the 1880s, one visitor to Manhattan Beach complained that sermons could not be heard over the ringing of beer glasses and the noises of shouting, dancing, laughing, playing, and love making. Religion and recreation, once closely integrated, competed at Coney not only for time but over values and clientele. Sabbath observance at Coney decreased throughout the Gilded Age, as the desire to maximize profits subverted the blue laws. The question of the propriety of doing business on Sunday periodically convulsed the island well into the twentieth century, but clearly secular amusements had put religious observance on the defensive.[18]

Prostitution at Coney also seemed a natural adjunct to the relative exemption of the resort from everyday rules. The presence of numerous bordellos and the easy availability of prostitutes revealed an unofficial acceptance of meretricious social behavior in the Gilded Age, and the preponderance of sex-for-money venues made Coney Island one of the carnal showcases of the country. "Men went to the seaside resort to be free, as they said, from the conventionalities of the city," reported one wit, "the said conventionalities being, apparently, the Ten Commandments." More than thirty concert saloons dotted the area near the beach, many of which made the bulk of their money from prostitution. When asked if Laura's Cottage, an infamous Coney bawdy house, was open for business in 1886, John McKane tactfully replied, "I do not make any inquiries." At another point, he reputedly claimed that "houses of prostitution are a necessity on Coney Island." McKane could be extremely strict with the pickpockets and counterfeiters whom he felt chased business away, but he told the Bacon Committee under oath, "I do not think it is my duty altogether to stop any people enjoying themselves that come down there in the summer season." Local juries agreed, refusing to convict proprietors for entertaining outsiders in a way that outsiders wanted to be entertained. Nineteenth-century America might be notorious for a suppression of sensuality, but as long as brothels remained spatially segregated at resorts, they failed to offend more than a few vociferous critics in the Gilded Age.[19]

Periodic outcries from reformers generated occasional farces of enforcement. When Oliver Cotter, an agent for the Society for the Prevention of Vice, went to the island on a summer Sunday, he found the bars operating at full capacity. He charged Charles Feltman, owner of the Coney Island Hotel, with keeping a disorderly house and allowing Sunday dancing and drinking; but a jury took no time in finding Feltman not guilty. Enraged, Cotter brought him up on charges less than two weeks later for selling liquor on Sunday. Again the charges did not stick, although, as the *New York Times* noted, "no effort was made by the defense to contradict the evidence offered by the prosecution that beer and whiskey were sold at Feltman's without any attempt at concealment." The Temperance Brotherhood brought charges against Feltman and twelve other violators in August, and in each case the jury found for the defendants. The newspaper reported that "several witnesses swore that they had purchased and drank lager in Feltman's house on Sunday, the 24th inst., and no testimony was offered for the defense, but notwithstanding this fact the jury brought in a verdict of not guilty."[20]

In his dependance on the easy sale of alcohol, Feltman helped popularize a commercialized version of German festival culture at Coney Island. In the 1860s, he had made a fortune by selling roasted frankfurters in small bread rolls, thereby "inventing" the hot dog. Feltman staked this money on the Ocean Pavilion, a restaurant and amusement palace with a pier that ran along West Tenth Street from Surf Avenue to the shore and with an ambience borrowed from urban beer gardens. Feltman advertised his enterprise extensively, lobbied the railroads to run late evening trains, and engaged Wannemacher's Seventy-first Regiment Band for the season, the first scheduled music performed on Coney at an eatery. His ballroom alone had room for two thousand dancers, and the restaurant could serve eight thousand people in a pleasant garden atmosphere, entertained by bands in lederhosen, Bavarian beer on tap, and a roller coaster and carousels. The Ocean Pavilion specialized in large excursion groups; a partial listing of arrangements made with Feltman for the 1883 season mentioned the Norddeutschen Bruder (2,500 tickets sold), the Brooklyn Young Butcher Guards (4,000), the German Order of Haragari (8,000), the Harmonica Mannerchor (4,000), the Scandinavian Singing Society (2,500), and Weber's Dancing Academy (3,000). The Ocean Pavilion served an average of two hundred thousand people every season in the 1880s, four hundred thousand in the 1890s, and two million from 1910 to 1920.[21]

Other Coney Island merchants relied even more heavily than Feltman on the sale of alcohol, the great lubricant of social discourse and relaxer of discipline. In 1890, a single inn claimed a seasonal rate of ten thousand kegs of lager beer (about 1.5 million glasses). The Mercantile Agency Reference Book listed forty-two hotels and saloons in 1888 in Coney Island and only eleven other businesses; in comparison, the section on Newport rated more than four hundred businesses but fewer hotels and drinking establishments. Even after the annexation of Gravesend to the City of Brooklyn in 1894, newspapers easily discovered saloons, gambling dens, and brothels (sometimes one and the same) operating with impunity. When the secretary of the Law and Order Society declared in 1897 that "Sodom was not a circumstance to the sin-debauched and crime-soaked Coney Island," Brooklyn's last mayor, Frederick Wurster, wryly replied, "If this advertising goes on, Coney Island won't be big enough to hold the crowds that want to go there."[22]

Although stories of perfidious Coney Island filled the written record of the nineteenth century, they almost always functioned as part of a rhetorical cycle that concluded with successful cleanups. "Stories of disturbances on the island have been greatly exaggerated," claimed the *New York Times* as early as 1868. The author of *Coney Island and the Jews* expressly compared the horrors of a trip in 1870 with "the peaceful and perfect pleasures of a trip to Coney Island in 1879." Another writer in 1880 recounted that "for many years, it had been a place for transient visitors, many of them of a low class. But lately it has become immensely improved." A reporter searching for crime on the notorious Norton's Point in 1870 found it "quiet and orderly." Yet several years later, an encyclopedic guidebook described Norton's Point in the 1870s as "notorious by the gamblers and blacklegs who infested the beach." Of course, the guidebook reported that now, "this has all been changed, and the beach at this point, if not attractive, is quiet and orderly." Journalists competing for a new angle on Coney Island could always find one in the rise and fall of the crime rate.[23]

During a single summer, newspapers might declare Coney Island to be one of the wickedest spots on earth and also as a model for proper behavior. In 1875, the *New York Times* complained about "the misconduct of the rowdy and the rough" but later that same season informed the public that the island was "rapidly losing the character for rowdyism which brought it into disrepute. A walk last Sunday a distance of more than two miles did not reveal a single instance of noisiness or drunkenness." The *Brooklyn Eagle,* usually staunchly anti-McKane, admitted in 1892 that "the island is cleaner now than it ever was before, morally and physically." In fact, serious offenses such as robbery or murder seem to have been no more common on the Coney Island shore than anywhere else in New York.[24]

Despite the best efforts of Coney's boosters, the upper-class patronage gradually deserted the island or vanished soundlessly beneath a flood of day-tripping workers. While the sojourners at the large hotels might occasionally go slumming at West Brighton, social mixing at the seaside inevitably implied, if not class conflict, at least the consciousness that other classes existed. This could make wealthy people very uncomfortable, as the Newport experience had demonstrated. At Rockaway Beach in the 1890s, William Dean Howells remarked that the thousands of excursionists made him uneasy, although they were an "entirely peaceable multitude." Members of the Four Hundred ran the Coney Island Jockey Club, but they rarely stayed at the island's grand hotels. According to the *Chicago Herald,* the Oriental housed "the same variety of people to be found at Saratoga or Long Branch caravanserais, where the sporting element is strong, and folks with sensitive fastidiousness are constantly shocked by touching elbows with human miscellany."[25]

The mass of visitors to Coney Island were urbanites who worked in factories, shops, and offices for six days and some nights a week and then went to the seashore to take the boisterous pleasures that eased the strain of work and confinement. Union organizers attempted to utilize Coney's popularity, but the trade unionists discovered time and again that their most prominent speakers could not match the island's seductive counterattractions. Among the multitude attending a "monster labor demonstration" at the Sea Beach Palace in 1885, one labor reporter discovered workers

> exploring the interior of the wooden elephant; some sitting by the "sad sea waves"; some on hobby horses; some enjoying the racket of the downhill railroad near the speaker's stand; some meditating on the strains of the hurdy-gurdy; some devouring hard-shell raw or soft-shell fried in fat; some taking their chances, ten cents a chance; some consoling their weeping babes; some flirting with their perspiring sweethearts . . . but all anxious to dodge the orators who were no less anxious to uncork their elocution. The managers made some desperate efforts for two hours to force some of the picnickers upon the benches that fronted the speaker's stand . . . but the down grade cars and the rival showmen were too much for him.

"If the working man would only show half the interest in the bread and butter question that he showed in the recent slugging battle at Coney Island," complained the *International Woodworker* in 1899, "he would be doing something to benefit himself and those dependent on him."[26]

But workers were showing an interest in the bread and butter question; their very presence at Coney Island reflected the fact that Americans worked fewer hours as the nineteenth century wore on, yet they also had more money to spend. Despite periodic financial panics, real income generally rose after 1860 while mass production forced prices down. A hypothetical national consumer price index (1860 = 100) declined from 157 in 1870 to 123 in 1880, 109 in 1890, and 101 in 1900. At the same time, annual wages rose in Brooklyn from $473 in 1880 to $605 in 1890 (an increase of 28 percent) and in New York from $427 in 1880 to $653 in 1890 (an increase of 53 percent). A two-dollar day at Coney Island (or a fifteen-dollar week at Saratoga) now seemed feasible to many, although whether it constituted an acceptable "expenditure" of time to labor organizers remained an open question.[27]

In theory, a trip to Coney Island did not necessarily integrate the visitor into the capitalist economy in a significant way. Like other resorts, Coney offered many entertainment options of a public character that did not necessarily cost money: bathing in the ocean, promenading on piers, gazing at views, and collecting seashells and driftwood. In the prehistoric days of 1868, the *New York Times* advised readers that they might "enjoy themselves plentifully, and come away with . . . as much money as they landed with, after deducting the price of a bathing-dress and a dish of baked clams." A later guidebook from 1880 informed readers, "You may, if you please, go to Coney Island and spend the day, and enjoy yourself hugely, without expending one more cent than is required to pay your fares to and from the beach." In 1891, *Harper's Weekly* could still report that "West Brighton is the haunt of song and dance, trapeze acting and juggling. . . . They all appeal to the great American public because they are *free*."[28]

This worldview made no sense to American business owners, who advocated spending money as a republican ideal and associated democracy with the collection of goods and experiences. A profusion of periodical articles, advertisements, and guidebooks popularized leisure travel for the masses, promoting its acquisition as an easily purchasable commodity. On one of the first electric billboards on Manhattan's Broadway, towering fifty feet high and eighteen feet wide, fifteen hundred multicolored lights blared Coney Island's attractions:

SWEPT BY OCEAN BREEZES

THE GREAT HOTELS

PAIN'S FIREWORKS

SOUSA'S BAND

SEIDL'S GREAT ORCHESTRA

THE RACES

NOW—MANHATTAN BEACH—NOW

For a young Theodore Dreiser, "this sign was an inspiration and an invitation. . . . It lifted Manhattan Beach into rivalry with fairyland."[29]

Although acquisitive consumption always existed, objects such as toys, novels, fashionable clothes, and leisure travel had for centuries been the possessions of a privileged elite. For eighteenth-century moralists, the very attractiveness of luxury caused it to be regarded in a negative light. But over the course of the nineteenth century, a "luxury" was transformed into a desirable object that, although unnecessary, did not merit condemnation on those grounds alone. A flood of factory-produced goods featured in popular literature, shopping areas, and grand hotels eroded the classical republican hostility toward private acquisitive behavior. For the lower socioeconomic classes, a Sunday excursion at Coney substituted for a trip to Saratoga or Newport. At the shore, workers avidly adopted the lifestyle of leisure travelers who defined personhood partially through the consumption of commodities and experiences.[30]

Gilded Age Coney Island served as a main point at which this consumer ethos reached the masses. Purchasable souvenirs such as racetrack programs, view books, embossed ashtrays, and scenic lithographs were omnipresent at Coney. George Tilyou, the island's greatest booster, inaugurated his career selling "genuine" bottled ocean water to tourists. Even the Oriental Hotel, that supposed bastion of exclusivity, mass-produced a children's souvenir alphabet plate. "Every inch of this part of the island," bragged one resident in 1883, "is rented to adventurers in commercial life of one kind or another." Department stores advertised in programs for the Brighton Beach Music Hall, beckoning women to buy summer dresses and bathing suits. Huge painted messages on the sails of "wretched advertising boats" implored promenaders to visit this or that store and buy, buy, buy. Even the Elephant Hotel, according to *Scientific American*, served primarily as a money-making venture to abstract "the unwary dime from the inquisitive sightseer." By purchasing souvenirs, day-trippers could then relive the trip vicariously at home just as if they had traveled to an overnight resort.[31]

For example, Milton Bradley created a game in 1881, entitled *A Wonderful Account of an Excursion to Coney Island*, to appeal "to those who are familiar with the beauties and fairy-like attractions of this metropolitan seaside resort." The game consisted of a large number of words and phrases on scraps of paper and a booklet with a story missing many key words. One player read the story while the others pulled words from the facedown pile to fit the blank spaces in hopes of generating laughable combinations. For the game to make sense for a mass market, the story had to present a stereotypical experience common to most visitors. In this case, the game told the tale of six tourists to New York City who visited Coney Island and began to purchase souvenirs and amusements from the moment they landed on the Iron Pier. Players understood, either consciously or unconsciously, that Americans visited Coney to buy material goods or to spend money to do things and that the entire experience could be reduced to cash exchange, that is, it could be commodified.[32]

As at Saratoga, travelers who had once collected specimens now purchased souvenirs and sent postcards. The latter, direct descendants of stereographic pictures, first appeared at the beach resort of Atlantic City in 1895. When the government reduced the postcard fee from two cents to a penny in 1898, people sent and collected postcards in overwhelming numbers; Americans bought 700 million postcards in 1906 and almost 1 billion in 1913. Travelers instinctively sent postcards from vacation destinations as a matter of ritual; visitors mailed an amazing two hundred thousand cards from Coney on a single day in 1906. The sacred charisma of the resort could now be purchased and sent through the mail not only to communicate but also to impress.[33]

Nor were postcards, souvenirs, or advertisements the only examples of infiltration of consumerism at the resort. Coney Island's Bowery, like its namesake in Manhattan, also offered a hurly-burly commercial ambience that from its inception appealed to vast crowds. The street owed its existence to Peter Tilyou and his son George, who in 1882 built Coney's first top-name vaudeville-style theater. They facilitated access by cutting an alley parallel to Surf Avenue but closer to the ocean front. Anyone walking from the avenue to the beach had to cross this newly planked Bowery, which immediately filled with barkers promoting cheap amusements, animal acts, freak shows, shooting galleries, small bathing pavilions, food stands, alfresco restaurants, and magic acts (one featuring a young Harry Houdini). For those without the money or time to vacation up the Hudson, a day on Coney Island's Bowery mimicked, albeit in a less disciplined way, the strange and irrepressible gaiety of Saratoga's Broadway (figure 55).[34]

Few claimed to experience ennui at Gilded Age Coney Island—at least not on their first visit. Manhattan and Brooklyn residents who went to Coney Island for relaxation on a Sunday reputedly needed something to

Figure 55. "The Bowery, Coney Island," 1903. The Bowery, uncrowded at midday, presented a multiplicity of things to see and buy. The Trocadero, here showing movies of the notorious Jeffries-Fitzsimmons fight, was the site of one of the first moving picture exhibitions in America in 1893. (Courtesy of the Brian Merlis Collection.)

quiet their nerves on Monday. The frenetic pace accelerated in the 1890s with the creation of even larger mass entertainment venues. The Manhattan Beach Hotel erected a two-thousand-seat theater in 1894 and a twelve-thousand-seat bicycle oval in 1895 and enlarged the fireworks arena to hold ten thousand people, while the Brighton Beach Hotel opened an eighteen-hundred-seat music hall in 1897. Entertainers at Coney performed as frequently as in an urban vaudeville show, and visitors could pay to amuse themselves around the clock. An exhausting itinerary, entitled "How to See

Coney Island in One Day," in *Percy's Pocket Dictionary of Coney Island* projected an expenditure of four dollars per person and virtually had its readers sprinting from one attraction to another.[35]

Commercialization also transformed the role of music. In the 1870s, marches, operatic medleys, patriotic airs, and other favorite songs of the day had been ubiquitous at Coney. The *New York Times* correspondent grew so sick of the clangor that he suggested that Coney's numerous regimental bands should play on rotating stands and be turned out to sea when their music became disagreeable. Gradually, entrepreneurs began to present music as a specific activity for spectators to pay for and consume. Coney led the way in developing the cult of American celebrity conductors after the Civil War, attracting (and creating) the biggest names in the business. The Manhattan Beach Hotel featured Patrick Gilmore, the most popular conductor of his time, from 1879 until his death in 1892. The hotel then hired the high-spirited John Philip Sousa and his Marine Band; "El Capitan" and several other Sousa marches saw their premieres at Coney, and he dedicated his "Manhattan Beach March" to Austin Corbin. Corbin lured Jules Levy, the dashing coronet virtuoso, from the Brighton Beach and made him a star by raising his salary from $350 to an unheard-of $750 a week and then widely publicizing the fact.[36]

Scrambling to catch up, the Brighton Beach built its own music pavilion and hired Anton Seidl, America's foremost disciple of the German composer Richard Wagner. Beginning in 1888, Seidl, assisted by Victor Herbert, conducted two concerts daily in the summer and regularly filled the three-thousand-seat pavilion (figure 56). As late as 1915, a crotchety James Huneker rhapsodized over memories of 1888, when "the Seidl music furnished an oasis in a dreary desert of vulgarity." The Seidl Society, a group of women from New York City organized by Laura Langford (married, not coincidentally, to the treasurer of the Brighton Beach and Coney Island Railroad) actively promoted the concerts. One writer complained that "on Coney Island, at the outset, the great bands played for free for all who cared to listen, but . . . [it is now] necessary to charge an admission fee, against which, I think, there has never been any protest."[37]

Just as concerts for fee replaced free music at Coney, mechanical amusements replaced noncommercial activities and became a mainstay well before the establishment of the amusement parks. In 1880, Joel Cook reported Coney Island filled with "flying-horses and velocipedes and swings, some of

Figure 56. Brighton Beach Concert Program, August 24, 1889. Coney's omnipresent music had been free in the 1870s but increasingly was presented in more formal venues and with an admission charge. The Brighton Beach Hotel built its own music pavilion and hired Anton Seidl, America's foremost disciple of Richard Wagner, to play two concerts daily for twenty-five cents a ticket. (Courtesy of the Brooklyn Historical Society.)

them being machines of great size, capable of riding fifty to a hundred people at one time; and the old folks as well as the children go merrily around." The *Eagle* described Coney in 1892 as "the home of all amusements which are actually insane or nearly so." Gilded Age Americans understood that mechanical amusements freed riders from inhibitions against physical contact; a journalist observed in 1889 that "no matter how frightened they get, the girls have to stay there once the machine is started, and that gives glorious opportunity to rescue them with both arms. Hence, the thing has made a hit."[38]

The basic forms of the carousel, Ferris wheel, and roller coaster were already fixed by 1890, and the twentieth century brought few changes to the concept of amalgamating thrills with opportunities for romantic intimacy. When George Tilyou failed in his bid to buy George Ferris's wheel at the Chicago Exposition of 1894, he returned to Coney, ordered a wheel half the size, and blithely claimed, "On this spot will be built the largest Ferris Wheel in the world." By the time the wheel arrived, Tilyou had sold enough concession space to pay for it, and some ten thousand people rode it every day. Coney's "two acres of merry-go-rounds, circular swings, roller coasters, [and] observation wheels" reinforced Stephen Crane in his 1894 opinion "that humanity only needs to be provided for ten minutes with a few whirligigs and things of that sort, and it can forget at least four centuries of misery."[39]

The American roller coaster dated from the conversion of the switchback railroad at Mauch Chunk, Pennsylvania, into a pleasure device that carried thirty-five thousand tourists in 1873. This idea stimulated LaMarcus Thompson, a Sunday school teacher from Philadelphia looking to entice young people away from the city's beer gardens. In 1884, he developed a similar railway at Coney, which cost $1,600 but grossed as much as $600 daily from avid customers. Within two years, a competitor originated the idea of a circular coaster that returned passengers to their starting position in front of the New Iron Pier, and then someone else invented a power-operated chain to convey the cars up the incline. "The new Coney Island roller coaster," *Frank Leslie's* announced in a featured cover article in 1886, "is a contrivance designed to give passengers, for the insignificant expenditure of five cents, all the sensation of being carried away by a cyclone, without the attendant sacrifice of life and limb." Riding on a roller coaster established an instantaneous informality between couples, and in case they failed to get the idea, Thompson built a popular Scenic Railway complete with tunnels conducive to quick embraces. So common were roller coasters at nineteenth-century Coney that they spawned odd variations to retain the customers' interest. One roller coaster circled the Elephant Hotel, a centrifugal Flip-Flap railway whirled riders in a complete loop-the-loop, and the Shoot-the-Chutes used boats to slide down a steep incline at high speed and bounce in the terminating pool in spectacular fashion.[40]

The carousel's appearance at Gravesend also predated the twentieth century by a generation. A German immigrant brought a primitive merry-go-round to America in 1847, and soon afterward, a Brooklyn man patented an overhead suspension to raise and lower the horse and give the illusion of galloping. Charles Looff, a woodcarver who emigrated to America in 1870, placed his first carousel on the grounds of Balmer's Pavilion at Coney as early as 1876 and then constructed a larger one for Charles Feltman's restaurant complex. Feltman introduced a double-decked "Greco-Roman" carousel in 1885, and yet a third one in 1892 filled with fanciful animals; he claimed carousels could consistently gross $500 a day during the summer and concluded that they paid "better than railroads or hotels. . . . I think it pays best of anything on the island." By 1900, more than ten carousels whirled visitors around at Coney Island. Manufacturers set up factories in Kings County, with Coney Island the undisputed showcase of carousel production, perhaps aided by the proximity to Coney's three racetracks.[41]

The success of the mechanical rides at Gilded Age Coney Island encouraged an even wider variety of fast-paced and time-structured spectacles. Lurid fireworks displays tapped into the American infatuation with the perils of nature and human-made disasters that had been a cultural staple since the antebellum fascination with steamboat explosions. The Manhattan Beach Hotel constructed a fireworks park in 1879, and the first of Henry Pain's sensational pyrotechnic shows lit up Coney's skies in 1883. Pain's dramatic extravaganzas became a standard feature on the island, presenting casts of hundreds of actors, clowns, and dancers in exotic or historic panoramas. Adoring crowds of five thousand to ten thousand necessitated the expansion of the fireworks enclosure to display the Mexican War, the Battle of Gettysburg, the defeat of the Spanish Armada, and the burning of Rome; tragedies such as the Johnstown and Galveston floods were godsends to an industry constantly strapped for new ideas. Pain capitalized on his fame by opening a mail-order business; by 1903 he had fireworks offices in New

York, Chicago, and Boston. Not to be outdone, the Brighton Beach used a cast of thousands to depict events such as the Battle of New Orleans. These theatrical worlds of destruction perpetuated the long tradition of communal participation organized around the act of staring. Yet at the same time, fabricated environments unmistakably represented a late-century turn to commercialized leisure, a more dramatic version of Saratoga's Indian encampment or Pompeia.[42]

Coney Island in the Gilded Age offered other encounters with spectacular and strange experiences (figure 57). The music halls, beer gardens, sideshows, shooting galleries, roller coasters, and preposterous architecture all seemed predicated on the crowd's insatiable longings and appetites for pleasure and release. Circuses and aquariums presented wild animal acts, and coarse and satirical Punch-and-Judy men adopted Coney's beach as their home, while bold visitors rose a thousand feet into the air in a balloon tethered to a steel cable. Dime museums materialized on the shore in the 1870s, and for the next sixty years, Coney Island reigned as the king of the American human oddity circuit, exhibiting casts of dwarfs, giants, Siamese twins, bearded ladies, savages, and snake charmers. Coney defined the American standard by which novelty and eccentricity were judged; when William Dean Howells witnessed lion taming at another resort in the 1890s, a spectator informed him "that you would not see anything like that on Coney Island."[43]

The license to stare, a prerogative of men in most settings, could also be claimed by women at seaside resorts (figure 58). On the one hand, women had to endure "the rude and vulgar gaze of those perfectly horrid folks who sit under umbrellas on the beach." The gauche gentleman who ogled women remained a stock figure of the shore, regularly depicted on stereographs. Both the Manhattan Beach and Brighton Beach Hotels eventually constructed covered walkways to allow women to enter the sea away from the ogling crowd of men. As at all resorts filled with strangers, a man might seem attractive and well-mannered, but his ultimate goal could be debauchery. In 1890, the *Eagle* condemned Coney's "whirlpool of democratization [whose] attractions make up a Vanity Fair at which young girls swarm, open-eyed, open-mouthed, wondering at everything and taking all the tinsel for gold. To their simple minds, the place is a fairyland, and it never dawns upon them that there can be any harm where there is so much good humor and laughter." Sensationalized stories such as that of "poor Bertha Barton,"

Figure 57. "Scenes and Incidents on Coney Island," *Harper's Weekly*, August 10, 1878. Note the contrast with *Frank Leslie's* depiction of Coney a generation earlier (figure 15). Yet the experience remained decentralized in the Gilded Age: Punch-and-Judy men, bathers, peddlers, children, petty thieves, jugglers, onlookers, and donkeys all shared space together. (Collection of the author.)

who either drowned or was murdered with her baby at Coney Island in 1877, served as a warning but also gave full vent to prurient voyeurism.[44]

If Coney's crowded beaches, dance halls, and Bowery held sexual danger for women, however, these public spaces also permitted them to participate in a public culture of flirtation and style. By manipulating men to "treat," working women could escape their own typically parochial and patriarchal ethnic cultures and enter the heterosocial resort world that well-to-do women had enjoyed throughout the century. An article in 1890 entitled "Promiscuous Bathing" inveighed against men and women who went into the water together, especially when they had just met. The female author grudgingly acknowledged that "tired shop girls come to the 'shore' to have a good time, to 'paint the town red,' and they begin early and end late. . . . Their companions, 'gentlemen friends' as they are called, are liberal to a

Figure 58. Women Bathing at Coney Island, ca. 1898. Other than at the races, illustrations and photographs of Gilded Age Coney Island do not lack for women. The ropes were necessary because bathing suits could weigh as much as fifteen pounds when wet, and few people could swim well. (Courtesy of the Brooklyn Historical Society [v1973.5.2728].)

fault; everything that the town affords is at the girl's service. They ride, they dance, they flirt, and when night has drawn her curtain, . . . they pass me in couples, he with his arm around her slim waist." Young women on the island, with their pretty dresses, bright talk, and coquettish manners, behaved in ways more akin to the gender relations of Saratoga than those of the typical working-class neighborhood. A trip to Coney in the Gilded Age took a young woman to a world far different from her home in the tenement districts only fifteen miles away.[45]

By extension, many Americans perceived Coney as a "naughty" place (figure 59). Trade cards, the nineteenth-century version of business cards,

Figure 59. "Ah There! Coney Island," 1897. This classic stereograph reveals the nineteenth-century American seaside in all its liminal glory. Americans of all classes enjoyed the beach with an abandon that was at odds with their supposed concern for disciplined rules of conduct. (Courtesy of the Museum of the City of New York.)

endorsed the idea that the resort offered unusual opportunities for sexual encounters. One card from the 1880s entitled "On the Road to Coney Island" advertised laundry soap by depicting a man on a train with an arm around a woman to whom his relationship was more than ambiguous. Resort postcards often inherited this trade card tradition by portraying sexually suggestive themes or messages. Some visitors used personal columns of the daily press to circumvent the boundaries of public conduct; one wrote, "Will stout blond lady, dressed in light suit, who floated while bathing at Manhattan Beach Saturday, communicate with ADMIRER." Another requested, "Brighton beach 'Smarty' would be pleased to rank as a friend of the 'Large Bodies' moving slowly for the 9:55 train Thursday evening. If the feelings are mutual, address, giving evidence to avoid mistakes." No wonder that the actress known as Little Egypt chose Coney Island as the venue in which to set up shop in 1895, fresh from her sensational act at the Columbian Exposition; this, in turn, inspired a re-creation of the streets of Cairo on Surf Avenue. To attract customers, Coney's sideshows and amusement concessions capitalized on the air of flirtation, permissiveness, and sexual innuendo. This voyeurism, so blatantly a part of the public resort experience, would eventually become a tacit reason for the success of motion pictures, and many of the earliest movies titillated their audiences with images of barely controlled female sexuality at Coney Island.[46]

Kings County reformers may have used Gravesend's roguish reputation as a means to extend Brooklyn's reach into the suburban towns, but they also believed John McKane's removal in 1893 would end the rule of "rowdyism and debauchery" at Coney Island, "the stupidest as well as vilest of resorts." Within two months of the court's sentencing of McKane in February 1894, the City of Brooklyn successfully annexed the town of Gravesend. The *Eagle* could hardly contain its glee: "The people of Gravesend have been rescued from barbarism. Civilization has been extended to that town." A month later, the paper editorialized, "Now that Coney Island is a part of the city, it will be cleaned out." In the end, however, these new developments had little effect on Coney's vices, which reflected the social desires of an age and not the work of a local boss or machine. When Brooklyn merged with Manhattan in 1898, Coney's political decline was complete. In five short years, the island went from being the major concern of the town of Gravesend (population 5,000) to just another neighborhood in the bureaucratic maze of a city of 3.5 million. As the new century dawned, the *Eagle* acknowledged the status quo in banner headlines: "Vice Is Supreme at Coney Island: The West End More Degraded To-Day than Ever in History." John McKane's ouster simply meant that outsiders would control the patronage and rule virtually all of Coney Island.[47]

The advent of the five-cent streetcar ride from Brooklyn to the beach in 1896 and the electrification of the Brooklyn Rapid Transit lines in 1899 affected the resort far more than any political changes. While baseball games struggled to attract ten thousand spectators, four hundred thousand people sometimes thronged Coney on weekends and holidays at the turn of the century, and eight million would visit in a season. On Luna Park's opening day in 1903, the park recorded an astounding forty-three thousand paid admissions in the first three hours, and in 1909, when all three amusement parks were still fairly new, an estimated twenty million people visited the island.[48]

The amusement park venture, however, turned out to be no gold mine. The industry was notoriously erratic, and a severe shaking-out process followed the park promotion hysteria of 1904 to 1908. Dreamland rarely turned a profit, and it was hardly missed as a drawing card after it burned to the ground in 1911 and the owners refused to rebuild it. Despite Frederic Thompson's profligate expenditures, Luna Park's formula grew stale, and he lost control of it to creditors in 1912, only nine years after that fabulous opening day. One manager after another failed to put the park on a paying basis, despite the absence of Dreamland's competition. In 1944, fire destroyed most of Luna Park, as well, and debris covered the area until 1949, when a parking lot replaced the burned-out remains.[49]

Yet Coney Island attendance continued to rise throughout the first half of the twentieth century, even though the amusement parks grew seedier or disappeared. Ever increasing hordes traveled by subway to Coney in the 1920s and 1930s and "dripped" their way back to Manhattan or Brooklyn with their bathing suits under their clothes; in 1928, the Stillwell Avenue subway depot collected more than twenty-four million fares. Attendance at Coney Island did not peak until after Dreamland and Luna Park burned down; on July 3, 1947, while Luna Park lay in ruins, an estimated 2.5 million people attended a United States Army air show and fireworks display. The next day, Coney registered 1.3 million visitors, almost 20 percent of the population of New York City. On one sweltering day in 1952, an astonishing 1.5 million came to the beach. Yearly attendance in these immediate postwar years probably approached 50 million. Thus, the early amusement park period represented no more than an incremental point in a steady line of ascending attendance at Coney Island.[50]

The presumed distinctiveness of the amusement park era proceeded directly from the desires of park owners to establish a dichotomy between the "new" Coney Island attractions and their supposedly disreputable predecessors in the Gilded Age. A procession of middle-class publications announced Coney transformed in the 1900s, a bastion of respectability possessing a new moral tenor that exuded wholesomeness. The attraction of the resort as a counterpoint to everyday life necessitated this ongoing promulgation of an attitude of moral ambiguity. Like its mechanized amusements, simultaneously advertised as life threatening and perfectly safe, Coney's semiotic richness contained within it the pleasure-loving "Sodom by the sea" and an innocuous family resort at the same time. This rhetoric followed the long tradition of ceaselessly promoting Coney's novelty and reassuring visitors that ameliorative efforts had successfully eradicated vice, eliminated brothels, and banished pool selling.

The amusement parks launched a massive publicity drive to reassure the public that undesirable persons would not be tolerated, and many writers took the bait, creating a mythic nineteenth-century Coney Island of chaotic and criminal disorder. The Tilyous, in particular, deadly enemies of John McKane, had a personal reason to exaggerate the nineteenth-century record. Peter Tilyou had tried to sully McKane's reputation by revealing the presence of gambling dens and brothels in 1883, and his son George had testified at length against McKane in the Bacon Committee hearings. The Minority Report had specifically noted George Tilyou's unreliability as a witness with a "grievance" against John McKane "because of certain legal proceedings by the local authorities against his father." After McKane's imprisonment, however, the Steeplechase owner won the propaganda war by default.[51]

Frederic Thompson, the owner of Luna Park, also helped rewrite Coney Island's history. For several seasons, he "spent upward of a hundred thousand dollars" in advertising Luna as "the place for your mother, your sister, your sweetheart." This public relations extravaganza temporarily paid off, as Thompson himself admitted: "Making Coney Island a decent, respectable place has increased the value of the property about five times in as many years." In 1902, Coney's business owners joined together to form a Board of

Trade to advertise the island's amusements as a whole instead of competing individually. No wonder some contemporaries actually believed Coney had been cleansed. Between 1903 and 1908, at least fifteen major articles appeared in national magazines serenading Coney Island with title words such as "apotheosis," "awakening," and "renaissance." This hoopla reflected less on the uniqueness of amusement park Coney Island than on the vast changes in the periodical industry at the turn of the century. The production of inexpensive mass-market magazines, appealing to a broad audience and surviving on advertising revenue, necessitated the constant promotion of novelty and an alliance with the forces of commerce.[52]

If before 1900 Coney was not nearly as rough as its reputation, neither was it as reformed after 1900 as its boosters wished. In fact, crime may have actually increased during the amusement park era. John McKane had taken great pride in his record on law and order; his lawyers opened their defense of his regime by reminding jurors that although criminals infested other resorts, "better order prevails in the town of Gravesend than in any similar locality in the world." Walter Creedmore, no friend of McKane, noted five years later that "the fallen chief certainly deserves credit for the skillful manner in which he policed the whole place. With a very small force of men under his command he preserved order among the thousands of Sunday visitors . . . and preserved such excellent order, too, that serious affrays were almost unknown during his term of office as chief of the local police." Criminals who had avoided McKane apparently moved to the island in droves after his deposition, and a string of notorious murders followed in the early 1900s, including the mysterious deaths of several local politicians. In 1901, the *New York Tribune*, in an article entitled "Coney Needs Cleansing," charged that visitors openly violated the law, with police connivance. The next year, the *Eagle* headlined, "Coney Island Still Is Rotten to the Core." Widely publicized investigations during the first years of the twentieth century confirmed the usual widespread vice at Coney: bawdy sideshows and displays of immorality on the beach during the day, rowdyism at night.[53]

Perceptive critics noted that little had changed at Coney Island with the creation of Luna Park and Dreamland except the ballyhoo. "The reprehensible and degrading resorts that disgraced old Coney are said to be wiped out," notes one character in an O. Henry short story. "The wipin' out process consists of raisin' the price from 10 cents to 25 cents, and hirin' a blonde named Maudie to sell tickets instead of Mickey, the Bowery Bite." If anywhere, a carnival spirit more closely dwelt outside the new parks than within; thousands of men and women continued to gravitate toward the raucous streets, alluring concession stands, and exotic sideshows. The Bowery and the Gut remained popular even after the erection of Dreamland by offering what the glittering parks could not: dozens of games of skill, shooting galleries with indecent animal figures, hole-in-the-wall joints with slot machines, and darkened dance and music halls where extravagant drinking was commonplace. Although reform groups found much to criticize, the vice-tinged attractions continued to lure New Yorkers into an older, exhilarating, shared public enjoyment. These places affronted middle-class decorum by their very existence, and they did not really decline at Coney until well into the twentieth century.[54]

Coney Island, with or without amusement parks, horrified the disparate intellectuals who inherited the mantle of the critics of nineteenth-century watering places. Robert Neal thought Coney reeked "with the stale foulness of past corruption [and] the deception of a newer vulgarity and cheap make-believe." James Huneker concluded that if Coney was "swept off the earth by some beneficent visitation of Providence, the thanksgivings of the community would be in order." Even after they closed the racetracks, the social architects of the early twentieth century envisioned greater reforms at Coney—perhaps even the complete removal of the noisome entertainments from the beachfront and reconstruction of the island as a noncommercial park, in line with the successful renovation of Revere Beach outside Boston. Ironically, the conservative critique of the carnivalesque atmosphere mirrored more radical attacks on the amusement parks. After Maxim Gorky visited Coney in 1907, the Russian author wrote a brutally disparaging article for *Independent* magazine, entitled "Boredom." Gorky noted that the essential contradiction of the island, the "intricate maze of motion and dazzling fire," was actually "organized as a paying business, as a means to extract . . . earnings from the pockets of the people."[55]

Yet no matter where they stood on the political spectrum, all analysts agreed that the amusement parks contributed to the ongoing commercialization of leisure. Coney's concessions and rides encouraged the impulse to consume; one reformer complained that amusement parks were "calculated to separate the people from money with the least possible return. Commercial profit is obviously the dominating factor in their provision." Edwin

Slosson, a visitor sympathetic to Coney, warned readers that "your pocket-book is not safe there yet, but it is not likely to be opened by another than yourself." Nothing personified this commodification more than a conversation he overheard between two young women in which "fun" was reified into a function of cash expenditure:

"What sort of time did you have?"
"Great. He blew in $5.00 on the blow out."
"You beat me again. My chump only spent $2.55."[56]

While the commercial aspect of the amusement parks merely amplified Gilded Age tendencies, their intensified top-down control represented something startling new. In the interests of the bottom line, the amusement parks attempted to rationalize leisure and eliminate spontaneity. Maxim Gorky yearned to see "a drunken man with a jovial face, who would push and sing and bawl, happy because he is drunk, and sincerely wishing all good people the same." This was impossible in a modern amusement park, where owners generally banned the sale of alcohol as a basic step in regulating crowd behavior. The Tilyou family found the gullibility of the masses amusing but believed that only people who used "harmless hoodwinking" to profit from that belief were legitimate capitalists. Edward Tilyou excluded himself when he declared that "the day of the confidence men and sharpers in amusement places is practically over." Frederic Thompson allowed that though Luna Park might be "frisky," *he* knew where to "draw the line." The amusement parks promulgated the dictum that "fun must be innocent" and never cross unwritten forbidden limits, thereby weakening the Gilded Age resort aura of more relaxed sexuality and easy familiarity with strangers.[57]

Amusement park owners also prided themselves on their application of popular psychology to maximize profit. Thompson shortened rides to one minute and theatrical shows to less than twenty and urged his employees to keep visitors moving because "to keep up the carnival spirit everybody must be on the 'go.' The moment a crowd of folk . . . catch this spirit they walk faster, they laugh, they spend money." At Steeplechase, the Tilyous noticed people took "great glee in seeing other folks in embarrassing positions. Not only does it seem funny to them, but it stirs up a soothing complacency that *they* are not the victims." George Tilyou's most famous "amusement" at Steeplechase, the notorious Blowhole Theater, allowed visitors to laugh as a blast of wind blew women's skirts skyward, while a dwarf shocked men with cattle prods. Tilyou therefore retained the voyeurism that had always defined the resort but loaded his park with activities that encouraged audience participation in the humiliation of strangers.[58]

Although the distance between Luna Park and the Breakers seems insurmountable, the urge to privatize leisure space in order to confer status affected all Americans. The monumental entrances of Coney's three amusement parks accentuated the separation of the play world from the real one but also provided symbolic assurance to visitors that they were secure within the private, policed park to which they had paid admission. In contrast, Coney Island outside the park (in the Gilded Age, the entire realm) lacked almost any physical boundaries. Visitors walked from beer gardens through photograph galleries and into minstrel shows without passing through any doors; as one observer explained, "the phrase 'next door' is used with writer's license. . . . There are very few doors." When the entire experience seemed unique, there was no need for grandiose proclamations.[59]

The urge to privatize and profit from leisure space was a basic principle of amusement park creation. Under the guise of improving the neighborhood, the politicians who built Dreamland deviously rammed a proposal through the New York Board of Estimate in 1903 awarding themselves not only the 850 feet of West Eighth Street from Surf Avenue to the ocean but the pier as well. The next year, visitors paid ten cents admission for what had formerly been city property, and those who wanted to get their feet wet without paying for the privilege had to walk to Twenty-third Street. Shortly after the Dreamland conflagration of 1911, New York City actually bought back the property for $1.8 million, including the street that the city had given away for nothing.[60]

Amusement parks tried to append the image of patrician glamour to plebeian venues, but this required a considerable expenditure of money. These semipublic spaces brought to the masses an elegance and scale previously the exclusive property of the privileged but, like vaudeville theaters and then movie palaces, in an environment dedicated to consumption. Steeplechase, Luna, and Dreamland had more in common with the extravaganza of the department store than with parodic discourse or communal fete. If the amusement park offered people an experience less dependent on individual privacy and consumption than its upper-class counterparts in Newport and Saratoga, those traits were more closely related to the limited economic resources of most of Coney's visitors than to a different worldview.[61]

Amusement park promoters, by transforming respectability from a barrier into an opportunity to tap wider markets, replicated the claims of other purveyors of commercialized leisure. For example, vaudeville also showcased fads and popular fashions, celebrated novelty as an end in itself, and eventually segmented into class-differentiated theaters and audiences. Vaudeville's profitability at the turn of the century depended upon widespread patronage, which it achieved only after shedding its rowdy reputation. As George Tilyou had done with amusement parks, Tony Pastor advertised his vaudeville theaters as great family resorts, and B. F. Keith restricted "all vulgarity and suggestiveness in words, action, and costume." Keith and Edward Albee eventually founded a vaudeville empire based on vertical integration, bureaucratic organization, and an economy of scale not unlike that of Standard Oil. The supposed purity of the self-censored vaudeville cartel remained one of its dominant characteristics throughout its golden age; its ascendancy perfectly paralleled the rise of amusement parks.[62]

In a capitalist society, people experiencing true festivity would strive to transcend the modern imperative to achieve, to work, to calculate cost, to seek the profitable and practical, by breaking with mundane cares and flying out of ordinary time. This type of pleasure can only rarely be willed into happening; "the true fetes," declared a turn-of-the-century French history book, "are those which improvise themselves." After witnessing the transformation of Coney Island wrought by the amusement parks, one of O. Henry's characters laments the loss:

> I walked far down on the beach, to the ruins of an old pavilion near one corner of this new private park, Dreamland. A year ago that old pavilion was standin' straight up and the old-style waiters was slammin' a week's supply of clam chowder down in front of you for a nickel and callin' you "cully" friendly, and vice was rampant, and you got back to New York with enough change to take a car at the bridge. . . . And that was Coney as we loved it, and as the hand of Satan was upon it, friendly and noisy and your money' worth, with no fence around the ocean and not too many electric lights.[63]

In 1891, *Harper's Weekly* had run a feature article entitled "A Pilgrimage to Coney's Isle." The journalist, like Charles Dudley Warner and so many others before him, used the secular pilgrimage motif to capture the resort experience in the Gilded Age. He walked past Coney's "revolving swings and merry-go-rounds, shooting galleries and concert halls, razzle-dazzles and switch-backs, toboggan-rollers and photographers, Frankfurters and pea-nuts, beer, music, [and] noise." The island seemed a mishmash of exotic landscapes, its architecture possessing "Alhambric turrets and minarets, garish decorations, and golden domes utterly at variance with each other." Factory workers and immigrant families squeezed pennies to afford the trip to Coney Island, for according to the author, "there was something exhilarating in the pilgrimage. . . . The cares of life were laid aside. The Pilgrims were in search of pleasure . . . [and] there was pleasure in watching the people."[64]

The Coney Island presided over by John McKane in the Gilded Age was hardly a utopia; it could be a racist, sexist, and occasionally dangerous place. For better or worse, it offered visitors a vibrant and unrestricted world of dance halls, racetracks, sexual teasing, boxing matches, brothels, and beach flirtation. The amusement parks retreated from the disorder, social leveling, and excess of the Gilded Age, thereby tempering the liminality of the resort experience. They instead elevated the commercial tendencies of Coney Island in the 1880s and 1890s and tried to contain visitors within an increasingly engineered environment in which patrons primarily played the role of active consumers of spectacles and material goods. In this sense, Steeplechase, Luna Park, and Dreamland were the true prototypes of the twentieth-century resort.

≈ CONCLUSION ≈

The Pursuit of Privacy, Profit, and Pleasure

ON LEAVING SARATOGA SPRINGS IN 1827 after a fortnight's stay, twenty-year-old Elizabeth Ruffin encountered a traffic jam created by the return of a huge crowd from the public execution of a murderer in nearby Albany. This entertaining diversion had drawn somewhere between fifteen thousand and forty thousand spectators, including numerous day-trippers from the resort. The horrified Virginia belle "counted 530 wagons that we met returning from the show," besides a number too great to calculate scattered about, and she concluded that the population of New York was completely depraved compared with the refined residents of the South. A local newspaper agreed, reporting that the execution was accompanied by "scenes of the most disgraceful drunkenness, gambling, profanity, and almost all kinds of debauchery."[1]

Ruffin's experience can be contrasted with another execution that took place almost a century later at Coney Island. Topsy the elephant, who had spent twenty-eight years under the big top, killed a circus follower who had fed her a lighted cigarette. "Skip" Dundy decided he could garner some free publicity for the soon-to-be-opened Luna Park by publicly executing her. Thomas Edison offered to use Topsy to demonstrate that electricity could be employed as a humane method for killing condemned criminals. The elephant was hooked up to the huge generators that ran the amusement park and electrocuted; newspapers covered the story on the front page. In a scene chillingly immortalized on film, a wisp of smoke wafted up from Topsy's flesh as the big elephant silently fell.[2]

The nineteenth-century resort thrived in the space between these two extremes. In colonial America, the requirements of the task, not the clock, had regulated the course of an everyday life dominated by the agricultural cycle. Religious and communal values and institutions restrained materialism and individualism, and the market economy, with its accompanying acquisitiveness, remained subordinate. Workers in preindustrial settings often performed their tasks free of haste, careless of exactitude, and not particularly concerned with productivity; "work" as a concept barely existed and was inextricably bound up with leisure. Like Albany's well-attended public execution, popular amusements before the Industrial Revolution were usually informally organized, drew celebrants mainly from the immediate area, and contained high levels of emotional spontaneity and often socially tolerated physical violence.[3]

In journeying all the way to Saratoga from Virginia, which certainly did not lack for mineral water springs, Elizabeth Ruffin participated in a new form of leisure. At the beginning of the nineteenth century, Americans generally did not take their pleasures away from home, but a nation at peace, a degree of prosperity, and technological improvements in transportation spurred travel to distant locales. Specialized modes of production gradually induced people to divide their lives into distinct compartments for work, household duties, and leisure activities, each with its own appropriate setting. Despite the stereotype of nineteenth-century domesticity, most Americans came to view taking a "vacation" at home as vaguely improper, if not dishonorable; the word itself derives from the Latin *vacare*, "to leave." Legends arose of families who pretended they had gone off to Saratoga or Newport while actually living in the back of the house and emerging furtively only by night.

Urban-style culture and amusements characterized these new watering places. Undeniably, scores of enthusiastic guests assembled to witness the "must-see" sunrise at the Catskill Mountain House or exclaimed in awe at God's majesty before the falls at Niagara. After "doing" the site, however, visitors returned to hotels to encounter the same tourists playing cards in the parlor, drinking champagne on the veranda, and comparing notes on the latest fashions in the city. As George Curtis commented, "None more than the Americans make it a principle to desert the city, and none less than the Americans know how to dispense with it. So we compromise by taking the city with us." Even when the grand tour later took the adventurous traveler to the West, the majority of tourists clung to their Pullman cars and lodged in cities, notwithstanding their alleged desire to experience primeval wilderness and the sublime.[4]

Nor did anyone go to a resort for solitude. The social dislocations of the nineteenth century led to a hunger for public life at the beach and the park, in the parlor and dining room, and on the veranda and the street. "There are few great summer hotels in the country," the *Nation* editorialized, "which are not conducted on the theory that all Americans like, whenever they leave home for recreation, a tremendous 'racket,' well lighted up, and a large crowd of people to enjoy it with." Grand resort hotels were private places only in the strictly legal sense; in every other way they celebrated the public realm. "The rule of sociability completely dominates," determined German traveler Friedrich Ratzel while staying at the United States Hotel. "The bedrooms in such an establishment are seldom such that one enjoys spending time in them," he noted of the finest hotel at Saratoga, but "the common rooms are stocked with every luxury." Reporters repeatedly praised hotels as palaces of the public, open to virtually anyone who could pay the bill and pass supposedly elementary tests of social acceptability. The major exceptions—African Americans and single women—confirmed their marginality in mainstream American society. The resort experience retained the communal spirit of preindustrial festivities, but it offered a far more emotionally disciplined routine than Elizabeth Ruffin witnessed outside of Albany.[5]

Summer journeys to Saratoga Springs, Newport, and Coney Island can be characterized as rituals—deliberately repeated acts that order or control the chaos of human experience. The ritual journey to the watering place, whether for a day, a week, or the summer, served as the modern secular equivalent of the sequences of festivals or religious pilgrimages of preindustrial societies. Ritual action may not be self-expression, but neither is it meaningless routine, for rituals translate enduring messages, values, and sentiments into observable action. These journeys to resorts shared some of the attributes of liminality often found in rites of passage: a sense of ordeal, release from structure, the partial leveling of status, reflection on the meaning of basic cultural values, and movement from a mundane center to a magical periphery that suddenly became central for the individual, at least temporarily. In traveling to the resort, visitors and local residents combined to create a "sacred" location, enshrining certain behaviors as American ideals.[6]

Like pilgrimage sites, the resort worlds of Saratoga, Newport, and Coney

Island were potentially liminal places. Their very existence implicitly challenged the "normal" values of American society in the nineteenth century—thrift, sobriety, utility, production—by suggesting that these values were neither necessarily eternal nor inevitable. At hotels, one service worker noted, sojourners tended to change their habits and "forget their dignity and self-respect. Everyone goes off standard when he gets into a hotel." The beaches at Newport and Coney Island especially created an enclave that partially exempted the visitor from everyday etiquette. Conceptually, this type of "leisure" really did derive from the idea of the Latin *licere*, "to be permitted," implying the freedom to do something stimulating, not just time off from work.[7]

A culture of see-and-be-seen voyeurism initially linked these resort destinations. "The crowd goes [to Saratoga] mainly because the crowd is there," reported the *Times* of London in a typical passage, "and this makes the crush so great upon the hotel piazzas and drawing-rooms. . . . Days are devoted to ease and amusement, and the nights to mirth and pleasure. . . . The place is almost perpetually en fete." Stephen Crane singled out the exact same element in seaside culture: "The huge wooden hotels empty themselves directly after dinner. . . . All hie to the big boardwalk. For there is joy in the heart in a crowd. One is in life and of life then. Nothing escapes; the world is going on and one is there to perceive it." At these very public resorts, the visitor observed "all the world" on the beach or the veranda and simultaneously enjoyed, or at least tolerated, the gaze returned by the heterogeneous crowd. Yet no single person or organization controlled this diffuse experience, and nothing as extraordinary as a public execution was necessary to attract secular pilgrims. The promenade demanded only the disciplined amiability necessary to interact in a world of strangers, and flirtation required no grand or violent spectacles to provide titillating pleasures.[8]

Visitors urgently tried to communicate the intoxicating nature of Saratoga, Newport, and Coney Island through words such as "enchantment," "fairyland," "paradise," "elysium," "heaven," "magic spell," and "perpetual fete." Resorts appropriated the music, feasting, and dancing that had previously accompanied religious pilgrimages to provide the extraordinary peaks of sensation that marked the participant's behavior and made it exceptional. Virtually by definition, the resort held out expectations in excess of fulfillment: illusions of social mobility, diminution of customary restrictions, and sexual license. Anxious visitors may have dreaded meeting numerous strangers without clear guidelines on interaction, but the potential for exhilaration lured them on throughout the nineteenth century.[9]

The emphasis on flirtation and disguise, the provocative tension of masquerade balls, and the ambivalent feelings toward confidence men and the sporting life identify resorts as places where nineteenth-century Americans expressed their fascination with the fluidity of personal identity. In the large city, anonymity reduced the depressed urbanite to insignificance; at the playful resort, it permitted the visitor to meet new people and try out new ideas and behaviors. While a journey to Saratoga, Newport, or Coney Island obviously did not offer absolute freedom, it did mitigate some of the demeaning sexual, racial, and class-bound ideologies that permeated everyday life in America. The sophistication of this type of watering place experience reveals considerable distance from the idea of a public execution as a major form of entertainment.

The frisson of the American resort displayed signs of fragility at its very creation and did not survive the nineteenth century. The Industrial Revolution disrupted leisure time in ways that would eventually be broadly shared across barriers of race, class, and gender. Boundaries evolved between secular and religious life, older holidays lost their meaning, and time thrift replaced task orientation. Some leisure activities were now condemned as a "waste of time," and most self-generated activity outside capitalism was dismissed as "doing nothing." Time itself became commodified and rationalized, to be used, priced, measured, adjusted, and, in the case of vacations, "spent." Greater individual freedom and the ubiquity of money wages fueled an entertainment explosion, and a colossal industry developed to supply the nation's diversions. Leisure entrepreneurs targeted "free time," systematically searching for ways to merchandise it.[10]

Because capitalism required not only a work ethic of self-restraint but also a mentality of self-indulgence, resorts profited greatly from the market revolution. After the Civil War, an informal coalition of doctors, social scientists, and transportation companies disputed the republican equation of the watering place with moral disease. They instead promoted leisure travel as a cure for the boredom of time discipline and the torpor of people's everyday lives. Religious leaders defended prosperity as God's favorable judgment on the American nation and popularized travel to resorts as a palliative to societal stress and excessive competition. Steamship lines and railroad companies commissioned guidebooks, issued excursion rates, and built trunk lines to resorts. Urban summer visitors appropriated abandoned or underpopulated sections of decayed seaport towns and backcountry villages, transforming them into cottage communities and vacation destinations. Newspapers initiated columns of travel tips, oceans of ink catalogued the names of visitors at hotels and cottages, and soon whole sections in weekend editions described the goings-on at Saratoga, Newport, and Coney Island.[11]

Two major characteristics of modern American society—privatization and commercialization—greatly altered the resort experience in the Gilded Age. The former resulted in the stratification of resorts by social class and broke down the communal sense of interacting with "all the world." Americans may not have been pleased with the democracy of the early American inn, but without an alternative, they acquiesced and declared themselves delighted to eat at the table with the stage driver, drink at the bar with the drover, dodge the logger's tobacco juice by the fire, and share a bed with several wagoners. Gradually, visitors began to assign hotels to innumerable, if impermanent, niches: style (fashionable, aristocratic, or democratic), duration (short stay or all summer), and companionship (the home of clergy, savants, or worst of all, invalids and dull people). Guidebooks made it a practice to note the ever widening divergence of prices of hotels and boardinghouses and proffered varied itineraries depending on the traveler's financial and temporal resources. As the century progressed, travelers abandoned talk of equality and used resorts to create and legitimate social differences. Newport's hotel industry, the rival of Saratoga's in the 1850s, collapsed with a suddenness that astonished contemporaries, to be replaced with expensive private housing.

By 1900, a hierarchy of resorts had evolved, with Newport at the head and Coney Island at the tail, offering prestige to visitors of varied socioeconomic groups. Grand hotels, where for the price of a minimal tariff virtually all were accepted as equals, no longer provided satisfactory distinction for most people. In Marietta Holley's best-selling satire on fashionable Saratoga, one country bumpkin voices the American creed: "I'm bound to be fashionable. W[h]ile I can go with the upper 10, it is my duty and privilege to go with 'em, and not mingle in the lower classes." From the middle of the social scale, William Dean Howells delineated his staid vacation colony from a nearby beach area filled with "inland people of little social importance . . . a resort of people several grades of gentility lower than ours: so many, in fact, that we never can speak of the Beach without averting our faces, or, at the best, with a tolerant smile." At the same time, elite tourists abandoned locations such as Coney Island or erected social demarcations within tourist areas. Only private mansions could escape the social vulgarity of commercial and public resorts, sniffed the author of an article in *Independent* magazine, "which in the end must leave its stamp on every person who frequents them." For most Americans, aspiring to the economic standard of those above and fearful of being mistaken for those below, the choice of resorts helped establish social position and create identity. In fact, modern tourist marketing teaches that reducing prices is often counterproductive, since most visitors positively correlate high prices with the quality of vacation destinations and hotels. A crucial factor in assuring repeat visitation is the visitors' belief that at tourist sites they will find "their kind of people."[12]

The commercialization of leisure dealt the second blow to the see-and-be-seen culture of resorts. The presence of large hotels and a complex network of interdependent advertisers, suppliers, entertainers, and service personnel identify antebellum Saratoga, Newport, and Coney Island as precursors of the modern tourist industry. On this level, the resort seems banal rather than extraordinary, visited by conformists following a pre-established itinerary laid out in commercial guidebooks and mass-produced to fill manufactured desires. Yet irregular entertainments and informal activities in the streets or on the beaches generally characterized these resorts in the antebellum period. The rubrics of ritual did not constrain nineteenth-century Americans to the degree that modern readers of their etiquette books imagine. Customary channels provided the structure yet allowed plenty of room for inventiveness and imagination. Visitor behavior at resorts originally stood somewhat outside the market, dependent upon "older" pleasures such as walking, talking, riding, and drinking.

By the late nineteenth century, however, commercialized places of action replaced these activities, now viewed as "boring." On Saratoga's Broadway, hotels rented out their ground floors to stores and turned promenaders into shoppers. At Coney, mechanical novelties, cheap amusements, and purchased souvenirs superseded the pleasures of the beach and the veranda. At both these sites, prominent gambling venues announced the decline of aimless strolling. Racetracks, casinos, and finally amusement parks all provided safe thrills and socially approved moderate excitement for those who visited resots at the end of the century. Visitors still yearned for a public life amid crowds, but they combined with resort entrepreneurs to create spaces in which citizens interacted primarily in relation to the private act of purchasing commodities. Coney Island's freak shows and disaster spectacles capitalized on the innate voyeurism of the masses of Americans who paid to view and evaluate the misfortunes of others; this became a cornerstone of the attraction of the new mass media.[13]

While it may have been an extreme case, the electrocution of Topsy the elephant exemplified not only the ceaseless search for technological novelty and gross spectacle that would characterize many twentieth-century leisure trends but also the new predominance of commercial values. The Gilded Age had loved elephants, and Coney Island's Elephant Hotel was arguably its most recognizable image until it was destroyed by fire in 1896. After P. T. Barnum spirited Jumbo away from England in 1882, elephants became national celebrities, not only for their size, as perfect metaphors for an expanding nation, but also because they were quiet animals easily endowed with human qualities by a sentimental public. Topsy's electrocution at Luna Park, therefore, had symbolic overtones; it reasserted the principle that animals, and indeed the entire natural environment, existed to be manipulated for human aggrandizement. In this case, however, the elephant was killed primarily as a publicity gimmick to entice people to spend money at an amusement park. The act may or may not have been as cruel as Albany's public execution seventy-five years earlier, but it did represent the triumph of commercial values over the course of the century.[14]

This commercialization of leisure benefited American society in at least two ways. Monetarized culture liberated recreation from the circumscribed mores and collective obligations of preindustrial social life, dominated by magic or religious festivals in rural or small village settings. When nineteenth-century Americans walked out of their homes, factories, or offices in the large industrial city, they experienced fewer cultural restraints than people in any previous age. The alliance of profit and pleasure gradually loosened the official moral strictures against many activities and produced any number of novel entertainments. Consumerism not only reflected the aesthetics and desires of the majority but also served as a means to self-creation. Many nineteenth-century "Victorians," who officially preached the rejection of sensuality and materialism in favor of self-discipline and the work ethic, visited resorts predicated on fashion, status, and self-indulgence. Quite simply, people seem to have had a great deal of fun at Saratoga Springs, Newport, and Coney Island in the Gilded Age.[15]

The marketplace also worked to democratize leisure in American society. "Probably no great business enterprise," editorialized one newspaper in 1880, "combining in so large a degree public benefit and private profit has ever been conducted in a more liberal spirit or with greater intelligence than the transformation of Coney Island from a dreary waste to a summer city by the sea." If leisure culture existed primarily to generate a profit, it would obviously be a shame to waste the consumptive possibilities of economic outgroups such as women and African Americans. Resorts, especially, pioneered the heterosocial leisure so essential to the expansion of capitalism and encouraged women to step into their influential role as chief familial consumer. By 1902, the magazine *World's Work* could devote an entire August issue to summer vacation play, reporting that Americans had "gone at it as a business and . . . brought [it] within the reach of everybody." The desire of some to exclude Jews at Coney Island and Saratoga was ultimately unsuccessful, for it conflicted not only with the desire to meet "all the world" at the resort but, more important, worked against the logic of profit making.[16]

On the other hand, privatization and commercialization undermined the liminal possibilities of the resort. Although the daily experiences of Newport cottagers, Saratoga hotel guests, and Coney Island day-trippers may have diverged, at the resort they all learned to participate as consumers of goods, services, and spectacles. Travel had long been acknowledged to be morally dangerous, and the antebellum watering place pilgrimage displayed potentially "subversive" manifestations of community. The capitalist "vacation" tempered these tendencies so that the journey retained its outward form surrounding an emasculated core. At Gilded Age resorts, the pilgrim's longing for exhilaration and community evolved into the modern traveler's search for the much tamer ideal of purchased pleasure; to witness the execution of an elephant was certainly an atypical experience, but it could hardly be classified as a liminal one in a psychological sense.[17]

In this way, pilgrimages to Saratoga, Newport, and Coney Island served a conservative purpose. The resort obviously could not stand entirely apart from reality, and different social groups occasionally battled over physical possession. Unwelcome Jews, African Americans, or single women often forced their way into watering places and hotels from which dominant groups had desired to exclude them. This squabbling, however, took place within a capitalist system in which there might be dispute about distributions of power but not about the structure of the system itself. Americans, regardless of race, class, or gender, accepted the resort's symbolic endorsement of commodification as well as the choice of destination as a building block of American social position.[18]

The liminal world is by definition a temporary moment in time, and despite the emphasis on breach and collectivity, the resort journey concluded with the reintegration of travelers into an unchanged American society. The transient existence of egalitarian antistructure at resorts did not fundamentally alter the normative consensus and may, as in the case of the medieval carnival, actually have reinforced it. Rites of protest rarely exist when the social order is seriously questioned, for they would be too dangerous. Although license in ritual can momentarily lift taboos, it generally affirms and preserves the status quo. For this reason, Coney Island of the amusement park era cannot accurately be characterized as contested space or oppositional subculture. A trip to the amusement park, no more or less than one to the seaside or the springs, directed excess energies into safe channels and fostered the myth of shared prosperity and upward social mobility in ways that strengthened the established order in America.[19]

The vicissitudes of the twentieth century wreaked havoc on Coney's amusement parks as much as on Saratoga's hotels and Newport's mansions. In 1890, *Harper's Weekly* asked, "Can there be decayed watering places? Comes there the ebb tide of fashion, which, after a time receding, leaves a resort once thronged, high, dry, stranded, and deserted?" Twenty years later, the *New York Times* responded, disdainfully recalling "summer spa days" dominated by vast hotels with soaring wood porticos as "rather old-fashioned and of a piece with the Gothic villas of the day." In the new century, no one would stay in a hotel, "still lit by gas, which has no porcelain tubs, no motorbus at the station, and no restaurant *a la carte*." Travelers expressed concern about the heavy food, outmoded sanitary facilities, and badly ventilated rooms of these anachronistic establishments. Some could not deal with the so-called idleness of traditional grand hotel life and looked instead to vacations promising more vigorous activity. The proliferation of automobiles and highways undercut the extended stay at one location by opening North America to unscheduled rambling. So-called automobilists, imagining themselves to be creating an adventurous alternative to slow-paced routines of the Gilded Age, collected sites the way a previous generation collected stereographs.[20]

Yet mechanically antiquated hotels could be rebuilt, as they always had been, if the market still promised a good financial return. It was not automobiles or obsolescence that threatened the old-fashioned resorts; of all the obloquy hurled at watering places, complaints about their sociability predominated. Saratoga, Newport, and Coney Island had all been created with the interaction of strangers in mind, whereas their twentieth-century counterparts almost always provided greater insularity. Automobile travelers completely reversed the traditional hotel's use of space; they judged motels by the amenities available in private rooms rather than in the virtually nonexistent public space. The new arrangements helped guarantee social segregation and severely restricted interaction with people from different classes or races. Even a Club Med–type vacation, perhaps the closest modern equivalent to a "cashless" holiday (beyond the initial expenditure), invariably takes place in exotic locales, fenced off from native populations, and far enough from home and at sufficient cost to eliminate those from the lower socioeconomic classes. Movies, television, and finally the Internet all supplanted the see-and-be-seen culture of resorts by conferring anonymity upon the viewer while permitting a socially acceptable voyeuristic experience, in the last case, controllable from the safety of one's own home.

At the midpoint of the twentieth century, it seemed as if Saratoga Springs would not survive much longer as a resort. Richard Canfield closed the Casino in the early years of the twentieth century, and most of the gambling houses moved out to Saratoga Lake, where the roulette wheels spun until the Kefauver Commission put them out of business in 1951. A state-of-the-art park complex built with New Deal money never succeeded in rivaling the great European spas. The United States Hotel was razed in 1945, and the Grand Union followed in 1953; huge parking lots essentially replaced both structures and stood out like gaping sores in Saratoga's most prominent locations. But just when it appeared the city might go to seed in the way of Sharon Springs, the powers-that-be decided to route the proposed superhighway from Albany to Montreal by way of Saratoga and thereby made the resort easily accessible by private automobile. A five-thousand-seat Performing Arts Center followed in 1966, offering both highbrow and lowbrow entertainment throughout the summer. The racetrack survived all the ups and downs; daily racetrack attendance in the 1990s exceeded twenty thousand horseplayers for an enlarged six-week season. Saratoga continues to promote itself as "the August place to be," appealing to American nostalgia for Queen Anne–style houses, the remains of the old-moneyed elite, and a main street lined with enticing stores. Though no longer quite "the queen of spas," Saratoga Springs seems likely to extend its reputation as a resort city into a third century.[21]

Newport also weathered an uncertain twentieth-century leisure market. The Fall River Line went bankrupt in 1937, and the Old Colony Railroad died soon afterward. In 1969, the two-mile-long Newport Bridge across the bay to Aquidneck Island finally permitted a direct overland route from New York and points south by automobile. Profligate living, marriage to adventurers, and indifference to business affairs dissipated Newport patrimonies and weakened the economic dominance of the city's visiting plutocrats. Income tax, a shortage of servants, the Depression, and increased ease of airplane travel all took their toll on Newport cottage life. In 1925, the city assessed the ten largest mansions at a total of more than $2.7 million, but by 1950, they were valued at only $823,000. The children and grandchildren of the owners rarely wished to live in these "white elephants," as Henry James called them, and they were converted to colleges, offices, charitable institutions, or museums. In 1900, summer estates accounted for 50 percent of all Newport taxes; by 1950 that figure was less than 20 percent. A new generation of geographically dispersed moguls and technocrats generally patronized more secluded resorts and relied for fame on the *Forbes Magazine* rankings, which reduced complex blue-blood formulas to simple cold-blooded accounting. The virtual withdrawal of the Navy left tourism as the area's economic mainstay; the Bellevue Avenue cottages are now the city's main attraction, and in an age that revels in conspicuous consumption, few tourists find them in bad taste. A recent guidebook informed readers that "much of what there is to do in Newport is connected with its history— which isn't as dull as it may sound."[22]

Coney Island's visitors retained their preference for group activity longer than cottagers at Newport, but most of them also succumbed to the siren song of greater class cohesion and individual privacy. Despite the construction of the Wonder Wheel (in 1920), the Cyclone (in 1927), and the Parachute Jump (in 1939), Coney had difficulty competing with suburban amusement parks or more car-friendly beaches on Long Island. Kings County's railroads ultimately reinforced the marketability of the local real estate that lay so close to the expanding metropolis. Consequently, developers gobbled up the boarded-up racetracks and hotels in the 1920s and turned Brighton and Manhattan Beaches into residential areas. The erection of large, high-rise housing projects in the 1960s marginalized Coney Island in the eyes of many New Yorkers; Steeplechase Park closed in 1965, and the twenty oceanfront blocks of amusements have now shrunk to three. Still, Coney Island continues to entice five million people a year, although most of the visitors are from the lower socioeconomic classes, and they cease to return as soon as their financial means or sense of social status permits them to rise in the resort world.[23]

Twentieth-century resorts may have jettisoned the old community-based and seasonal travel experience, but they still owed a great deal to their nineteenth-century progenitors. The public execution of an elephant would hardly surprise visitors to modern Las Vegas, the home of twenty-four-hour spectacles in an environment complete with fire-breathing dragons, shark-filled aquariums, and grandiose recreations of exotic foreign environments. As at nineteenth-century resorts, the calculated manipulation of Las Vegas's architecture and fantasy-land environment encourages disengagement from reality and creates both a stage upon which to act and an environment amenable to spending money. High and low rollers alike participate in a money-drenched carnival of extravagance by visiting an eye-popping array of retail shops on and off the Strip, including the most hallowed names in consumerism. Thirteen hotels boast more than one thousand rooms, capped by the self-proclaimed "world's largest hotel," with more than five thousand. In 1996, thirty million people passed through the hundred thousand hotel and motel rooms in Clark County, leaving a profit of more than $15 billion for the gaming and tourism industry. The entire Las Vegas experience harkens back to Morrissey's Club House and Coney Island's racetracks. A stroller transplanted from Saratoga's Broadway or Coney's Bowery in the 1890s would not feel out of place.[24]

Modern theme parks, however, achieve the type of total control of space, movement, and mood that leisure entrepreneurs could only aspire to in Gravesend. At Disneyland in Anaheim and Disney World in Orlando, orderly motion eliminates the chaos typical of the midway, technological wizardry replaces the sexualized atmosphere of the beach, and twenty-five million relatively well-to-do guests, a large proportion of them children, substitute for urban laborers. Modern theme parks have perfected the lure of safe thrills; asked to assess thirty-two desirable characteristics of the amusement park, patrons chose "cleanliness," and "line control" as the two most important. Just as late-nineteenth-century Americans strove to establish privacy and restrict unwanted strangers from their leisure activities, modern theme parks run by huge corporations erect fences, charge admission, design rides to avoid excessive contact between strangers, and move far enough from the central city and its dangerous classes and races to lend prestige to the journey.[25]

Visits to casinos and theme parks in the early-twenty-first century retain their sense of pilgrimage for participants, drawing acolytes great distances to bounded places distinct from ordinary settlements. Their popularity reveals the continued hunger for great spaces that can provide dramatic settings for collective action. This instinct, however, has been tempered by the hostility of most Americans to public space, also inherited from the nineteenth century. Unrestricted streets and beaches are increasingly associated with danger and dirt and seen as areas to pass through or view from a distance rather than use. More privatized spaces such as self-contained megamalls (which often have incorporated the arcade and rides of the amusement park), enormous sports arenas, skyscraper atriums, and pseudo-historical marketplaces all attempt to fill the gap partially left vacant by the demise of the nineteenth-century grand hotels. Journeys to resorts are now typically oriented to consumption; a 1998 poll ranked shopping as the most popular vacation activity (32 percent) by a margin of two to one over ten other possibilities. Even this vestige of communal culture is now threatened by the commercial power of the Internet. The aimless masses rocking on the veranda, gossiping in the parlor, and "doing nothing" on the beach have moved on.[26]

Saratoga, Newport, and Coney Island in the mid-nineteenth century served as appealing secular pilgrimage destinations. They transformed simple walking into a communal promenade and gave participants a chance to see and be seen by "all the world." For most of the nineteenth century, these resorts tapped into the desire for pleasure travel and community that captivated Americans across class, racial, ethnic, and gender divides. They held out the possibility of a fascinating, dangerous, democratic, and erotic public realm, albeit in a world spatially distinct from everyday life. Gradually, commercialization and privatization took their toll, all the world went their separate ways, and novel entertainments replaced other faces and other people. By the dawn of the twentieth century, a journey to Saratoga Springs, Newport, or Coney Island fortified rather than subverted the strictures of everyday life. Instead of idiosyncratic laboratories for the rethinking and reworking of American norms, resorts had been transformed into mundane places where visitors bought souvenirs, gambled for money, partied in private mansions, and witnessed spectacles akin to the execution of a circus elephant.

Notes

UNC	Southern Historical Collection, University of North Carolina, Chapel Hill, North Carolina

YC	Yates Collection, Skidmore College, Saratoga Springs, New York

Introduction

1. *Harper's Weekly (HW)*, 10 Aug. 1878.

2. Charles Dudley Warner, "Their Pilgrimage," *Harper's Monthly (HM)* 72 (1886): 670; and 73 (1886): 170–71, 184.

3. T. Jackson Lears, "Beyond Veblen: Rethinking Consumer Culture in America," in *Consuming Visions: Accumulation and Display of Goods in America, 1880–1920*, ed. Simon Bronner (New York: Norton, 1989), 76–77. For overemphasis on the uniqueness of the period from 1890 to 1920, see Lewis Erenberg, *Steppin' Out: New York Nightlife and the Transformation of American Culture, 1890–1930* (Chicago: Univ. of Chicago Press, 1981), xi–xv, 5–31; Stanley Coben, *Rebellion against Victorianism: The Impetus for Cultural Change in 1920s America* (Oxford: Oxford Univ. Press, 1991), 3–36; John Kasson, *Amusing the Million: Coney Island at the Turn of the Century* (New York: Hill and Wang, 1978), 3–9.

4. Arnold van Gennep, *The Rites of Passage,* trans. Monica Vizedom and Gabrielle Cafee (1908; Chicago: Univ. of Chicago Press, 1960), 1–25, 189–94; Victor Turner, "Liminal to Liminoid in Play, Flow, and Ritual: An Essay in Comparative Symbology," *Rice University Studies* 60 (Summer 1974): 53–92; Victor Turner and Edith Turner, *Image and Pilgrimage in Christian Culture* (New York: Columbia Univ. Press, 1978), 1–34, 231–54; Sally Moore and Barbara Myerhoff, eds., *Secular Ritual* (Amsterdam: Van Gorcum, 1977), 3–70; Dean MacCannell, *Empty Meeting Grounds: The Tourist Papers* (New York: Routledge, 1993), 255–79; Donald Weber, "From Limen to Border: A Meditation on the Legacy of Victor Turner for American Cultural Studies," *American Quarterly* 47 (Sept. 1995): 525–36.

The Turners' linkage of rites of passage, pilgrimage, and tourism has been challenged as ahistorical or lacking nuance; see John Eade and Michael Sallnow, eds., *Contesting the Sacred: The Anthropology of Christian Pilgrims* (London: Routledge, 1991), 1–29; Tom Driver, *The Magic of Ritual: Our Need for Liberating Rites That Transform Our Lives and Our Communities* (New York: HarperCollins, 1991), 227–38; Barbara Aziz, "Personal Dimensions of the Sacred Journey: What Pilgrims Say," *Religious Studies* 23 (1987): 247–61; Surinder Bhardwaj and Gisbert Rinschede, *Pilgrimage in World Religions* (Berlin: D. Reimer, 1988); Michael Pearson, *Pilgrimage to Mecca: The Indian Experience, 1500–1800* (Princeton, N.J.: Marcus Wiener, 1996).

5. John Watson, *Historic Tales of Olden Time: Concerning the Early Settlement and Advancement of New York City and State* (New York, 1832), 203–7.

6. Edward Hungerford, "Our Summer Migration: A Social Study," *Century* 42 (Aug. 1891): 569 ("the rich"); "The Summer Exodus and What It Testifies," *Century* 38 (July 1889): 469–70.

7. "Why Can't We Get Away?" *Newsweek*, 27 July 1998, 40–44; *New York Times (NYT)*, 12 Apr. 1998.

8. *NYT*, 28 Aug. 1982; 21 May 1995; "Why Can't We Get Away?" 40–44.

CHAPTER ONE   *The Creation of Saratoga Springs*

1. Putnam Family Papers, 1791–1918, New York State Historical Association Library, Cooperstown, N.Y. (NYSHAL); "Map of a Number of Building Lots . . . Being the Property of Gideon Putnam," Apr. 1810, drawn by James Scott, Saratoga County Clerk's Office, Ballston Spa, N.Y. (SCCO); John Steel, *An Analysis of the Mineral Waters of Saratoga and Ballston . . . Together with a History of These Watering Places*, 2d ed. (Saratoga Springs, 1838), 41–43; Nathaniel Sylvester, *History of Saratoga County, New York* (Philadelphia, 1878), 152–67; George Anderson, *Our County and Its People: A Descriptive Biographical Record of Saratoga County, New York* (Boston, 1899), 134–36; William Stone, *Reminiscences of Saratoga and Ballston* (New York, 1890), 55–65.

2. Phyllis Hembry, *The English Spa, 1560–1815: A Social History* (London: Athlone, 1990), 1–3, 302–4; Sylvia McIntyre, "Bath: The Rise of a Resort Town, 1660–1800," in *Country Towns in Pre-Industrial England*, ed. Peter Clark (Leicester, Eng.: Leicester Univ. Press, 1981), 214–43; Penelope Corfield, *The Impact of English Towns, 1700–1800* (Oxford: Oxford Univ. Press, 1982), 51–66.

3. Carl Bridenbaugh, "Baths and Watering Places of Colonial America," *William and Mary Quarterly* 3 (Apr. 1946): 153–74; Henry Lawrence, "Southern Spas: Source of the American Resort Tradition," *Landscape* 28 (1983): 1–12; Carol Roark, "Historic Yellow Springs: The Restoration of an American Spa," *Pennsylvania Folklife* 24 (1974): 28–34; Estrellita Karsh, "Taking the Waters at Stafford Springs," *Harvard Library Bulletin* 28 (1980): 264–81; Donald Yacovone, "A New England Bath: The Nation's First Resort at Stafford Springs," *Connecticut Historical Society Bulletin* 41 (Jan. 1976): 1–11.

4. Milo North, *An Analysis of Saratoga Waters . . .* (Saratoga Springs, 1858), 6–11. To this day, scientists cannot pinpoint the origin of the carbonation; see Donald Siegel, "Natural Bubbling Brew: The Carbonated Springs of Saratoga," *Geotimes* 41 (May 1996): 21; George Putnam and James Young, "The Bubbles Revisited: The Geology and Geochemistry of 'Saratoga' Mineral Waters," *Northeastern Geology* 7 (Apr. 1985): 53–56.

5. Samuel Tenney, "An Account of a Number of Mineral Springs at Saratoga in the State of New York," *Memoirs of the American Academy of Arts and Sciences* 2 (1793): 43–61; Valentine Seaman, *A Dissertation on the Mineral Waters of Saratoga . . .* (New York, 1793); "Natural History, Mineral Springs, at Saratoga," *Rural Magazine, or Vermont Repository* 1 (Sept. 1795): 451–53; Timothy Howe, *A History of the Medicinal Springs at Saratoga and Ballstown . . .* (Brattleboro, Vt., 1804); Isaac Weld, *Travels through the States of North America and the Provinces of Upper and Lower*

Canada (New York, 1799), 1:276; Abigail May, "Aunt Abby May's Ballstown Journal," entry at 20 June 1800, NYSHAL; Nathan Fiske, *The Moral Monitor* (Worcester, Mass., 1801), 2:204–9; Henry Sigerist, "The Early Medicinal History of Saratoga Springs," *Bulletin of the History of Medicine* 13 (May 1943): 572–84.

6. Philip Stansbury, *A Pedestrian Tour of Two Thousand Three Hundred Miles in North America* (New York, 1822), 50–51; Eliza Bridgham, "A Journey through New England and New York in 1818," *Magazine of History* 2 (July 1905): 23 ("unpleasant"); Jacques Milbert, *Picturesque Itinerary of the Hudson River*, trans. Constance Sherman (1828; Ridgewood, N.J.: Gregg, 1968), 49; Gideon Davison, *The Fashionable Tour; or, A Trip to the Springs, Niagara, Quebeck, and Boston in the Summer of 1821* (Saratoga Springs, 1822), 33–58; Edward Talbott, *Five Years Residence in the Canadas: Including a Tour through Part of the United States of America in the Year 1823* (London, 1824), 2:348–49; Reuben Sears, *A Poem on the Mineral Waters of Ballston and Saratoga . . .* (Ballston Spa, 1819), 89–90; John Duncan [John Morison], *Travels through Part of the United States and Canada in 1818 and 1819* (Glasgow, 1823), 2:234–35.

7. Milbert, 50.

8. Elihu Hoyt, "Journal of a Tour of Saratoga Springs," entry at 5 Aug. 1827, photocopy ed. by Peter Rippe, from original manuscript in Pocumtuck Valley Memorial Association, Deerfield, Mass., 1973, Saratoga Springs Historical Museum, Saratoga Springs, N.Y. (SSHM); Almira Read, "A Visit to Saratoga: 1826," ed. Genevieve Darden, *New York History* 50 (July 1969): 286–90, entry at 18 Aug. 1826; James Gilliam, "A Trip to the North," *Tyler's Quarterly Historical and Genealogical Magazine* 2 (1920): 297–305; Valentine Seaman, *A Dissertation on the Mineral Waters of Saratoga . . . ,* 2d ed. (New York, 1809), 81–82; George Temple, *The American Tourists' Pocket Companion, or a Guide to the Springs . . .* (New York, 1812), 45.

9. Stone, 287–97; "Carpenter's Saratoga Powders, for Making Congress Spring or Saratoga Waters," *American Journal of Science* 16 (1829): 370; Jonathan Constable to James Livingston, 29 Aug. 1828, file 17981, New York State Library Archives, Albany (NYSLA); William Meade, *An Experimental Enquiry into the Chemical Properties and Medicinal Qualities of the Principal Mineral Waters of Ballston and Saratoga* (Philadelphia, 1817), 64–65; Steel, 126, 79–127.

10. "Map of Lands Lately Owned by J. Clarke . . . ," 1851, drawn by H. Scofield, SCCO; Fitz-Greene Halleck, *The Poetical Works of Fitz-Greene Halleck* (New York, 1847), 241; James Stuart, *Three Years in North America* (Edinburgh, 1833), 1:192; North, 8–9; Cornelius Durkee, *Reminiscences of Saratoga* (Saratoga Springs: Saratogian, 1928), 126, 152–63.

11. Timothy Bigelow, *Journal of a Tour to Niagara Falls in the Year 1805* (Boston, 1876), 12–14; Henry Gilpin, *The Northern Tour: Being a Guide to Saratoga . . .* (Philadelphia, 1825), 60–65; Washington Irving, *Salmagundi* no. 16 (15 Oct. 1807); Timothy Dwight, *Travels in New England and New York* (1822; Cambridge: Harvard Univ. Press, 1969), 3:290–93; Theodore Dwight, *The Northern Traveller, Containing*

the Routes to the Springs, Niagara, Quebec, and the Coal Mines . . ., 6th ed. (New York, 1841), 140–51; Bernhard Puckhaber, ed., *Through the Years: A Pictorial History of the Village of Ballston Spa* (Ballston Spa: Bicentennial Commission, 1976), 3–17; Nancy Evans, "The Sans Souci: A Fashionable Resort Hotel in Ballston Spa," *Winterthur Portfolio* 6 (1970): 111–26; Thomas Chambers, "Seduction and Sensibility: The Refined Society of Ballston, New York, 1800," *New York History* 78 (July 1997): 245–72.

12. Elkanah Watson, *Men and Times of the Revolution* (New York, 1856), 349–51; Cohen quoted in Edward Grose, *Centennial History of the Village of Ballston Spa* (Ballston Spa: Ballston Journal, 1907), 53–73; "James Morrell's Account of a Trip to Ballston and Saratoga Springs in August, 1813," *Pennsylvania Magazine of History* 39 (19 Oct. 1915): 431; John Griscom, *Memoir of John Griscom* (New York, 1859), 76–78; Eliza Bowne, *A Girl's Life Eighty Years Ago: Selections from the Letters of Eliza Southgate Bowne* (1887; New York: Scribner's Sons, 1903), 128–30; John Melish, *Travels through the United States . . .* (1815; New York: Johnson Reprint, 1970), 551–53.

13. Evans, 121; [William Hay], *A History of Temperance in Saratoga County, N.Y.* (Saratoga Springs, 1855), 3–41, 112 ("unsunk Sodom"); *New York Observer*, 13 Aug. 1836; Whitman Mead, *Travels in North America* (New York, 1820), 155; Sans Souci Hotel ledger, June 1823 to Aug. 1826, Brookside Saratoga County History Center, Ballston Spa, N.Y.

14. *Act of Incorporation of the Village of Saratoga Springs, 17 April 1826 (with amendments to 1847)*, nos. 9–11, 13–14, Amendment to Act in 1829, no. 8, Saratoga Springs City Historian's Office, Saratoga Springs, N.Y. (SSCHO).

15. Town of Saratoga, Minutes of the Commissioners of Excise, 1836–54, 1–2, SSCHO; George Waller, *Saratoga: Saga of an Impious Era* (Englewood Cliffs: Prentice-Hall, 1966), 62–67; Hugh Bradley, *Such Was Saratoga* (New York: Doubleday, Doran, 1940), 71–81; Charles Jones and Lorenzo Greenwich II, *A Choice Collection of the Works of Francis Johnson* (New York: Point Two, 1983), 14–41.

16. "First Impressions of Saratoga," pt. 5, *National Era* 13 (8 Sept. 1859): 1; Michael O'Brien, ed., *An Evening When Alone: Four Journals of Single Women in the South, 1827–1867* (Charlottesville: Univ. Press of Virginia, 1993), 86; Stuart, 1:194–95; *HW*, 8 Aug. 1857 ("devil"); *New York Herald*, 13 Aug. 1848; Read, entry at 28 Aug. 1826; Samuel Sombre [James Gerard], *Aquarelles: Or Summer Sketches* (New York, 1858), 44–45; Caroline Gilman, *The Poetry of Travelling in the United States* (New York, 1838), 86.

17. Robert Vandewater, *The Tourist, or Pocket Manual for Travellers . . .*, 6th ed. (New York, 1838), 82; Barbara Shupe, Janet Steins, and Jyoti Pandit, *New York State Population, 1790–1980* (New York: Neal-Schuman, 1987), 264; George Templeton Strong, *Diary*, ed. Alan Nevins and Milton Thomas (New York: Macmillan, 1952), entry at 30 July 1841; Wellington Williams, *Appleton's Northern and Eastern Traveller's Guide* (New York, 1850), 169–71; Henry Tudor, *Narrative of a Tour in North*

America (London, 1834), 1:191; Carl Arfwedson, *The United States in 1832, 1833, and 1834* (London, 1834), 269; Grose, 67–70, 177; Samuel De Veaux, *The Travellers' Own Book to Saratoga Springs, Niagara Falls, and Canada . . .* (Buffalo, 1841), 29; *New York Weekly Tribune,* 6 Sept. 1851.

18. Daniel Benedict diary, entry at 5 July 1830, in *Saratoga Sentinel,* 14 Apr. to 30 June 1881; Saratoga Springs Town Board Minutes, 1820–64, SSCHO; Minutes of the [Village of Saratoga Springs] Board of Trustees, 26 Mar. 1844, SSCHO; Andrew Reed and James Matheson, *A Narrative of a Visit to the American Churches from the Congregational Union of England and Wales* (London, 1835), 318–19 ("redeemed"); Durkee, 145–47; [Beaufoy], *Tour through Parts of the United States and Canada, by a British Subject* (London, 1828), 135; map of Saratoga Springs (about 1820) drawn by J. Davison Jr. in 1890, Local History Room, Saratoga Springs Public Library, Saratoga Springs, N.Y. (SSPL); Thomas Gordon, *Gazetteer of the State of New York* (Philadelphia, 1836), 675–85; Thomas Hamilton, *Men and Manners in America* (1833; New York: Augustus Kelley, 1968), 2:372; Sarah Joseph Hale, *Sketches of American Character,* 4th ed. (Boston, 1833), 183–85. See chattel mortgages in SSCHO: Railroad House (1833), Pavilion House (1833), Pavilion Hotel (1836), Congress Hall (1837), Northern Hotel (1844), and the marvelous "List of items belonging to Putnam and Hathorn Contained in Union Hall premises" recorded in "To the Protection Insurance Co., 12 October 1848," NYSHAL.

19. Temple, 16. Jane Austen's *Sanditon* (1817) begins with a carriage being overturned on the way to a seaside resort; *Lady Susan; The Watsons; Sanditon* (New York: Penguin, 1974), 155.

20. O'Brien, 81 ("dust"); Basil Hall, *Travels in North America in the Years 1827, 1828* (London, 1829), 2:7; William Hoyt, ed., "Saratoga Jaunt, 1827: The Journal of Francis Johnson Dallam," *New York History* 28 (July 1947), entry at 5 Aug. 1827; Gilliam, 294–97; "Journey to Saratoga Springs, 1820," *Proceedings of the Massachusetts Historical Society* 50 (Feb. 1917): 189–96 (Fitch family); Tudor, 1:188–89; Margaret Davidson, "Sentimental Journey: The Diary of Margaret Miller Davidson," ed. Walter Harding, *Journal of the Rutgers University Library* 13 (Dec. 1949): 21–22, entry at 6 June 1833; Gilman, *Poetry,* 77, 88; Clement Moore to Mother, 14 Aug. 1830, Moore Papers, New York State Historical Society (NYSHS); Charles Griffin, "A Trip to Saratoga in 1833," SSPL.

21. *NYT,* 29–30 July 1852; Nathaniel Hawthorne, *The Centenary Edition of the Works of Nathaniel Hawthorne* (Columbus: Ohio State Univ. Press, 1974), 15:20; Donald Ringwald, *Hudson River Day Lines* (Berkeley, Calif.: Howell-North, 1965), 1–11.

22. Sarah Joseph Hale, *Traits of American Life* (Philadelphia, 1835), 187; *Tourist's Guide to the Hudson River, by Steamboat and Railroad . . .* (New York, 1852); Achille Murat, *The United States of North America* (London, 1833), 357; William Dunlap, *A Trip to Niagara; or, Travellers in America: A Farce, in Three Acts* (New York, 1830), 26–27; Alfred Weber, Beth Lueck, and Dennis Berthold, *Hawthorne's Travel*

Sketches (Hanover: Univ. Press of New England, 1989), 1–23; Dona Brown, *Inventing New England: Regional Tourism in the Nineteenth Century* (Washington, D.C.: Smithsonian Institution Press, 1995), 1–40.

23. "Swimming: A Dialogue between Philonao and Colymbao," *New England Magazine* 2 (June 1832): 507; on railroads and New Jersey resorts, see Emil Salvini, *The Summer City by the Sea: Cape May, New Jersey, An Illustrated History* (New Brunswick: Rutgers Univ. Press, 1995), 17–36; Charles Funnell, *By the Beautiful Sea: The Rise and High Times of That Great American Resort, Atlantic City* (New York: Knopf, 1975), 3–23; Maryann Brent, "Coastal Resort Morphology as a Response to Transportation Technology" (Ph.D. diss., Univ. of Waterloo [Ontario], 1997), 64–142, 199–200.

24. F. Daniel Larkin, *Pioneer American Railroads: The Mohawk & Hudson and the Saratoga & Schenectady* (Fleischmanns, N.Y.: Purple Mountain Press, 1995), 49–66, 80; Durkee, 89–91; Edward Abdy, *Journal of a Residence and Tour in the United States of North America, from April 1833 to October 1834* (1835; New York: Negro Universities Press, 1969), 1:262–63; Jim Shaughnessy, *Delaware and Hudson* (Berkeley, Calif.: Howell-North, 1967), 89–97; *Annual Report of the Saratoga & Washington Railroad* (Saratoga Springs, 1850); *Annual Report . . . of the Railroad Corporations for the Year Ending September 30, 1858* (Albany, 1859); Anderson, 176–84, 547; Stone, 176–86.

25. Stone, 313–20; Davison quoted in Bradley, 89; [Freeman Hunt], *Letters about the Hudson River and Its Vicinity* (New York, 1836), 79–80; *Frank Leslie's*, 27 Aug. 1859; De Veaux, 53; Durkee, 68; "First Impressions of Saratoga," pt. 1, *National Era* 13 (11 Aug. 1859).

26. Clement Moore, *Poems* (New York, 1844), 18; Charles Dickens, *American Notes* (New York, 1842), chap. 15; Strong, entries at 28–30 July 1841; Philip Hone, *Diary of Philip Hone,* ed. Bayard Tuckerman (New York, 1889), entries at 29 July 1843, 29 Aug. 1832; Richard White's summer tour in 1839 covered eighteen hundred miles in nineteen days; see *Narrative of a Journey from Quebec to Niagara, through the State of New York . . .* (Exeter, Mass., 1896).

27. James Kirke Paulding, *The New Mirror for Travellers; and Guide to the Springs* (New York, 1828), 3–6, 290–91; Temple, 23–24; John Watson, *Historic Tales of Olden Time: Concerning the Early Settlement and Advancement of New York City and State* (New York, 1832), 205–8; Michael Rockland, ed., *Sarmiento's Travels in the United States in 1847* (Princeton: Princeton Univ. Press, 1970), 137, 219, 239, 312; Francis Grund, *The Americans in Their Moral, Social, and Political Relations* (1837; New York: Johnson Reprint, 1968), 323; George Towle, *American Society* (London, 1870), 1:313–15; Frederick Marryat, *A Diary in America: With Remarks on Its Institutions* (1839; New York: Knopf, 1962), 45, 366 ("locomotive people"), 452.

28. Francis Hall, *Travels in Canada, and the United States, in 1816 and 1817* (Boston, 1818), 29; [Hunt], 201; William Peck and Charles Peck, *Peck's Tourist Companion to Niagara Falls, Saratoga Springs, the Lakes, Canada, Etc.* (Buffalo, 1845),

162 ("most celebrated"); Jacob Delameter, "Thesis on the Use and Abuse of the Saratoga Waters," *New York Journal of Medicine* 3 (July 1844): 55–65; "Diary of a Trip from Boston to Canada and Return through New York," entries at 14 Aug. 1822 to 8 Oct. 1822, NYSLA; De Veaux, 64–65.

29. O'Brien, 81 ("Elysium?"); Eleanor Grosvenor to Charlotte and Sarah Holcombe, 5 June 1833, file FM11336, George Holcombe Papers, NYSLA; Mrs. Lucy Wooster to Ann, 11 July 1844, Southern Historical Collection, University of North Carolina, Chapel Hill (UNC); *New York Tribune,* 7 July 1848; Ira Bean to Eliza Bean, 6 June 1830, file 13886, NYSLA.

30. Letter to "Dear Mother," 21 Aug. 1833, NYSHAL; Barnes Lathrop, ed., "A Southern Girl at Saratoga Springs, 1834," *North Carolina Historical Review* 15 (Apr. 1938): 161 ("shoemaker"); Robert Wickham, *A Saratoga Boyhood* (Syracuse: Orange Publishing, 1948), 6; *New York Mirror,* 3 Aug. 1839; Stone, 190–96, 222–43; Henry Clay, *The Papers of Henry Clay* (Lexington: Univ. Press of Kentucky, 1988), 9:325–37; Hone, entries at 19 July to 12 Aug. 1839; Bradley, 94–102; Elizabeth Ellet, *The Court Circles of the Republic* (Philadelphia, 1872), 274–76; Edmund Huling diary, entries at 1 Aug. to 4 Dec. 1840, SSPL.

31. *New York Post,* 7 Aug. 1843, quoted in Jack Kofoed, *Brandy for Heroes: A Biography of the Honorable John Morrissey* (New York: Dutton, 1938), 225; Hone, entries at 10 Aug. 1839, 24 July 1839; *Saratoga Sentinel,* 21 July 1835; John Disturnell, *Springs, Water-Falls, Sea Bathing Resorts, and Mountain Scenery of the United States and Canada* (New York, 1855), 360–62; Orville Holley, ed., *The Picturesque Tourist* (New York, 1844), 97; John Godley, *Letters from America, 1844* (London, 1844), 42; *Albany Argus,* 6 Aug. 1847.

32. *Frank Leslie's,* 4 Sept. 1859; Washington Irving, *Letters* (Boston: Twayne, 1978–82), 4:325; *Our Summer Retreats: A Handbook to All of the Chief Waterfalls, Springs . . .* (New York, 1858); Anderson, 185–87; "Announcement on Opening of New United States Hotel," SSHM; *National Era,* 8 Sept. 1850; "Congress Hall, Saratoga," *Eclectic Magazine* (July 1860), SSPL; Shupe, Steins, and Pandit, 264. For colonization, see letter to "Dear Mother," 21 Aug. 1833; *Frank Leslie's,* 27 Aug. 1859; *New York Herald,* 13 , 27 Aug. 1853; O'Brien, 83; Milbert, 49–51.

33. Minutes of the [Village of Saratoga Springs] Board of Trustees, 11, 25 Apr. 1846, 30 Jan. 1847; Anderson, 188–90; Bradley, 107–8; *Charter and By-Laws of the Village of Saratoga Springs* (Saratoga Springs, 1866), Village Ordinances of 1850 (187–88), and 31 Mar. 1857 (379).

34. *New York Evening Express,* 21 Aug. 1847, quoted in Landon Manning, *The Noble Animals: Tales of Saratoga Turf* (Saratoga Springs, 1973), 37; Durkee, 78–79, 93–96; Minutes of the [Village of Saratoga Springs] Board of Trustees, "Annual Report," 15 Nov. 1844 (42), 12 May 1846 (69–70), 25 Mar. 1856 (341), 2 Apr. 1866 (503–4); *Act of Incorporation* [Saratoga Springs], 10–11, and Amendments to Charter in 1844 and 1846, 12–13. For grumbling, see *The Petition of John Taxdodger and One Other, to the Legislature of the State of New York, for a City Charter for the New City of*

Sarahaha, formerly Saratoga Springs (Sarahaha [Saratoga Springs], 1859), 3–12, and "Notice to Taxpayers of Saratoga, 1866," Yates Collection, Skidmore College, Saratoga Springs (YC).

35. Grosvenor to Charlotte and Sarah Holcombe, 5 June 1833, George Holcombe Papers; Ellen Bond, "Journal of a Trip Made with My Dear Mother, Father, and Sisters and L.S. and Sue, July–Aug. 1850," entry at 29 July 1850, file 13389, NYSLA; Abigail May, entry at 20 June 1800; *Albany Statesman*, 6 Sept. 1820; Tudor, 1:191; *New York Tribune*, 9 June 1847; *Gleason's Pictorial Drawing-Room Companion*, 28 Aug. 1852; Durkee, 62, 72–75; *New York Herald*, 19 July 1848; 13 Aug. 1853.

36. Irving, *Letters*, 4:325; De Veaux, 92; "The Great Van Broeck Property," *Leisure Hour* 752 (26 May 1866): 322 ("great rush"); Mary Lynn and William Fox, eds., "The 1850 Census of Saratoga Springs," rev. ed. 1991, SSPL; Sylvester, *History*, 192; Anderson, 502–4; Lee Soltow, *Men and Wealth in the United States, 1850–1870* (New Haven: Yale Univ. Press, 1975), 178–80.

37. "Map of Lands Called 'The Homestead' Belonging to Samuel Twitchell at Saratoga Springs, 1840," SCCO; George Endicott, *Endicott's Pictures of Saratoga for 1843* (New York, 1843); *Sentinel* quoted in Grace Swanner, *Saratoga: Queen of Spas* (Utica: North Country, 1988), 126–27. On the "progress" motif, see Records and Proceedings of the Saratoga County Agricultural Society, 1844, address by Daniel Shepherd, 24–25, NYSLA; *Plattsburgh Republican*, 9 Sept. 1826; De Veaux, 89; Sears, *Poem*, 35.

38. Lynn and Fox, SSPL; William Fox and Mary Lynn, eds., "The 1860 Census of Saratoga Springs," 1991, SSPL.

39. *New York Herald*, 21 Aug. 1847; Charles Latrobe, *The Rambler in North America, 1832–1833* (1835; New York: Johnson Reprint, 1970), 2:127; Godley, 42–45; Patrick Shirreff, *A Tour through North America . . .* (Edinburgh, 1835), 57–58; Moore, *Poems*, 15–19; [Beaufoy], 135, 41–42; *HW*, 15 Aug. 1857.

40. Benjamin Perry, *Letters of Gov. Benjamin Franklin Perry to His Wife* (Greenville, N.C., 1890), 103–7; Frederick Olmsted, *The Cotton Kingdom* (1861; New York: Knopf, 1953), 416; "Art. IV.: 'The Northern Lakes . . .,' " *North American Review* 57 (July 1843): 112–23; Murat, 357; Daniel Drake, *The Northern Lakes: A Summer Resort for Invalids of the South* (1842; Cedar Rapids, Iowa: Torch, 1954); Lawrence Brewster, *Summer Migrations and Resorts of South Carolina Low-Country Planters* (Durham: Duke Univ. Press, 1947), 82.

41. Davison, *Fashionable*, 5; Gideon Davison, *Routes and Tables of Distances Embraced in the Traveller's Guide through the Northern and Middle States and the Canadas* (Saratoga Springs, 1833), 5; John Buckingham, *America: Historical, Statistic, and Descriptive* (London, 1841), 2:437; George Curtis, *Lotus Eating: A Summer Book* (New York, 1856), 114; "South Carolina, No. 2," *New England Magazine* 1 (Sept. 1831): 34–41.

42. Christopher Jenkins to his wife, 13 July 1826, Mrs. Christopher Jenkins Papers, Duke University Manuscripts Collection, Durham, N.C. (DUMC); Sarah Alexander

to A. Leopold Alexander, 30 July 1828, Alexander-Hillhouse Papers, UNC; William Lord to Eliza Lord (Wilmington, N.C.), 18 Aug. 1817, Lord Family Papers, UNC.

43. Union Hall register, 20 May 1852 to 27 Sept. 1856, SSHM: for example, 2 July 1853, 58 northerners and 3 southerners; 1 July 1854, 46 northerners and 3 southerners; 2 July 1855, 25 northerners, no southerners; 9 Aug. 1853, 96 northerners, 11 southerners; 7 Aug. 1854, 32 northerners, 5 southerners; 8 Aug. 1855, 46 northerners, 5 southerners. See also Peter Bulkley, "Identifying the White Mountain Tourist: Origin, Occupation, and Wealth as a Definition of the Early Hotel Trade, 1853–1854," *Historical New Hampshire* 35 (1980): 11, 124, 153–54; Darrell Norris, "Reaching the Sublime: Niagara Falls Visitor Origins, 1831–1854," *Journal of American Culture* 9 (Spring 1986): 53–59.

44. Camden *Journal* and New York *Mirror* quoted in Brewster, 103, 118–20; "Summer Travel in the South," *Southern Quarterly Review* 26 (Oct. 1854): 24–40, 60–65; "The Prospects and Policy of the South . . . ," *Southern Quarterly Review* 26 (Oct. 1854): 437; "Domestic Tourism," *Southern Literary Messenger* 17 (June 1851): 376–77; Hiram Fuller, *Belle Brittan on a Tour, at Newport and Here and There* (New York, 1858), 181; Nathaniel Willis, *The Rag Bag: A Collection of Ephemera* (New York, 1855), 271–73; Paul Finkelman, *An Imperfect Union: Slavery, Federalism, and Comity* (Chapel Hill: Univ. of North Carolina Press, 1981), 71–76, 131–36, 296–312.

45. *NYT,* 5 Aug. 1856; "Editor's Table," *Southern Literary Messenger* 31 (Nov. 1860): 390–91; Henry Ravenal, *The Private Journal of Henry William Ravenal, 1859–1887* (Columbia: Univ. of South Carolina Press, 1947), 26–28; Brewster, 101–2, 121–22; John Hope Franklin, *A Southern Odyssey: Travelers in the Antebellum North* (Baton Rouge: Louisiana State Univ. Press, 1976), 28, 143–68, 206–9, 255; *HW,* 15 Aug. 1857; *New York World,* 11 Aug. 1860.

46. Lynn and Fox, 1850, table 2; Fox and Lynn, 1860, table 2; Myra Armstead, *"Lord, Please Don't Take Me in August": African Americans in Newport and Saratoga Springs, 1870–1930* (Chicago: Univ. of Illinois Press, 1999), 19–37; J. Davison, map of Saratoga Springs; Theodore Corbett, "Saratoga County Blacks, 1720–1870," *Grist Mill* 20 (1986): 1–6; Solomon Northup, *Twelve Years a Slave,* ed. Sue Eakin and Joseph Logsdon (1854; Baton Rouge: Louisiana State Univ. Press, 1968), 9–11.

47. Jane North quoted in O'Brien, 201; *Saratogian,* 27 July 1855, quoted in Manning, *Noble,* 65; *Saratogian,* 14 Aug. 1888; *NYT,* 15 June 1877; 29 July 1865; Stuart, 1:229; Gretchen Sorin and Jane Rehl, *Honorable Work: African Americans in the Resort Community of Saratoga Springs, 1870–1970* (Saratoga Springs: Historical Society, 1992), 10; Armstead, 28; "The Grave of a Slave," lyrics by Sarah Furton, music by Francis Johnson, in *Tippecanoe and Tyler Too: A Collection of American Political Marches, Songs, and Dirges,* Newport Classic NPD85548, compact sound disk.

48. *NYT,* 6 June 1868; Lynn and Fox, 1850, table 1; Fox and Lynn, 1860, table 1; United States Hotel help book, 1880–82, NYSHAL; *Patterns: Saratoga's Nineteenth-Century Women* (Saratoga Springs: Historical Society, 1989), 3–18.

49. G. Terry Scharrer, "Farming in Saratoga County, 1860–1920," *Grist Mill* 14

(Winter 1980): 1–6; Durkee, 135–36; Helen McKearin, "Saratoga Glass and Its Personality, Oscar Granger," *Antiquarian* 14 (Mar. 1930): 44–45, 98–102; Fenton Keyes, "The Springs, Glass Houses, and Bottles of Saratoga Springs, N.Y.," *New York History* 38 (Apr. 1957): 214–16; Swanner, 140–49.

50. Michel Chevalier, *Society, Manners, and Politics in the United States*, trans. T. G. Bradford (1836; Gloucester, Mass.: Peter Smith, 1967), 304 (see the identical thought in Harriet Martineau, *Retrospect of Western Travel* [London, 1838], 2:221–22); George Morris, *The Little Frenchmen and His Water Lots; with Other Sketches of the Times* (Philadelphia, 1839), 57, 41–50; Curtis, 122; *Plattsburgh Republican*, 9 Sept. 1826; Vandewater, 84.

51. Mary Murray diary, entry at 7 Aug. 1825, NYSHS; O'Brien, 83 ("form"); "First Impressions of Saratoga," pt. 2, *National Era* 13 (18 Aug. 1859) ("faces"); *NYT*, 30 July 1866; Bigelow, 13; Steel, 122, 184; Marietta Holley, *Samantha at Saratoga or, "Racin' after Fashion" by Josiah Allen's Wife* (Philadelphia, 1887), 102; Gideon Davison, *The Traveller's Guide through the Middle and Northern States and the Province of Canada*, 8th ed. (Saratoga Springs, 1840), 139. For trips to Congress Spring, see De Veaux, 54; Griscom, 77–78; Latrobe, 2:128; Abbey Goodwin to Stephen Goodwin, 17 Aug. 1848, file 17996, NYSLA; Towle, 2:75; Peck and Peck, 168; Morris, *Frenchmen*, 69–83; Thomas Richards, "Saratoga," *Knickerbocker* 54 (Sept. 1859): 250–52; Bronson Howard, *Saratoga; or, "Pistols for Seven"* (New York, 1870), 20–21; Bond, entry at 30 July 1850. For some "typical" Saratoga days, see Lucy Wright Wooster to Ann Wooster, 21 Aug. 1846, Wooster Family Papers, UNC; Curtis, 113–21; Buckingham, 2:432–54; Sombre, 5–51; "Glances at Men and Things, Saratoga Springs," *New Yorker* 8 (24 Aug. 1839): 366; Griffin, entry at 10–15 May 1833; *HW*, 8 Aug. 1857; Read, entries at 23–25 Aug. 1826.

52. Daniel McLaren, *The Saratoga Pavilion Fountain* (New York, 1842), 102–5; Benedict diary, entries at 12 July 1841, 11 Oct. 1843.

53. United States Hotel menus, 16 Aug. 1854, 31 July 1855, SSHS; Alexander MacKay, *The Western World; or, Travels in the United States in 1846–1847*, 2d ed. (1849; New York: Negro Universities Press, 1968), 3:199–201; Charles Weld, *A Vacation Tour in the United States and Canada* (London, 1855), 74–76; John Irwin, *Hydrotherapy at Saratoga: A Treatise on the Natural Mineral Waters* (New York, 1892), 142–43. On dyspepsia, see Hamilton, *Men and Manners*, 2:379; "Why We Get Sick," *HM* 13 (Oct. 1856): 645; Tudor, 1:193–94; "Glances at Men and Things," 366; "First Impressions of Saratoga," pt. 3, *National Era* 13 (25 Aug. 1859); Paulding, *Mirror*, 20–21.

54. *Frank Leslie's*, 27 Aug. 1859; 3 Sept. 1859; Bond, entry at 1 Aug. 1850; *New York Herald*, 27 Aug. 1847; Gilman, *Poetry*, 85–86; Weld, *Vacation*, 72; Martineau, 2:221–22; *Brooklyn Eagle*, 15 Aug. 1844; Buckingham, 2:433; Percy Pyne diary, 1843, NYSHS.

55. Durkee, 121; *Saratoga Whig*, 11 Aug. 1843; account books for Panorama of Geneva at Saratoga Springs, 1834–35, SSCHO; Reed and Matheson, 320.

56. *Saratogian,* 14 Jan. 1880 ("nature"); *HW,* 24 Aug. 1872; Moore, *Poems,* 35–36.

57. Union Hall register, 1852–56; *New York Herald,* 20 July 1857; Strong, entry at 30 July 1841. This finding is in line with studies of the origins of tourists for both the White Mountains and Niagara Falls; Bulkley, 113, 153; Norris, 56.

58. *New York Daily News,* 21 July 1855; Stansbury, 48–50 ("barren"); John Bachelder, *Popular Resorts and How to Reach Them* (Boston, 1875), 176 ("surpassed"). On Saratoga's lack of natural attractions, see William Chambers, *Things as They Are in America* (New York, 1854), 57; De Veaux, 88; Hale, *Sketches,* 186; Charles Lyell, *A Second Visit to the United States of North America* (London, 1849), 2:263; Sears, *Poem,* 31–32; Richards, "Saratoga," 255–56; Bridgham, 26; *Wilson's Illustrated Guide to the Hudson River* (New York, 1848), 58; O'Brien, 86, 90.

59. "First Impressions," pt. 1. For overemphasis on the tourist's search for "nature," see John Sears, *Sacred Places: American Tourist Attractions in the Nineteenth Century* (New York: Oxford Univ. Press, 1989), 12–32, 156–81, 209–16; W. Douglas McCombs, "Therapeutic Rusticity: Antimodernism, Health, and the Wilderness Vacation," *New York History* 76 (Oct. 1995): 415–27.

60. Grund, *Americans,* 323, 17–40; Disturnell, *Springs;* Alexis de Tocqueville, *Democracy in America,* trans. Henry Reeve (1835–40; New York: Schocken, 1972), 1:153–61. For killjoy Americans, see Frances Trollope, *Domestic Manners of the Americans* (1832; New York: Knopf, 1949), 209, 305; Dickens, *Notes,* chap. 18; Lyell, 2:91; "Disjointed Gossip from the Other Side of the Big Pond," *Bentley's Magazine* 39 (1856): 583; Buckingham, 2:43–44, 351–52; "Why We Get Sick," 642.

61. Henry Ward Beecher, *Lectures to Young Men, on Various Important Subjects,* 3d ed. (New York, 1852), passim; Henry Ward Beecher, *Star Papers; or, Experiences of Art and Nature* (New York, 1855), passim; Clifford Clark, *Henry Ward Beecher: Spokesman for a Middle-Class America* (Urbana: Univ. of Illinois Press, 1978), 2–5, 57–59, 197–229, 275–80. See *Brooklyn Eagle,* 13 July 1879, for Beecher at Coney Island.

62. Irving, *Salmagundi* no. 16 (15 Oct. 1807); Irving, *Letters,* 4:321, 330; Curtis, 14; *New York Herald,* 27 July 1848; Pyne diary, 28–29; *Our Summer Retreats,* 32–34.

CHAPTER TWO   *The Revival of Newport*

1. James Fenimore Cooper, *The Red Rover: A Tale* (Philadelphia, 1828), 1; James Fenimore Cooper, *The Letters and Journals of James Fenimore Cooper,* ed. J. Beard (Cambridge: Harvard Univ. Press, 1968), 2:295; Adam Hodgson, *Letters from North America* (London, 1824), 2:132–33; Edward Kendall, *Travels through the Northern Parts of the United States* (New York, 1809), 2:8–11; Tyrone Power, *Impressions of America during the Years 1833, 1834, and 1835* (London, 1836), 1:95; George Templeton Strong, *Diary,* ed. and trans. Alan Nevins and Milton Thomas (New York: Macmillan, 1852), entry at 7 May 1836; James Stuart, *Three Years in North Amer-*

ica (Edinburgh, 1833), 1:357–60; Thomas Hamilton, *Men and Manners in America* (1833; New York: Augustus Kelley, 1968), 134–55; Anne Royall, *Sketches of History, Life, and Manners in the United States* (New Haven, 1826), 364–72.

2. "A British Navy Yard Contemplated in Newport, R.I., in 1764," *Rhode Island Historical Magazine (RIHM)* 6 (July 1885): 42–47; "Newport Society in the Last Century," *HM* 59 (Sept. 1879): 497; Carl Bridenbaugh, "Colonial Newport as a Summer Resort," *Rhode Island Historical Society Collections* 26 (Jan. 1933): 5–17; Bruce Daniels, *Puritans at Play: Leisure and Recreation in Colonial New England* (New York: St. Martin's, 1995), 141–59; Peter Coleman, *The Transformation of Rhode Island, 1790–1861* (Providence: Brown Univ. Press, 1963), 9–36, 93, 123–24; Elaine Crane, *A Dependent People: Newport, Rhode Island, in the Revolutionary Era* (New York: Fordham Univ. Press, 1985), 53–59; Lynne Withey, *Urban Growth in Colonial Rhode Island: Newport and Providence in the Eighteenth Century* (Albany: State Univ. of New York Press, 1984), 99–122.

3. Melville quoted in Bridenbaugh, "Newport," 2–6; John Williams to John Malbone (Augusta, Ga.), 18 Dec. 1769, Malbone Papers, box 174, Newport Historical Society, Newport, R.I. (NHS); Hamilton quoted in Wendy Martin, ed., *Colonial American Travel Narratives* (New York: Penguin, 1994), 252–53, 288–94; "A Chapter from Arthur Brown's Miscellaneous Sketches, London, 1798," *RIHM* 6 (Jan. 1886): 165. Sheila Skemp, "George Berkeley's Newport Experience," *Rhode Island History (RIH)* 37 (May 1978): 52–63; Edwin Gaustad, *George Berkeley in America* (New Haven: Yale Univ. Press, 1979), 1–18.

4. De Warville quoted in *Newport, Block Island, and Narragansett Pier* (Boston, 1895), 16; Judith Boss, *Newport: A Pictorial History* (Virginia Beach: Donning, 1981), 64–79.

5. John Pease and John Miles, *Gazetteer of the States of Connecticut and Rhode Island* (Hartford, 1819), 2:354; Douglass quoted in Carl Bridenbaugh, *Cities in Revolt: Urban Life in America, 1743–1776* (New York: Knopf, 1955), 53; Paul Bourcier, "Prosperity at the Wharves: Providence Shipping, 1780–1850," *RIH* 48 (May 1990): 35–49; Harold Hurst, "The Elite Class of Newport, Rhode Island; 1830–1860" (Ph.D. diss., New York University, 1975), 4; Withey, 33–107.

6. Theodore Dwight, *The Northern Traveller, Containing the Routes to the Springs, Niagara, Quebec, and the Coal Mines . . .* , 6th ed. (New York, 1841), 281; George Mason, *Annals of Trinity Church, Newport, Rhode Island* (Newport, 1894), 2:45–46 (tax); Philip Stansbury, *A Pedestrian Tour of Two Thousand Three Hundred Miles in North America* (New York, 1822), 267–68; Coleman, 36; Anthony Nicolosi, "The Newport Asylum for the Poor: A Successful Nineteenth-Century Institutional Response to Social Dependency," *RIH* 47 (Feb. 1989): 8. On the lack of new construction, see Wilfred Munro, *Picturesque Rhode Island* (Providence, 1881), 51; *Newport Mercury*, 20 Oct. 1860; George Channing, *Early Recollections of Newport, R.I.* (Newport, 1868), 149; Richard Bayles, *History of Newport County, Rhode Island* (New York, 1888), 1:488, 535; Charles Dow, *Newport: The City by the Sea* (Newport,

1880), 53. Dow later worked on Wall Street and helped create the stock index that bears his name.

7. George Smith, "Memories of Long Ago, 1833–1925," *Bulletin of the Newport Historical Society (BNHS)* 56 (Jan. 1926): 10; Coleman, 35, 62–70, 135–39, 178, 201, 220; Anna Hunter, "A Decade of Newport as Seen by Two Wandering Sons," *Newport Historical Society Bulletin (NHSB)* 53 (Apr. 1925): 4; *Newport Mercury,* 6 July 1850; 19 Oct. 1850; 15 Nov. 1856; 6 Nov. 1858; *Acts and Resolves of the Rhode Island Assembly,* 80–95 (May 1846), Rhode Island Historical Society, Providence (RIHS); Bayles, 1:537; George Mason, *Newport Illustrated, in a Series of Pen and Pencil Sketches* (New York, 1854), 79; Timothy Dwight, *Travels in New England and New York* (1822; Cambridge: Harvard Univ. Press, 1969), 3:30; Pease and Miles, 2:351–55.

8. Power, 2:26; *Herald of the Times,* 21 Aug. 1834; Dow, 54–56; Samuel Ward to [?], 20 Oct. 1793, Peck ms., RIHS; *Newport Mercury,* 14 June 1828; *Rhode Island Republican,* 17 Jan. 1828; 2 Oct. 1828; Bayles, 1:488–89; Hunter, "Decade," 2–7; *Newport Daily News,* 24–25 Mar. 1897; Osmand Tiffany, "Old Newport," *Cosmopolitan* (Oct. 1893): 665; Howe quoted in Maud Howe Elliott, *This Was My Newport* (Cambridge: Mythology, 1944), 53.

9. J. Maxwell to Adam Alexander, 6 Sept. 1822, Adam Alexander Papers, UNC; Robert Habersham diary, entries at 30 July–1 Aug. 1831, UNC; John Calhoun, *The Papers of John C. Calhoun* (Columbia: Univ. of South Carolina Press, 1958–88), 1:12–13, 24; Marian Gouverneur, *As I Remember: Recollections of American Society during the Nineteenth Century* (New York: Appleton, 1911), 100–101.

10. Hugh S. Ball (Newport) to brother John Ball (Charleston), 29 Sept. 1826; John's reply, 12 Oct. 1826; Hugh S. Ball, 2 Sept. 1831, to John Ball, John Ball Sr. and John Ball Jr. Papers, DUMC; *Newport Mercury,* 30 June 1821; 5 Aug. 1826 ("thronged"); 16 Feb. 1884; Ball (1830) quoted in Lawrence Brewster, *Summer Migrations and Resorts of South Carolina Low-Country Planters* (Durham: Duke Univ. Press, 1947), 33; George Mason, *Reminiscences of Newport* (Newport, 1884), 9–18.

11. Dow, 69–70; *Newport Mercury,* 21 May 1859; Myra Armstead, *"Lord, Please Don't Take Me in August": African Americans in Newport and Saratoga Springs, 1870–1930* (Chicago: Univ. of Illinois Press, 1999), 19–34.

12. *Acts and Resolves,* 50–51 (Oct. 1845); *Newport Daily News,* 7 Nov. 1860; William Lloyd Garrison, *The Letters of William Lloyd Garrison,* ed. Louis Ruchames (Cambridge: Belknap, 1971), 2:97, 123–33; Salomon de Rothschild, *A Casual View of America: The Home Letters of Salomon de Rothschild, 1859–1861,* ed. and trans. Sigmund Diamond (London: Cresset, 1962), 67; Strong, entry at 31 May 1856; [George Curtis], "Editor's Easy Chair," *Harpers Monthly* 61 (Sept. 1880): 631; Bayles, 1:422–30; William McLoughlin, *Rhode Island: A History* (New York: Norton, 1978), 142–47; Marvin Gettleman, *The Dorr Rebellion: A Study in American Radicalism, 1833–1849* (New York: Random House, 1973), 161–62.

13. *Rhode Island Republican,* 28 May 1829 ("cheaper"); 3 Sept. 1829; "Newport:

Historical and Social," *HM* 9 (Aug. 1854): 315; Elliott, 71–77, 41–43; Channing, *Recollections*, 164; *Herald of the Times*, 21 Aug. 1834; Anna Burgwyn (Newport) to mother (Boston), undated letters in Burgwyn Family Papers, UNC; Hunter, "Decade," 8–20; *Acts and Resolves*, 6–8 (June 1833), 55–57 (Oct. 1840); Tiffany, 673; Henry Turner, "Reminiscences of Newport, 1881," NHS; John Smith, *The Illustrated Hand-Book: A New Guide for Travellers* (New York, 1850), 35; Dwight, *Traveller*, 3:33–34.

14. *Acts and Resolves*, 59 (Jan. 1844), 20–22 (May 1844); Dow, 61–66; *NYT*, 6 Aug. 1876; Charles Sweetser, *Book of Summer Resorts* (New York, 1868), 10; *Newport Mercury*, 9 Aug. 1845; 14 June 1884; Sidney Fisher, *A Philadelphia Perspective: The Diary of Sidney George Fisher Covering the Years 1834–1871*, ed. Nicholas Wainwright (Philadelphia: Historical Society of Pennsylvania, 1967), 176, 190; Antoinette Downing and Vincent Scully Jr., *The Architectural Heritage of Newport, Rhode Island, 1640–1915* (New York: Clarkson Potter, 1967), 120–31; Thomas Richards, "Newport," *Knickerbocker* 54 (Oct. 1859): 350 ("epitome").

15. James Harrison (New York) to daughter, 15 Aug. 1853, James Harrison Papers, UNC; Channing, *Recollections*, 264, v; Edward Peterson, *History of Rhode Island and Newport* (New York, 1853), 285–86; *Newport Mercury*, 17 Aug. 1844; 21 July 1849; 2 Aug. 1851; 26 Aug. 1854; 2 Aug. 1856; *Newport Daily News*, 8 Aug. 1851; 15–18 Sept. 1851; *HW*, 4 Sept. 1858; Mary Powel, "Presidential Visits to Newport," *BNHS* 45 (July 1923): 16–31.

16. John Dix [George Phillips], *A Handbook of Newport, and Rhode Island* (Newport, 1852), 20–21, 154–56; *HW*, 30 Sept. 1893; Ronald Potvin, ed., "In His Own Words: Henry Williams Returns to Newport," *Newport History (NH)* 65 (1993): 40–43; Brewster, 34; *Newport Mercury*, 3 Nov. 1849; 5 Mar. 1853; 16 Feb. 1884; 14 June 1884; Mason, *Illustrated*, 12; Armstead, 23, 32–33.

17. *Newport Daily News*, 24–25 Mar. 1897; Frederick Marryat, *A Diary in America: With Remarks on Its Institutions* (1839; New York: Knopf, 1962), 45; Charles Jefferys, *Newport: A Short History* (Newport: Newport Historical Society, 1992), 43–45; Hunter, "Decade," 16; Francis Grund shared Hunter's sentiment almost verbatim in *The Americans in Their Moral, Social, and Political Relations* (1837; New York: Johnson Reprint, 1968), 323–24.

18. Roger McAdam, *Floating Palaces: New England to New York on the Old Fall River Line* (Providence: Mowbray, 1972), 11–21; Roger McAdam, *The Old Fall River Line* (New York: Stephen Daye, 1955), 13–95; Edwin Dunbaugh, *Night Boat to New England, 1815–1900* (New York: Greenwood, 1992), 6, 17, 103–31; Fisher, 198.

19. "Newport City Documents, 1853–54" (Newport, 1854), docs. 3, 17, NHS; "Tax Book of the City of Newport for 1854," NHS; "Tax Book of the City of Newport 1863," NHS; *Newport Mercury*, 17 Aug. 1844; 7 Sept. 1844; 28 Aug. 1852; 23 July 1853; 22 Apr. 1854 ("costly mansions"); 14 Oct. 1854; *Newport Daily News*, 19 Sept. 1851; 18 Oct. 1851.

20. Hurst, 62, 70, 81 (pattern); Alan Schumacher, "Newport's First Directory,"

NH 44 (1971): 93–105; *Newport City Directory for 1858* (Newport, 1858), 105–24; R. S. Neale, *Bath, 1680–1850: A Social History, or, A Valley of Pleasure yet a Sink of Iniquity* (London: Routledge, 1981), 12–94.

21. Power, 2:22; *Newport Mercury*, 15 May 1852; 14 Oct. 1854 (steam mills); 23 May 1874 ("dingy"); Rhode Island Historical Preservation Commission (RIHPC), *The Kay Street–Catherine Street–Old Beach Road Neighborhood, Newport, Rhode Island* (Providence, 1974), 16–19; RIHPC, *The West Broadway Neighborhood: Newport, Rhode Island* (Providence, 1977), 17–19; RIHPC, *The Southern Thames Street Neighborhood in Newport, Rhode Island* (Providence, 1980), 12–23.

22. *Acts and Resolves*, 20–22 (June 1839), 3 (Jan. 1847), 64–73 (May 1847), 12–13 (Jan. 1848), 72–79 (May 1848), 49–50 (June 1851); *Newport Daily News*, 13 July 1850; *Newport Mercury*, 27 Oct. 1849.

23. *Tax-Book for the City of Newport for 1859* (Newport, 1860); Charles Hammett, *A Contribution to the Bibliography and Literature of Newport, R.I.* (Newport, 1887), 99–101; "Newport City Documents for 1853–1854," docs. 3, 10, 16; "Newport City Documents for 1857–1858" (Newport, 1858), docs. 12, 69–70, NHS; *Newport Mercury*, 16, 30 Oct. 1852; 6 Nov. 1852; 5 Sept. 1857 ("capital"); 13 Nov. 1858 ("wealth"); Hurst, 93; Frank Harris, *History of the Re-union of the Sons and Daughters of Newport, R.I., July 4, 1884* (Newport, 1885), 36; Dix, *Handbook*, 20.

24. "Newport in Winter," *Putnam's Monthly* 1 (Feb. 1853): 150–52; *Newport City Directory for 1858;* Mason, *Illustrated*, 12; Hurst, 16–76, 150; *Newport Mercury*, 16 Feb. 1856; 3 Oct. 1857; William Chambers, *Things as They Are in America* (New York, 1854), 56–58. See also Charlene Lewis, "Ladies and Gentlemen on Display: Planter Society at the Virginia Springs, 1790–1860" (Ph.D. diss., Univ. of Virginia, 1997), 136–89.

25. Sarah Cohoone, *Visit to Grand-Papa; Or, A Week at Newport* (New York, 1840): 38; Cleveland Amory, *The Last Resorts* (1948; New York: Harper and Brothers, 1952), 183–84; *Newport, Block Island, and Narragansett Pier*, 49, 55. William Lawrence's heirs eventually sold Ochre Point in subdivided parcels for more than $800,000; "Ochre Point: The Home of an American Jurist," *Newport Historical Magazine* 3 (1882): 33–55.

26. *Newport Mercury*, 7 Sept. 1850 ("deplore"); 19 Oct. 1850; 8 Feb. 1851; 16 Aug. 1851; 17 July 1852.

27. Leila Lee [Rebecca Coe], *The Dales in Newport* (New York, 1854), 101–3; *NYT*, 29 Aug. 1866 ("strand"); *Frank Leslie's*, 29 Aug. 1857; Mason, *Illustrated*, 50, 91–100; Dix, *Handbook*, vii, 21, 69–80; Cohoone, 59–61; Mary Powel, "The Old Easton Farm," *BNHS* 64 (Jan. 1928): 6–8; *Newport Mercury*, 8 June 1822; 17 July 1852; *HW*, 28 Aug. 1858; 4 Sept. 1858; Dow, 78–83, 102–3.

28. Sadayoshi Omoto, "Berkeley and Whittredge at Newport," *Art Quarterly* 27 (Winter 1964): 42–56; William Channing, *The Works of William E. Channing* (Boston,

1882), 422; James Yarnall, *John La Farge in Paradise: The Painter and His Muse* (Newport: William Vareika, 1995), 2–18.

29. Nathaniel Hawthorne, *The Centenary Edition of the Works of Nathaniel Hawthorne* (Columbus: Ohio State Univ. Press, 1974), 9:451–62; William Ulyat, *Life at the Seashore* (Princeton, N.J., 1880), 26–43; Alan Corbin, *The Lure of the Sea: The Discovery of the Seaside in the Western World, 1750–1840*, trans. Jocelyn Phelps (Berkeley: Univ. of California Press, 1994), 18–21, 163–68, 229–63; John Walton, *The English Seaside Resort: A Social History* (New York: St. Martin's, 1983), 5–73, 216–18; William Cowper, *Poetical Works* (London: Oxford Univ. Press, 1959), 120; Robert Southey, *Letters from England*, 3d ed. (1807; London, 1814), 1:346–47 (letter 30); Jane Austen, *Lady Susan; The Watsons; Sanditon* (New York: Penguin, 1974), 155–211.

30. *Newport Mercury*, 16 Aug. 1856; Reed and Matheson, 318–19 ("run"); "Swimming: A Dialogue between Philonao and Colymbao," *New England Magazine* 2 (June 1832): 506–12; Charles Norton, *American Seaside Resorts* (New York, 1883), 5–8; George Walton, *Mineral Springs of the United States* (New York, 1873), 373–78; Ellen Bond, "Journal of a Trip Made with My Dear Mother, Father, and Sisters and L.S. and Sue, July–Aug. 1850," entries at 10, 12 Aug. 1850, file 13389, NYSLA; Towle, 2:83; "Disjointed," 581; Katherine Wormeley, "Reminiscences of Newport in the Fifties," *NH* 41 (1968): 14–16; Samuel Sombre [James Gerard], *Aquarelles: Or Summer Sketches* (New York, 1858), 55–56.

31. George Curtis, *Lotus-Eating: A Summer Book* (New York, 1856), 149; Anthony Trollope, *North America* (New York: Knopf, 1951), 25–28; *Rhode Island Republican*, 14 Aug. 1828; *Newport Daily News*, 16 May 1850; Ocean House Omnibus, ca. 1850, NHS; Henry David Thoreau, *Cape Cod* (1865; Princeton: Princeton Univ. Press, 1988), 214.

32. *NYT*, 1 Aug. 1866 ("appearance"); Lee, 51–55; *Rhode Island Republican*, 7 Aug. 1828; Powel, "Easton," 8; Emil Salvini, *The Summer City by the Sea: Cape May, New Jersey, An Illustrated History* (New Brunswick: Rutgers Univ. Press, 1995), 6–28; George Thomas and Carl Doebly, *Cape May, Queen of Seaside Resorts: Its History and Architecture* (Philadelphia: Art Alliance, 1976), 19–29, 65; Joseph Garland, *Boston's North Shore: Being an Account of Life among the Noteworthy, Fashionable, Wealthy, Eccentric, and Ordinary, 1823–1890* (Boston: Little, Brown, 1978), 29–73.

33. John Watson, *Historic Tales of Olden Time: Concerning the Early Settlement and Advancement of New York City and State* (New York, 1832), 204–5; Bond, entry at 10 Aug. 1850; Potvin, 40; "Newport City Documents, 1857–58," docs. 103, 114; *Newport Mercury*, 14 Aug. 1852; 16 July 1853; 12 Aug. 1854; 21 July 1855; Trollope, *North America*, 27–28; Orr's quoted in Claudia Kidwell, *Women's Bathing and Swimming Costume in the United States* (Washington, D.C.: Smithsonian Institution Press, 1968), 8; Norton, 5–7 ("ball-room"); John Stilgoe, *Alongshore* (New Haven: Yale Univ. Press, 1994), 335–57. Newport beaches still used the flag system in the late 1800s; see James Bowditch, *Newport: The City by the Sea* (Providence, 1880), 39, and *Newport*,

Block Island, and Narragansett Pier, 48. A sign at Coney Island warned that "Bathing without full suits positively prohibited by law," in 1870, *NYT,* 29 Aug. 1870.

34. Richards, "Newport," 337–52; Henry Tuckerman, "Newport Out of Season," *Knickerbocker* 52 (July 1858): 24–35; "Disjointed," 575–84; Mason, *Illustrated,* 7–10, 49–100; Hammett, 54–56; Rebecca Harding Davis, "The Wife's Story," *Atlantic Monthly* 14 (July 1864): 1–19. On romantic Newport, see Dow, 85–98; "Newport: Historical and Social," 291–315; Dix, *Handbook,* 72–75; Cohoone, 87–123; Elliott, 45–46; Henry Tuckerman, "The Graves at Newport," *HM* 39 (Aug. 1869): 372–88; Samuel Longfellow, ed., *The Life of Henry Wadsworth Longfellow with Extracts from His Journals and Correspondence* (Boston, 1891), 2:239–41; Philip Means, *Newport Tower* (New York: Henry Holt, 1942), 27–85; Henry Wadsworth Longfellow, *The Complete Poetical Works* (Boston: Houghton Mifflin, 1922), 13–14; Lee, 105–24, 209–11.

35. Mark Sullivan, "John F. Kensett at Newport: The Making of a Luminist Painter," *Antiques* 138 (Nov. 1990): 1030–41; Linda Ferber, "William Trost Richards at Newport," *NH* 51 (1978): 1–15; Gibson Danes, "William Morris Hunt and His Newport Circle," *Magazine of Art* 43 (Apr. 1950): 144–50; John Driscoll and John Howat, *John Frederick Kensett: An American Master* (New York: Norton, 1985), 42, 168–80; Cheryl Cibulka, *Quiet Places: The American Landscapes of Worthington Whittredge* (Washington, D.C.: Garamond Pridemark, 1982), 24–28, 60–74; Yarnall, *La Farge,* 21–134; Daniel Sachs, "Alfred Thompson Bricher and the Social Implications of Romantic Images of the American Victorian Summer Watering Place" (Ph.D. diss., Case Western Reserve Univ., 1996), 70–131.

36. Curtis, *Lotus-Eating,* 47–49; see the identical thought in Thomas Starr King, *The White Hills: Their Legends, Landscape, and Poetry* (1859; New York, 1870), 17, 57, 72. For Henry James in Newport, see *Autobiography,* ed. Frederick Dupee (New York: Criterion, 1956), 299; Robert Le Clair, *Young Henry James: 1843–1870* (New York: Bookman, 1955), 280–94, 481–87; Leon Edel, *Henry James: The Untried Years, 1843–1870* (Philadelphia: Lippincott, 1953), 136–83, 139; Wormeley, 1–17; Virginia Covell, "In the Footsteps of Henry James," *NH* 61 (Summer 1988): 69–75.

37. Hiram Fuller, *Belle Brittan on a Tour, at Newport and Here and There* (New York, 1858), 162–79, 211; "The Queen of Aquidneck," *HM* 44 (Aug. 1874): 315–16; John La Farge, *The Manner Is Ordinary* (New York: Harcourt, Brace, 1954), 17.

38. Curtis, *Lotus-Eating,* 192–96; Fisher, 82; Ward McAllister, *Society as I Have Found It* (New York, 1890), 191–203; Trollope, *North America,* 28; *Newport Mercury,* 27 Oct. 1849; 21 Aug. 1852; 4 Sept. 1852; 21 July 1855 (*Transcript*); 16 Aug. 1856 (Trinity); 14 June 1884; 21 Dec. 1889; Lee, 73–78; Mason, *Illustrated,* 20, 71; *Frank Leslie's,* 29 Aug. 1857; "Newport: Historical and Social," 290; *NYT,* 13 Aug. 1857; Tuckerman, "Season," 26.

39. Bond, entries at 9–10 Aug. 1850; Dix, *Handbook,* 152–70; Fuller, 157–214; Richards, "Newport," 337–52; Hammett, 110–11; *Acts and Resolves,* 190–91 (June 1853).

40. "Letter of the Late Joseph Wharton, 1864," *NHSB* 71 (Oct. 1929): 23; For typical days, see *Newport Mercury*, 2 Aug. 1856; "Disjointed," 582; Hunter, "Decade," 21; *New York Herald*, 29 Aug. 1848; 23 Aug. 1853; *NYT*, 7 July 1875; Mary King Van Rensselaer, *Newport: Our Social Capital* (Philadelphia: Lippincott, 1905), 30–33.

41. "Newport in Winter," 152 ("great white pile"); Henry Ward Beecher, *Star Papers; or, Experiences of Art and Nature* (New York, 1855), 111–13; Brewster, 34, 102 ("rusticate"); Power, 2:26–31; *Newport Mercury*, 6 Aug. 1853; James Lowell, *Letters of James Russell Lowell*, ed. Charles Norton (New York, 1894), 1:214–17.

42. Fitz-Greene Halleck, *The Poetical Works of Fitz-Greene Halleck* (New York, 1847), 241; "American Country Life," *Crayon* 5 (Oct. 1858): 280; *New York Herald*, 13, 29 Aug. 1848; "Chit-Chat upon Philadelphia Fashions for August," *Godey's Lady's Book* 37 (Aug. 1848): 119. For the watering place round, see "All Baggage at the Risk of Owner: A Story of the Watering-Places," *HM* 5 (Aug. 1852): 337; Charles Murray, *Travels in North America during the Years 1834, 1835, and 1836* (New York, 1839), 62; Fisher, 200; Benjamin Perry, *Letters of Gov. Benjamin Franklin Perry to His Wife* (Greenville, N.C., 1890), 103; "The Great Van Broek Property," *Leisure Hour* 751–52 (26 May 1866): 322; Thomas Nichols, *Forty Years of American Life* (London, 1864), 401; Bayard Taylor, "The Chiropodist: A Story of the Watering-places," *HM* 24 (Mar. 1862): 460–66; Brewster, 101–10.

43. Victor Turner and Edith Turner, *Image and Pilgrimage in Christian Culture* (New York: Columbia Univ. Press, 1978), 241–44, 1–39; Emile Durkheim, *The Elementary Forms of Religious Life*, trans. J. Swain (1912; New York: Allen and Unwin, 1915), 346, 337–65; Aristotle, *Nichomachean Ethics*, 8, vi, 4. The social dynamics of pilgrimage has become the subject of much fruitful inquiry: N. Crumrine and Alan Morinis, eds., *Pilgrimage in Latin America* (New York: Greenwood, 1991); Mary Nolan and Sidney Nolan, *Christian Pilgrimage in Modern Western Europe* (Chapel Hill: Univ. of North Carolina Press, 1989); Simon Coleman and John Elsner, *Pilgrimage: Past and Present in the World Religions* (Cambridge: Harvard Univ. Press, 1995); Bardwell Smith and Holly Reynolds, *The City as a Sacred Center: Essays on Six Asian Contexts* (New York: E. Brill, 1987). Medieval pilgrimage is considered in Donald Howard, *Writers and Pilgrims: Medieval Pilgrimage Narratives and Their Posterity* (Berkeley: Univ. of California Press, 1980); Jonathan Sumption, *Pilgrimage: An Image of Medieval Religion* (Totowa, N.J.: Rowman and Littlefield, 1975); and Margaret Labarge, *Medieval Travellers* (New York: Norton, 1982).

44. Georg Roppen and R. Sommer, *Strangers and Pilgrims: An Essay on the Metaphor of Journey* (New York: Humanities, 1964); Frans Amelinckx and J. Megay, eds., *Travel, Quest, and Pilgrimage as a Literary Theme* (Ann Arbor, Mich.: Univ. Microfilms, 1978), 7–24; Janis Stout, *The Journey Narrative in American Literature: Patterns and Departures* (Westport, Conn.: Greenwood Press, 1983), ix–32, 123–57.

45. Lester Vogel, *To See a Promised Land: Americans and the Holy Land in the Nineteenth Century* (University Park: Pennsylvania State Univ. Press, 1993), 41–60;

William Stowe, *Going Abroad: European Travel in Nineteenth-Century American Culture* (Princeton: Princeton Univ. Press, 1994), 3–28.

46. William Truettner and Alan Wallach, eds., *Thomas Cole: Landscape into History* (New Haven: Yale Univ. Press, 1994), 90–128; Patrick McGreevy, "Niagara as Jerusalem," *Landscape* 28 (1985): 26–32; John Sears, *Sacred Places: American Tourist Attractions in the Nineteenth Century* (New York: Oxford Univ. Press, 1989), 5–7; Alfred Weber, Beth Lueck, and Dennis Berthold, *Hawthorne's Travel Sketches* (Hanover: Univ. Press of New England, 1989), 55–61, 119–23, 169–80; Jacob Delameter, "Thesis on the Use and Abuse of the Saratoga Waters," *New York Journal of Medicine* 3 (July 1844): 62; Henry Gilpin, *The Northern Tour: Being a Guide to Saratoga . . .* (Philadelphia, 1825), 66; R. F. Dearborn, *Saratoga and How to See It* (Saratoga Springs, 1871), 52.

47. "American Country Life," 280 ("infatuated Moslem," "irresistible craving"); Sophie Sparkle [Jennie Hicks], *Sparkles from Saratoga* (New York, 1873), 5; Curtis, *Lotus-Eating,* 111; Lyman Powell, ed., *Historic Towns of New England* (New York, 1898), 466; Hartley Davis, "Magnificent Newport," *Munsey's* 23 (July 1900): 482; see also Charles Bristed, *The Upper Ten Thousand: Sketches of American Society* (New York, 1852), 172; "First Impressions of Saratoga," pt. 1, *National Era* 13 (11 Aug. 1859); *Frank Leslie's,* 5 Sept. 1857; Lucy Comfort, *The Belle of Saratoga* (New York, 1876), 17; *NYT,* 21 July 1868; *HW,* 12 Sept. 1891.

48. Max Weber, *From Max Weber: Essays in Sociology,* ed. and trans. Hans Gerth and C. Wright Mills (New York: Oxford Univ. Press, 1946), 139–55, 282, 350–57 (the phrase is actually Friedrich von Schiller's); Leigh Schmidt, *Consumer Rites: The Buying and Selling of American Holidays* (Princeton: Princeton Univ. Press, 1995), 3–32, 122–68, 194–234.

49. B. Weed Gorham, *Camp Meeting Manual: A Practical Book for the Camp Ground* (Boston, 1854), 31–32, 17; Robert Louis Stevenson, *Across the Plains with Other Memories and Essays* (New York, 1892), 83; Ellen Weiss, *City in the Woods: The Life and Design of an American Camp Meeting on Martha's Vineyard* (New York: Oxford Univ. Press, 1987), xi–113; Kathryn Grover, ed., *Hard at Play: Leisure in America, 1840–1940* (Rochester: Strong Museum, 1992), 9–27. Round Lake, fifteen miles south of Saratoga Springs, exemplified the stages in this evolution from a communal, tented camp meeting site founded in 1868 to a resort with individually owned cottages; *Frank Leslie's,* 31 July 1869; 31 Aug. 1878; Mary Snyder, *The Round Lake Association, 1868–1968* (Albany: The Center, 1968), 3–16.

50. See Turner and Turner, 1–39, 231–54; Graham Dann, "Tourist Motivation: An Appraisal," *Annals of Tourism Research (ATR)* 8 (1981): 184–201; Nelson Graburn, "The Anthropology of Tourism," *ATR* 10 (1983): 9–33; Dennison Nash, "The Ritualization of Tourism: Comment on Graburn's *The Anthropology of Tourism,*" *ATR* 11 (1984): 504–6; Stowe, 3–5, 55–56; Michael Pearson, "Pilgrims, Travellers, Tourists: The Meanings of Journeys," *Australian Cultural History* 10 (1991), 125–34.

51. Samuel De Veaux, *The Traveller's Own Book to Saratoga Springs, Niagara*

Falls, and Canada . . . (Buffalo, 1841), 64–65; Joanna Anthon diary, 1867–83, New York City Public Library, Main Branch, Manhattan, N.Y. (NYCPL); Barnes Lathrop, ed., "A Southern Girl at Saratoga Springs, 1834," *North Carolina Historical Review* 15 (Apr. 1938): 159; Edith Wharton, *A Backward Glance* (New York: Appleton-Century, 1934), 82–91. See Jemima Morrell's thoughts on traveling in *Miss Jemima's Swiss Journal: The First Conducted Tour of Switzerland* (1863; London: Putnam, 1963), 67–68: "Our lives needed no other romance than was afforded by the perfect freedom we enjoyed. It was an entire change; the usual routine of life was gone. All memories of times and seasons faded away and we lived only in the enjoyment of the present. We all felt that the recollection of these pleasant days would form a precious possession for the rest of our life."

52. Thursty McQuill [Wallace Bruce], *The Hudson River by Daylight* (New York, 1874), 106–11; William Fox and Mae Banner, "Social and Economic Contexts of Folklore Variants: The Case of Potato Chip Legends," *Western Folklore* 42 (Apr. 1983): 114–26; *Saratogian*, 27 July 1914; George Waller, *Saratoga: Saga of an Impious Era* (Englewood Cliffs: Prentice-Hall, 1966), 3–13, 190–94; Arthur Vanderbilt II, *Fortune's Children: The Fall of the House of Vanderbilt* (New York: William Morrow, 1989), 399–408; Richard Barrett, *Good Old Summer Days: Newport, Narragansett Pier, Saratoga, Long Branch, Bar Harbor* (New York: Appleton-Century, 1941), 160–62; Grace Swanner, *Saratoga: Queen of Spas* (Utica: North Country, 1988), 103; James Kettlewell, *Saratoga Springs: An Architectural History* (Saratoga Springs: Lyrical Ballad, 1991), 4.

53. *New York Express* quoted in *Newport Mercury*, 8 July 1848; Judith Adler, "Travel as Performed Art," *American Journal of Sociology* 94 (May 1989): 1382–85.

54. *New York Herald*, 23 Aug. 1853 ("vicious"); *NYT*, 8 Sept. 1856 ("gathering"); 21 May 1877; Potvin, 39–40; *Acts and Resolves*, 64 (Oct. 1842), 7 (Jan. 1847); "Newport City Documents, 1857–58," doc. 6; "Newport City Documents, 1858–59" (Newport, 1859), doc. 42, NHS; Nicolosi, 13–14; Hurst, 93; Peterson, *History*, 277–79; *Newport Daily News*, 19 June 1855. For examples of street crime, see *Newport Mercury*, 28 Aug. 1852; 9 Sept. 1854 (bell); 14 Oct. 1854; 19 Apr. 1856; 12 July 1856; 15 Nov. 1856; *Newport Daily News*, 8 Dec. 1851; 10 Dec. 1853.

55. Curtis, *Lotus-Eating*, 165–66; George Mason, ed., *Re-Union of the Sons and Daughters of Newport, R.I., August 23, 1859* (Newport, 1859), 10.

56. *Acts and Resolves*, 110–14 (Jan. 1838), 75–79 (Jan. 1839), 3–8 (Jan. 1844), 3–17 (May 1852); Coleman, 249; "Editor's Easy Chair," *HM* 5 (July 1852): 267; *Newport Mercury*, 15, 29 May 1853 ("rum-suckers"); 5 Mar. 1853; 10 July 1886; "Why We Get Sick," *HM* 13 (Oct. 1856): 645; *New York Herald*, 13 Aug. 1853; *New York Tribune*, 18 July 1886. The *Herald of the Times*, a Whig newspaper in Newport, consistently supported temperance; see, e.g., 18 Sept. 1834; 2 Mar. 1837; 6 June 1844.

57. Fisher, 82, 124, 136, 140–41, 176, 190, 199, 213, 250.

58. "Newport: Historical and Social," 290, 316–17 ("realm"); *NYT*, 8 Sept. 1856; *Newport Mercury*, 31 July 1852; 7 Aug. 1852; Coleman, 21, 220–25.

59. *Newport Mercury,* 26 July 1851; 19 July 1856; 13 Nov. 1858 ("gayest"); *Newport Daily News,* 21 Aug. 1851 ("hum"); "Newport in Winter," 149; Mason, *Re-Union,* passim; *NYT,* 22–26 Aug. 1859; 13–15 Aug. 1857; Cooper, *Letters,* 5:163.

CHAPTER THREE   *The Rise of Coney Island*

1. *HW,* 10 Aug. 1878; 9 Aug. 1890; José Martí, *The America of José Martí,* trans. Juan de Onís (New York: Noonday, 1953), 107–8; Joel Cook, *Brief Summer Rambles near Philadelphia* (Philadelphia, 1882), 96–99; William Ulyat, *Life at the Seashore* (Princeton, N.J., 1880), 49; William Bishop, "To Coney Island," *Scribner's* 20 (July 1880): 359–63; *NYT,* 10, 27 Aug. 1877; 24 June 1878; 30 June 1879; *Coney Island and the Jews* (New York, 1879), 18.

2. Gravesend Town Records, 1646–1705, vols. 300–305, New York City Municipal Archives, Manhattan, N.Y. (NYCMA); Jaspar Dankers and Peter Sluyter, *Journal of a Voyage to New York . . . in 1679–1680,* ed. and trans. Henry Murphy (Brooklyn, 1867), 118; J. T. Bailey, *Historical Sketch of the City of Brooklyn and the Surrounding Neighborhood* (Brooklyn, 1840), 43–51; Peter Ross, *A History of Long Island* (New York: Lewis, 1902), 1:354–72; Henry Stiles, ed., *The Civil, Political, Professional, and Ecclesiastical History and Commercial and Industrial Record of the County of Kings and the City of Brooklyn from 1683 to 1884* (New York, 1884), 189–92; Carl Bridenbaugh, "Baths and Watering Places of Colonial America," *William and Mary Quarterly* 3 (Apr. 1946): 174; "Shifting Shapes of Coney Island," *Brooklyn Bridge* 1 (Sept. 1995): 16. Rem Koolhaas called Coney "a clitoral appendage at the entrance to New York Harbor," in *Delirious New York: A Retroactive Manifesto for Manhattan* (1978; New York: Monacelli, 1994), 31.

3. David Tallman to John Terhune, 30 July 1814, Brooklyn Historical Society (BHS); Terhune-Wycoff Family Papers, 1747–1932, BHS; *Long Island Star,* 1 July 1824; 21 July 1825.

4. Thomas Field to John Terhune, 20 Aug. 1827, Terhune-Wycoff Papers, BHS; Ross, *History,* 1:367–68; Walt Whitman, *The Gathering of the Forces* (New York: Putnam's Sons, 1920), 2:151–55; Walt Whitman, *The Complete Writings of Walt Whitman* (New York: Henry Knight, 1902), 4:17, 8:56; Stiles, *History,* 192; *Brooklyn before the Bridge: American Paintings from the Long Island Historical Society* (Brooklyn: Brooklyn Museum, 1982), 15–22, 54–60; *NYT,* 3, 6 Feb. 1878; see also Robert Herbert, *Monet on the Normandy Coast: Tourism and Painting, 1867–1886* (New Haven: Yale Univ. Press, 1994), 1–7.

5. Thomas Gordon, *Gazetteer of the State of New York* (Philadelphia, 1836), 497–98 ("frugality"); Stiles, *History,* 194; Horatio Spafford, *Gazetteer of the State of New York* (Albany, 1824), 203–4; Stephen Ostrander, *History of the City of Brooklyn and Kings County* (Brooklyn, 1894), 2:33; Nathaniel Prime, *A History of Long Island* (New York, 1845), 68, 333; John Disturnell, *A Gazetteer of the State of New-York,* 2d ed.

(Albany, 1843), 129; John French, *Gazetteer of the State of New York* (Syracuse, 1860), 372 ("families").

6. Thomas Garrett, "A History of Pleasure Gardens in New York City, 1700–1865" (Ph.D. diss., New York University, 1978), 10–99, 279–408, 599–638; John Durand, *The Life and Times of A. B. Durand* (New York: Scribner's Sons, 1894), 39–40; Bailey, 51–52 ("strangers"); John Watson, *Historic Tales of Olden Time: Concerning the Early Settlement and Advancement of New York City and State* (New York, 1832), 204; Philip Hone, *The Diary of Philip Hone,* ed. Bayard Tuckerman (New York, 1889), entries at 6 Apr. 1833, 31 May 1838, 30 June 1839; Charles Murray, *Travels in North America during the Years 1834, 1835, and 1836* (New York, 1839), 1:55–56; Orville Holley, ed., *The Picturesque Tourist* (New York, 1844), 39; John Godley, *Letters from America, 1844* (London, 1844), 28–29; Charles Sweetser, *Book of Summer Resorts* (New York, 1868), 43–44; Spafford, 204.

7. Coney Island Plank Road, bundle 87, Gravesend Town Documents, NYCMA; "Midsummer Holidays," *Scribner's* 12 (Aug. 1876): 595–97; Wellington Williams, *Appleton's Northern and Eastern Traveller's Guide* (New York, 1850), 134; *New York Herald,* 4 July 1850; 2 July 1851; *Long Island Star,* 23 June 1836; *Brooklyn Eagle,* 27 June 1844; 21 June 1848; Disturnell, *Gazetteer,* 129; John Barber and Henry Howe, *Historical Collections of the State of New York* (New York, 1842), 237; *NYT,* 30 July 1855; *Frank Leslie's,* 20 Sept. 1856; *HW,* 20 Aug. 1859; *New York Herald,* 2 July 1851; Daniel Tredwell, "Kings County in Fact, Legend, and Tradition," chap. 2 ("attractions"), BHS.

8. Coney Island House register, Special Collections, Brooklyn Public Library (BPL); *Brooklyn Eagle,* 5 Mar. 1939; *New York Herald,* 7, 17 July 1848; 13 Aug. 1848.

9. *Coney Island Pavilion,* lithograph (26 July 1845), BHS; George Templeton Strong, *Diary,* ed. Alan Nevins and Milton Thomas (New York: Macmillan, 1952), entry at 12 Aug. 1851; Charles Shanley, "Coney Island," *Atlantic Monthly* 34 (Sept. 1874): 307–9; *NYT,* 14 July 1873; 20, 27 Aug. 1877; 14 Mar. 1878; 1 May 1878; 29 July 1878; Charles Norton, *American Seaside Resorts* (New York, 1883), 96; Townsend Percy, *Percy's Pocket Dictionary of Coney Island* (New York, 1880), 56–57; *Coney Island and the Jews,* 13; Walter Creedmore, "The Real Coney Island," *Munsey's* 21 (Aug. 1899): 745–47; Julian Ralph, "Coney Island," *Scribner's* 20 (July 1896): 9–17; Lindsay Denison, "The Biggest Playground in the World," *Munsey's* 33 (Aug. 1905): 558–60.

10. *New York Herald,* 16 July 1865; John Disturnell, *Springs, Water-Falls, Sea Bathing Resorts, and Mountain Scenery of the United States and Canada* (New York, 1855), 63; Sweetser, 38–44 ("best"); Ross, *History,* 2:40–42; *NYT,* 3 July 1863; 10 July 1866 ("swelter," "supreme"); 16 July 1866; 21 July 1868; Eric Ierardi, *Gravesend: The Home of Coney Island* (New York: Vantage, 1975), 66–68.

11. *Our Summer Retreats, a Hand Book to all the Chief Waterfalls, Springs...* (New York, 1858), 5–7; Strong, entry at 19 Oct. 1867; Marc Linder and Lawrence Zacha-

rias, *Of Cabbages and Kings: Agriculture and the Formation of Modern Brooklyn* (Iowa City: Univ. of Iowa Press, 1999), 115–23, 139–40.

12. *NYT,* 6 May 1877; 1 May 1878; Ross, *History,* 1:368–69; Percy, 17, 59.

13. Stiles, *History,* 195; *Coney Island and the Jews,* 13–15; *Coney Island* (New York: [Iron Steamboat Co.], 1883), 23–24; Walter Marshall, *Through America; or, Nine Months in the United States* (London, 1881), 43; Brian Cudahy, *Around Manhattan Island and Maritime Tales of New York* (New York: Fordham Univ. Press, 1997), 120–55; Kathy Peiss, *Cheap Amusements: Working Women and Leisure in Turn-of-the-Century New York* (Philadelphia: Temple Univ. Press, 1986), 117–21.

14. National Construction Co., *Iron Piers* (New York, 1879), 15–18; Percy, 46; *NYT,* 20 Mar. 1879; 23 Apr. 1879; 3 July 1879; *Coney Island and the Jews,* 15; Cook, 85–91; *HW,* 9 Aug. 1879; 29 July 1882; Bishop, 353, 359.

15. Stiles, *History,* 419–25; New York State, *Board of Railroad Commissioners: Annual Report, 1884* (Albany, 1885): 2:421–60; *By Narrow Gauge to Bay Ridge and Coney Island: The Old New York and Manhattan Beach* (Hoboken, N.J.: Railroadiana Library, 1947), 2–7; *NYT,* 5 Apr. 1877; 9 Mar. 1878; 16, 18 Apr. 1878; 2, 10 July 1878; 11 Sept. 1878; 25 Jan. 1879; 28 June 1879; 8 Dec. 1881; "Railroads, 1877–93," vol. 45, Gravesend Town Documents; *Brooklyn Eagle,* 26 Sept. 1891; Zacharias and Linder, 141–49, 381–87; Brian Merlis et al., *Brooklyn's Gold Coast: The Sheepshead Bay Communities* (New York: Sheepshead Bay Historical Society, 1997), 33–35.

16. *NYT,* 6 May 1877; 20 Aug. 1877; 1 May 1878; 11 July 1906; Percy, 30, 42; Ralph, 9–10; William Younger, *Old Brooklyn in Early Photographs, 1865–1929* (New York: Dover, 1978), 114–15; *Coney Island Souvenir: How to Get There and Where to Go* (Brooklyn, 1883), 33–39.

17. *NYT,* 5 June 1896; *Coney Island and the Jews,* 10–11; Stiles, *History,* 195–96; Cook, 93; *Brooklyn Eagle,* 28, 30 June 1878; 2 Aug. 1891. Corbin's railroad was reorganized as the New York, [Brooklyn], & Manhattan Beach in 1885.

18. Gravesend Town Meetings, 1736–1864, bundle 9, and Town Records, 1704–1872, vol. 306, NYCMA; *NYT,* 29 Aug. 1870; 8, 25 Aug. 1878; 22 Aug. 1879; Stiles, *History,* 195–97; Stephen Weinstein, "The Nickel Empire: Coney Island and the Creation of Urban Seaside Resorts in the United States" (Ph.D. diss., Columbia Univ., 1984), 117–18.

19. *NYT,* 24 Dec. 1878; 22 Aug. 1879; Weinstein, "Nickel Empire," 53–59; *Brooklyn Eagle,* 2 Aug. 1891; *Prospectus of the Manhattan Beach Improvement Co.* (New York, 1879).

20. Percy, 50–53; *HW,* 10 Aug. 1878; Henry Howard, ed., *The Eagle and Brooklyn: The Record of the Progress of the Brooklyn Daily Eagle* (Brooklyn, 1893), 1139; *Brooklyn Eagle,* 12 July 1877; 24, 28 May 1880; 26, 28 June 1880; 8 July 1880; *NYT,* 13, 20 Aug. 1877; 1, 16 May 1878; 24 Sept. 1878; 14 July 1884; Henry Pierrepont diary, entry at 20 June 1879, BHS; Merlis, 26–37.

21. Theodore Dreiser, *The Color of a Great City* (New York: Boni and Liveright, 1923), 121–29; *The Story of Manhattan Beach . . .* (New York, 1879), 26–36; *Brooklyn Eagle*, 28 May 1880.

22. Percy, 53; *The Story of Manhattan Beach*, 33–40; Bishop, 359; *Coney Island and the Jews*, 17–18; Cook, 93–98; Norton, 92–94; *Frank Leslie's*, 9, 16 Aug. 1879; *Brooklyn Eagle*, 14 July 1879; 1 Aug. 1893; Martí, 108.

23. Percy, 45–46, 54; Merlis, 33–34. For linear stratification, see *Adirondack News*, 4 Aug. 1888; *Coney Island*, 13–14; Norton, 92–96; Bishop, 357; Ross, *History*, 1:373–75, 578; *Brooklyn Eagle*, 14 July 1879; 7 July 1892.

24. *NYT*, 29 July 1878; Percy, 18–19; Cook, 93–95; *Brooklyn Eagle*, 6 July 1876; 30 June to 2 July 1878; 13 Aug. 1880; 3 Apr. 1888; *Coney Island and the Jews*, 16; *Coney Island Souvenir*, 19; Hotel Brighton menu, 14 Aug. 1879, NYCPL; *Hotel Brighton*, lithograph (Graphic Co., ca. 1880), BHS; Robert Foster, *Brighton Beach Hotel and Its March from the Sea* (Brooklyn, 1888), 12; Eric Ierardi, *Gravesend, Brooklyn: Coney Island and Sheepshead Bay* (Dover, N.H.: Arcadia, 1996), 56–59.

25. Sea Beach Palace Hotel menu, 1881, BPL; Weinstein, "Nickel Empire," 98; Gravesend Town Documents, vol. 321, 8, 152, 176–77; *Brooklyn Eagle*, 16 July 1880; 6 Sept. 1890.

26. "The Summer Exodus and What It Testifies," *Century* 38 (July 1889): 469; Percy, 43, 68–73; Parks Department Records, City and Borough of Brooklyn, file 72, BHS; Gravesend Common Lands, Trustees' Minutes, 1880–94, NYCMA; *A Wonderful Account of an Excursion to Coney Island* (game) (Springfield, Mass.: Milton Bradley, 1881), 10 ("Teutonic"), NYSHS; Stiles, *History*, 198–207; *NYT*, 1 May 1878; 17 July 1879; *Coney Island and the Jews*, 14; Norton, 95; Bishop, 359–60; *HW*, 10 Aug. 1878.

27. *Brooklyn Eagle*, 1 July 1878, 10 July 1879 ("pilgrim"); Percy, 58; J. P. Sweet, *A Day on Coney Island* (New York, 1880), 8; *Coney Island Souvenir*, 36; *Coney Island*, 9, 21–22; James McCabe, *Illustrated History of the Centennial Exhibition* (Philadelphia, 1876), 414–24, 543–48.

28. Bishop, 363; McCabe, *History*, 296–315, 433–69, 845–51; James Gilbert, *Perfect Cities: Chicago's Utopias of 1893* (Chicago: Univ. of Chicago Press, 1991), 94–130. Walter Benjamin famously noted that "world exhibitions were places of pilgrimage to the fetish Commodity," in *Charles Baudelaire: A Lyric Poet in the Era of High Capitalism*, ed. Jean Lacoste, trans. Harry Zohn (London: N.L.B., 1973), 165.

29. "The Colossal Elephant of Coney Island," *Scientific American* 53 (11 July 1885): 1, 21; *HW*, 12 Sept. 1891; *NYT*, 21 Feb. 1884; 30 May 1885; 28 Sept. 1896; *Brooklyn Eagle*, 28 Sept. 1896.

30. *Kings County Rural Gazette*, 3 Aug. 1878, in Linder and Zacharias, 155; assessment role, 1859, vol. 3055, and assessment role, 1883, vol. 3079, Gravesend Town Records; *HW*, 10 Aug. 1878; *Coney Island and the Jews*, 8, 19; Cook, 87–91, 98; *Coney Island Souvenir*, 31; *NYT*, 1 May 1878; 16 Sept. 1878; *Brooklyn Eagle*, 12 May

1879. For the slow rate of change before 1880, compare the *Census of the State of New York for 1855* (Albany, 1857), 235, 272 and *Census of New York for 1875* (Albany, 1877), 244, 324.

31. Lucy Gillman, "Coney Island," *New York History* 36 (July 1955): 261 (cartoon); Stiles, *History,* 203 (Babel); *Brooklyn Union,* 5 July 1883; *NYT,* 14 July 1873; 6 May 1877; 27 Aug. 1877; 1, 27 May 1878; 26, 29 July 1878; 30 Aug. 1878; 24 Sept. 1878; *Brooklyn Eagle,* 8 July 1889; *New York State Board of Railroad Commissioners,* 2:902–5, 991–93, 1073–76; Norton, 92; Howard, *Eagle,* 1139; Cook, 93; Weinstein, "Nickel Empire," 135–36, 329.

32. *Evening Mail,* 23 July 1879, quoted in *Coney Island and the Jews,* 30; Strong, entry at 15 Aug. 1851; Shanley, 306–12; John Hutcheson, "Summer Life in the States," *Belgravia Magazine* 15 (1871): 349–51.

33. *New York Herald,* 21 July 1884; *Brooklyn Citizen,* 9 July 1887; Weinstein, "Nickel Empire," 99, 158; *NYT,* 31 Aug. 1874; 7 July 1875; Peter Hales, *Silver Cities: The Photography of American Urbanization, 1839–1915* (Philadelphia: Temple Univ. Press, 1984), 180, 267–69.

34. *Brooklyn Eagle,* 28 June 1892; Joel Benton, "The Holiday Hallucination," *North American Review* 146 (Apr. 1888): 472–73; U.S. Dept. of Commerce, *Historical Statistics of the United States: Colonial Times to 1970* (1976; White Plains: Kraus International, 1989), vol. 1, 165 (D728–38), 201–2 (E52–63), 210–13 (E135–202); Joshua Brown and David Ment, *Factories, Foundries, and Refineries: A History of Five Brooklyn Industries* (New York: Brooklyn Educational and Cultural Alliance, 1980), 5; New York [State], *Annual Report of the Bureau of Labor Statistics . . . for the Year 1886* (New York, 1887), 661–64; New York [State], *Annual Report of the Bureau of Labor Statistics . . . for the Year 1900* (New York, 1901), 18, 43, 173, 232; Witold Rybczynski, *Waiting for the Weekend* (New York: Viking, 1991), 109–61; Juliet Schor, *The Overworked American: The Unexpected Decline of Leisure* (New York: Basic, 1991), 45, 60–78. The *New York Times,* 31 July 1910, asked several business executives, "How long should a man's vacation be?" Henry Clews (financier), Frank Hedley (I.R.T.), John Archbold (Standard Oil), and Joseph Davis (American Locomotive Works) thought that businessmen required at least a month, but anything more than two weeks would spoil a good clerk. Davis felt workers could take their vacations when they were laid off.

35. *NYT,* 31 Aug. 1874; 20 Aug. 1877; Bishop, 358, 364; Cook, 101; *Brooklyn Times,* 16 June 1890; *Saratogian Almanac for 1881* (Saratoga Springs, 1881), 34; Martí, 108.

36. Bishop, 364. On the question of who is a tourist, see Valene Smith, ed., *Hosts and Guests: The Anthropology of Tourism,* 2d ed. (Philadelphia: Univ. of Pennsylvania Press, 1989), 1–4; Erik Cohen, "Who Is a Tourist: A Conceptual Clarification," *Sociological Review* 22 (Nov. 1974): 532–46; Neil Leiper, "The Framework of Tourism: Towards a Definition of Tourism, Tourist, and the Tourist Industry," *ATR* 6 (1979): 395, 404; Christopher Law, *Urban Tourism: Attracting Visitors to Large Cities*

(New York: Mansell, 1994), 4–15, 156–59. In 1992, the multinational World Tourism Organization defined tourism as comprising "the activities of persons travelling to and staying in places outside their usual environment for not more than one consecutive year for leisure, business, and other purposes." This definition emphatically included same-day visits; see Victor Middleton, *Marketing in Travel and Tourism* (London: Butterworth-Heinemann, 1995), 7.

37. U.S. Dept. of Commerce, *Historical Statistics,* vol. 1, 10–12 (A29–72); *Oxford English Dictionary,* 2d ed., s.v. "stranger"; Louis Wirth, "Urbanism as a Way of Life," *American Journal of Sociology* 44 (1938): 1–24; Georg Simmel, "The Metropolis and Mental Life," in *The Sociology of Georg Simmel* (New York: Free Press, 1950), 409–24; Sally Merry, *Urban Danger: Life in a Neighborhood of Strangers* (Philadelphia: Temple Univ. Press, 1981), 234–38; Anthony Marsella, "Urbanization, Mental Health, and Social Deviancy," *American Psychologist* 53 (June 1998): 624–34.

38. Herman Melville, *The Writings of Herman Melville* (Evanston: Northwestern Univ. Press, 1968–89), 9:13–45; Lydia Maria Child, *Letters from New York,* ed. Bruce Mills (1843; Athens: Univ. of Georgia Press, 1998), 59 (letter 13; 17 Feb. 1842); see also 43–45 (letter 10; 21 Oct. 1841); Henry Ward Beecher, *Star Papers; or, Experiences of Art and Nature* (New York, 1855), 106; Emerson quoted in Morton White and Lucia White, *The Intellectual versus the City* (Cambridge: Harvard Univ. Press, 1962), 29, 36–53.

39. *NYT,* 21 July 1868; Percy, 16; Kenneth Greenberg, *Honor and Slavery: Lies, Duels, Masks, Dressing as Women, Gifts, Strangers, . . . and Gambling in the Old South* (Princeton: Princeton Univ. Press, 1996), 81–86.

40. *Oxford English Dictionary,* 2d ed., s.v. "tourist"; Erving Goffman, *Encounters: Two Studies in the Sociology of Interaction* (Indianapolis: Bobbs-Merrill, 1961), 7–14, 79–81; Daniel Boorstin, *The Image: A Guide to Pseudo-Events in America* (1961; New York: Atheneum, 1987), 85; Simmel, 402.

41. Sarah Joseph Hale, *Sketches of American Character,* 4th ed. (Boston, 1833), 185; William Hoyt, ed., "Saratoga Jaunt, 1827: The Journal of Francis Joseph Dallam," *New York History* 28 (July 1947): 332; *New York Post,* 7 Aug. 1843, in Jack Kofoed, *Brandy for Heroes: A Biography of the Honorable John Morrissey* (New York: Dutton, 1938), 225; also Hone, entry at 7 Aug. 1835; Abbey Goodwin to Stephen Goodwin, 17 Aug. 1848, file 17996, NYSLA; Jacques Milbert, *Picturesque Itinerary of the Hudson River,* trans. Constance Sherman (1828; Ridgewood, N.J.: Gregg, 1968), 49–51; Timothy Dwight, *Travels in New York and New England* (1822; Cambridge: Harvard Univ. Press, 1969), 3:290; John Buckingham, *America: Historical, Statistic, and Descriptive* (London, 1841), 2:432; Theodore Dwight, *The Northern Traveller, Containing the Routes to the Springs, Niagara, Quebec, and the Coal Mines . . . ,* 6th ed. (New York, 1841), 86, 307; Philip Stansbury, *A Pedestrian Tour of Two Thousand Three Hundred Miles in North America* (New York, 1822), 50.

42. George Mason, *Newport Illustrated, in a Series of Pen and Pencil Sketches* (New York, 1854), 8, 49; John Dix [George Phillips], *A Handbook of Newport, and Rhode*

Island (Newport, 1852), advertisement in back; "Newport City Documents, 1853–54" (Newport, 1854), doc. 1, NHS; also *Rhode Island Republican,* 28 May 1829; 3 Sept. 1829; Edward Peterson, *History of Rhode Island and Newport* (New York, 1853), 286; Thomas Richards, "Newport," *Knickerbocker* 54 (Oct. 1859): 350; George Curtis, *Lotus-Eating: A Summer Book* (New York, 1856), 165; Anna Hunter, "A Decade of Newport as Seen by Two Wandering Sons," *NHSB* 53 (Apr. 1925): 8–16; Hugh Ball to John Ball, 8 Aug. 1831, Ball and Ball Papers, DUMC; *Newport Daily News,* 15 July 1850; *Newport Journal,* 21 July 1883.

43. Bailey, 51–52; *NYT,* 21 July 1868; 29 Aug. 1870; 14 July 1873; Percy, 17, 66, 30 (*Appleton's*).

44. I. Eaton, *The History of Coney Island, from Its Discovery in 4.11.44 Down to High Tide Last Night* (New York, 1879), 19, 32–36 ("sights"); Dreiser, 120–21; John Erskine, *The Memory of Certain Persons* (Philadelphia: Lippincott, 1947), 10; Bishop, 355–61; Cook, 100; *Wonderful Account,* 9 ("jollity"); Howard, *Eagle,* 1139; Percy, 63–64; stereographs 14 and 44, 91–F177, Dennis Collection; NYCPL; *Brooklyn Eagle,* 28 July 1880.

45. *NYT,* 21 July 1868 ("levels"); 13 Aug. 1877 ("true republic"); 20 Aug. 1877; 1 May 1878; *HW,* 10 Aug. 1878; Ulyat, 136–38; Howard, *Eagle,* 1138–39; *Brooklyn Standard Union,* 1 July 1890; J. Howe Adams, "Bathing at the American Sea-Shore Resorts," *Cosmopolitan* 19 (July 1895): 316, 324.

46. Martí, 107; Stephen Crane, *The Works of Stephen Crane: Tales, Sketches, and Reports,* ed. Fredson Bowers (Charlottesville: Univ. Press of Virginia, 1973), 8:322–38, 516; *HW,* 12 Sept. 1891; Percy, 21; Colin Berry, "Futura Obscura," *Preservation* (July 1999): 21.

47. Garrett, 489–95; Harrison Rhodes, "American Holidays: The Sea Shore," *HM* 129 (June 1914): 8; J. Ellis Voss, "Summer Resort: An Ecological Analysis of a Satellite Community" (Ph.D. diss., Indiana Univ., 1941), 39, 134; Oliver Pilat and Jo Ranson, *Sodom by the Sea: An Affectionate History of Coney Island* (Garden City, N.Y.: Doubleday, Doran, 1941), 315; Martin Paulsson, *The Social Anxieties of Progressive Reform: Atlantic City, 1854–1920* (New York: New York Univ. Press, 1994), 32–41. For "Kill the Coon," see Denison, 560; Day Willey, "The Trolley Park," *Cosmopolitan* 33 (June 1902): 269; William Mangels, *The Outdoor Amusement Industry* (New York: Vantage, 1952), 196–97; Martí, 108; Crane, 8:183; Ralph, 16–17; David Nasaw, *Going Out: The Rise and Fall of Public Amusements* (New York: Basic, 1993), 91–94; game depicted in *Coney Island: A Documentary Film* (Santa Monica, 1991), produced by Ric Burns and Buddy Squires.

48. Photograph from Saratoga Springs Historical Museum, in Gretchen Sorin and Jane Rehl, *Honorable Work: African Americans in the Resort Community of Saratoga Springs, 1870–1970* (Saratoga Springs: Historical Society, 1992), 28–29; Willard Gatewood, *Aristocrats of Color: The Black Elite, 1880–1920* (Bloomington: Indiana Univ. Press, 1990), 45, 111–14, 114 ("respectable"), 200–202, 248; William Stowe,

Going Abroad: European Travel in Nineteenth-Century American Culture (Princeton: Princeton Univ. Press, 1994), 61–73; Myra Armstead, *"Lord, Please Don't Take Me in August": African Americans in Newport and Saratoga Springs, 1870–1930* (Chicago: Univ. of Illinois Press, 1999), 18–19.

49. Newport, the site of the nation's first synagogue, had no Jewish residents from 1822 to 1870; members of the once flourishing Sephardic community had either been assimilated into Christian families or left the city. They survived as a romantic theme in Henry Wadsworth Longfellow, "The Jewish Cemetery in Newport" (1858), in *The Complete Poetical Works* (Boston: Houghton Mifflin, 1922), 191–92, and in a similar work by Emma Lazarus (1867), *Selections from Her Poetry and Prose* (New York: Emma Lazarus Federation, 1967), 32–33, 99–100; see Morris Gutstein, *The Story of the Jews of Newport* (New York: Bloch, 1936), 214–63.

50. Lee Livney, "Let Us Now Praise Self-Made Men: A Reexamination of the Hilton-Seligman Affair," *New York History* 75 (Jan. 1994): 67–98; Stephen Elias, *Alexander T. Stewart: The Forgotten Merchant Prince* (London: Praeger, 1992), 189–222; *NYT*, 19–26 June 1877; *Saratogian*, 20–22 June 1877; *Saratoga Sentinel*, 21 June 1877; Elizabeth Drexel Lehr, *"King Lehr" and the Gilded Age* (Philadelphia: Lippincott, 1935), 22.

51. *Coney Island and the Jews*, 21; Joseph Smith, *Reminiscences of Saratoga, or Twelve Years at the "States"* (New York, 1897), 190; *Saratoga Sentinel*, 21 June 1877; Alice Rhine, "Race Prejudice at Summer Resorts," *Forum* 3 (July 1887): 523–31; Seneca Ray Stoddard, *Saratoga Springs: Its Hotels, Boarding Houses, and Health Institutions* . . . (Albany, 1882), 6; also Seneca Ray Stoddard, *Saratoga Springs* . . . (Glens Falls, 1889), 18; "August at Saratoga," *Fortune*, Aug. 1935, 65; Sander Gilman, *The Jew's Body* (New York: Routledge, 1991), 169–93; Naomi Cohen, *Encounter with Emancipation: The German Jews in the United States, 1830–1914* (Philadelphia: Jewish Publication Society, 1984), 249–98; Jacob Marcus, *United States Jewry, 1776–1985* (Detroit: Wayne State Univ. Press, 1991), 2:278, 3:156–59; Hugh Bradley, *Such Was Saratoga* (New York: Doubleday, Doran, 1940), 188; Alf Evers, *The Catskills: From Wilderness to Woodstock* (Garden City, N.Y.: Doubleday, 1972), 478–519. When Corbin needed a good lawyer several years later, he hired Louis Brandeis.

52. *New York Herald*, 22 July 1879; *Coney Island and the Jews*, 19–28; *NYT*, 23–25 July 1879; *Saratogian*, 23 July 1879; Leonard Dinnerstein, *Antisemitism in America* (New York: Oxford Univ. Press, 1994), 35–57. The Brighton Beach later flirted with excluding Jews; *NYT*, 21 July 1889.

53. *NYT*, 29 July 1878; Peiss, 115–27.

54. Nasaw, 47–61.

55. Cook, 92 ("jollity"); Bishop, 363 ("Sunday fete").

56. Shanley, 307–9; *Brooklyn Standard Union*, 8 July 1887; *Brooklyn Union*, 29 Aug. 1883; *New York Sun*, 16 July 1877; pamphlet quoted in Weinstein, "Nickel Empire," 180–81.

57. Kate Chopin, *The Awakening and Other Stories* (1899; New York: Holt, Rinehart and Winston, 1970), chaps. 10, 39; Dix, *Handbook*, 71–72; Ulyat, 39–40; Norton, 8; Percy, 11–16, 85–94; Dreiser, 122; Adams, "Bathing," 322.

58. Martí, 103.

59. Joseph Garland, *Boston's North Shore: Being an Account of Life among the Noteworthy, Fashionable, Wealthy, Eccentric, and Ordinary, 1823–1890* (Boston: Little, Brown, 1978), 157–75; Richard Guy Wilson, ed., *Victorian Resorts and Hotels* (Philadelphia: Victorian Society, 1982), 102; Mangels, 19; *Saratogian Almanac for 1881*, 34; Roger McAdam, *The Old Fall River Line* (New York: Stephen Daye, 1955), 60.

60. Tilyou quoted in Richard Snow, *Coney Island: A Postcard Journey to the City of Fire* (New York: Brightwaters, 1984), 11; Bishop, 365; Cook, 101.

CHAPTER FOUR   *The Public Resort*

1. Paton Yoder, "The American Inn, 1775–1850: Melting Pot or Stewing Kettle?" *Indiana Magazine of History* 59 (1963): 135–51; Jefferson Williamson, *The American Hotel: An Anecdotal History* (New York: Knopf, 1930), 3–37; Karen Spitulnik, "The Inn Crowd: The American Inn, 1730–1830," *Pennsylvania Folklife* 22 (Winter 1972): 25–41; Doris King, "The First-Class Hotel and the Age of the Common Man," *Journal of Southern History* 23 (May 1957): 173–88.

2. George Lewis, *Impressions of America and American Churches* (1848; New York: Negro Universities Press, 1968), 21; William Eliot, *A Description of Tremont House, with Architectural Illustrations* (Boston, 1830), 1–20; *New York Daily News*, 21 July 1855; Jane Knowles, "Luxury Hotels in American Cities, 1810–1860" (Ph.D. diss., Univ. of Pennsylvania, 1972), 69–206; for hotels without cities, see Charles Bristed, *The Upper Ten Thousand: Sketches of American Society* (New York, 1852), 91–92; Edward Dicey, *Spectator of America* (London, 1863), 218; Daniel Boorstin, *The Americans: The National Experience* (New York: Random House, 1965), 141–43.

3. Paul Blouet and Jack Allyn, *Jonathan and His Continent* (Bristol, 1889), 275–78 ("cathedrals"); "Melbourne Hotels," *Duffy's Hibernian Magazine* 5 (May 1864): 333 ("spitting"); Charles Weld, *A Vacation Tour in the United States and Canada* (London, 1855), 71; Frances Trollope, *Domestic Manners of the Americans* (1832; New York: Knopf, 1949), 24–25.

4. Francis Lieber, *Letters to a Gentleman in Germany, Written after a Trip from Philadelphia to Niagara* (Philadelphia, 1834), 60; Charles Lyell, *A Second Visit to the United States of North America* (London, 1849), 1:122; John Buckingham, *America: Historical, Statistic, and Descriptive* (London, 1841), 2:435, 103, 159, 1:473; Michel Chevalier, *Society, Manners, and Politics in the United States,* trans. T. G. Bradford (1836; Gloucester, Mass.: Peter Smith, 1967), 304–5. See Charles Dickens, "London Recreations," in *Sketches by Boz* (London, 1836), on emulation at English hotels.

5. Ellen Bond, "Journal of a Trip Made with My Dear Mother, Father, and Sisters and L.S. and Sue, July–Aug. 1850," entry at 29 July 1850, file 13389, NYSLA; Beatrice Sweeney, *The Grand Union Hotel: A Memorial and a Lament* (Saratoga Springs: Historical Society, 1982), 10; Thomas Nichols, *Forty Years of American Life* (London, 1864), 10; Michael Rockland, ed. and trans., *Sarmiento's Travels in the United States in 1847* (Princeton: Princeton Univ. Press, 1970), 141–45.

6. *Atkinson's Saturday Evening Post,* 3 Sept. 1836; Buckingham, 2:443–44, 513; *Frank Leslie's,* 5 Sept. 1857; Charles Latrobe, *The Rambler in North America* (1832; New York: Johnson Reprint, 1970), 2:129; Jacques Milbert, *Picturesque Itinerary of the Hudson River,* trans. Constance Sherman (1828; Ridgewood, N.J.: Gregg, 1968), 49–51; Achille Murat, *The United States of North America* (London, 1833), 357; *Gleason's Pictorial Drawing-Room Companion,* 25 Oct. 1851.

7. George Sala, *America Revisited* (London, 1882), 2:88 ("patient people"), 1:167–81; George Sala, *My Diary in America in the Midst of War* (London, 1865), 244–71; George Towle, *American Society* (London, 1870), 2:81–82; "Disjointed Gossip from the Other Side of the Big Pond," *Bentley's Magazine* 39 (1856): 582; Frederick Marryat, *A Diary in America: With Remarks on Its Institutions* (1839; New York: Knopf, 1962), 375–78; United States Hotel advertisement, Vertical Files, Bea Sweeney Archives, SSHM; Cornelius Durkee, *Reminiscences of Saratoga* (Saratoga Springs: Saratogian, 1928), 69–70; *NYT,* 8 July 1854; 5, 30 Aug. 1869.

8. *Newport Daily News,* 21 Oct. 1850; *NYT,* 8 July 1854 ("pleasures"); *HW,* 24 Aug. 1872 ("eaves"); "Editor's Easy Chair," *HM* 15 (Oct. 1857): 700; Chevalier, 304–5.

9. Joel Cook, *Brief Summer Rambles near Philadelphia* (Philadelphia, 1882), 94–95.

10. "Congress Hall, Saratoga," *Eclectic Magazine* (July 1860), in SSPL; Brian Merlis et al., *Brooklyn's Gold Coast: The Sheepshead Bay Communities* (Brooklyn: Sheepshead Bay Historical Society, 1997), 35.

11. "Narrative of the Travels of a Scot through the United States," 3:30, May 1824, NYSHS; Weld, *Vacation,* 76; Union Hall inventory, 1848, Putnam Family Papers, NYSHAL; John Dix [George Phillips], *A Handbook of Newport, and Rhode Island* (Newport, 1852), 21; Buckingham, 2:443; "First Impressions of Saratoga," pt. 1, *National Era* 13 (11 Aug. 1859), and pt. 6 (15 Sept. 1859); Mary Murray diary, entries at 7–9 Aug. 1825, NYSHS; Blouet and Allyn, 273–76; Sophie Sparkle [Jennie Hicks], *Sparkles from Saratoga* (New York, 1873), 21–24; *HM* quoted in Dominick Cavallo, *Muscles and Morals: Organized Playgrounds and Urban Reform, 1880–1920* (Philadelphia: Univ. of Penn. Press, 1981), 18–19. The bulk of William Dean Howells' utopian novel, *A Traveler from Altruria* (1894), takes place on a resort hotel veranda.

12. Margaret Davidson, "Sentimental Journey: The Diary of Margaret Miller Davidson," ed. Walter Harding, *Journal of the Rutgers Univ. Library* 13 (Dec. 1949): 21–22, entry at 7 June 1833; Milbert, 49–51; Union Hall inventory, 1848, Putnam

Family Papers; Merlis; 35; Anthony Trollope, *North America* (New York: Knopf, 1951), 24; Kenneth Ames, *Death in the Dining Room and Other Tales of Victorian Culture* (Philadelphia: Temple Univ. Press, 1992), 7–43, 150–84.

13. Bond, entry at 29 July 1850; Abbey Goodwin to Stephen Goodwin, 17 Aug. 1848, file 17996, NYSLA; Caroline Gilman, *The Poetry of Travelling in the United States* (New York, 1838), 88 ("heads"); Ernest de Hauranne, *A Frenchman in Lincoln's America: Huit Mois en Amérique, Lettres et Notes de Voyage, 1864–1865*, ed. and trans. Ralph Bowen (Chicago: R. Donnelly, 1984), 132.

14. Florence Achambault, "The Ocean House," *Old Rhode Island* 2 (July 1992): 29; *Atkinson's Saturday Evening Post*, 3 Sept. 1836 ("line"); Bayard Taylor, "The Chiropodist: A Story of the Watering-places," *HM* 24 (Mar. 1862): 461; collection of Union Hotel menus, SSPL; Mary Dunlop, *Sixty Miles from Contentment: Travelling the Nineteenth-Century Interior* (New York: Basic, 1995), 123–42. On dining rooms, see Elizabeth Shackleford diary, entry at 4 July 1861, NYSHAL; Samuel Sombre [James Girard], *Aquarelles: Or Summer Sketches* (New York, 1858), 36–38; Buckingham, 1:473, 2:103, 159, 441–42; Marianne Finch, *An Englishwoman's Experience in America* (London, 1853), 13–15; Susan Williams, *Savory Suppers and Fashionable Feasts: Dining in Victorian America* (New York: Pantheon, 1985), 51–90.

15. Alexander Mackay, *The Western World; or, Travels in the United States in 1846–1847*, 2d ed. (1849; New York: Negro Universities Press, 1968), 3:201 ("clatter"); Weld, *Vacation*, 74–75; Hugh Bradley, *Such Was Saratoga* (New York: Doubleday, Doran, 1940), 91–94; William Chambers, *Things as They Are in America* (New York, 1854), 55. No menus from the extensive Menu Collection at the Main Branch of the New York Public Library predate 1851. On American eating habits, see Patrick Shirreff, *A Tour through North America* . . . (Edinburgh, 1835), 34, 57–58; Sala, *Diary*, 2:265; Lewis, *Impressions*, 22; Marryat, 373; John Godley, *Letters from America, 1844* (London, 1844), 31; Nichols, 1:1; Towle, 1:259–62; Francis Grund, *The Americans in Their Moral, Social, and Political Relations* (1837; New York: Johnson Reprint, 1968), 324; Trollope, *Domestic Manners*, 24–25.

16. Michael O'Brien, ed., *An Evening When Alone: Four Journals of Single Women in the South, 1827–1867* (Charlottesville: Univ. Press of Virginia, 1993), 85; Mackay, 3:198; Milbert, 50; Washington Irving, *Letters* (Boston: Twayne, 1978–82), 4:324.

17. James Gilliam, "A Trip to the North," *Tyler's Quarterly Historical and Genealogical Magazine* 2 (1920): 297–305.

18. Nathaniel Willis, *Hurry-graphs; or, Sketches of Scenery, Celebrities, and Society, Taken from Life* (New York, 1851), 284–94; *The Two Brides*, in Janice Grover, "Luxury and Leisure in Early-Nineteenth-Century America: Saratoga Springs and the Rise of the Resort" (Ph.D. diss., Univ. of California, Davis, 1973), 111–12; *Newport Daily News*, 12 Aug. 1850 ("squirts"); *New York Herald*, 13 Aug. 1853.

19. Philip Hone, *The Diary of Philip Hone*, ed. Bayard Tuckerman (New York, 1889), entry at 22 July 1840; "From the Diary of John Quincy Adams," *Battlements* (Friends of Saratoga Battlefield) 11 (Summer 1999): 4.

20. O'Brien, 82–86.

21. Charles Griffin, "A Trip to Saratoga in 1833," SSPL; Weld, *Vacation,* 77; Godley, 28–29, 42; Mackay, 3:198; *NYT,* 10 Aug. 1868; O'Brien, 81; George Templeton Strong, *Diary,* ed. Alan Nevins and Milton Thomas (New York: Macmillan, 1952), entries at 28–30 July 1841; John MacGregor, *Our Brothers and Cousins: A Summer Tour in Canada and the States* (London, 1859), 44; Sparkle, 16; "All Baggage at the Risk of the Owner: A Story of the Watering-Places," *HM* 5 (Aug. 1852): 335; William Dean Howells, *A Hazard of New Fortunes* (New York, 1890), pt. 4, chap. 4; William Dean Howells, *An Open-Eyed Conspiracy: An Idyl of Saratoga* (New York, 1897), 27–38, 51–52.

22. Charles Dudley Warner, "Their Pilgrimage," *HM* 73 (1886): 666–67; Timothy Flint, *Recollections of the Last Ten Years* (1826; New York: Knopf, 1932), 377–80 ("restraints"); Plato, *The Laws* 2:658, and *Philebus* 50b, in *Plato: The Collected Dialogues,* ed. Edith Hamilton and Huntington Cairns (Princeton: Princeton Univ. Press, 1961); William Shakespeare, "The Merchant of Venice," act 1, scene 1, and "As You Like It," act 2, scene 7 ("stage"); Thomas Middleton, "A Game of Chess" (1624), in *The Works of Thomas Middleton,* ed. Arthur Bullen (New York: AMS Press, 1964), 7:114.

23. *NYT,* 8 July 1854 ("regard for appearances"); Erving Goffman, *The Presentation of Self in Everyday Life* (1959; Woodstock, N.Y.: Overlook, 1973), 17–140, 208–55; Erving Goffman, *Behavior in Public Places: Notes on Social Organization of Gatherings* (New York: Free Press of Glencoe, 1963), 3–12; Roy Wood, "Hotel Culture and Social Control," *ATR* 21 (1994): 71–75.

24. "Newport: Historical and Social," *HM* 9 (Aug. 1854): 317; "Domestic Tourism," *Southern Literary Messenger* 17 (June 1851): 377 ("coteries"); "Illustrations of American Society: The Parvenus," *Knickerbocker* (Mar. 1837): 277 (wealth); Sombre, 57–74; Marietta Holley, *Samantha at Saratoga or, "Racin' after Fashion" by Josiah Allen's Wife* (Philadelphia, 1887), 10–17; Jean Bancroft diary, entry at 12 June 1875, NYSLA; O'Brien, 86.

25. Paulding quoted in Dona Brown, *Inventing New England: Regional Tourism in the Nineteenth Century* (Washington, D.C.: Smithsonian Institution Press, 1995), 36; Lynn Lofland, *A World of Strangers: Order and Action in Urban Public Space* (New York: Basic, 1973), x–23.

26. [John Ruth], *Decorum: A Practical Treatise on Etiquette and Dress of the Best American Society* (New York, 1880), 11, 70–90; John Kasson, *Rudeness and Civility: Manners in Nineteenth-Century Urban America* (New York: Hill and Wang, 1991), 34–71; Beecher quoted in Robert Wiebe, *The Opening of American Society: From the Adoption of the Constitution to the Eve of Disunion* (New York: Knopf, 1984), 327–32; Marryat, 75; Charles Dudley Warner, "Their Pilgrimage," 72:660.

27. Ralph Waldo Emerson, *Selections from Ralph Waldo Emerson,* ed. Stephen Whicher (Boston: Houghton Mifflin, 1957), 42–56, 147–68; Robert Louis Stevenson, *The Complete Shorter Fiction* (New York: Carroll and Graf, 1991), 439–88; Karen

Halttunen, *Confidence Men and Painted Women: A Study of Middle-Class Culture in America, 1830–1870* (New Haven: Yale Univ. Press, 1982), 33–55, 92–133, 153, 170–87.

28. Taylor, "Chiropodist," 460–66; Towle, 2:89–90; *Hampden Post* (Springfield, Mass.), 17 Nov. 1847; Henry Gilpin, *The Northern Tour: Being a Guide to Saratoga . . .* (Philadelphia, 1825), 66. For a sampling of tales of uncertain identity, see *New York Daily Mirror*, 14 Aug. 1830; "Illustrations," 277–84; "First Impressions of Saratoga," pt. 5, *National Era* 13 (8 Sept. 1859); "How We Spend Our Money," *HM* 13 (Sept. 1856): 507–8; "Newport: Its Papers, Its Polkas, and Pugilists," *North American Miscellany* 5 (Apr. 1851): 471; Hiram Fuller, *Belle Brittan on a Tour, at Newport and Here and There* (New York, 1858), 182–87; James Kirke Paulding, *The New Mirror for Travellers; and Guide to the Springs* (New York, 1828), 264–72. The plot of William Dunlap's play, *A Trip to Niagara; or, Travellers in America: A Farce, in Three Acts* (New York, 1830), also hinged on a disguised traveler.

29. Lucy Comfort, *The Belle of Saratoga* (New York, 1876), 18–22; Willis paraphrased in Brown, *Inventing*, 38.

30. Charles Dickens, "The Tuggses at Ramsgate," in *Sketches;* Frances Trollope, *The Robertses on Their Travels* (London, 1846), 1:329–30, 6–7, 2:12, 107; Charles Lever, *The Dodd Family Abroad* (London, 1862), 1:1–14, 65–70, 2:623.

31. Edward Earle, ed., *Points of View: The Stereograph in America, A Cultural History* (Rochester: Visual Studies Workshop, 1979), 9–21, 30; David Johnson, *Illegal Tender: Counterfeiting and the Secret Service in Nineteenth-Century America* (Washington, D.C.: Smithsonian Institution Press, 1995), 1–64; David Henkin, *City Reading: Written Words and Public Spaces in Antebellum New York* (New York: Columbia Univ. Press, 1998), 137–65; Theodore Weld, *American Slavery as It Is* (1839; New York: Arno Press, 1968), 7–10; Harriet Beecher Stowe, preface to *Uncle Tom's Cabin* (1852; New York: Signet, 1981).

32. For Newport Tower, see Alan Schumacher, "Hammett's Bibliography," *NH* 41 (1968): 109; Philip Means, *Newport Tower* (New York: Henry Holt, 1942), 18–85; Leila Lee [Rebecca Coe], *The Dales in Newport* (New York, 1854), 115–24, 209–11; for hoaxes, see Gordon Stein, *Encyclopedia of Hoaxes* (Detroit: Gale Research, 1993), 127–33, 252, 284–301; Andie Tucher, *Froth and Scum: Truth, Beauty, Goodness, and the Ax Murder in America's First Mass Medium* (Chapel Hill: Univ. of North Carolina Press, 1994), 46–61; Geoffrey Buerger, "Parson, Pretender, Pauper: Eleazer Williams Reconsidered," *Voyageur* 5 (Winter 1988–89): 13; Neil Harris, *Humbug: The Art of P. T. Barnum* (Chicago: Univ. of Chicago Press, 1973), 61–89; John Dizikes, *Sportsmen and Gamesmen* (Boston: Houghton Mifflin, 1981), 38–42; Barbara Franco, "The Cardiff Giant: A Hundred-Year-Old Hoax," *New York History* 50 (Oct. 1969): 420–40. For Mark Twain, see *Huckleberry Finn* (New York, 1884), chaps. 19–33; Randall Knoper, *Acting Naturally: Mark Twain in the Culture of Performance* (Berkeley: Univ. of California Press, 1995), 74–169; Susan Gillman, *Dark Twins: Imposture and Identity in Mark Twain's America* (Chicago: Univ. of Chicago Press, 1989), 14–52.

33. Edgar Allan Poe, *The Imaginary Voyages* (Boston: Twayne, 1981), xiii–16;

Edgar Allan Poe, *The Works of Edgar Allan Poe* (Chicago, 1895), 234–48 ("Diddling"); Edgar Allan Poe, "Maelzel's Chess-Player," *Southern Literary Messenger* 2 (Apr. 1836): 318–26; O'Brien, 82, 408; Harris, *Humbug*, 23, 62–88; *New York Daily Graphic*, 4 Sept. 1878; Stein, 45–60, 141–42. According to local legend (Marjorie Waite, *Yaddoo: Yesterday and Today* [Albany: Argus, 1933], 16–23), Poe wrote the first draft of "The Raven" in Saratoga in the summer of 1843.

34. Percy Adams, *Travellers and Travel Liars* (Berkeley: Univ. of California Press, 1962), 1–18, 223–37; for some pseudonymous accounts, see Sparkle; Thursty Mc-Quill [Wallace Bruce], *The Hudson River by Daylight* (New York, 1874); Sombre; Mark Pencil, *White Sulphur Papers; or, Life at the Springs of Western Virginia* (New York, 1839).

35. Gary Lindberg, *The Confidence Man in American Literature* (New York: Oxford Univ. Press, 1982), 6–7, 48–107, 142–66; Susan Kuhlmann, *Knave, Fool, and Genius: The Confidence Man as He Appears in Nineteenth-Century American Fiction* (Chapel Hill: Univ. of North Carolina Press, 1973); James McCabe, *Lights and Shadows of New York Life; or, The Sights and Sensations of a Great City* (Philadelphia, 1872), 314–15; Henry Ward Beecher, *Lectures to Young Men, on Various Important Subjects*, 3d ed. (New York, 1852), 225–26.

36. "First Impressions," pt. 1; Herman Melville, *The Writings of Herman Melville* (Evanston: Northwestern Univ. Press, 1968–89), vol. 10, chaps. 1–3, 24; John Blair, *The Confidence Man in Modern Fiction: A Rogue's Gallery with Six Portraits* (New York: Barnes and Noble, 1979), 33–52; Harris, *Humbug*, 219–31; Lindberg, 15–47. In a climactic scene of Melville's *Moby Dick* (chap. 36), Captain Ahab reminds Starbuck, "All visible objects, man, are but as pasteboard masks. . . . If man will strike, strike through the mask."

37. Lindberg, 3–11; Johnson Hooper, *Adventures of Captain Simon Suggs* (1845; Chapel Hill: Univ. of North Carolina Press, 1969), 8; Charles Dickens, *American Notes* (New York, 1842), chap. 18.

38. *NYT*, 9 July 1865; 5, 17 Aug. 1869; 9 Dec. 1881; Arnold Schrier and Joyce Story, eds., *A Russian Looks at America: The Journey of Alexsandr Borisovitch Lakier in 1857* (Chicago: Univ. of Chicago Press, 1979), 19–23; Bradley, 313–15. For monte, see *HW*, 8 Sept. 1866; Charles Shanley, "Coney Island," *Atlantic Monthly* 34 (Sept. 1874): 308 ("fool"); *The Story of Manhattan Beach . . .* (New York, 1879), 25; Townsend Percy, *Percy's Pocket Dictionary of Coney Island* (New York, 1880), 42; *NYT*, 14 July 1873; 27 May 1878; 17 Sept. 1878; 30 June 1879.

39. Flint, 380; Lydia Maria Child, *Letters from New York*, ed. Bruce Mills (1843; Athens: Univ. of Georgia Press, 1998), 44 (letter 10; 21 Oct. 1841); *Plattsburgh Republican*, 9 Sept. 1826; Lucy Wright Wooster to Ann Wooster, 21 Aug. 1846, Wooster Family Papers, UNC; Almira Read, "A Visit to Saratoga: 1826," ed. Genevieve Darden, *New York History* 50 (July 1969): entry at 21 Aug. 1826; "First Impressions of Saratoga," pt. 4, *National Era* 13 (1 Sept. 1859); O'Brien, 85–89 ("ridiculous"); Mary Murray diary, entry at 12 Aug. 1825.

40. C. B. Moon's Lake House register, 25 June 1880; 17 June 1882, SSHM;

Coney Island House register, 1848–52, Special Collections, BPL; "Domestic Tourism," 378; Boorstin, *Americans,* 140; Dickens, *Notes,* chap. 15; Peter Bulkley, "Identifying the White Mountain Tourist: Origin, Occupation, and Wealth as a Definition of the Early Hotel Trade, 1853–1854," *Historical New Hampshire* 35 (1980): 140.

41. Warner, 72:664.

42. Charles Baldwin diary, entry at 21 July 1866, 1:184–85, NYSLA; Warner, 72:662. At the hot springs at Ruapeka Bay in New Zealand, bathers dispensed with the strict moral codes of Maori society; a proverbial local saying declared, "There is no law in Ruapeka"; Ian Rockel, *Taking the Waters: Early Spas in New Zealand* (Wellington, N.Z.: Government Printing Office, 1986), 154–55; see also Constantine Vaporis, *Breaking Barriers: Travel and the State in Early Modern Japan* (Cambridge: Harvard Univ. Press, 1994), 198–216, 236–42.

43. Griffin, "A Trip to Saratoga"; Perceval Reniers, *The Springs of Virginia: Life, Love, and Death at the Waters, 1775–1900* (Chapel Hill: Univ. of North Carolina Press, 1941), 75–77 ("dull"); Robert Habersham diary, entry at 29 July 1832, UNC; O'Brien, 24–27; Shanley, 307.

44. Mary Ryan, *Women in Public: Between Banners and Ballots, 1825–1880* (Baltimore: Johns Hopkins Univ. Press, 1990), 58–94, 172–80; David Scobey, "Anatomy of the Promenade: The Politics of Bourgeois Sociability in Nineteenth-Century New York," *Social History* 17 (May 1992): 220; Jane Donegan, *"Hydropathic Highway to Health": Women and the Water-Cure in Antebellum America* (New York: Greenwood, 1986), xi–14, 185–97; Susan Cayleff, *Wash and Be Healed: The Water-Cure Movement and Women's Health* (Philadelphia: Temple Univ. Press, 1987), 2–16, 74–108, 159–63; Charlene Lewis, "Ladies and Gentlemen on Display: Planter Society at the Virginia Springs, 1790–1860" (Ph.D. diss., Univ. of Virginia, 1997), 481–554.

45. Richard Cobden, *American Diaries* (Princeton: Princeton Univ. Press, 1952), 121; Theodore Corbett, "Women at the Spas, 1790–1850," *Local History: Brookside Saratoga County Historical Center* 1 (Sept. 1991): 1–8; Sans Souci Hotel ledger, June 1823 to Aug. 1826, Brookside Saratoga County History Center, Ballston Spa. For some reluctant men, see Clement Moore, *Poems* (New York, 1844), 15–24; Holley, *Racin',* 1–17; Sombre, 13–15; *New York Daily Graphic,* 9 Aug. 1873; Sparkle, 5–8; "The Great Van Broek Property," *Leisure Hour* 751 (19 May 1866): 307–8; Bancroft diary, entry at 12 June 1875. As a woman alone, Lillian Foster had trouble getting a hotel room in 1860; *Way-side Glimpses, North and South* (New York, 1860), 42, 193–94. Harvey Levenstein discusses the feminization of American international travel in *Seductive Journey: American Tourists in France from Jefferson to the Jazz Age* (Chicago: Univ. of Chicago Press, 1998), 107–21.

46. MacGregor, 43; "Disjointed Gossip," 581–84; Tyrone Power, *Impressions of America during the Years 1833, 1834, and 1835* (London, 1836), 2:25; *HW,* 15 Aug. 1857; Harriet Martineau, *Retrospect of Western Travel* (London, 1838), 2:216; Paulding, *Mirror,* 228–43; Salomon de Rothschild, *A Casual View of America: The Home Letters of Salomon de Rothschild, 1859–1861,* ed. and trans. Sigmund Diamond (Lon-

don: Cresset, 1962), 68; Strong, 3:40, entry at 16 Aug. 1860 ("lewd"); Henry Sienkiewicz, *Portrait of America: Letters of Henry Sienkiewicz*, ed. and trans. Charles
Morley (New York: Columbia Univ. Press, 1959), 3–6, 26–28, 120–22; Rockland,
136–38.

47. "Painted Angels at Saratoga," *Godey's Magazine* 71 (Nov. 1865): 451; *New-
port Mercury*, 26 July 1851; Lois Banner, *American Beauty* (New York: Knopf, 1983),
68; Miss Willie Creagh to her sister, 17 July 1870; also 2 July [Aug.] 1870, Creagh
Family Papers, UNC; Marian Gouverneur, *As I Remember: Recollections of American
Society during the Nineteenth Century* (New York: Appleton, 1911), 98; Robert Wickham, *A Saratoga Boyhood* (Syracuse: Orange Publishing, 1948), 73; "The Grecian
Bend" (Philadelphia, 1868), sheet music in National Museum of Racing, Saratoga
Springs, N.Y. (NMR). For woman's rights conventions at Saratoga and Newport, see
Elizabeth Cady Stanton et al., *History of Woman Suffrage* (1882; New York: Arno,
1969), 2:402–4, 1:620–28; *Newport Mercury*, 28 Aug. 1869; *Newport Daily News*, 26–
27 Aug. 1869; *HW*, 28 Aug. 1858; 3 Sept. 1859.

48. Thomas Grattan, *Civilized America* (London, 1859), 2:58–62; *Newport Daily
News*, 28 Aug. 1850; *Gleason's Pictorial Drawing-Room Companion*, 25 Oct. 1851; *New
York Herald*, 19 July 1848; 13 Aug. 1853; Towle, 2:75, 86; *HW*, 23 Aug. 1857; 20 Aug.
1859; de Hauranne, 133; Sarah Joseph Hale, *Sketches of American Character*, 4th ed.
(Boston, 1833), 179–98; Benjamin Perry, *Letters of Gov. Benjamin Franklin Perry to
His Wife* (Greenville, N.C., 1890), 109; William Dodd, *The Cotton Kingdom* (New
Haven: Yale Univ. Press, 1921), 41.

49. Murat, 356–57; Willis, *Hurry-graphs*, 276–93; Paulding, *Mirror*, 228–39;
HW, 28 Aug. 1858 ("flirt"); Barnes Lathrop, ed., "A Southern Girl at Saratoga
Springs, 1834," *North Carolina Historical Review* 15 (Apr. 1938): 159 ("prayers");
Nathaniel Willis, "The Ghost Ball at Congress Hall," *Ladies' Companion* 18 (Oct.
1842): 13. At Newport, the musicians flirted with female guests; *Newport Daily News*,
30 July 1851; 2 Aug. 1851.

50. "All Baggage," 336–39; *New York Weekly Tribune*, 6 Sept. 1851; "First Impressions," pt. 4 ("mask"); Mary Murray diary, entries at 12–13 Aug. 1825.

51. John Saxe, *Poetical Works* (Boston, 1882), 49 (sheet music in YC); Bristed,
139–40; Paulding, *Mirror*, 239–43; David Black, *The King of Fifth Avenue: The
Fortunes of August Belmont* (New York: Dial, 1981), 37–44; Sidney Fisher, *A Philadelphia Perspective: The Diary of Sidney George Fisher Covering the Years 1834–1871*,
ed. Nicholas Wainwright (Philadelphia: Historical Society of Pennsylvania, 1967),
124, 176; Margaret Gillespie, "Havens for the Fashionable and Sickly: Society, Sick-
ness, and Space at Nineteenth-Century Southern Spring Resorts" (Ph.D. diss., Univ.
of North Carolina, 1998), 71–73. Guy de Maupassant's spa romance, *Mount Oriol*
(1887; Paris: Louis Conard, 1911), ended in the birth of a child out of wedlock.

52. *Faxon's Illustrated Handbook of Travel* (Boston, 1874), 18, 55 ("elysium").

53. *NYT*, 5 Aug. 1856; 8 Sept. 1856 ("carnival"); Sombre, 20–28, 43–44; Saxe,
49; *Newport Mercury*, 3, 10, 17 Aug. 1844; Fuller, 184; *Newport Daily News*, 13 Aug.

1851; 1 Sept. 1851; George Curtis, *Lotus-Eating: A Summer Book* (New York, 1856), 114–18; Durkee, 177–78; Paulding, *Mirror,* 37 ("windings"); Charles Dow, *Newport: The City by the Sea* (Newport, 1880), 64–66.

54. *World* quoted in McCabe, *Lights,* 604; *New York Herald,* 13 Aug. to 2 Sept. 1848; 22 Aug. 1853; Anna Hunter, "A Decade of Newport as Seen by Two Wandering Sons," *NHSB* 53 (Apr. 1925): 21 (royalty); Fisher, 176; *Newport Mercury,* 21, 28 Aug. 1847; *Newport Daily News,* 27 Aug. to 5 Sept. 1850; Towle, 2:25; *Saratoga Daily Register,* 1 Sept. 1889; Lewis, "On Display," 379–87.

55. "First Impressions of Saratoga," pt. 3, *National Era* 13 (25 Aug. 1859) ("dressing"), and pt. 7 (22 Sept. 1859); Comfort, 19, 23; *New York Herald,* 22 Aug. 1853; William Butler, *Nothing to Wear, and Other Poems* (New York, 1899), 16; *New York Herald,* 3 Aug. 1844; *HW,* 8, 15 Aug. 1857; Buckingham, 2:441–45; Fuller, 173; Stevenson, *Fiction,* 122; Foster, *Glimpses,* 42; Martineau, 2:216; Thackeray's daughter ("overdress") in Stephens Papers, Aug. 1868, DUMC; Godley, 43–44; Latrobe, 2:126; Sombre, 42; Weld, *Vacation,* 73; Abbey Goodwin to Stephen Goodwin, 17 Aug. 1848; *NYT,* 31 July 1854; "Chit-Chat upon Philadelphia Fashions for August," *Godey's Lady's Book* 37 (Aug. 1848): 119; Henry Brown, *Brownstone Fronts and Saratoga Trunks* (New York: Dutton, 1935), 160–62.

56. *Brooklyn Eagle,* 4 Aug. 1877.

57. On *flâneurs,* see Walter Benjamin, *Charles Baudelaire: A Lyric Poet in the Era of High Capitalism,* ed. Jean Lacoste, trans. Harry Zohn (London: N.L.B., 1973), 35–66; Keith Tester, ed., *The Flâneur* (London: Routledge, 1994), 1–80, 181–87; Priscilla Ferguson, *Paris as Revolution: Writing the Nineteenth-Century City* (Berkeley: Univ. of California Press, 1994), 80–114; Susan Buck-Morss, *The Dialectics of Seeing: Walter Benjamin and the Arcades Project* (Cambridge: MIT Press, 1989), 304–7; Deborah Nord, *Walking the Victorian Streets: Women, Representation, and the City* (Ithaca: Cornell Univ. Press, 1995), 11–48; Vanessa Schwartz, *Spectacular Realities: Early Mass Culture in Fin-de-Siècle Paris* (Berkeley: Univ. of California Press, 1998).

At Lourdes, France, the peasant girl Bernadette Soubirous discovered the most famous of all nineteenth-century springs in 1858. It quickly became the focus of pilgrimages on a scale unknown since medieval times. The crowds harassed Bernadette to such a degree that she reversed the usual watering place motto by lamenting, "If I could only see without being seen!"; Ernest Turner, *Taking the Cure* (London: Michael Joseph, 1967), 233–53.

58. Poe, *Works,* 1:131–39; Nathaniel Hawthorne, *The Centenary Edition of the Works of Nathaniel Hawthorne* (Columbus: Ohio State Univ. Press, 1974), 3:146, 9:130; Walt Whitman, *The Complete Writings* (New York: Henry Knight, 1902), 1:191–93, 2:1–5, 307.

59. Washington Irving, *Salmagundi* no. 12 (27 June 1807); Gilpin, 66.

60. *NYT,* 21 July 1868; Hone, entries at 1 June 1835, 12 Aug. 1839; Perry, 107; Strong, entry at 30 July 1841; *Albany Statesman,* 6 Sept. 1820; *HW,* 3 Sept. 1859;

"Newport: Historical and Social," *HM*, 289; Mrs. S. S. Colt, *The Tourist's Guide through the Empire State* (Albany, 1871), 137; Buckingham, 2:435. For some other examples of "all the world," see Rothschild, 66–67; George Morris, *The Little Frenchman and His Water Lots; with Other Sketches of the Times* (Philadelphia, 1839), 51, 56, 62–69; "Glances at Men and Things, Saratoga Springs," *New Yorker* 8 (24 Aug. 1839): 366; *Plattsburgh Republican*, 9 Sept. 1826; Carl Arfwedson, *The United States in 1832, 1833, and 1834* (London, 1834), 272–75; Latrobe, 2:143–44; Moore, *Poems*, 28, 52–55; *NYT*, 9 July 1865; Eliza Bowne, *A Girl's Life Eighty Years Ago: Selections from the Letters of Eliza Southgate Bowne* (1887; New York: Scribner's Sons, 1903), 128; "Travels of a Scot," entry at 30 May 1824, NYSHS; *Frank Leslie's*, 27 Aug. 1859; I. Eaton, *The History of Coney Island, from Its Discovery in 4.11.44 Down to High Tide Last Night* (New York, 1879), 32–33; *Our Summer Retreats, a Hand Book to all the Chief Waterfalls, Springs . . .* (New York, 1858), 29–32.

61. *Frank Leslie's*, 27 Aug. 1859, 9 July 1864; Gilman, *Poetry*, 84; Melville, 14:322, 459–62, 659; *NYT*, 29 July 1878; 16 Sept. 1878. For other examples, see *New York Herald*, 13 Aug. 1848; *NYT*, 7, 15, 18 Aug. 1856; 16 July 1867; Mackay, 3:198; *New York Tribune*, 22 June 1853; Murat, 357; Morris, *Frenchman*, 50; Colt, 137; Sparkle, 12, 21; *Brooklyn Eagle*, 9 July 1882.

62. John Watson, *Historic Tales of Olden Time: Concerning the Early Settlement and Advancement of New York City and State* (New York, 1832), 206; John Hutcheson, "Summer Life in the States," *Belgravia Magazine* 15 (1871): 353–54; "American Country Life," *Crayon* 5 (Oct. 1858): 280; Solomon Northup, *Twelve Years a Slave*, ed. Sue Eakin and Joseph Logsdon (1854; Baton Rouge: Louisiana State Univ. Press, 1968), 9–11; Thomas quoted in John Hope Franklin, *A Southern Odyssey: Travellers in the Antebellum North* (Baton Rouge: Louisiana State Univ. Press, 1976), 143.

63. Patricia Spacks, *Boredom: The Literary History of a State of Mind* (Chicago: Univ. of Chicago Press, 1994), 1–30, 268. For ennui, see *New York Weekly Tribune*, 6 Sept. 1851; Buckingham, 2:454; Daniel Drake, *The Northern Lakes: A Summer Resort for Invalids of the South* (1842; Cedar Rapids, Iowa: Torch, 1954), 112–14, 123; James Stuart, *Three Years in North America* (Edinburgh, 1833), 1:193–94; Latrobe, 2:128; Thomas Hamilton, *Men and Manners in America* (1833; New York: Augustus Kelley, 1968), 2:380; Sombre, 31; "First Impressions," pt. 5; *NYT*, 15 Aug. 1857.

64. "Illustrations," 279; Hone, entry at 2 Aug. 1839; Mel Heimer, *Fabulous Bawd: The Story of Saratoga* (New York: Henry Holt, 1952), 60–61; "All Baggage," 334.

65. Hale, *Sketches*, 178–93; James Kirke Paulding, "American Society: Number Two," *Knickerbocker* 8 (Aug. 1836): 210–13; Moore, *Poems*, 45; *New York Tribune*, 25 Aug. 1853; Sombre, 5–74; Flint, 375–80; Child, *Letters*, 109–29; Beecher, *Lectures*, 22; Willis, *Hurry-graphs;* Bristed, passim; Watson, 207–8; Thomas Hamilton, *Men and Manners*, 2:379–81; "Domestic Tourism," 377.

66. "American Country," 280.

67. Ibid.

1. *Wilkes' Spirit of the Times*, 15, 22 Aug. 1863; *New York Herald*, 6, 7, 23 Aug. 1863; 31 May 1880; *Frank Leslie's*, 8 July 1865; Charles Dawson, *Saratoga: Its Mineral Waters and Their Uses in Preventing and Eradicating Disease and as a Refreshing Beverage* (New York, 1868), 8–15.

2. Union Hall register, 19–30 July 1869, SSPL; *New York World*, 8 Aug. 1865; John Hope Franklin, *A Southern Odyssey: Travellers in the Antebellum North* (Baton Rouge: Louisiana State Univ. Press, 1976), 265–71.

3. William Leach, *Land of Desire: Merchants, Power, and the Rise of a New American Culture* (New York: Pantheon, 1993), 3.

4. William Harding, *John Morrissey: His Life, Battles, and Wrangles* (New York, 1881), 8–49; Edward Van Every, *Sins of New York as "Exposed" by the Police Gazette* (New York: Frederick Stokes, 1930), 72–90; *Life of John Morrissey, the Irish Boy Who Fought His Way to Fame and Fortune* (New York, 1878), 3–16; "Gambling Houses of New York," *St. James Magazine* 20 (1867): 252–56; Luc Sante, *Low Life: Lures and Snares of Old New York* (New York: Vintage, 1991), 163–66.

5. *Wilkes' Spirit of the Times*, 22 Aug. 1863; Jack Kofoed, *Brandy for Heroes: A Biography of the Honorable John Morrissey* (New York: Dutton, 1938), 217–29; *Boston Journal* quoted in Arthur Train, *Puritan's Progress* (New York: Scribner's Sons, 1931), 272; *NYT*, 3–9 Aug. 1864; *New York Herald*, 3, 10 Aug. 1864.

6. Union Hall menus, 15 June to 24 Sept. 1865, SSPL; *Frank Leslie's*, 26 Aug. 1865; *New York Herald*, 11 Aug. 1865; *NYT*, 9 July 1865; 26 June 1866; 16, 25, 30 July 1866; 2 Aug. 1866; 22 July 1867; 8 Aug. 1867; 5–6 Aug. 1868; 13–14 July 1869; 1, 5, 15, 30 Aug. 1869; *New York Tribune*, 14 Aug. 1865 (9,000 glasses); 6–7 Aug. 1868; *HW*, 26 Aug. 1865; 24 Aug. 1867; 11 Sept. 1869; *Wilkes' Spirit of the Times*, 19 Aug. 1865; 4, 11 Aug. 1866; Records and Proceedings of the Saratoga County Agricultural Society, 1865–68, NYSLA; Melvin Adelman, *A Sporting Time: New York City and the Rise of Modern Athletics* (Urbana: Univ. of Illinois Press, 1990), 80.

7. *NYT*, 3, 17 July 1872; 5 Aug. 1873; William Stone, *Saratoga Springs, Being a Complete Guide . . .* (New York, 1866), 18; Charles Webb, *Sea-Weed and What We Seed: My Vacation at Long Branch and Saratoga* (New York, 1876), 71, 81–86; Edward Hotaling, *They're Off: Horse Racing at Saratoga* (Syracuse: Syracuse Univ. Press, 1995), 88–100; Landon Manning, *The Noble Animals: Tales of the Saratoga Turf* (Saratoga Springs, 1973), 67–94; Mel Heimer, *Fabulous Bawd: The Story of Saratoga* (New York: Henry Holt, 1952), 91–95; John Hervey, *Racing in America, 1665–1865* (New York: Jockey Club, 1944), 2:355.

8. Eli Perkins [Melville Landon], *Saratoga in 1901* (New York, 1872), 24, 46 ("Baden-Baden"); *Every Saturday*, 9 Sept. 1871; *Saratogian*, 28 June 1871; Mrs. S. S. Colt, *The Tourist's Guide through the Empire State* (Albany, 1871), 147–48; Kofoed, 229–33; Hugh Bradley, *Such Was Saratoga* (New York: Doubleday, Doran, 1940), 145–50.

9. *New York Herald,* 7 July 1848; 13 Aug. 1853; 21–24 Sept. 1853; *NYT,* 30 Aug. 1854; Daniel Benedict diary, entry at 15 Aug. 1847, SSPL; Two Englishmen [Alexander Rivington and Mr. Harris], *Reminiscences of America in 1869* (London, 1870), 75; *Herald* quoted in Manning, *Noble,* 15, 3–55; *Saratoga Sentinel,* 19 July 1883; Samuel De Veaux, *The Travellers' Own Book to Saratoga Springs, Niagara Falls, and Canada . . .* (Buffalo, 1841), 92 ("apparatus"); Edmund Huling, "Gambling in Saratoga," 1889 ("roulette"), SSCHO.

10. Stuart Reid, "Society at Saratoga," *Tinsley's Magazine* 34 (Feb. 1884): 240–41; *Champlain Interview and Rouse's Point Star,* 1 Sept. 1882; *NYT,* 17 Aug. 1868; Robert Wickham, *A Saratoga Boyhood* (Syracuse: Orange Publishing, 1948), 18–21; *Adirondack News,* 2 Aug. 1890; Thomas Richards, *Miller's Guide to Saratoga Springs and Vicinity* (1867; New York, [1877?]), 60–62; William Dean Howells, *An Open-Eyed Conspiracy: An Idyl of Saratoga* (New York, 1897), 6–8; Marietta Holley, *Samantha at Saratoga or, "Racin' after Fashion" by Josiah Allen's Wife* (Philadelphia, 1887), 199–206. For some postbellum days, see Charles Sweetser, *Book of Summer Resorts* (New York, 1868), 20–21; Friedrich Ratzel, *Sketches of Urban and Cultural Life in North America,* ed. and trans. Stewart Stehlin (New Brunswick: Rutgers Univ. Press, 1988), 66–73; R. F. Dearborn, *Saratoga and How to See It* (Saratoga Springs, 1871), 57; Perkins, 82–88; *Faxon's Illustrated Handbook of Travel* (Boston, 1874), 54–55; *Saratoga Illustrated: The Visitor's Guide of Saratoga Springs* (New York, 1890), 98–100.

11. Sidney Fisher, *A Philadelphia Perspective: The Diary of Sidney George Fisher Covering the Years 1834–1871,* ed. Nicholas Wainwright (Philadelphia: Historical Society of Pennsylvania, 1967), 530–31; Richards, *Miller's,* 28–29; *NYT,* 16 July 1866; 5, 30 Aug. 1869 ("dazzle"); 28 June 1875; John Hutcheson, "Summer Life in the States," *Belgravia Magazine* 15 (1871): 352; Andrew Boyd, *Boyd's Saratoga Springs Directory for 1868–1869* (Albany, 1868), xviii; Edward Hall, "A Week at an American Water Cure," *St. James Magazine* 10 (Oct. 1872): 34; [Henry James], "Saratoga," *Nation* (11 Aug. 1870): 87–89.

12. *Life of John Morrissey,* 16–18; *Saratogian,* 17 June 1871 ("I have lived"); 9, 26 Aug. 1871; 2 May 1878; *NYT,* 13 July 1869, 18 Aug. 1871; Bradley, 145–50.

13. Patrick Shireff, *A Tour through North America . . .* (Edinburgh, 1835), 10–12; Manning, *Noble,* 89 ("Sunday School"); *Wilkes' Spirit of the Times,* 15 Aug. 1863; 13 Aug. 1864; Howells, *Saratoga,* 129; Hotaling, *They're Off,* 151–64; for women at the track, see Miss Willie Creagh to her sister, 17 July 1870, Creagh Family Papers, UNC; Bronson Howard, *Saratoga; or, "Pistols for Seven"* (New York, 1870), 25–29; *NYT,* 30 July 1866; 2 Aug. 1866; 1 Aug. 1869; Jesse Williams, "Saratoga," *Outing* 41 (Dec. 1902): 273; *HW,* 26 Aug. 1865; *Frank Leslie's,* 16 Aug. 1879; Louis Howe, "Saratoga Springs," *New England Magazine* 32 (June 1905): 482–84; "Coney Island Jockey Club," *Blood Horse* 5 (Sept. 1977): 3999; *Chicago Herald* quoted in *St. Regis Falls Adirondack News,* 4 Aug. 1888; Brooke Kroeger, *Nellie Bly: Daredevil, Reporter, Feminist* (New York: Times Books, 1994), 229.

14. "Gambling Houses," 254; James McCabe, *Lights and Shadows of New York*

Life; or, the Sights and Sensations of a Great City (Philadelphia, 1872), 715–30; Edward Crapsey, *The Nether Side of New York . . .* (1872; Montclair, N.J.: Patterson Smith, 1969), 92–100; Matthew Smith, *Sunshine and Shadow in New York* (Hartford, 1869), 394–411; Henry Chafetz, *Play the Devil: A History of Gambling in the United States from 1492 to 1950* (New York: Clarkson Potter, 1960), 32–36, 292–96; John Dizikes, *Sportsmen and Gamesmen* (Boston: Houghton Mifflin, 1981), 39–41; John Findlay, *People of Chance: Gambling in American Society from Jamestown to Las Vegas* (New York: Oxford Univ. Press, 1986), 11–78.

15. *HW*, 23 Sept. 1876 (Nast); 18 May 1878; Fisher, 530–31; Kofoed, 249–75; *NYT*, 16 July 1866; *Saratogian*, 29 Apr. to 4 May 1878; *Saratoga Sentinel*, 2 May 1878; *New York Herald*, 2 May 1878; Russel Crouse, *Mr. Currier and Mr. Ives: A Note on Their Lives and Times* (Garden City, N.Y.: Garden City Publishing, 1936); Carl Sandburg, *American Songbag* (New York: Harcourt, Brace, 1927), 398–99. In *Troy's One Hundred Years: 1789–1889,* Arthur Weise indexed four thousand names but did not mention Morrissey (see Richard Sasuly, *Bookies and Bettors: Two Hundred Years of Gambling* [New York: Holt, Rinehart, and Winston, 1982], 63).

16. Criminal Dockets, 1876–77, 1887, SSCHO; *Charter and By-Laws of the Village of Saratoga Springs* (Saratoga Springs, 1866), secs. 10–16, 31–35, 47–53; Anthony Comstock, "Pool Rooms and Pool Selling," *North American Review* 157 (Nov. 1893): 606; *Saratogian*, 2 May 1878; *Saratoga Sentinel*, 31 July 1879; *Saratoga Daily Journal*, 8 Aug. 1883; 12 Aug. 1886.

17. Katrina Trask, *Yaddo* (Boston: T. Todd, 1923), 129–38; *NYT*, 31 Aug. 1890; Alexander Gardiner, *Canfield: The True Story of the Greatest Gambler* (Garden City, N.Y.: Doubleday, Doran, 1930), 258–60; Heimer, 149–87; *New York World*, 19, 26 Aug. 1894; 8 Oct. 1893; *The Story of Nellie Bly* (New York: American Flange and Manufacturing, 1951); Kroeger, 215–16, 243–44.

18. Gardiner, 263–74; *Adirondack News*, 2 Aug. 1890; Wickham, 10, 29–49; Chris Carola et al., *George S. Bolster's Saratoga* (Virginia Beach: Donning, 1990), 190–92.

19. *Wilkes' Spirit of the Times*, 10 Aug. 1895; 1 Feb. 1896; Chafetz, 319–39, 87–95; Gardiner, 1–166; 262–97; Bradley, 210–75; Williams, "Saratoga," 266–75; Herbert Asbury, *Sucker's Progress: An Informal History of Gambling in America from the Colonies to Canfield* (New York: Dodd, Mead, 1938), 419–51. For the track in these years, see Gottfried Walbaum, "Reminiscences," transcribed by Frank Tannehill, 1931, NMR; Hotaling, *They're Off,* 146–64; Bradley, 232–40; Manning, 83–89.

20. Holley, *Racin',* 218; Seneca Ray Stoddard, *Saratoga Springs: Its Hotels, Boarding Houses, and Health Institutions . . .* (Albany, 1882), 1; Colt, 138; *Frank Leslie's,* 1 Aug. 1895; *Times* (London), 9 Dec. 1887; *Chisolm's All-Round Route and Panoramic Guide* (Montreal, 1880), 45; Howe, "Saratoga," 480 ("nothing stranger"); Joseph Smith, *Reminiscences of Saratoga, or Twelve Seasons at the "States"* (New York, 1897), 90–91. For price gouging, see *NYT*, 7 July 1865; 14 July 1875.

21. Towle, 2:76; *NYT*, 18–19 June 1865; 25 June 1866; 12 July 1866; 16 July 1867;

6 Sept. 1869; 18 July 1871; *HW,* 23 June 1866; *Plattsburgh Sentinel,* 30 Aug. 1866. For the Grand Central Hotel, see Benjamin Butler, *From New York to Montreal* (New York, 1873), 23; *New York Daily Graphic,* 23 June 1873; 27 Oct. 1873; R. F. Dearborn, *Saratoga, and What to See There: An Annual Guide with a Treatise on the Mineral Waters* (New York, 1874), 13; Robert Joki, *Saratoga Lost: Images of Victorian America* (Hensonville, N.Y.: Black Dome, 1998), 16, 98–99.

22. *New York Tribune,* 12 Aug. 1876; *Frank Leslie's,* 8 July 1865; 7 Aug. 1869; 28 May 1870 ("paradise"); *NYT,* 9–14, 29 July 1865; 26 June 1866; 5, 30 Aug. 1869; *Chisolm's,* 33–34; *HW,* 29 July 1865; 7 Aug. 1869; Richards, *Miller's,* 32; Sweetser, 5–7.

23. Thursty McQuill [Wallace Bruce], *The Hudson River by Daylight* (New York, 1874), 118–22; *Saratogian,* 30 July 1874; Benjamin Butler, *The Summer Tourist* (Boston, 1880), 56–61; *NYT,* 24 June 1876; *Yvon's Great Picture . . .* (Saratoga Springs: n.d.); *New York Daily Graphic,* 27 Oct. 1873; 15 Aug. 1878; *Frank Leslie's,* 2 Sept. 1876; *New York Tribune,* 12 Aug. 1876; Beatrice Sweeney, *The Grand Union Hotel: A Memorial and a Lament* (Saratoga Springs: Historical Society, 1982), 1–13.

24. Elizabeth Phelps, *The Gates Ajar* (Boston, 1869), 169–91; McQuill, 66; McCabe, *Lights,* 375–85, 464–69; Michael Miller, *The Bon Marché: Bourgeois Culture and the Department Store, 1869–1920* (Princeton: Princeton Univ. Press, 1981), 19–72; Rosalind Williams, *Dream Worlds: Mass Consumption in Late-Nineteenth-Century France* (Berkeley: Univ. of California Press, 1982), 86–102; Elaine Abelson, *When Ladies Go A Thieving: Middle-Class Shoplifters in the Victorian Department Store* (New York: Oxford Univ. Press, 1989), 42–128; Leach, 76, 20–35.

25. Minutes of the [Village of Saratoga Springs] Board of Trustees, 15 July 1854, SSCHO; *New York Herald,* 7 July 1848 ("luxury"); Ellen Bond, "Journal of a Trip Made with My Dear Mother, Father, and Sisters and L.S. and Sue, July–August 1850," entries at 30 July to 6 Aug. 1850, file 13389, NYSLA; Eleanor Grosvenor to Charlotte and Sarah Holcombe, 5 June 1833, file FM11336, George Holcombe Papers, NYSLA; Michael O'Brien, ed., *An Evening When Alone: Four Journals of Single Women in the South, 1827–1867* (Charlottesville: Univ. Press of Virginia, 1993), 89–90. For vendors and souvenirs in antebellum Newport, see *Newport Mercury,* 2 Aug. 1856.

26. Carola et al., 73; Joki, 15; "The Great Van Broek Property," *Leisure Hour* 752 (26 May 1866): 322 ("pockets"); *Saratoga Springs Directory 1894* (Saratoga Springs, 1894), 37; *Frank Leslie's,* 8 July 1865; Howells, *Saratoga,* 37–38; *New York Daily Graphic,* 27 Oct. 1873.

27. Records and Proceedings of the Saratoga County Agricultural Society, 1862; *Adirondack News,* 20 Dec. 1890 (ministers).

28. Stoddard (1882), 1–4; Seneca Ray Stoddard, *Saratoga Springs . . .* (Glens Falls, 1889), 10; Seneca Ray Stoddard, *Saratoga Springs . . .* (Glens Falls, 1897), 3; Sophie Sparkle [Jennie Hicks], *Sparkles from Saratoga* (New York, 1873), 44; Holley,

Racin', 116; [James], "Saratoga," 87; *NYT*, 2 May 1874; Reid, 240; *Saratoga Illustrated*, 4; Prentiss Ingraham, ed., *Saratoga: Winter and Summer* (New York, 1885), 26–27; *Frank Leslie's*, 21 Aug. 1875.

29. Butler, *Tourist*, 55–62; *Chisolm's*, 29–33; ephemera from United States Hotel and Congress Hall, SSHM; *Saratoga Union*, 25 Dec. 1889; John Leng, *America in 1876* (New York, 1877), 41, 78–79; 252–70; *Saratoga Sentinel*, 22 Apr. 1875; 6 May 1875; Nathaniel Sylvester, *History of Saratoga County, New York* (Philadelphia, 1878), 165–67; *NYT*, 6 June 1868; 13 July 1869 ("best built"); 24 June 1876; *New York Daily Graphic*, 11 Aug. 1883; Sweetser, 4–5; anonymous speech (1866) and Congress Hall bonds in YC.

30. *NYT*, 4 July 1874; 20 June 1875; Karl Baedeker, ed., *The United States, with an Excursion into Mexico* (New York, 1893), 180; Henry Vivian, *Notes of a Tour in America* (London, 1878), 32–33, 218–22; Ratzel, 73; Holley, *Racin'*, 94–95; Dawson, 12–15; Dearborn, *What to See*, 9–20; Stoddard (1882), 6–19; *Saratoga Illustrated*, 16–32; Philip Wakely, *Saratoga in a Nutshell: A Guide to Saratoga Sights* (Saratoga Springs, 1892), 19; Floyd Rinhart and Marion Rinhart, *Summertime: Photographs of Americans at Play, 1850–1900* (New York: Clarkson Potter, 1978), 24 ("nowhere else"); "Grand Union Hotel: Season of 1890," NYCPL; *Saratogian*, 6 July 1877; Henry Sienkiewicz, *Portrait of America: Letters of Henry Sienkiewicz*, ed. and trans. Charles Morley (New York: Columbia Univ. Press, 1959), 3–6; *Frank Leslie's*, 4 July 1874; 28 June 1875; Sparkle, 100–159.

31. John Disturnell, *Springs, Water-falls, Sea Bathing Resorts, and Mountain Scenery of the United States and Canada* (New York, 1855), vi; advertisement, United States Hotel, Vertical Files, Bea Sweeney Archives, SSHM; *Faxon's*, 16–18; Sylvester, *History*, 166–68; *Frank Leslie's*, 31 July 1875; Fisher, 530–31; Bradley, 194–99.

32. Bennett quoted in Catherine Donzel et al., *Grand American Hotels* (New York: Vendome, 1989), 22; Cleveland Amory, *The Last Resorts* (1948; New York: Harper and Brothers, 1952), 416–18; Smith, *Reminiscences*, 64; *NYT*, 2 May 1874; Wickham, 25.

33. Gerald Carson, *A Good Day at Saratoga* (Chicago: American Bar Association, 1978), 42, 4–52; *Times* (London), 9 Dec. 1887; Leng, 41; *Champlain Interview and Rouse's Point Star*, 1 Sept. 1882; John Reeves, "The Way of a Realist: A Study of Howells' Use of the Saratoga Scene," *PMLA* 65 (Dec. 1950): 1038–44.

34. Boyd, 122–36; *Saratogian*, 22 Aug. 1888; *Kirwin and Williams' Saratoga Springs Directory* (Saratoga Springs, 1890), 277–99; *Census of New York for 1875* (Albany, 1877), 248–49.

35. Ingraham, 43; William Fox and Mary Lynn, eds., "The 1860 Census of Saratoga Springs: A Numerical Listing," table 1, SSPL; Sylvester, *History*, 135–36; *Saratogian Almanac for 1881* (Saratoga Springs, 1881), 20 May 1880. For strikes, see Sweeney, 10; *Saratoga Journal*, 4 Sept. 1880; 21 July 1883; *NYT*, 4 May 1874; *Saratogian*, 21–26 July 1877.

36. *Saratogian*, 15 June 1888; Perkins, 4, 9, 35–37; *Saratoga Sentinel*, 2 Sept.

1880; *NYT,* 15 June 1877; 10 May 1891; William Rogers to Dolly Smith, June 1871, Dolly Smith Papers, SSHM; Howells, *Saratoga,* 104–9; Reeves, 1035–51; Emma Waite diary, entries at 3, 6 June 1870, 12 July 1870, NYSLA; Holley, *Racin',* 92–93; Gretchen Sorin and Jane Rehl, *Honorable Work: African Americans in the Resort Community of Saratoga Springs, 1870–1970* (Saratoga Springs: Historical Society, 1992), 10–19, 28; Joan Baldwin, "Saratoga County Blacks in the Civil War," *Grist Mill* 21 (1987): 1–6; Myra Armstead, *"Lord, Please Don't Take Me in August":* *African Americans in Newport and Saratoga Springs, 1870–1930* (Chicago: Univ. of Illinois Press, 1999), passim; Bradley, 163.

37. Minutes . . . of the Board of Water Commissioners, 1872–1900, 1:1–9, SSCHO; *Frank Leslie's,* 30 Aug. 1879; *Saratoga Sentinel,* 25 June 1878; 9, 30 June 1881; 22 June 1882; *Saratogian,* 6 June 1881; Sweetser, 20. For sewage, see *The Sewage Question in Saratoga* (Saratoga Springs, 1885), passim. The Paris Ritz in 1906 was the first hotel to attach a bathroom to every room; Alev Croutier, *Taking the Waters: Spirit, Art, Sensuality* (New York: Abbeville, 1992), 98.

38. Charles Dudley Warner, "Their Pilgrimage," *HM* 73 (1886): 600; Avenue Commissioners of Construction, vol. 2, Oct. 1870, SSCHO; Union Ave. Association Records, SSCHO; *NYT,* 25 June 1866; 18 July 1871; 4 May 1874; *NYT,* 25 June 1876 ("devolve"). For Saratoga Lake, see *Gleason's Pictorial Drawing-Room Companion,* 25 Oct. 1851; *Frank Leslie's,* 4 Sept. 1859; 26 July 1862; 6 Sept. 1879; *New York Tribune,* 10 July 1865; 27 Dec. 1891; Colt, 145–47; Holley, *Racin',* 136–43.

39. *New York Tribune,* 12 Aug. 1876; *Saratogian,* 6 Oct. 1875; 27 May 1878; *Saratoga Illustrated,* 82; Warner, 73:593–95; Joki, 59–77; *Saratoga Register,* 6–8 Aug. 1878; stereograph in YC.

40. Phyllis Hembry, *The English Spa, 1560–1815: A Social History* (London: Athlone, 1990), 1–3, 302–4; Barry Cunliffe, *The City of Bath* (New Haven: Yale Univ. Press, 1987), 112–45; Oliver Goldsmith, *"The Bee" and Other Essays by Oliver Goldsmith, Together with the "Life of Nash"* (London: Oxford Univ. Press, 1914), 289–310.

41. Hotaling, *They're Off,* 27; for examples of some of these amusements, see Elihu Hoyt, "Journal of a Tour of Saratoga Springs," entry at 9 Aug. 1827, photocopy ed. by Peter Rippe from original manuscript in Pocumtuck Valley Memorial Association, Deerfield, Mass., 1973, SSHM; De Veaux, 92; Philip Hone, *The Diary of Philip Hone,* ed. Bayard Tuckerman (New York, 1889), entries at 19 July and 9 Aug. 1839; "First Impressions of Saratoga," pt. 4, *National Era* 13 (1 Sept. 1859): 1; Shackleford diary, entry at 3 June 1861; *Saratoga Whig,* 17 Aug. 1841; "Public Diversions: From the Beginning Up to the Present Time," 25 Dec. 1889, SSCHO; Benedict diary, entries at 4 Aug. 1835, 20–31 Aug. 1846, 27 July 1847, and 1, 8 Sept. 1859.

42. Bruce Manzer, "Saratoga County Bibliography" (1977), 22–33, 182–86, SSPL; Herman Melville, *The Writings of Herman Melville* (Evanston: Northwestern Univ. Press, 1968–89), 4:157, 141–60, 328–29.

43. Diana Webb, *Pilgrims and Pilgrimage in the Medieval West* (London: I. B. Tauris, 1999), 124–32; William Dean Howells, "Confessions of a Summer Colonist,"

Atlantic Monthly 82 (Dec. 1898): 742; Holley, *Racin'*, 323–24; *Saratoga Springs: America's Greatest Watering Places* (New York, 1888); *Saratoga Album* (New York, 1881); *Souvenir Views of Saratoga*, 4th ed. (Portland, Me.: L. Nelson, 1905); *Views of Saratoga* (New York: T. Nelson, n.d); Ingraham, 7; souvenir candy boxes, glasses, pin cushions, and wooden storage boxes in YC; see also Richard Hamilton, "The Hotel Marketing Phenomenon: Souvenirs, Mementos, Advertising, and Promotional Materials," in "The Grand Resort Hotels and Tourism in the White Mountains," ed. Bryant Tolles, *Historical New Hampshire* 50 (Summer 1995): 95–108; sheet music in SSPL, SSHM, YC, and NHS.

44. Flowers in the Bond journal.

45. Stereographs in Dennis Collection, NYCPL; Carola et al., 14–15; Stuart Stiles, *Stereoscopic Saratoga Springs: Approaching and Entering the Twentieth Century* (Middletown, N.Y.: Prior King, 1998); Joki, xii–xiv, 22; Rinhart and Rinhart, 8–13; *NYT,* 14 July 1865; *New York Tribune,* 10 July 1865. On stereographs, see Austin Abbot, "The Eye and the Camera," *HM* (July 1869): 482; William Darrah, *The World of Stereographs* (Gettysburg, Pa., 1977), 1–73; Edward Earle, ed., *Points of View: The Stereograph in America, A Cultural History* (Rochester: Visual Studies Workshop, 1979), 9–21, 90–115.

46. Daniel Shepherd, *Saratoga. A Story of 1787* (Boston, 1856), reprinted as *Saratoga. The Famous Springs* (Philadelphia, 1866); Nathaniel Sylvester, *Indian Legends of Saratoga and of the Upper Hudson Valley* (Troy, N.Y., 1884), 11; Nathaniel Sylvester, *Saratoga and Kay-ad-ros-se-re* (Troy, N.Y., 1876), 51; also Charles Peterson, *Grace Dudley; or, Arnold at Saratoga: An Historical Novel* (Philadelphia, ca. 1849).

47. O'Brien, 202; Todd DeGarmo, "Indian Camps and Upstate Tourism," *New York Folklore Newsletter* 14 (Summer 1993): 4–5; Marianne Finch, *An Englishwoman's Experience in America* (London, 1853), 115–17; *Saratoga Journal,* 31 July 1883; 8 Aug. 1883; Bond, entry at 6 Aug. 1850; *New York Herald,* 30 Aug. 1848; 27 Aug. 1853; Wickham, 53–58; Richards, *Miller's,* 53–54; *Saratogian,* 22 Aug. 1888; William Dix, "American Summer Resorts in the Seventies," *Independent* 70 (1 June 1911): 1212; Holley, *Racin',* 175–92, 303–4; Ratzel, 72; *Saratoga Illustrated,* 84; Joki, 112–13. The battlefield tour merited only one sentence in John Bachelder, *Popular Resorts and How to Reach Them* (Boston, 1875), 175–77.

48. *The Pompeia: A Reproduction of the House of Pansa . . .* (New York, 1890); *Handbook of the Pompeia: A Grand Roman House* (Saratoga Springs, 1892); *New York Herald,* 3 Aug. 1889; Baedeker, 180–82; Howells, *Saratoga,* 92–94; *Saratogian,* 10 Aug. 1891; Carola et al., 123; *Saratoga News,* 17 Aug. 1889. The House of Pansa closed in 1906, but the building still stands.

49. *Mount McGregor: The Popular Summer Sanitarium Forty Minutes from Saratoga* (Buffalo, 1884), 7–31; Nathaniel Sylvester, *The Historic Muse on Mount McGregor, One of the Adirondacks near Saratoga* (Troy, N.Y., 1885), 8–26; *Frank Leslie's,* 1 July 1882; 8 Aug. 1885; *HW,* 14 July 1883; 27 June 1885; 1 Aug. 1885; *Saratoga*

Sentinel, 22 June 1882; Thomas Pitkin, *The Captain Departs: Ulysses S. Grant's Last Campaign* (Carbondale: Southern Illinois Univ. Press, 1973), 46–129; Lloyd Lewis and Henry Smith, *Oscar Wilde Discovers America [1882]* (1936; New York: Benjamin Blom, 1967), 385–88; O. Clarke, *General Grant at Mount McGregor* (Saratoga Springs: Saratogian, 1906), 9–46; Richard Goldhurst, *Many Are the Hearts: The Agony and Triumph of Ulysses S. Grant* (New York: Reader's Digest, 1975), 204–54; Holley, *Racin'*, 232–40; "A Visit to Mount McGregor," *Grant Cottage Chronicles* 4 (Spring 1993): 2–3 ("banished").

50. Ingraham, 9–10, 28, 99–103; *HW*, 7 Feb. 1885; 13 Feb. 1904 ("Saratoga as a Winter Resort,"); *Saratoga Springs* (Saratoga: Businessmen's Association, n.d.); Holley, *Racin'*, 212–27; W. B. Westcott, *Dedicated to the Saratoga Toboggan Club* (Saratoga Springs, 1887), 3–15; *Saratoga Guide Illustrated* (Saratoga Springs, 1886), 46–48; letter from J.Z. to Mrs. Blanding, 8 Aug. 1881, NYSLA.

51. *NYT*, 2, 5, 9 Sept. 1894; 5, 6 Sept. 1895; 2 Sept. 1896; 8 Sept. 1897; 2 Sept. 1924; *Saratogian*, 2 Sept. 1894; 7 Sept. 1897; 16 July 1902; collection of photos, programs, and souvenirs in SSPL.

52. *Frank Leslie's*, 11 Sept. 1875; 5 Aug. 1876; 16 Aug. 1879; *HW*, 30 Sept. 1871; 25 July 1874; 1 Aug. 1874; 31 July 1875; 5 Aug. 1876; 2 Aug. 1879; *New York Herald*, 15 July 1874; *New York Daily Graphic*, 14–15 July 1874; 10–17 July 1875; *NYT*, 28 June 1875; 14–19 July 1875; 16–17 July 1876; 5 July 1884; *Saratogian*, 9 July 1874; 11–12 July 1879; *Saratoga Sentinel*, 24 June 1875; 3, 15, 22 July 1875; 10 July 1879; Webb, *Sea-Weed*, 64–67. On rowing, see Charles Peverelly, *The Book of American Pastimes* (New York, 1866), 115–334; Robert Kelly, *American Rowing: Its Background and Traditions* (New York: Putnam's Sons, 1932), 14–95; Samuel Crowther and Arthur Ruhl, *Rowing and Track Athletics* (New York: Macmillan, 1905), 47–58, 159–60, 268.

53. Clarence Rice, "A Report on the Mineral Waters of the United States by the Committee Appointed by the American Climatological Association," *Medical Record* (15 June 1889): 646–49; "Report of Committee on Sanataria and on Mineral Springs," *American Medical Association Transactions* 31 (1880): 537–65; Ronald Foresta, *America's National Parks* (Washington, D.C.: Resources for the Future, 1975), 11–12; Charles Chandler, *Lecture on Water* (Albany, 1871), 20–21; John Moorman, *Mineral Springs of North America* (Philadelphia, 1873), 229; James Bacon, *On the Medicinal Character of Hathorn Spring Water* (Albany, 1878), 1–31; Charles Fish, "The Mineral Springs of Saratoga," *Popular Science Monthly* 19 (May 1881): 24–33; *Annuaire des Eaux Minérales et des Bains de la France et de L'Étranger*, 28th ed. (Paris, 1886), 120; Titus Coan, "Home Uses of Mineral Waters," *HM* 77 (Oct. 1888): 722; Thomas Burchard, *The Saratoga Waters: A Clinical Essay* (Saratoga Springs, 1892), 36–53; James Crook, *The Mineral Waters of the United States and Their Therapeutic Uses* (New York, 1899), 341–67.

54. *Saratoga Sentinel*, 9 Aug. 1883; Bernhard Puckhaber, *Saratogas* (1976; Ballston Spa, 1993), 4–11, 25–105; Dawson, 22–25, 47–60; *New York Daily Graphic*, 19

Aug. 1878; Henry McGuier, *Concise History of High Rock Spring* (Saratoga Springs, 1867), 21–23; *NYT,* 26 June 1866; 24 Aug. 1866; Sweetser, 8–17; Butler, *Tourist,* 65–76; Sylvester, *History,* 160; Ebenezer Emmons, *The Empire Spring: Its Composition and Medical Uses* (Albany, 1849), 28–37; Carola et al., 13–14, 150–58; *New York Sun,* 2 Aug. 1896; *Saratoga Illustrated,* 112; Ratzel, 73.

55. Manzer, 22–26, 182–86; John Steel, *An Analysis of the Mineral Waters of Saratoga and Ballston . . . Together with a History of These Watering Places,* 2d ed. (Saratoga Springs, 1838); Richard Allen, *Hand-Book of Saratoga, and Stranger's Guide* (New York, 1869); Milo North, *An Analysis of Saratoga Waters; also of Sharon, Avon, Virginia, and Other Mineral Waters of the United States* (Saratoga Springs, 1858); Norman Bedortha, *Practical Medication, or, The Invalid's Guide: With Directions for the Treatment of Disease* (Albany, 1860); Sylvester Strong, *Lung, Female, and Chronic Diseases* (New York, 1861); J. P. Butler, *Secrets of the Medicinal Waters of Saratoga Springs* (Saratoga Springs, 1888), 7–33; Morris Franklin, *The Eureka White Sulphur Spring Bathing Pavilion and Park* (Saratoga Springs, 1897), 6–8; John Irwin, *Hydrotherapy at Saratoga: A Treatise on the Natural Mineral Waters* (New York, 1892), iv–2.

56. *Saratoga Sentinel,* 9 Aug. 1883; Grace Swanner, *Saratoga: Queen of Spas* (Utica: North Country, 1988), 150–62; Irwin, 259–61; James Kemp, "The Mineral Springs of Saratoga," *New York State Museum Bulletin* 159 (1912): 5–79; Douglas Moriarta, "Practical Side of Saratoga Springs as a Health Resort," *Albany Medical College Annals* (Oct. 1920): 334–36; William Back et al., "Bottled Water, Spas, and Early Years of Water Chemistry," *Ground Water* 33 (July 1995): 608–9.

57. Stoddard (1882), 1–4; *New York Daily Graphic,* 3 June 1878; on free entertainment, see *New York Tribune,* 12 Aug. 1876; Smith, *Reminiscences,* 125; Howells, *Saratoga,* 6–8, 39–52, 104, 134; Charles Snyder diary, entries at 7, 9 July 1883, NYSLA.

58. *NYT,* 6 July 1875 ("ferment"); Baedeker, 180; Holley, *Racin',* 271.

59. *Saratogian Annual for the Year 1883* (Saratoga Springs, 1883); *NYT,* 16 July 1867; Howells, *Saratoga,* 36–37; Vivian, 35; *Saratogian,* 23 July 1879.

60. Letter dated 24 Apr. 1878 to "Petty," NYSHAL; Smith, *Reminiscences,* 91; *Times* (London), 9 Dec. 1887; Parker Morrell, *Diamond Jim: The Life and Times of James Buchanan Brady* (Garden City, N.Y.: Garden City Publishing, 1934), 22–30; *Sparkle,* 12; George Waller, *Saratoga: Saga of an Impious Era* (Englewood Cliffs: Prentice-Hall, 1966), 200–258.

61. *National Police Gazette,* 25 Sept. 1880, quoted in Mary Blanchard, *Oscar Wilde's America: Counterculture in the Gilded Age* (New Haven: Yale Univ. Press, 1998), 10–19; Heimer, 165–66; Perkins, 78–79; Lewis and Smith, 383–88; Bradley, 188–94, 241–53; Evander Berry Wall, *Neither Pest nor Puritan: The Memoirs of E. Berry Wall* (New York: Dial, 1940), 75–77; *Essex County Republican,* 2 Aug. 1883; Albert Crockett, *Peacocks on Parade* (New York: Sears, 1931), 36–39, 310–12.

62. *New York Recorder,* 26 July 1891; Warner, 73:594; *Saratoga Union,* 25 Dec.

1889; Smith, *Reminiscences*, 64, 80, 90, 99; Kofoed, 230; stereographs 12–13, F–149, Dennis Collection; *NYT*, 4 July 1874; *New York Tribune*, 10 Aug. 1876; Heimer, 141; Gardiner, 277–80. For Nathaniel Willis's role in creating "celebrity" culture, see his *Hurry-graphs; or, Sketches of Scenery, Celebrities, and Society* (New York, 1851), and Thomas Baker, *Sentiment and Celebrity: Nathaniel Parker Willis and the Trials of Literary Fame* (New York: Oxford Univ. Press, 1999), 6–14, 70–96, 189–91.

63. *Champlain Interview and Rouse's Point Star*, 1 Sept. 1882 ("stare"); Williams, "Saratoga," 266–67; Howe, "Saratoga," 472; Ingraham, 25; *New York Tribune*, 27 July 1878; *NYT*, 24 July 1876; Howells, *Saratoga*, 65–66, 6–16, 38–39; Smith, *Reminiscences*, 109, 191; Colt, 138 ("festival"); Irwin, 150; Leng, 41 ("freedom"). For continued use of the "all the world" motif, see *Faxon's*, 53–54; J. David Williams, *America Illustrated* (Boston, 1883), 73; Reid, 240; *HW*, 6 Sept. 1890; *Frank Leslie's*, 28 Aug. 1875; 23 Aug. 1879.

CHAPTER SIX   *The Privatization of Newport*

1. [Henry James], "Saratoga," *Nation* 11 (11 Aug. 1870): 87–89 ("spectacle"); "Lake George," *Nation* (25 Aug. 1870): 119–20; "From Lake George to Burlington," *Nation* 11 (1 Sept. 1870): 135–36; "Newport," *Nation* (15 Sept. 1870): 170–72 ("sunstantial"; "villas"); Henry James, *Autobiography*, ed. Frederick Dupee (New York: Criterion, 1956), 495; Mildred Howells, ed., *Life in Letters of William Dean Howells* (New York: Doubleday, Doran, 1928), 2:6–7.

2. *Newport Daily News*, 23 Aug. 1869 ("Saratoga"); 28 Aug. 1869; Saxe quoted in *Faxon's Illustrated Handbook of Travel* (Boston, 1874), 55; Oramel Senter, "Civic and Scenic New England: Newport in 1877," *Potter's American Monthly* 9 (July 1877): 14 ("stress"); "The Queen of Aquidneck," *HM* 44 (Aug. 1874): 311 ("blacklegs"); *NYT*, 4 Aug. 1873; *Newport Daily News*, 5 Sept. 1878; *HW*, 6 Sept. 1890.

3. *Newport Mercury*, 21 Aug. 1875; George Towle, *American Society* (London, 1870), 1:80; *Newport: Season of 1874; with Map, List of Summer Residents, and Tide Table* (Newport, 1874), 32–34 ("wonder"); Senter, 14; *NYT*, 3 Aug. 1875.

4. Atlantic House Papers, box 4, 1861–67, NHS; John Pegram, "Recollections of the United States Naval Academy," in *Personal Narratives of Events in the War of Rebellion* (Providence, 1891): 36–49; *Newport Mercury*, 21 Sept. 1861; 27 May 1865; 10 June 1865; 22 July 1865; 9 Sept. 1865; *HW*, 5 Feb. 1876; *NYT*, 29 July 1865; 2 Jan. 1873; 16 June 1873; 15 May 1874.

5. Lionel Casson, *Travel in the Ancient World* (Baltimore: Johns Hopkins Univ. Press, 1974), 138–48; *Herald of the Times*, 25 Sept. 1845; Kenneth Jackson, *Crabgrass Frontier: The Suburbanization of the United States* (New York: Oxford Univ. Press, 1985), 58–79.

6. Charles Dudley Warner, "Their Pilgrimage," *HM* 73 (1886): 424; Tyrone Power, *Impressions of America during the Years 1833, 1834, and 1835* (London, 1836), 2:23; *NYT*, 3 Aug. 1875 ("delusions"); *Newport, Block Island, and Narragansett Pier*

(Boston, 1895), 20 ("absence"); "The Evolution of the Summer Resort," *Nation* 37 (19 July 1883): 47; "Private vs. Public Resorts," *Independent* 53 (6 June 1901): 1332; Whitman quoted in Jackson, *Crabgrass*, 50; Russell Conwell, *Acres of Diamonds* (Old Tappan, N.J.: Fleming Revell, 1960), 25.

7. Anna Hunter, "Kay Street during My Life," *BNHS* 83 (Apr. 1932): 1–6; Ann Benway, *A Guide to Newport Mansions* (Newport: Preservation Society of Newport County, 1984), 12–23; Jane Mulvagh and Mark Weber, *Newport Houses* (New York: Rizzoli, 1989), 66–75.

8. *Herald of the Times*, 29 Aug. 1844; Richard Bayles, *History of Newport County, Rhode Island* (New York, 1888), 1:489–90; Charles Dow, *Newport: The City by the Sea* (Newport, 1880), 56–68; George Smith, "Memories of Long Ago, 1839–1925," *BNHS* 56 (Jan. 1926): 4; Alan Schumacher, "Newport's Real Estate King," *NH* 61 (1988): 36–45; Nathaniel Willis, *The Rag Bag: A Collection of Ephemera* (New York, 1855), 276; Sidney Fisher, *A Philadelphia Perspective: The Diary of Sidney George Fisher Covering the Years 1834–1871*, ed. Nicholas Wainwright (Philadelphia: Historical Society of Pennsylvania, 1967), 199, 213, 250.

9. *Newport Mercury*, 10 July 1852; 28 Aug. 1852; 16 July 1853; *New York Herald*, 13 Aug. 1853; John Dix [George Phillips], *A Handbook of Newport, and Rhode Island* (Newport, 1852), 20, 169; "Newport in Winter," *Putnam's Monthly* 1 (Feb. 1853): 154 ("How fiercely"); Henry Cabot Lodge, *Early Memories* (New York: Scribner's Sons, 1913), 88.

10. Julia Ward Howe, *Reminiscences: 1819–1899* (Boston, 1899), 238; Dow, 57; *NYT*, 10 Aug. 1868; Maud Howe Elliott, *This Was My Newport* (Cambridge: Mythology, 1944), 171; Schumacher, "King," 46–50.

11. *Newport Mercury*, 29 June 1861; 15 Aug. 1863 (*Republican*); 6 Aug. 1864; John Disturnell, *Springs, Water-falls, Sea Bathing Resorts, and Mountain Scenery of the United States and Canada* (New York, 1855), 223–24; "Newport City Documents, 1853–54" (Newport, 1854), doc. 3, 17, NHS; *Newport Daily News*, 19 Aug. 1851; 19 June 1854; *NYT*, 13, 22 Aug. 1866; Mary King Van Rensselaer, *Newport: Our Social Capital* (Philadelphia: Lippincott, 1905), 27–37; Mrs. William Birckhead, "Recollections of My Uncle Edward King," *NHSB* 71 (Oct. 1929): 2–10; *New York Herald*, 13 Aug. 1853; George Mason, *Newport and Its Cottages* (Boston, 1875), 29–30; Mary La Farge and James Yarnall, "Nurturing Art and Family: The Newport Life of Margaret Mason Perry La Farge," *NH* 67 (1995): 58–74.

12. Schumacher, "King," 47; William Brownell, "Newport," *Scribner's* 16 (Aug. 1894): 142–43; *NYT*, 12 July 1873; 3 June 1878; *HW*, 18 Sept. 1886; Van Rensselaer, *Newport*, 73–85; Mason, *Cottages*, 55–57; *Newport: Season of 1874*, 12, 20–26; Shari Benstock, *No Gifts from Chance: A Biography of Edith Wharton* (New York: Scribner's Sons, 1994), 429–30.

13. Lee Soltow, *Men and Wealth in the United States, 1850–1870* (New Haven: Yale Univ. Press, 1975), 105; Harold Hurst, "The Elite Class of Newport, Rhode Island: 1830–1860" (Ph.D. diss., New York University, 1975), 47–76.

14. Mason, *Cottages*, 9–10; *Newport Mercury*, 26 Sept. 1874; Dow, 72–77; Charles Hammett, *A Contribution to the Bibliography and Literature of Newport, R.I.* (Newport, 1887), 112; Anthony Trollope, *North America* (New York: Knopf, 1951), 28; Salomon de Rothschild, *A Casual View of America: The Home Letters of Salomon de Rothschild, 1859–1861*, ed. and trans. Sigmund Diamond (London: Cresset, 1962), 69; Van Rensselaer, *Newport*, 39–54; "Queen of Aquidneck," 307–11 ("the time"); David Black, *The King of Fifth Avenue: The Fortunes of August Belmont* (New York: Dial, 1981), 192.

15. Benway, 18–24; McAllister quoted in Cleveland Amory, *The Last Resorts* (1948; New York: Harper and Brothers, 1952), 184–90.

16. Elizabeth Drexel Lehr, *"King Lehr" and the Gilded Age* (Philadelphia: Lippincott, 1935), 113; Ward McAllister, *Society as I Have Found It* (New York, 1890), 245, 6–10, 117, 170, 239–52, 335–38; Elliott, 38–47; Arthur Train, *Puritan's Progress* (New York: Scribner's Sons, 1931), 377–82; Mary King Van Rensselaer, *The Social Ladder* (New York: Henry Holt, 1924), 219–20; 244–46.

17. *Newport Daily News*, 17, 23 July 1869; *Newport Mercury*, 7 Aug. 1869 (convention); *NYT*, 29 July 1865 ("degenerated"); 10 Aug. 1868 ("poorest"); 20 July 1866; 22 Aug. 1866; 16 June 1877. For antebellum complaints, see Fisher, 136, 213; "Newport: Historical and Social," *HM* 9 (Aug. 1854): 289, 317; *Newport Mercury*, 12 Aug. 1854; 2 Aug. 1856; *Newport Daily News*, 19 Aug. 1851.

18. Charles Sweetser, *Book of Summer Resorts* (New York, 1868), 12; *NYT*, 20 July 1866; 22 Aug. 1866; 13 Aug. 1868; 4 Aug. 1873; 25 May 1874; 10 June 1875; 26 July 1875; 3 Aug. 1875; 20 June 1877 ("Irish king"); 27 Jan. 1878; 3 June 1878; 16 June 1879; Senter, 14–15; *Newport: Season of 1874*, 32; *Newport and How to See It . . . 1872* (Newport, 1872), 49–57; *Newport Mercury*, 2 Aug. 1856; "Queen of Aquidneck," 305 ("shadowy"); *Newport Daily News*, 15 July 1850; 17, 23 July 1869.

19. Mark Twain and Charles Dudley Warner, *The Gilded Age: A Tale of Today* (New York, 1873), chap. 33; Lehr, 142; Amory, 178; Richard Barrett, *Good Old Summer Days: Newport, Narragansett Pier, Saratoga, Long Branch, Bar Harbor* (New York: Appleton-Century, 1941), 275–77.

20. Warner, 73:110–15.

21. "Queen of Aquidneck," 312; *HW*, 31 July 1869; *NYT*, 8 Aug. 1875; "Where Life Is Like a Story: Fashionable Summer Life at Gay Newport," *Ladies Home Journal* 7 (Aug. 1890): 2; *New York Recorder*, 19 July 1891 ("exploded"); John Hutcheson, "Summer Life in the States," *Belgravia Magazine* 15 (1871): 353; Brownell, 151–53 ("bathing . . . is over"); *Newport, Block Island, and Narragansett Pier*, 71; *Every Saturday*, 28 July 1870.

22. *Newport Mercury*, 21 Aug. 1886 ("jeering"); Gouverneur Morris, "Newport the Maligned," *Everybody's* 29 (Sept. 1908): 323–24; Amory, 250–56.

23. "Newport: Historical and Social," 112; *HW*, 4 Sept. 1858. For rambunctious behavior, see Thomas Edison's short, "Cakewalk at Coney Island," filmed in the 1890s and excerpted in *Coney Island: A Documentary Film* (Santa Monica, 1991),

produced by Ric Burns and Buddy Squires; *Brooklyn Eagle,* 11 July 1899; photograph of cross-dressing at Coney Island, file V.19735.1209, BHS.

24. "Disjointed Gossip from the Other Side of the Big Pond," *Bentley's Magazine* 39 (1856): 582–83 ("Hegira"); "Evolution," 47–48 ("pity"); *NYT,* 16 June 1877.

25. Henry Pierrepont diary, entries at 23 June 1883, 3–7 Oct. 1882, BHS; George Templeton Strong, *Diary,* ed. Alan Nevins and Milton Thomas (New York: Macmillan, 1952), entries at 8–17 May 1858; John Chadwick diary, 1881, 21–28, John Oldfield Chadwick papers, DUMC.

26. Edward Bok, "Summers of Our Discontent," *Ladies Home Journal* 18 (May 1901): 16; "Summer Hotels," *Nation* 39 (11 Sept. 1884): 217 ("killed"); "The Summer Exodus and What It Testifies," *Century* 38 (July 1889): 469 ("elastic"); Robert Grant, "The Art of Living: The Summer Problem," *Scribner's* 18 (July 1895): 52; "Changes in Summer Migration," *Nation* 53 (17 Sept. 1891): 210–11.

27. Thomas Wentworth Higginson, "Julia Ward Howe," *Outlook* 85 (26 Jan. 1907): 167–78; Thomas Wentworth Higginson, "Old Newport Days," *Outlook* 91 (17 Apr. 1909): 876–80; Washington Irving, *Letters* (Boston: Twayne, 1978–82), 4:629; *NYT,* 4 Aug. 1873; Samuel Longfellow, ed., *The Life of Henry Wadsworth Longfellow with Extracts from His Journals and Correspondence* (Boston, 1891), 2:238–41, 3:203; James Russell Lowell, *Letters of James Russell Lowell,* ed. Charles Norton (New York, 1894), 1:214–17, 2:59; Howe, *Reminiscences,* 400–409, 402 ("evaporate"); Elliott, 99, 79–114; Maud Stevens, "Colonel Higginson and His Friends in Newport," *BNHS* 24 (Apr. 1924): 1–15; Mary Higginson, ed., *Letters and Journals of Thomas Wentworth Higginson* (Boston: Houghton Mifflin, 1921), 228–74; James Yarnall, "Edwin Booth's Life in Paradise," *NH* 68 (1997): 113–36; Gary Scharnhorst, "'How Genuinely Unaffected a Man He Was': Bret Harte in Newport," *NH* 69 (1998): 1–17.

28. McAllister, 110–20, 174–75, 199; *NYT,* 8 Aug. 1875; 16 June 1877 ("formalities"); Maude Cooke, *Social Etiquette or Manners and Customs of Polite Society* (Boston, 1896), 258; *Newport Daily News,* 19 Aug. 1851; "Queen of Aquidneck," 318 ("courses"); Elliott, 157; *HW,* 30 Sept. 1893; William Dix, "American Summer Resorts in the Seventies," *Independent* 70 (1 June 1911): 1214.

29. Benway, 24–32; "Editor's Easy Chair" (Sept. 1880): 631 ("comparable"); *NYT,* 3 May 1873; Mulvagh and Weber, 66–75, 110–19; Mason, *Cottages,* 25–26; Birckhead, 6.

30. *NYT,* 18 Aug. 1868; Two Englishmen [Alexander Rivington and Mr. Harris], *Reminiscences of America in 1869* (London, 1870), 65; *HW,* 14 Aug. 1869; 18 Sept. 1886; Elliott, 132, 234; Edith Wharton, *A Backward Glance* (New York: Appleton-Century, 1934), 82–85.

31. *HW,* 30 Sept. 1893 (tea); *Evening Standard* quoted in Arnold Lewis, *American Country Houses of the Gilded Age: Sheldon's "Artistic Country Seats"* (Mineola, N.Y.: Dover, 1982), 100; Hammett, 54–56.

Ida Lewis, the lighthouse keeper's daughter, was for a time the equal of any cottager as a Newport celebrity. Lewis rescued eighteen people from drowning between 1850 and 1906 and in doing so became a national celebrity. President Grant, General Sherman, and Susan B. Anthony all met with her, and visitors bought Ida Lewis hats and scarves, stereoscopic views of her house, and even her picture. One summer, an astonishing nine thousand admirers came to visit her at Lime Rock Lighthouse; *Newport Mercury*, 27 Nov. 1869; 14 Dec. 1869; *Newport Daily News*, 13 Aug. 1869; James Graham, "Ida Lewis Waltz" (Newport, 1869), RIHS; James Clauson, "A Half-Forgotten Heroine: Ida Lewis, the Lighthouse Keeper in Newport Harbor," *Putnam's Magazine* 7 (Feb. 1910): 515–23; Ellen Le Garde, "A Day with Ida Lewis," *Ladies Home Journal* 7 (July 1890): 1–2.

32. "Summer Travel in the South," *Southern Quarterly Review* 26 (Oct. 1854), 40 ("puppydom"); Rothschild, 68; *NYT*, 1 Aug. 1866; "Disjointed Gossip," 581–82.

33. George Curtis, *Lotus-Eating: A Summer Book* (New York, 1856), 145, 164; Richard O'Connor, *The Golden Summers: An Antic History of Newport* (New York: Putnam's Sons, 1974), 109–13.

34. *Newport Mercury*, 30 Aug. 1879; *Newport Daily News*, 23 Aug. 1869; 12 Aug. 1881 ("difficult"); McAllister, 355–57; James Bowditch, *Newport: The City by the Sea* (Providence, 1880), 59–61; *NYT*, 8 Feb. 1878 ("necessity"); Alan Schumacher, *The Newport Casino: Its History* (Newport: Newport Historical Society, 1987), 46–55.

35. George Lathrop, *Newport* (New York, 1884); Elliott, 154–57; Dow, 114–15; Cecelia Manning, "A Physical History of the Newport Casino" (1987), 3–12, 31–37, Newport Public Library, Newport, R.I.; *Times* quoted in Lewis, *Sheldon's*, 16–17; Sarah Woolsey, "Isle of Peace," *Scribner's* 22 (Aug. 1881): 490–91; Chadwick diary, 21–28.

36. Evander Berry Wall, *Neither Pest nor Puritan: The Memoirs of E. Berry Wall* (New York: Dial, 1940), 102.

37. Paul Baker, *Richard Morris Hunt* (Cambridge: MIT Press, 1980), 120–35, 236–47; Gibson Danes, "William Morris Hunt and His Newport Circle," *Magazine of Art* 43 (Apr. 1950): 150; Antoinette Downing and Vincent Scully Jr., *The Architectural Heritage of Newport, Rhode Island, 1640–1915* (New York: Clarkson Potter, 1967), 129–75.

38. Memoir of Alva Vanderbilt Belmont, 1933, Matilda Young Papers, 114–18, DUMC; Baker, *Hunt*, 348–64; Mulvagh and Weber, 80–83, 106–221; Benway, 36–45.

39. *HW*, 10 Dec. 1892; "The Business of Leisure: The Gilded Age in Newport," *NH* 62 (Summer 1989): 122–25; Benway, 46–59; Baker, *Hunt*, 227, 364–72.

40. *HW*, 30 Sept. 1893; Barrett, 38–51; Richard Wilson, ed., *Victorian Resorts and Hotels* (Philadelphia: Victorian Society, 1982), 111–16; Elliott, 154–57; *Newport, Block Island, and Narragansett Pier*, 51–54; Lathrop, *Newport*, 33–34; *Newport Mercury*, 3, 17 Aug. 1895.

41. Dow, 117 ("fashionable"); Harrison Rhodes, "American Holidays: The Sea

Shore," *HM* 129 (June 1914): 12 ("no hotels"); *NYT,* 24 June 1878; *HW,* 30 Sept. 1893 ("passers-by"); Lathrop, *Newport,* 80.

42. Lewis, *Sheldon's,* viii–ix, 93–99; *NYT,* 2, 4 May 1874 ("mistake"); J. David Williams, *America Illustrated* (Boston, 1883), 74 ("delightful").

43. Alexis de Tocqueville, *Democracy in America,* trans. Henry Reeve (1835–40; New York: Schocken, 1972), 2:256, 1:155; James Kirke Paulding, *The New Mirror for Travellers; and Guide to the Springs* (New York, 1828); Charles Bristed, *The Upper Ten Thousand: Sketches of American Society* (New York, 1852); McAllister, 157, 349; Abram Dayton, *Last Days of Knickerbocker Life in New York* (New York, 1882), 147–74; Frederic Jaher, *The Urban Establishment: Upper Strata in Boston, New York, Charleston, Chicago, and Los Angeles* (Urbana: Univ. of Illinois Press, 1982), 57–97, 202–8, 245–81; Soltow, 90–91, 122–23, 178–83.

44. Mrs. Harrison Burton, "The Myth of the Four Hundred," *Cosmopolitan* 19 (July 1895): 329–34; *New York Weekly Tribune,* 6 Sept. 1851; Francis Grund, *Aristocracy in America: From the Sketch-Book of a German Nobleman* (1839; Gloucester, Mass.: Peter Smith, 1968), 14–15, 3–135.

45. Thorstein Veblen, *The Theory of the Leisure Class* (1899; New York: Mentor, 1963), chap. 2; William Dean Howells, *The Rise of Silas Lapham* (New York, 1885), chap. 2; Thomas Higginson, *Malbone: An Oldport Romance* (1869; Boston, 1882), 121.

46. Lawrence Levine, *Highbrow / Lowbrow: The Emergence of Cultural Hierarchy in America* (Cambridge: Harvard Univ. Press, 1988), 60, 85–168.

47. Judith Adler, "Origins of Sightseeing," *ATR* 16 (1989): 24; Isobel Cosgrove and Richard Jackson, *The Geography of Recreation and Leisure* (London: Hutchinson Univ. Library, 1972), 33–40; John Towner, "The Grand Tour: A Key Phase in the History of Tourism," *ATR* 12 (1985): 297–326; Robert Elleray, introduction to *Brighton: A Pictorial History* (Chichester, Eng.: Phillimore, 1987), n.p.

48. Hugh DeSantis, "The Democratization of Travel: The Travel Agent in American History," *Journal of American Culture* 1 (Spring 1978): 4–10.

49. Melvil Dewey, "Co-operation in Vacations," *Outlook* 52 (27 July 1895): 135; Warner, 73:416–27, 598; William Dean Howells, *An Open-Eyed Conspiracy: An Idyl of Saratoga* (New York, 1897), 67; Frank Kintrea, "Tuxedo Park," *American Heritage* 29 (Aug. 1978): 69–77; Richard Hale, *The Story of Bar Harbour* (New York: Ives Washburn, 1949), 167–89.

50. Charles Norton, *American Seaside Resorts* (New York, 1883), 65–67 ("tedious"); *NYT,* 11–12 Aug. 1872; 20 July 1877; Joanna Anthon diary, entries at 18 June to 16 Sept. 1869, NYCPL; Charles Carroll, "Narragansett Pier," *HM* 59 (July 1879): 166; Frederic Denison, *Picturesque Narragansett: Sea and Shore, with Illustrated Providence and Newport* (Providence, 1879); New York, New Haven, & Hartford Railroad, *Sketch of Narragansett Pier* (Boston, 1896).

51. *Newport Mercury,* 9 July 1887; Bayles, 1:505; Lathrop, *Newport,* 97–99; *NYT,*

6 Aug. 1876; 5 Aug. 1887; *Newport, Block Island, and Narragansett Pier*, 20 ("humble"); Hartley Davis, "Magnificent Newport," *Munsey's* 23 (July 1900): 482; Bowditch, 23–35; Lyman Powell, ed., *Historic Towns of New England* (New York, 1898), 466.

52. Mason quoted in Frank Harris, *History of the Re-Union of the Sons and Daughters of Newport, R.I., July 4, 1884* (Newport, 1885), 35 ("commerce"), 35–46, 125–26; Power, 2:22 (line); *Newport Mercury*, 18 May 1872; Hunter, "Kay Street," 8–12; RIHPC, *The West Broadway Neighborhood: Newport, Rhode Island* (Providence, 1977), 20–25; Smith, *"Memories,"* 9; *NYT,* 23 Dec. 1878; 28 Apr. 1879; 16 June 1879.

53. Harris, *History*, 9–72, 125–26; *NYT,* 6 July 1884; *Newport Journal,* 5 July 1884; Brownell, 154; *Newport Mercury*, 23 June 1894; *Newport: Season of 1874*, 50–58; John Bachelder, *Popular Resorts and How to Reach Them* (Boston, 1875), 104–7; *Newport, Block Island, and Narragansett Pier*, 78–111; Bowditch, 13–22; Roger McAdam, *The Old Fall River Line* (New York: Stephen Daye, 1955), 8–25, 54–72; Edwin Dunbaugh, *Night Boat to New England, 1815–1900* (New York: Greenwood, 1992), 177–234, 273–326.

54. *Newport Mercury*, 23 July 1853; 13 Aug. 1887; Lehr, 139–40; Brownell, 135–36; *NYT,* 15 May 1874; 2 Aug. 1875; 2 Apr. 1877; 21 May 1877; Consuelo Vanderbilt Balsan, *The Glitter and the Gold* (New York: Harper and Brothers, 1952), 28; *HW,* 7 Feb. 1885; Amory, 188–90 ("villagers"); Bayard Taylor, "Travel in the United States," *Atlantic Monthly* 19 (Apr. 1867): 483. John La Farge's son painted an appealing picture of growing up in Newport circa 1890, in John S. La Farge, *The Manner Is Ordinary* (New York: Harcourt, Brace, 1954), 34–44.

55. *HW,* 30 Sept. 1893; *Newport Daily News*, 17 July 1869; *Newport Mercury*, 23 Mar. 1889; 10 Aug. 1889; J. Stedman Ward, "The Trolley Car Days of Newport, R.I.," *NH* 47 (1974): 129–31; Brownell, 143; Florence Hall, "Changes in Newport Life and Forms of Entertainment," *Harper's Bazaar* 39 (Nov. 1905): 1034.

56. Lehr, 114; Elliott, 154–55; Gladys Bolhouse, "The Muenchinger-King Hotel," *NH* 41 (1968): 57–66. On hotels, see *NYT,* 30 June 1872; 2 Jan. 1873; 16 June 1873; 4 Aug. 1873; 15, 23 May 1874; 10 June 1875; 26 July 1875; 28 July 1876; 29 Apr. 1877; 4 June 1877; 16 Nov. 1877; *Newport: Season of 1874*, 11; "Queen of Aquidneck," 311; "Sayings and Doings," *Harper's Bazar* 12 (23 Aug. 1879): 539; *Newport Mercury*, 20 Aug. 1887; 3 Sept. 1887. For gambling, see "Newport: Historical and Social," 317; *Frank Leslie's*, 29 Aug. 1857; Leila Lee [Rebecca Coe], *The Dales in Newport* (New York, 1854), 99–101; Alexander Gardiner, *Canfield: The True Story of the Greatest Gambler* (Garden City, N.Y.: Doubleday, Doran, 1930), 267–69.

57. Schumacher, "King," 45; *Newport Herald*, 14 Sept. 1895; 10 Sept. 1898; *Newport Mercury*, 10, 17 Sept. 1898; Harris, *History*, 40–41; Wilfred Munro, *Picturesque Rhode Island* (Providence, 1881), 53; *NYT,* 3 Aug. 1875 ("Saratoga"); 6 Aug. 1876; 24 June 1878; Norton, 67 (Ocean House hops); Senter, 14–15; Bushrod James, *American Resorts; with Notes upon Their Climate* (Philadelphia, 1889), 34–35.

58. Lodge, 89, 208–12; "Reminiscences of Newport, 50–60 Years Ago," *NHSB* 57 (Apr. 1926): 4–6 ("dull"); Tiffany quoted in *Newport Mercury,* 21 Dec. 1889; Howe, *Reminiscences,* 408–9; Higginson, *Letters,* 226, 234; Warner, 73:116–17; Henry James, *The Europeans* (London, 1878), chap. 9; "Editor's Easy Chair," *HM* 61 (Sept. 1880): 630; Henry Adams, *The Education of Henry Adams* (1906; Cambridge: Riverside, 1961), 241–42; Henry James, *The American Scene* (1907; Bloomington: Indiana Univ. Press, 1968), 209–26; Jonathan Lincoln, *The City of the Dinner-Pail* (New York, 1909), 186; Edwin Godkin, "The Expenditure of Rich Men," *Scribner's* 20 (Oct. 1896): 500; Davis, "Newport," 472–88; Robert Walker, *The Poet and the Gilded Age: Social Themes in Late-Nineteenth-Century Verse* (New York: Octagon, 1969), 89–93; James Yarnall, *John La Farge in Paradise: The Painter and His Muse* (Newport: William Vareika, 1995), 12–17; Linda Ferber, "William Trost Richards at Newport," *NH* 51 (1978): 9.

59. Wall, 102–3; Lehr, 112; Wharton, *Backward,* 90, 106; Powell, 466 ("homestead").

60. Washington Irving, *Salmagundi* no. 16 (15 Oct. 1807). For other comments on how the masses turned gentility into vulgarity, see Alexander Mackay, *The Western World; or, Travels in the United States in 1846–47,* 2d. ed. (1849; New York: Negro Universities Press, 1968), 3:197; James Kirke Paulding, "American Society: Number Two," *Knickerbocker* 8 (Aug. 1836): 212; Timothy Flint, *Recollections of the Last Ten Years* (1826; New York: Knopf, 1932), 372–75; Nathaniel Willis, *Hurry-graphs; or, Sketches of Scenery, Celebrities, and Society, Taken from Life* (New York, 1851), 284–94.

61. Godkin, 495; Emily Faithfull, *Three Visits to America* (New York, 1884), 35–36; Paul Blouet and Jack Allyn, *Jonathan and His Continent* (Bristol, Eng., 1889), 13, 52–61; William Dean Howells, *A Traveller from Altruria* (New York, 1894), chap. 5.

62. Hall, "Newport Life," 1034–35; Grant, 50; Godkin, 499–500; Dixon Wecter, *The Saga of American Society: A Record of Social Aspiration, 1607–1937* (New York: Scribner's Sons, 1937), 456; *NYT,* 15 May 1874.

63. *Newport Herald,* 29 Aug. 1895; Gail MacColl and Carol Wallace, *To Marry an English Lord* (New York: Workman, 1989), 141–76; O'Connor, 83–85, 267–85; Elliot, 13–37; Balsan, 25–54; Cornelius Vanderbilt Jr., *Queen of the Golden Age: The Fabulous Story of Grace Wilson Vanderbilt* (New York: McGraw Hill, 1956), 16–17; Arthur Vanderbilt II, *Fortune's Children: The Fall of the House of Vanderbilt* (New York: William Morrow, 1989), 157–63, 216–17.

64. Lehr, 138; Wecter, 331–44; Davis, "Newport," 472–74; "Where Life," 2.

65. Tocqueville, 2:44; Strong, 4:94; Myra Armstead, *"Lord, Please Don't Take Me in August": African Americans in Newport and Saratoga Springs, 1870–1930* (Chicago: Univ. of Illinois Press, 1999), 67–84; Train, 239; Mason, *Cottages,* 80; McCallister, 202–3.

66. Robert Dunn, "Newport, the Blessed of Sport," *Outing* 52 (Sept. 1908): 689–

99; Paul Bourget, *Outre-Mer; Impressions of America* (New York, 1895), 47–57, 327; Elliott, 197–227; Brownell, 144–45; Hall, "Newport Life," 1032–33; Donald Mrozek, *Sport and American Mentality, 1880–1910* (Knoxville: Univ. of Tennessee Press, 1983), 118–29; "History of Yachting in Newport," *NH* 47 (1974): 121–26 (reprinted from the *Providence Journal*, 2 Aug. 1885); Lathrop, *Newport*, 147–61; "Yacht Race Game" (New York: McLaughlin Brothers, ca. 1891), Mystic Seaport Museum, Mystic, Conn.

67. Schumacher, "Casino," 55–72; Barrett, 52–62; *Newport, Block Island, and Narragansett Pier*, 68–70; Mrozek, 129–35.

68. Lydia Child, *The Mother's Book* (Boston, 1831), 59; Grant, 56; Lois Banner, *American Beauty* (New York: Knopf, 1983), 142–46, 187; Eileen Slocum, "Memories of Bellevue Avenue: The Story of a Newport Family," *NH* 67 (Summer 1995): 38–39; Frederick Martin, *Passing of the Idle Rich* (1911; New York: Arno Press, 1975), 230–31.

69. O'Connor, 175–215; Wector, 368–71; Blouet and Allyn, 46–48; Amory, 175, 205–28; Barrett, 81–117; Michael Strange, *Who Tells Me True* (New York: Scribner's Sons, 1940), 57–58.

70. Memoir of Alva Vanderbilt Belmont, 158–64; Woolsey, 494; Lewis Erenberg, *Steppin' Out: New York Nightlife and the Transformation of American Culture, 1890–1930* (Chicago: Univ. of Chicago Press, 1981), 146–71; Virginia Jenkins, *The Lawn: A History of an American Obsession* (Washington, D.C.: Smithsonian Institution Press, 1994), 1–6, 183–87; Deborah Turbeville and Louis Auchincloss, *Newport Remembered* (New York: Harry Abrams, 1994), 38–41.

Veblen's discussion of emulation, shorn of its pseudoanthropological foundation, explains a great deal of nineteenth-century behavior, but the concept has a certain vagueness. For criticism, see Rick Tilman, *Thorstein Veblen and His Critics, 1891–1963* (Princeton: Princeton Univ. Press, 1992), 190–225; Colin Campbell, *The Romantic Ethic and the Spirit of Modern Consumerism* (Oxford: Basil Blackwell, 1987), 49–57; and Theodor Adorno, "Veblen's Attack on Culture," in *Prisms* (London: Neville Spearman, 1967): 75–94. Many recent analysts, although varying in their acceptance of emulation as the driving force behind consumer culture, have picked up on Veblen's portrayal of consumption as an act of identity; see Mary Douglas and Baron Isherwood, *The World of Goods* (New York: Basic, 1979), 56–84; Grant McCracken, *Culture and Consumption: New Approaches to the Symbolic Character of Consumer Goods and Activities* (Bloomington: Indiana Univ. Press, 1990), 6–25, 88–103. Although Veblen's theories seem vulnerable regarding the transmission of fashion (Elizabeth Wilson, *Adorned in Dreams: Fashion and Modernity* [Berkeley: Univ. of California Press, 1985], 49–57), Joan Severa makes an impressive case for emulation as the chief engine of nineteenth-century fashion diffusion, in *Dressed for the Photographer: Ordinary Americans and Fashion, 1840–1900* (Kent: Kent State Univ. Press, 1995), xv–xix.

71. *Mercury* quoted in MacColl and Wallace, 146.

CHAPTER SEVEN *"That Was Coney As We Loved It, and As the Hand of Satan Was upon It"*

1. *NYT,* 7 July 1895; Eric Ierardi, *Gravesend: The Home of Coney Island* (New York: Vantage, 1975), 77–84, 121–33; Edo McCullough, *Good Old Coney Island* (1957; New York: Fordham Univ. Press, 2000), 183–233, 296–327.

2. The public relations construction of Coney Island as "new" after 1900 is congenial to many historians because they wish to see hegemony as contested and thereby to culturally empower workers and immigrants. For some interpretations that emphasize the uniqueness of amusement park Coney Island, see John Kasson, *Amusing the Million: Coney Island at the Turn of the Century* (New York: Hill and Wang, 1978), 3–9, 63–112; Richard Snow, *Coney Island: A Postcard Journey to the City of Fire* (New York: Brightwaters, 1984), 11–20; Robert Snow and David Wright, "Coney Island: A Case Study in Popular Culture," *Journal of Popular Culture* 9 (Spring 1976): 970–71; Raymond Weinstein, "Disneyland and Coney Island: Reflections on the Evolution of the Modern Amusement Park," *Journal of Popular Culture* 26 (Summer 1992): 136, 144–46.

3. McCullough, 114–53; *NYT,* 30 June 1879; *Brooklyn Eagle,* 6, 16 July 1880; 14 Aug. 1880; 8 July 1882; 10 July 1890; 31 July 1893; Oliver Pilat and Jo Ranson, *Sodom by the Sea: An Affectionate History of Coney Island* (Garden City, N.Y.: Doubleday, Doran, 1941), 66–80; *Brooklyn Daily Eagle Almanac, 1888* (Brooklyn, 1888), 31.

4. Lyman Weeks, *The American Turf: An Historical Account of Racing in the United States* (New York, 1898), 471–75; *Brooklyn Eagle,* 2 July 1883; Evander Berry Wall, *Neither Pest nor Puritan: The Memoirs of E. Berry Wall* (New York: Dial, 1940), 29–32; Brian Merlis et al., *Brooklyn's Gold Coast: The Sheepshead Bay Communities* (Brooklyn: Sheepshead Bay Historical Society, 1997), 21–24, 53–62; Eric Ierardi, *Gravesend, Brooklyn: Coney Island and Sheepshead Bay* (Dover, N.H.: Arcadia, 1996), 59–62. Frederic Remington sketched the CIJC, *HW,* 18 June 1887.

5. *Wilkes' Spirit of the Times,* 10 Aug. 1895; 1 Feb. 1896; Townsend Percy, *Percy's Pocket Dictionary of Coney Island* (New York, 1880), 26; Peter Ross, *A History of Long Island* (New York: Lewis, 1902), 1:369; Walter Vosburgh, *Racing in America, 1866–1921* (New York: Jockey Club, 1922), 26–31; Ierardi, *Sheepshead Bay,* 55.

6. Collection of programs, railway tickets, and passes, 1880s and 1890s, in NMR, NYSHS, and BHS; Henry Howard, ed., *The Eagle and Brooklyn: The Record of the Progress of the Brooklyn Daily Eagle* (New York, 1893), 1012; John Hervey, *Racing in America, 1665–1865* (New York: Jockey Club, 1944), 2:339–64; Steven Riess, *City Games: The Evolution of American Urban Society and the Rise of Sports* (Urbana: Univ. of Illinois Press, 1991), 182–85; *Frank Leslie's,* 1888, in Ellen Snyder-Grenier, *Brooklyn! An Illustrated History* (Philadelphia: Temple Univ. Press, 1996), 181; New York [State], *Proceedings before Committee of Assembly of the State of New York Appointed to Investigate Municipal Affairs of Brooklyn . . . ,* 2 vols. (New York, 1887), Majority Report (doc. 110), 2:9–11, file Leg. 506.7, NYSLA; *Brooklyn Eagle,* 29 July 1882; 13

July 1952; Anthony Comstock, "Pool Rooms and Pool Selling," *North American Review* 157 (Nov. 1893): 602; Melvin Adelman, *A Sporting Time: New York City and the Rise of Modern Athletics, 1820–1870* (Urbana: Univ. of Illinois Press, 1990), 31–52, 75–89.

When Leonard Jerome imported parimutuel wagering to horse racing in 1871, bettors resisted not only the changeable odds of the new system but also their meta-morphosis from "customers" with a face-to-face and continuing relationship with bookies into "consumers" in an abstract market ruled by rational calculation. None-theless, the new system seemed less corruptible and eventually triumphed.

7. *Chicago Herald* quoted in *St. Regis Falls Adirondack News*, 4 Aug. 1888 ("hardly a woman"). In the short poem, "At Galway Races" (1910), William Butler Yeats yearns for life "before the merchant and the clerk breathed on the world with timid breath." Yeats finds it symbolically at the racetrack, "There where the course is, delight makes all of the one mind"; William Butler Yeats, *The Collected Poems of W. B. Yeats* (New York: Macmillan, 1974), 95.

8. Howard, *Eagle*, 1041; Riess, 174; *NYT*, 4, 21 Nov. 1899; *Brooklyn Eagle*, 28 June 1892; 1 July 1892; 14 Aug. 1892; 8 Aug. 1893; 25 Sept. 1893; McCullough, 89–90, 154–82; Snyder-Grenier, 185.

9. Walter Creedmore, "The Real Coney Island," *Munsey's* 21 (Aug. 1899): 746 ("flotsam"); *Brooklyn Times*, 12 July 1890 ("overrated"); Barbara Shupe, Janet Steins, and Jyoti Pandit, *New York State Population, 1790–1980* (New York: Neal-Schuman, 1987), 100, 118, 200; *Census of New York for 1855* (Albany, 1857), 7; *Census of New York for the Year 1875* (Albany, 1877), 19, 36; *New York Herald*, 20 Sept. 1889; McCullough, 70–73; *Brooklyn Union* quoted in Stephen Weinstein, "The Nickel Empire: Coney Island and the Creation of Urban Seaside Resorts in the United States" (Ph.D. diss., Columbia Univ., 1984), 183, 114, 123; New York [State], *Proceedings*, 1:577–78; Robert Neal, "New York's City of Play," *World To-Day* 11 (Aug. 1906): 824; Charles Shanley, "Coney Island," *Atlantic Monthly* 34 (Sept. 1874): 310; Edward Hotaling, *The Great Black Jockeys: The Lives and Times of the Men Who Dominated America's First National Sport* (Rocklin, Calif.: Forum, 1999), 239–309. For comparison, see Herbert Foster, "The Urban Experience of Blacks in Atlantic City, New Jersey, 1850–1915 (Ph.D. diss., Rutgers Univ., 1981), 17–21, 40–59, 232–43.

10. *New York World*, 23 Apr. 1884; *Brooklyn Union*, 24 Sept. 1883; 22 Apr. 1884; *Brooklyn Eagle*, 8, 11 Apr. 1887; 27 May 1887; *NYT*, 13 July 1885; Riess, 182; Harold Syrett, *The City of Brooklyn, 1865–1898: A Political History* (New York: Columbia Univ. Press, 1944), 182–85; Pilat and Ransom, 66–70; *Brooklyn Daily Citizen*, 6 June 1891; Weinstein, "Nickel Empire," 202 (resolution); New York [State], *Proceedings*, 1:531–51.

11. *Brooklyn Eagle*, 29 July 1882; *NYT*, 31 Mar. 1887; 1 Apr. 1887; John Mc-Kane's accounts, 1883–94, bundle 75, Gravesend Town Documents, NYCMA.

12. Ross, *History*, 1:370; New York [State], *Proceedings*, 1:525–31; Creedmore,

749; Gravesend Railroads, Suits, 1888–92, vol. 46, NYCMA; *Census of New York for 1875*, 36; Henry Stiles, ed., *The Civil, Political, Professional, and Ecclesiastical History and Commercial and Industrial Record of the County of Kings and the City of Brooklyn from 1683 to 1884* (New York, 1884), 195–207; *Brooklyn Eagle*, 7 July 1892; Merlis, 18–19, 27, 37; Gravesend Board of Health Minutes, 1880–93, vols. 323–25, 315, NYCMA.

13. Gravesend Town Meetings, 1879–88, bundles 10–13, NYCMA; *NYT*, 22 Aug. 1879; 3–14 Oct. 1882; 27–28 Feb. 1886; *The Coney Island Souvenir: How to Get There and Where to Go* (Brooklyn, 1883), 29; New York [State], *Proceedings*, 1:521–22, Majority Report (doc. 110), 2:16–18; Weinstein, "Nickel Empire," 88–90.

14. *NYT*, 31 Mar. 1887; New York [State], *Proceedings*, 1:507–97, 525, Majority Report (docs. 110–11), 2:7–41, and Minority Report (doc. 111), 2:1–20; *Brooklyn Eagle*, 17 Mar. 1887; 8, 11, 14, 16, 23 Apr. 1887; 9, 11 May 1887.

15. *Brooklyn Eagle*, 6, 7 ("for my sake") Nov. 1888; 7 Sept. 1890; 6–7 Nov. 1893; *Brooklyn Daily Citizen*, 3, 6 ("monarch") Sept. 1890; Ross, *History*, 1:370–71; Pilat and Ranson, 38–49; Creedmore, 749; *Brooklyn Eagle Almanac, 1888*, 178, 193; *NYT*, 6 Nov. 1888; 23 Jan. to 15 Feb. 1894.

16. *New York World*, 23 Jan. to 16 Feb. 1894; *Brooklyn Eagle*, 3, 6–9 Nov. 1893; 15 Feb. 1894; 27 July 1894; *New York Tribune*, 16 Feb. 1894; Ross, *History*, 1:371–72. The BHS contains two large volumes of newspaper clippings relating to McKane's trial.

17. *HW*, 8 Sept. 1866; *NYT*, 14 July 1873; 27 Aug. 1877; 26 June 1878; 30 June 1879; 10 June 1885; 4 July 1885; James Ford, "The Old-Fashioned Summer Hotel," *Munsey's* (June 1899): 477; *The Sewage Question in Saratoga* (Saratoga Springs, 1885), 40–45, appendix, 30–31; *Brooklyn Union*, 1 Aug. 1884; 10 June 1885; *Brooklyn Eagle*, 9 July 1877; 24 May 1880; 10 May 1894; Gravesend Town Meetings, 1879–88, bundle 11, and 1888–94, bundle 13; Harold Perkin, in "The 'Social Tone' of Victorian Seaside Resorts in the North-West," *Northern History* 11 (1975): 180–94, attributes the class stratification of English resorts primarily to patterns of land ownership.

18. New York [State], *Proceedings*, 1:550–52; Ross, *History*, 1:374; *Brooklyn Standard Union*, 7 May 1894; *NYT*, 13 Aug. 1877; 18–31 May 1909; Weinstein, "Nickel Empire," 76–77 (beer glasses), 136–37; Michael Marks Davis, *The Exploitation of Pleasure: A Study of Commercial Recreations in New York City* (New York: Russell Sage Foundation, 1911), 59–61; Manfred Jonas, "The American Sabbath in the Gilded Age," *Jahrbuch für Amerikastudien* 6 (1961): 91–113.

19. Edwin Slosson, "The Amusement Business," *Independent* 59 (21 July 1904): 134 ("free"); Stiles, *History*, 209; New York [State], *Proceedings*, 1:546–59, 555 ("inquiries"), 551 ("duty"); Howard, *Eagle*, 451–53; Pilat and Ranson, 33–34, 71 ("necessity"); Ierardi, *Home*, 94–120; Ross, *History*, 1:370; Edward Crapsey, *The Nether Side of New York . . .* (1872; Montclair, N.J.: Patterson Smith, 1969), 138–46; *Brooklyn Eagle*, 27 June 1892.

20. *NYT,* 25 June 1877; 6, 10, 17 July 1877 ("no effort"); 7 Aug. 1877 ("lager"); Percy, 64.

21. *Coney Island: An Illustrated Guide to the Sea* (Brooklyn, 1883), in Snyder-Grenier, 183; Percy, 30, 34; Stiles, *History,* 199–200; *Brooklyn Eagle,* 24 May 1880; 23 June 1882; 7 July 1892; Lucy Gillman, "Coney Island," *New York History* 36 (July 1955): 260–66; Weinstein, "Nickel Empire," 178–79; Snow, 50–51; David Gerber, "The Germans Take Care of Our Celebrations," in *Hard at Play: Leisure in America, 1840–1940,* ed. Kathryn Grover (Rochester: Strong Museum, 1992), 39–60.

22. *Mercantile Agency Reference Book* (Boston, 1888); *Brooklyn Eagle Almanac, 1888,* 123; Syrett, 193; *Brooklyn Eagle,* 5–9 May 1894; 18 Aug. 1897; *Brooklyn Standard-Union,* 7 May 1894; *NYT,* 13 Apr. 1896; Weinstein, "Nickel Empire," 179–80, 215–16; Pilat and Ranson, 112–20 ("Sodom"); Gillman, "Coney Island," 268.

23. *Coney Island and the Jews* (New York, 1879), 7–9; Percy, 58 ("blacklegs"; "changed"); *Brooklyn Daily Times,* 12 July 1890; William Ulyat, *Life at the Seashore* (Princeton, 1880), 136–38; *NYT,* 21 July 1868 ("disturbances"); 29 Aug. 1870 ("quiet and orderly"); 12 May 1879; Snyder-Grenier, 175; *The Story of Manhattan Beach . . .* (New York, 1879), 24–25.

24. *Brooklyn Eagle,* 21 June 1892; 1 Aug. 1893; Weinstein, "Nickel Empire," 328; *Brooklyn Daily Times,* 16 June 1890; 12 July 1890; *NYT,* 7 July 1875; 25 Aug. 1875; 6 May 1877; 13 Aug. 1877.

25. *Chicago Herald* quoted in *St. Regis Falls Adirondack News,* 4 Aug. 1888 ("el-bows"); William Dean Howells, *Literature and Life* (New York: Harper and Brothers, 1902), 161–72; *NYT,* 29 July 1878; James Huneker, *New Cosmopolis: A Book of Images* (New York: Scribner's Sons, 1915), 153; Dana Gatlin, "Amusing America's Millions," *World's Work* 26 (July 1913): 332; Julian Ralph, "Coney Island," *Scribner's* 20 (July 1896): 17; David Nasaw, *Going Out: The Rise and Fall of Public Amusements* (New York: Basic, 1993), 81.

26. *International Woodworker* (Chicago), June 1899, quoted in Kathy Peiss, *Cheap Amusements: Working Women and Leisure in Turn-of-the-Century New York* (Phila-delphia: Temple Univ. Press, 1986): 124; *New York Herald,* 21 July 1884; *NYT,* 31 Aug. 1874; 7 July 1875; reporter quoted in Weinstein, "Nickel Empire," 151.

27. Weinstein, "Nickel Empire," 130–33; James Henretta et al., *America's History,* 3d ed. (New York: Worth, 1997), 1:A13.

28. *NYT,* 21 July 1868; 29 Aug. 1870; *HW,* 12 Sept. 1891; Percy, 53, 62 ("without").

29. Theodore Dreiser, *The Color of a Great City* (New York: Boni and Liveright, 1923), 119.

30. Simon Bronner, ed., *Consuming Visions: Accumulation and Display of Goods in America, 1880–1920* (New York: Norton, 1989), 55–71; Daniel Rodgers, *The Work Ethic in Industrial America, 1850–1920* (Chicago: Univ. of Chicago Press, 1974), 94–124; Christopher Berry, *The Idea of Luxury: A Conceptual and Historical Investigation* (New York: Cambridge Univ. Press, 1994), 242; Chandra Mukerji, *From Graven Images: Patterns of Modern Materialism* (New York: Columbia Univ. Press, 1983), 8–

12, 166–209, 246–61; Neil McKendrick, John Brewer, and J. H. Plumb, *The Birth of a Consumer Society: The Commercialization of Eighteenth-Century England* (Bloomington: Indiana Univ. Press, 1982), 1–33. In *The English Urban Renaissance: Culture and Society in the Provincial Town, 1660–1760* (New York: Clarendon, 1989), 225–56, 312–18, Peter Borsay singles out emulation as the engine that drives consumerism; for dissents, see Colin Campbell, *The Romantic Ethic and the Spirit of Modern Consumerism* (Oxford: Basil Blackwell, 1987), 17–35, and Lorna Weatherill, *Consumer Behavior and Material Culture in Britain, 1660–1760* (London: Routledge, 1989), 25–42, 191–200.

31. *Kings County Rural Gazette,* 23 June 1883, in Weinstein, "Nickel Empire," 170 ("every inch"); George Brunswick, *Coney Island and Rockaway* (New York, 1880); "The Colossal Elephant of Coney Island," *Scientific American* 53 (11 July 1885): 1; Lyon, 18; *Coney Island Souvenir,* 2; Snyder-Grenier, 179; Ralph, 10–12; William Bishop, "To Coney Island," *Scribner's* 20 (July 1880): 356; "Brighton Beach Music Hall Programs," 1894, BHS; *A Wonderful Account of an Excursion to Coney Island* (game) (Springfield, Mass.: Milton Bradley, 1881), 15 ("wretched"), NYSHS; I. Eaton, *The History of Coney Island, from Its Discovery in 4.11.44 Down to High Tide Last Night* (New York, 1879), passim; J. P. Sweet, *A Day on Coney Island* (New York, 1880), 9–10; souvenir items in BHS, such as child's alphabet plate, Oriental Hotel, ca. 1890; Manhattan Beach Hotel medal, ca. 1877; trade cards, stereograph views, silk scarf commemorating first seven winners of Suburban Handicap, 1890, in NMR. See Percy, 31–32, 45–46, 66, who obsessed over the relative costs of à la carte meals.

32. *Wonderful Account,* 3–15.

33. Collection of stereoscopic views of Coney Island, 91–F177, Dennis Collection, NYCPL; *Wonderful Account,* 11; Snow, 20.

34. Photograph of Bowery, ca. 1903, V1973.5.2726, BHS; Ross, *History,* 2:40–42; Ralph, 16–18; Creedmore, 746–47; Peter Lyon, "The Master Showman of Coney Island," *American Heritage* 9 (June 1958): 14–21, 92–95. For Surf Avenue, see Snow, 32–35; William Younger, *Old Brooklyn in Early Photographs, 1865–1929* (New York: Dover, 1978), 114–15.

35. *Brooklyn Eagle,* 8 July 1889; 5 July 1895 (advertisement); Weinstein, "Nickel Empire," 76–77; Percy, 45–46; *Brooklyn Daily Citizen,* 18 Aug. 1895.

36. *Brooklyn Eagle,* 28 May 1880; 16 July 1882; 2 July 1888; 31 July 1893; 13, 20 June 1897; *NYT,* 30 Aug. 1878; 18 July 1880; 25 Aug. 1884; 13 Aug. 1886; *New York Tribune,* 31 May 1880; "Manhattan Beach Program for Gilmore's Band Grand Concerts," 21 July 1889, BHS; Joel Cook, *Brief Summer Rambles near Philadelphia* (Philadelphia, 1882), 94; Percy, 11–12, 55; Lloyd Morris, *Postscript to Yesterday* (New York: Random House, 1940), 113–15.

37. Ralph, 16 ("protest"); *Brooklyn Eagle,* 29 Apr. 1894; *NYT,* 4 July 1888; 17 June 1889; Joseph Horowitz, *Wagner Nights: An American History* (Berkeley: Univ. of California Press, 1994), 191–213, 302–3; Henry Finck, *Anton Seidl: A Memorial by His Friends* (New York, 1899), 35, 42, 102; Huneker, 158; Ralph, 15–16. The Seidl

Society Archive, BHS, contains four clipping books, numerous programs, and voluminous correspondence relating to these concerts.

38. *Brooklyn Eagle*, 21 June 1892 ("rescue"); 7 July 1892 ("insane"); Cook, 87–99.

39. Stephen Crane, *The Works of Stephen Crane: Tales, Sketches, and Reports*, ed. Fredson Bowers (Charlottesville: Univ. Press of Virginia, 1973), 8:324; Norman Anderson and Walter Brown, *Ferris Wheels: An Illustrated History* (New York: Pantheon, 1983), 5–31; William Mangels, *The Outdoor Amusement Industry* (New York: Vantage, 1952), 105–15; Snow, 13, 76; stereograph 52, F91–183, and 58 ("Razzle-Dazzle," ca. 1895), 91–F177, Dennis Collection.

40. *Brooklyn Eagle*, 21 June 1892; *New York Herald*, 2 June 1884; *Frank Leslie's*, 24 July 1886; Mangels, 81–102; *NYT*, 28 Sept. 1896; 9 Mar. 1919; John Sears, *Sacred Places: American Tourist Attractions in the Nineteenth Century* (New York: Oxford Univ. Press, 1989), 192–96; Snow, 36–43, 84–85; photograph of Elephant Hotel and coaster, V1974.22.442, BHS. For mechanical novelties at amusement park Coney, see *Scientific American* articles: "Looping the Double Loop" (90 [25 June 1904]: 493); "Leap-Frog Railway" (93 [8 July 1905]: 29–30); "Mechanical Joys of Coney Island" (99 [15 Aug. 1908]: 101, 108–10); "Mechanical Side of Coney Island" (103 [6 Aug. 1910]: 104–5, 112–13).

41. *Brooklyn Eagle*, 28 June 1892 ("better than railroads"); *Brooklyn Union*, 18 Aug. 1884; 18 June 1885; 25 July 1885; William Manns et al., *Painted Ponies: American Carousel Art* (Millwood, N.Y.: Zon, 1986), 9–25, 100–177.

42. *HW*, 6 Aug. 1881; 14 Sept. 1889; *Brooklyn Eagle*, 2, 10, 17 July 1880; 7, 14 Aug. 1880; 8, 29 July 1882; 20 June 1897; *NYT*, 13–14 Aug. 1883; 11 July 1888; 27 June 1894; 26 May 1895; 6 June 1896; Weinstein, "Nickel Empire," 76–77, 85; Andrea Dennett and Nina Warnke, "Disaster Spectacles at the Turn of the Century," *Film History* 4 (1990): 101–11.

43. Crane, *Works*, 8:322–28; *Wonderful Account*, 10; *NYT*, 6 May 1877; 20, 27 Aug. 1877; 30 May 1879; Sweet, 29; Percy, 12–13; Charles Norton, *American Seaside Resorts* (New York, 1883), 95; Robert Bogdan, *Freak Show: Presenting Human Oddities for Fun and Profit* (Chicago: Univ. of Chicago Press, 1988), 55–58; Andrea Dennett, *Weird and Wonderful: The Dime Museum in America* (New York: New York Univ. Press, 1997), 66–85.

44. Ralph, 10; *The Story of Manhattan Beach*, 37; *Chicago Herald* quoted in *St. Regis Falls Adirondack News*, 4 Aug. 1888; Weinstein, "Nickel Empire," 73–74 ("horrid"); 197 ("whirlpool"); "Watching the Bathers," stereograph 38, 91–F177, Dennis Collection; *Coney Island Souvenir*, 12; *Poor Bertha Barton; or, The Coney Island Mystery* (New York, 1877). See Mary Dunlop, *Sixty Miles from Contentment: Travelling the Nineteenth-Century American Interior* (New York: Basic, 1995), 161–67, for the rarely recorded (but probably common) case of men sneaking below the decks of steamboats to peek up women's skirts through holes in the floor.

45. Felicia Holt, "Promiscuous Bathing," *Ladies Home Journal* 7 (Aug. 1890): 6–7; Peiss, 115–38.

46. *Adirondack News*, 4 Aug. 1888; trade card in BHS; personals from *Coney Island Sun*, 14 Sept. 1878, quoted in Weinstein, "Nickel Empire," 72; Lauren Rabinovitz, *For the Love of Pleasure: Women, Movies, and Culture in Turn-of-the-Century Chicago* (New Brunswick: Rutgers Univ. Press, 1998), 154–67; see Thomas Edison's short, "Cakewalk at Coney Island," filmed in the 1890s and excerpted in *Coney Island: A Documentary Film* (Santa Monica, 1991), produced by Ric Burns and Buddy Squires.

47. Crane, *Works*, 8:326; "The Looker On," *Brooklyn Life* 13 (27 June 1896); *Brooklyn Eagle*, 25 Apr. 1894 ("rowdyism"); 27 Apr. 1894 ("barbarism"; "stupidest"); 3, 5 May 1894 ("cleaned out"); 12 Aug. 1895; 12 June 1897; 23 July 1900 ("Vice Supreme"); *NYT*, 24–30 Mar. 1894; 23–27 Apr. 1894; 24 June 1895; 8 July 1895; Ralph, 3.

48. *Seeing Coney Island of Today: An Illustrated Guide and Souvenir* (New York: Cupples and Leon, 1904): 1; Lindsay Denison, "The Biggest Playground in the World," *Munsey's* 33 (Aug. 1905): 562; Albert Paine, "The New Coney Island," *Century* 68 (Aug. 1904): 537; Slosson, 135; *HW*, 8 July 1905; *NYT*, 2 Sept. 1909; 24 Oct. 1909. For transit, see *Brooklyn Life*, 8 Aug. 1896; *Brooklyn Eagle*, 28 June 1892; 12 Aug. 1895; 12 June 1896; 29 Mar. 1899; *NYT*, 8–10 July 1897.

49. *Brooklyn Eagle*, 27–28 May 1911; 5 July 1911; Snow, 113; Gatlin, 330–35.

50. Gillman, "Coney Island," 283; *New York Tribune*, 30 June 1901; McCullough, 191–98, 328; *NYT*, 16 July 1939; Nasaw, 243–55; Weinstein, "Nickel Empire," 286–90; Bruce Watson, "Three's a Crowd, They Say, but Not at Coney Island," *Smithsonian* 27 (Dec. 1996): 101–2.

51. Ross, 2:40–42; *Brooklyn Union*, 25, 30 July 1883; 4, 18 Aug. 1883; 12 Aug. 1884; *Brooklyn Eagle*, 8 Apr. 1887; New York [State], *Proceedings*, 2:1453–99; Minority Report (doc. 111), 2: 17–18; Lyon, 19; Weinstein, "Nickel Empire," 109–11, 205. One of the most frequently used histories of Coney Island was written by George Tilyou's nephew and takes a particularly dim view of McKane's reign; McCullough, vi, 113.

52. Frederic Thompson, "Amusing the Million," *Everybody's* 19 (Sept. 1908): 385–86; Weinstein, "Nickel Empire," 255–56; for a sampling, see "Apotheosis of Coney Island," *Current Literature* 35 (Sept. 1903): 326; "The Awakening of Coney Island," *HW*, 4 May 1901; Charles Davis, "The Renaissance of Coney," *Outing* (Aug. 1906): 513–22; Rollin Hartt, "The Amusement Park," *Atlantic Monthly* 99 (May 1907): 677; Richard LeGallienne, "Human Need for Coney," *Cosmopolitan* 39 (July 1905): 239–46; Neal, 825; Denison, 557–62; Paine, 537–38; Slosson, 135.

53. McKane trial scrapbook, vol. 1, BHS; William Allen, "Opportunities at Coney Island," *Charities* 12 (4 June 1904): 580–82; Denison, 557–66; Elmer Harris, "The Day of Rest at Coney Island," *Everybody's* 19 (July 1908): 34; Creedmore, 745–48; *New York Tribune*, 15, 19 July 1901; Pilat and Ranson, 33–34, 53–56; *Brooklyn Eagle*, 9 July 1902.

54. O. Henry [William Sydney Porter], "The Greater Coney Island," in *Complete*

Works of O. Henry (Garden City, N.Y.: Garden City Publishing, 1937), 889; Neal, 824–25; "Mechanical Side of Coney Island," 112–13; Snyder-Grenier, 193–94; Marietta Holley, *"Samantha at Coney Island and a Thousand Other Islands" by Josiah Allen's Wife* (Norwood, Mass.: Christian Herald, 1911), 312–13. The Bowery was also periodically "reformed"; *NYT*, 30 Apr. 1894; 6, 14 May 1894; Denison, 564.

55. Maxim Gorky, "Boredom," *Independent* 63 (8 Aug. 1907): 309–17; Huneker, 152–64; Neal, 819–25; LeGallienne, 239–41; Richard Edwards, *Popular Amusements* (New York: Association Press, 1915), 105–9; Guy Carryl, "Marvelous Coney Island," *Munsey's* 25 (Sept. 1901): 815; *Brooklyn Eagle*, 11 July 1899; Sylvester Baxter, "Seaside Pleasure-Grounds for Cities," *Scribner's* 23 (June 1898): 676–87.

Gorky's critique anticipated the Frankfurt school's emphasis on consumption as a compensation for boredom and social entrapment. Theorists such as Herbert Marcuse and Theodor Adorno posited mass leisure as a monolithic oppressor that encouraged political passivity. Leisure culture legitimated the existing order and mystified the sources of exploitation in the system, resulting in a false consciousness based on false needs. Culture suppressed the consumer-oriented proletariat's capacity for resistance and rendered the concept of a revolutionary class struggle obsolete; see Theodor Adorno, *The Culture Industry: Selected Essays on Mass Culture* (London: Routledge, 1991): 53–92; 182–88, 213–14; Herbert Marcuse, *One-Dimensional Man* (Boston: Beacon, 1964), 5, 246. The not-so-subtle elitism of intellectuals is skewered in Paul Gorman, *Left Intellectuals and Popular Culture in Twentieth-Century America* (Chapel Hill: Univ. of North Carolina Press, 1996), Patrick Brantlinger's *Bread and Circuses: Theories of Mass Culture as Social Decay* (Ithaca: Cornell Univ. Press, 1983), and Andrew Ross, *No Respect: Intellectuals and Popular Culture* (New York: Routledge, 1989). Pierre Bourdieu argued in *Distinction: A Social Critique of the Judgment of Taste*, trans. Richard Nice (1979; Cambridge: Harvard Univ. Press, 1984), that systems of domination find expression in virtually all areas of cultural practice, including choices of food, dress, music, and by extension, resorts and vacations.

56. Edwards, 107 ("profit"); Slosson, 135–39; Edward Tilyou, "Human Nature with the Brakes Off; Or: Why the Schoolma'am Walked into the Sea," *American Magazine* 94 (July 1922): 19–21, 92–94. The *New York Times*, 24 Oct. 1909, reported the average visitor to Coney Island spent $2.25.

57. Gorky, 316; Lyon, 15 ("damn"); Thompson, "Amusing," 378–86; Tilyou, 92–94 ("hardworking"; "confidence men"); Frederic Thompson, "Summer Show," *Independent* 62 (20 June 1907): 1462 ("fun"); Peiss, 128–29.

58. Thompson, "Summer Show," 1460–63; Kasson, *Amusing*, 60–61; Tilyou, 19 ("great glee"), 91–94; Thompson, "Amusing," 378–87 ("carnival spirit").

59. Carryl, 809 ("doors").

60. Pilat and Ranson, 160–61, 173, 311–24; Snow, 31.

61. Nasaw, 86, 221–40.

62. Gatlin, 326; Albert McLean, *American Vaudeville as Ritual* (Lexington: Univ.

Press of Kentucky, 1968), 1–37, 66–90; Robert Snyder, *The Voice of the City: Vaude-ville and Popular Culture in New York* (New York: Oxford Univ. Press, 1989), 9–41, 84, 101–2, 130–54; Richard Butsch, "Bowery B'hoys and Matinee Ladies: The Re-Gendering of Nineteenth-Century American Theater Audiences," *American Quar-terly* 46 (Sept. 1994): 374–77; Nasaw, 19–33 ("vulgarity").

63. Charles Rearick, *Pleasures of the Belle Époque: Entertainment and Festivity in Turn-of-the-Century France* (New Haven: Yale Univ. Press, 1985), 201, 219–20 ("true fetes"); Thompson, "Summer," 1463; O. Henry, "Greater Coney," 890. O. Henry also satirized Coney Island in "A Lickpenny Lover," in *Complete Works*, 1228–32.

64. *HW*, 12 Sept. 1891; 14 Sept. 1889; Ralph, 16–18; Crane, *Works*, 8:322–28.

Conclusion

1. *Albany Daily Advertiser,* 25 Aug. 1827; Michael O'Brien, ed., *An Evening When Alone: Four Journals of Single Women in the South, 1826–1867* (Charlottesville: Univ. Press of Virginia, 1993), 89.

2. *NYT,* 5 Jan. 1903; *Coney Island: A Documentary Film,* produced by Ric Burns and Buddy Squires, written by Richard Snow (Santa Monica, 1991); John Doyle, "Looking through a Trunk Full of Memories," *Brooklyn Bridge* 3 (Oct. 1997): 68–69.

3. Nancy Struna, *People of Prowess: Sport, Leisure, and Labor in Early Anglo-America* (Chicago: Univ. of Illinois Press, 1996), 1–33, 74–95, 119–42; Bruce Dan-iels, *Puritans at Play: Leisure and Recreation in Colonial New England* (New York: St. Martin's, 1995), 141–59, 215–21; Robert Malcolmson, *Popular Recreations in English Society, 1700–1850* (Cambridge: Cambridge Univ. Press, 1973), 1–14.

4. George Curtis, *Lotus-Eating: A Summer Book* (New York, 1856), 12, 29–56, 188–89; Pierre Berton, *Niagara: A History of the Falls* (New York: Kodansha, 1992), 19–51. For the West, see John Muir, *Letters to a Friend* (1915; Dunwoody, Ga.: Norman Berg, 1973), 80–81; Rudyard Kipling, *American Notes* (Norman: Univ. of Oklahoma Press, 1981), xvii, 87–104; Samuel Bowles, *Across the Continent* (New York, 1865), 280; Earl Pomeroy, *In Search of the Golden West: The Tourist in Western America* (New York: Knopf, 1957), 52–72; Sally Kabat, "Home Away from Home: The Architectural Geography of Hotels in the American Southwest, 1880–1920" (Ph.D. diss., Univ. of New Mexico, 1994), 66–227.

5. "Summer Hotels," *Nation* 39 (11 Sept. 1884): 217; Friedrich Ratzel, *Sketches of Urban and Cultural Life in North America,* ed. and trans. Stewart Stehlin (New Brunswick: Rutgers Univ. Press, 1988), 67.

6. Victor Turner and Edith Turner, *Image and Pilgrimage in Christian Culture* (New York: Columbia Univ. Press, 1978), 34, 251; Mark Carnes, *Secret Ritual and Manhood in Victorian America* (New Haven: Yale Univ. Press, 1989), 2–36.

7. Worker quoted in Jefferson Williamson, *The American Hotel: An Anecdotal His-tory* (New York: Knopf, 1930), 135; *Oxford English Dictionary,* 2d ed., s.v. "leisure."

8. Stephen Crane, *The Works of Stephen Crane: Tales, Sketches, and Reports,* ed.

Fredson Bowers (Charlottesville: Univ. Press of Virginia, 1973), 8:516; *Times* (London), 9 Dec. 1887. Michel Foucault places far too much theoretical emphasis on Jeremy Bentham's "panopticon," a circular prison project designed by Bentham in 1791 (though it was never built) in which prisoners could at all times be observed; voyeuristic curiosity was a nineteenth-century commonplace; see Michel Foucault, *Discipline and Punish: The Birth of the Prison,* trans. Alan Sheridan (New York: Pantheon, 1977), 200–209; Richard Hamilton, *The Social Misconstruction of Reality: Validity and Verification in the Scholarly Community* (New Haven: Yale Univ. Press, 1996), 175–81.

9. See Guy de Maupassant, *Mount Oriol* (1887; Paris: Louis Canard, 1911), 304, on European spas: "They are the only fairylands left upon the earth! In two months more things happen in them than in the rest of the universe during the remainder of the year. One might say with truth that the springs are not mineralized, but bewitched."

10. Chris Rojek, *Capitalism and Leisure Theory* (London: Tavistock, 1985), 13–33; Juliet Schor, *The Overworked American: The Unexpected Decline of Leisure* (New York: Basic, 1991), 12–15, 50–56; E. P. Thompson, "Time, Work-Discipline, and Industrial Capitalism," *Past and Present* 38 (1967): 56–97. Paradoxically, the preposterously wealthy industrial capitalists who built palaces at Newport could best step outside the resort market and the time thrift that characterized the modern era. One Bellevue Avenue resident never wore a watch in her life, for as she said, "It makes me nervous to think I have to be somewhere at exactly a certain minute"; Eileen Slocum, "Memories of Bellevue Avenue: The Story of a Newport Family," *NH* 67 (Summer 1995): 43, 50.

11. Washington Gladden, *From the Hub to the Hudson* (Boston, 1869), iv; Charles Murray, *Adventures in the Wilderness; or, Camp-Life in the Adirondacks* (Boston, 1869), 1–64; Robert Taylor, *Saranac: America's Magic Mountain* (New York: Paragon, 1988), 25–54. Minister Russell Conwell delivered the lecture *Acres of Diamonds* (Old Tappan, N.J.: Fleming Revell, 1960), 24, more than six thousand times from 1870 to 1930, preaching the social acceptability of wealth; Reverend Caleb Winchester allegorized his European tour in *Gospel of Foreign Travel* (Rochester, 1891). The treatment of neurasthenia, a popular pseudodisease of the nineteenth century, centered around travel as a form of "climatotherapy"; Francis Gosling, *Before Freud: Neurasthenia and the American Medical Community, 1870–1910* (Chicago: Univ. of Illinois Press, 1987), 1–32, 108–35.

12. "Private vs. Public Resorts," *Independent* 53 (6 June 1901): 1331–33 ("in the end"); William Dean Howells, "Confessions of a Summer Colonist," *Atlantic Monthly* 82 (Dec. 1898): 742–46; Marietta Holley, *Samantha at Saratoga or, "Racin' after Fashion" by Josiah Allen's Wife* (Philadelphia, 1887), 129–35, 227, 242; Melvyn Greene, *Marketing Hotels and Restaurants into the Nineties: A Systematic Approach to Increasing Sales* (London: Heinemann, 1987), 47–48. Richard Gittelson and John Crompton, "Insights into the Repeat Vacation Phenomenon," *ATR* 11 (1984): 199–

217 ("their kind"); Roy Wood, "Hotel Culture and Social Control," *ATR* 21 (1994): 67, 77–79.

13. Norbert Elias and Eric Dunning, *Quest for Excitement: Sport and Leisure in the Civilizing Process* (Oxford: Basil Blackwell, 1986), 63–74, 116–25; Erving Goffman, *Interaction Ritual: Essays in Face-to-Face Behavior* (Chicago: Aldine, 1967), 196, 262–70.

14. Neil Harris, *Humbug!: The Art of P. T. Barnum* (Chicago: Univ. of Chicago Press, 1973), 256–70; Charles Funnell, *By the Beautiful Sea: The Rise and High Times of That Great American Resort, Atlantic City* (New York: Knopf, 1975), 56–59.

15. For a worker's view, see "Review of Boot Cotton Mills Museum, Lowell National Historical Park," *Journal of American History* (June 1993): 198–202.

16. *NYT*, 18 July 1880; "The People at Play," *World's Work* 4 (Aug. 1902): 2373–78; Kathy Peiss, "Commercial Leisure and the 'Woman Question,'" in *For Fun and Profit: The Transformation of Leisure into Consumption*, ed. Richard Butsch (Philadelphia: Temple Univ. Press, 1990), 105–17.

17. The vestiges of this liminality account for the vacation's enduring hold on the American consciousness. In *Signatures of the Visible* (New York: Routledge, 1990), 25, 34, and *The Ideologies of Theory: Essays, 1971–1986* (Minneapolis: Univ. of Minnesota Press, 1988), 2:61–74, Fredric Jameson notes that although mass culture's capitalist processes reify cultural expression into commodity, they still must address utopian hopes and dreams in order to appeal to modern audiences.

18. Italian political theorist Antonio Gramsci speculates that hegemonic groups have utilized economic and cultural means to legitimate the current social order through negotiation and compromise. In a sense, this is a functionalist analysis, for Gramsci implies that once the system has been installed, mechanisms that serve the interest of the dominant group reproduce unequal social relations without any conscious effort; Antonio Gramsci, *Selections from the Prison Notebooks*, trans. Quintin Hoare and Geoffrey Smith (New York: International, 1971), 286, 12, 333, 181–82, 269–72, 277–318. The literature on the nature and validity of Gramsci's theory of hegemony is voluminous; for a sampling, see Stuart Hall and Tony Jefferson, eds., *Resistance through Rituals: Youth Subcultures in Postwar Britain* (London: HarperCollins Academic, 1976), 9–74; T. Jackson Lears, "The Concept of Cultural Hegemony: Problems and Possibilities," *American Historical Review* 90 (June 1985): 567–93; John Diggins, "Comrades and Citizens: New Mythologies in American Historiography," *American Historical Review* 90 (June 1985): 614–34; James Scott, *Domination and the Art of Resistance: Hidden Transcripts* (New Haven: Yale Univ. Press, 1990), 70–107; Chris Rojek, *Ways of Escape: Modern Transformations in Leisure and Travel* (Lanham, Md.: Rowman and Littlefield, 1994), 10–50.

19. Max Gluckman, *Order and Rebellion in Tribal Africa* (New York: Free Press, 1963), 110–36; Peter Burke, *Popular Culture in Early Modern Europe* (New York: Harper and Row, 1978), 199–204; Victor Turner, ed., *Celebration: Studies in Festivity and Ritual* (Washington, D.C.: Smithsonian Institution Press, 1982), 27–28; Bruce

Lincoln, *Discourse and the Construction of Society: Comparative Studies of Myth, Ritual, and Classification* (New York: Oxford Univ. Press, 1989), 53–90. People can, in fact, refashion the objects and messages created for them by the dominant cultural order to fit their own values and needs; see John Fiske, *Understanding Popular Culture* (Boston: Unwin Hyman, 1989), 5, 133–62; T. Jackson Lears, "Making Fun of Popular Culture," *American Historical Review* 97 (Dec. 1992): 1417. Not all aspects of culture and consumption, however, are polysemic texts open to negotiation. In the *Chronicle of Higher Education* 43 (14 Feb. 1997): A16, Lears attacks the "cultural slumming" of scholars who engage in "pseudopopulist celebration of corporate-sponsored entertainment as an expression of popular taste." Warren Susman defends popular culture in *Culture as History: The Transformation of American Society in the Twentieth Century* (New York: Pantheon, 1984), xxix, 162, but concedes that most of it is "manipulative, coercive, vulgar, and intolerable."

20. *HW,* 9 Aug. 1890 ("ebb tide"); *NYT,* 3 July 1910; Harrison Rhodes, *In Vacation America* (New York: Harper and Bros., 1915), 65–71; John Jakle, *The Tourist: Travel in Twentieth-Century North America* (Lincoln: Univ. of Nebraska Press, 1985), 53–54, 301–8; Dona Brown, "The Twentieth-Century Tour: The Decline of the Great Hotels," in "The Grand Resort Hotels and Tourism in the White Mountains," ed. Bryant Tolles, *Historical New Hampshire* 50 (Summer 1995): 125–40.

21. Robert Joki, *Saratoga Lost: Images of Victorian America* (Hensonville, N.Y.: Black Dome, 1998), 160–71. For snippets of Saratoga in the twentieth century, see David Steele, *Vacation Journeys East and West: Descriptive and Discursive Stories of American Summer Resorts* (New York: Putnam's Sons, 1918), 23–43; Mortimer Fraith, "Our Sporting Spa: The Lure of the Races and Laces at Saratoga," *Forum* 62 (Sept. 1919): 345–49; Edith Wharton, *The Buccaneers* (New York: Appleton-Century, 1938), 3–4; Cleveland Amory, *The Last Resorts* (1948; New York: Harper and Brothers, 1952), 412–16; James Kunstler, *The Geography of Nowhere: The Rise and Decline of America's Man-Made Landscape* (New York: Simon and Schuster, 1993), 133–46, 181.

22. Henry James, *The American Scene* (1907; Bloomington: Indiana Univ. Press, 1968), 222–24; Richard O'Connor, *The Golden Summers: An Antic History of Newport* (New York: Putnam's Sons, 1974), 66, 315; Amory, 169–74, 32–48; Charles Jefferys, *Newport: A Short History* (Newport: Newport Historical Society, 1992), 75–93; Tom Gannon and Richard Cheek, *Newport: The City by the Sea* (Woodstock, Vt.: Countryman, 1992), 23.

23. Michael Onorato, "Epilogue," in Edo McCullough, *Good Old Coney Island* (1957; New York: Fordham Univ. Press, 2000), 339–52; *New York Post,* 2 Sept. 1994.

24. *NYT,* 13 June 1999; Hal Rothman, *Devil's Bargains: Tourism in the Twentieth-Century American West* (Lawrence: Univ. Press of Kansas, 1998), 313–37; Sharon Zukin et al., "From Coney Island to Las Vegas in the Urban Imaginary: Discursive Practices of Growth and Decline," *Urban Affairs Review* 33 (May 1998): 627–54; Robert Parker, "Las Vegas: Casino Gambling and Local Culture," in *The Tourist City,* ed. Dennis Judd and Susan Fainstein (New Haven: Yale Univ. Press, 1999), 107–23.

25. Raymond Weinstein, "Disneyland and Coney Island: Reflections on the Evolution of the Modern Amusement Park," *Journal of Popular Culture* 26 (Summer 1992): 131–33; *NYT*, 30 Mar. 1997; Susan Davis, *Spectacular Nature: Corporate Culture and the Sea World Experience* (Berkeley: Univ. of California Press, 1997), 21; John Findlay, *Magic Lands: Western Cityscapes and American Culture after 1940* (Berkeley: Univ. of California Press, 1992), 52–116; Sharon Thach and Catherine Axinn, "Patron Assessments of Amusement Park Attributes," *Journal of Travel Research* 32 (Winter 1994): 51–54.

26. Alexander Moore, "Walt Disney World: Bounded Ritual Space and the Playful Pilgrimage Center," *Anthropological Quarterly* 53 (Oct. 1980): 207–18; "Why Can't We Get Away?" *Newsweek*, 27 July 1998, 43; Neil Harris, *Cultural Excursions: Marketing Appetites and Cultural Tastes in Modern America* (Chicago: Univ. of Chicago Press, 1990), 278–96; Michael Sorkin, ed., *Variations on a Theme Park: The New American City and the End of Public Space* (New York: Noonday, 1992), xiii–xv, 204–32.

Bibliographical Essay

The diaries, letters, visitor accounts, newspaper articles, hotel records, and hundreds of other primary sources consulted in the writing of this book can best be traced in the endnotes to each chapter. In the following essay, I have tried not to duplicate these references but instead to give readers some sense of the secondary literature, emphasizing more recent works on tourism, specific resorts, and leisure culture in nineteenth-century America.

Bruce Manzer's voluminous bibliography entitled "Saratoga County, New York: 1757–1995" (2d ed., 1996) is the starting place for all research on Saratoga Springs. Like many other hard-to-find works on the city, it can be located in the Local History Room at the Saratoga Springs Public Library. Although their lack of documentation can make them frustrating to use, three older books on Saratoga stand out: Hugh Bradley, *Such Was Saratoga* (New York: Doubleday, Doran, 1940), Mel Heimer, *Fabulous Bawd: The Story of Saratoga* (New York: Henry Holt, 1952), and George Waller, *Saratoga: Saga of an Impious Era* (Englewood Cliffs, N.J.: Prentice-Hall, 1966). Several more recent works capture the resort's charm and architectural playfulness, including Robert Joki, *Saratoga Lost: Images of Victorian America* (Hensonville, N.Y.: Black Dome, 1998), and James Kettlewell, *Saratoga Springs: An Architectural History* (Saratoga Springs: Lyrical Ballad, 1991). Janice Grover mines many obscure sources in "Luxury and Leisure in Early-Nineteenth-Century America: Saratoga Springs and the Rise of the Resort" (Ph.D. diss., Univ. of California, Davis, 1973). Theodore Corbett emphasizes Saratoga's resort workers and infrastructure in *The Making of American Resorts: Saratoga Springs, Ballston Spa, Lake George* (New Brunswick: Rutgers Univ. Press, 2001).

Almost any volume of *Newport History* turns up some interesting tidbit on that city, especially the issue entitled "The Business of Leisure: The Gilded Age in Newport" (*Newport History* 62 [Summer 1989]: 3–21). The Providence-oriented *Rhode Island History* is occasionally relevant, for example, Barbara Schreier and Michele Major's article, "The Resort of Pure Fashion: Newport, Rhode Island, 1890–1914" (*Rhode Island History* 47 [February 1989]: 22–34). The best overviews are the aptly titled *Newport: A Short History*, by Charles Jefferys (Newport: Newport Historical Society, 1992), and Judith Boss, *Newport: A Pictorial History* (Virginia Beach: Donning, 1981). Roger Parks edited the useful *Rhode Island: A Bibliography of*

Its History (Hanover: Univ. Press of New England, 1983), but only 3 of the 626 entries on Newport concern hotels; this bibliography was updated in 1989 and in 1995. The city's antebellum period is discussed in Peter Coleman, *The Transformation of Rhode Island, 1790–1861* (Providence: Brown Univ. Press, 1963). I have benefited immeasurably from reading Harold Hurst's fine dissertation, "The Elite Class at Newport, Rhode Island: 1830–1860" (Ph.D. diss., New York Univ., 1975). Antebellum Southern visitors make an appearance in an entertaining chapter in John Hope Franklin's *A Southern Odyssey: Travelers in the Antebellum North* (Baton Rouge: Louisiana State Univ. Press, 1976).

Jane Mulvagh and Mark Weber's *Newport Houses* (New York: Rizzoli, 1989) beautifully depicts the Gilded Age cottages, and Ann Benway's little *Guidebook to Newport Mansions* (Newport: Preservation Society of Newport County, 1984) contains more than enough background information. Paul Baker's *Richard Morris Hunt* (Cambridge: MIT Press, 1980) chronicles this shaper of Gilded Age Newport. The classic text for Newport's role in the creation of a unique American summer architecture is *The Architectural Heritage of Newport, Rhode Island, 1640–1915* (New York: Clarkson Potter, 1967), by Antoinette Downing and Vincent Scully Jr. Two contrasting yet complementary views of Gilded Age Newport are presented in Elizabeth Drexel Lehr, *"King Lehr" and the Gilded Age* (Philadelphia: Lippincott, 1935), and Mary Murphy-Schlichting, "A Summer Salon: Literary and Cultural Circles in Newport, R.I." (Ph.D. diss., New York Univ., 1992). For minority culture, see Richard Youngken, *African Americans in Newport* (Newport: Rhode Island Historical Preservation and Heritage Commission, 1995), and Myra Armstead, *"Lord, Please Don't Take Me in August": African Americans in Newport and Saratoga Springs, 1870–1930* (Chicago: Univ. of Illinois Press, 1999).

Older works on resorts, unencumbered by theory and closer to an oral tradition, can often be invaluable. Richard Barrett's *Good Old Summer Days: Newport, Narragansett Pier, Saratoga, Long Branch, Bar Harbor* (New York: Appleton-Century, 1941) and Cleveland Amory's *The Last Resorts* (1948; New York: Harper and Brothers, 1952) both contain extensive coverage of Newport and Saratoga. A longer and equally entertaining version is Richard O'Connor's *The Golden Summers: An Antic History of Newport* (New York: Putnam's Sons, 1974). Edith Wharton's novels are wonderful sources for examining the Newport plutocracy, but she devotes only a few pages specifically to the city: some passing references in *The House of Mirth* (New York: Scribner's Sons, 1905) and a brief chapter 21 in *The Age of Innocence* (New York: Appleton, 1920). A century has hardly dulled the incisive wit of Thorstein Veblen's *The Theory of the Leisure Class* (1899; New York: Mentor, 1963), which concludes that conspicuous consumption is status-seeking behavior; see also John Diggins' masterful *The Bard of Savagery: Thorstein Veblen and Modern Social Theory* (New York: Seabury, 1978) for analysis.

Almost all accounts of Coney Island tend to overstate the importance of the amusement parks as a cultural phenomenon. John Kasson's *Amusing the Million:*

Coney Island at the Turn of the Century (New York: Hill and Wang, 1978) continues to dominate analysis of the island's history; Robert Snow and David Wright's "Coney Island: A Case Study in Popular Culture" (*Journal of Popular Culture* 9 [Spring 1976]: 960–75) is a shorter version. Two older Coney Island histories that are heavy on wonderful anecdotes but light on documentation are Oliver Pilat and Jo Ranson, *Sodom by the Sea: An Affectionate History of Coney Island* (Garden City, N.Y.: Doubleday, Doran, 1941), and Edo McCullough's *Good Old Coney Island* (New York: Scribner's Sons, 1957). The latter, reprinted by Fordham University Press in 2000, needs to be read with a grain of salt since the author was George Tilyou's nephew. Despite the lack of a central thesis, Stephen Weinstein's historical research shines in his fine dissertation, "The Nickel Empire: Coney Island and the Creation of Urban Seaside Resorts in the United States" (Ph.D. diss., Columbia Univ., 1984). Excellent pictorial material can be found in Richard Snow's *Coney Island: A Postcard Journey to the City of Fire* (New York: Brightwaters Press, 1984); Snow also wrote the screenplay for the entertaining video, *Coney Island: A Documentary Film* (Santa Monica, 1991), produced by Ric Burns and Buddy Squires. Kathy Peiss ponders the role of gender at Coney in a great chapter in *Cheap Amusements: Working Women and Leisure in Turn-of-the-Century New York* (Philadelphia: Temple Univ. Press, 1986). Rem Koolhaas's *Delirious New York: A Retroactive Manifesto for Manhattan* ([1978; New York: Monacelli, 1994], 28–79) contains a stream-of-consciousness essay on Coney Island filled with interesting insights and transpositions.

Raymond Weinstein's "Disneyland and Coney Island: Reflections on the Evolution of the Modern Amusement Park" (*Journal of Popular Culture* 26 [Summer 1992]: 113–64), tends to overdraw the differences between the two. Russel Nye's "Eight Ways of Looking at an Amusement Park" (*Journal of Popular Culture* 15 [1981]: 63–75) fails even to consider that the experience might be hegemonic in nature; a special edition of the *South Atlantic Quarterly* (92 [Winter 1993]), edited by Susan Willis, entitled "The World According to Disney," generally takes a more pessimistic view. The pioneering study of "the outdoor amusement industry" was William Mangel's book of the same name (New York: Vantage, 1952); less useful is Judith Adams, *The American Amusement Park Industry: A History of Technology and Thrills* (Boston: Twayne, 1991). For the world of carnival and the fete, no one can now escape Mikhail Bakhtin's *Rabelais and His World* (trans. Helene Iswolsky [1965; Cambridge: MIT Press, 1968]).

Beaches and shores have drawn a great deal of attention recently. Although it focuses on the European setting, the best analysis by far is Alan Corbin's *The Lure of the Sea: The Discovery of the Seaside in the Western World, 1750–1840* (trans. Jocelyn Phelps [Berkeley: Univ. of California Press, 1994]). Two breezier accounts are Lena Lencek and Gideon Bosker, *The Beach: The History of Paradise on Earth* (New York: Viking, 1998), and John Stilgoe's *Alongshore* (New Haven: Yale Univ. Press, 1994). The history of Coney Island draws immediate comparison with the beach resort of Atlantic City. Charles Funnell's *By the Beautiful Sea: The Rise and High Times of That*

Great American Resort, Atlantic City (New York: Knopf, 1975) is one of the first (and best) serious studies of an American resort. The desire on the part of New York reformers to turn Coney Island into a seaside park was hardly unique, as is made clear in Martin Paulsson's *The Social Anxieties of Progressive Reform: Atlantic City, 1854–1920* (New York: New York Univ. Press, 1994).

Only two decades ago, the study of American resorts and leisure travel could be called a nascent field. Now, there is no shortage of imaginative work on a host of nineteenth-century watering places. Cindy Aron's *Working at Play: A History of Vacations in the United States* (New York: Oxford Univ. Press, 1999) stresses the supposed American wariness toward leisure. Two of the finest books on the American desire for destinations that transcend mundane reality are John Sears, *Sacred Places: American Tourist Attractions in the Nineteenth Century* (New York: Oxford Univ. Press, 1989), and Dona Brown, *Inventing New England: Regional Tourism in the Nineteenth Century* (Washington, D.C.: Smithsonian Institution Press, 1995), although both authors stack the deck by intentionally excluding Saratoga and Coney Island. For the nearby New Hampshire resorts, "The Grand Resort Hotels and Tourism in the White Mountains" (*Historical New Hampshire* 50 [Summer 1995]), edited by Bryant Tolles, contains nine essays of varying quality. Eric Purchase's *Out of Nowhere: Disaster and Tourism in the White Mountains* (Baltimore: Johns Hopkins Univ. Press, 1999) concentrates on the appropriation of cultural imagery by business interests and speculators. The domestic-traveler-turned-tourist is often portrayed as a nitwit, easy to please and happy with a superficial, sanitized, and contrived experience: see Daniel Boorstin, *The Image: A Guide to Pseudo-Events in America* (1961; New York: Atheneum, 1987).

As Elizabeth McKinsey notes in *Niagara Falls: Icon of the American Sublime* (Cambridge: Cambridge Univ. Press, 1985), the "sublimity" of the site made Niagara not only the foremost American nineteenth-century tourist site but perhaps the most unique. William Irwin, *The New Niagara: Tourism, Technology, and the Landscape of Niagara Falls, 1776–1917* (University Park: Pennsylvania State Univ. Press, 1995), takes up the story where McKinsey leaves off, dealing with the transformation from sublime nature to sublime technology. Karen Dubinsky, *The Second Greatest Disappointment: Honeymooning and Tourism at Niagara Falls* (New Brunswick: Rutgers Univ. Press, 1999), is especially convincing in portraying the nineteenth-century falls as a gendered place replete with the forbidden pleasures of (hetero)sexuality, romance, and danger. In *Places on the Margin: Alternative Geographies of Modernity* (London: Routledge, 1991), Rob Shields offers a provocative analysis of the movement of Niagara Falls from a liminal site to a commercial cliché emptied of meaning.

Some useful books on miscellaneous nineteenth-century resorts and tourism include *Victorian Resorts and Hotels,* edited by Richard Guy Wilson (Philadelphia: Victorian Society, 1982); Ellen Weiss, *City in the Woods: The Life and Design of an American Camp Meeting on Martha's Vineyard* (New York: Oxford Univ. Press, 1987); Harold Hochschild, *An Adirondack Resort in the Nineteenth Century: Blue Mountain*

Lake, 1870–1900 (Blue Mountain Lake, N.Y.: Adirondack Museum, 1962); Stuart Blumin and Hansi Durlach, *The Short Season of Sharon Springs: Portrait of Another New York* (Ithaca: Cornell Univ. Press, 1980); Earl Pomeroy, *In Search of the Golden West: The Tourist in Western America* (New York: Knopf, 1957); Roland Van Zandt, *The Catskill Mountain House* (1966; Hensonville, N.Y.: Black Dome Press, 1991); Alf Evers et al., *Resorts of the Catskills* (New York: St. Martin's, 1979); and Harry Weiss and Howard Kemble, *They Took to the Waters: The Forgotten Mineral Spring Resorts of New Jersey and Nearby Pennsylvania and Delaware* (Trenton, N.J.: Past Times Press, 1962). The female presence at the hydropathic resort is discussed in detail in Jane Donegan's *"Hydropathic Highway to Health": Women and the Water-Cure in Antebellum America* (New York: Greenwood, 1986) and Susan Cayleff's *Wash and Be Healed: The Water-Cure Movement and Women's Health* (Philadelphia: Temple Univ. Press, 1987). An examination of the activities of Americans abroad also sheds light on the secular pilgrimage; see Lester Vogel, *To See a Promised Land: Americans and the Holy Land in the Nineteenth Century* (University Park: Pennsylvania State Univ. Press, 1993), William Stowe, *Going Abroad: European Travel in the Nineteenth Century American Culture* (Princeton: Princeton Univ. Press, 1994), and Terry Caesar's insights on guidebooks in *Forgiving the Boundaries: Home as Abroad in American Travel Writing* (Athens: Univ. of Georgia Press, 1995).

In searching for analogs to the hotel, the seductive department store stands out as another reconfiguration of nineteenth-century public space that brought together a heterogeneous crowd oriented to consumption. These stores are ably considered in William Leach, *Land of Desire: Merchants, Power, and the Rise of a New American Culture* (New York: Pantheon, 1993), and there is a fine chapter on A. T. Stewart in Mona Domosh, *Invented Cities: The Creation of Landscape in Nineteenth-Century New York and Boston* (New Haven: Yale Univ. Press, 1996). In "Everything under One Roof: World's Fairs and Department Stores in Paris and Chicago" (*Chicago History* 12 [Fall 1983]: 28–47), Russell Lewis overtly connects the two sites through their emphasis on consumption. Robert Rydell's *All the World's a Fair: Visions of Empire at American International Expositions, 1876–1916* (Chicago: Univ. of Chicago Press, 1984) stresses the way these fairs worked to extend ruling-class hegemony and to legitimate racism.

The role of horse racing and gambling in American society has not drawn much serious interest; the best work to date is Ann Fabian's *Card Sharps, Dream Books, and Bucket Shops: Gambling in Nineteenth-Century America* (Ithaca: Cornell Univ. Press, 1990). Howard Chudacoff portrays the shadowy bachelor world of womanizing, fighting, and boozing in *The Age of the Bachelor: Creating an American Subculture* (Princeton: Princeton Univ. Press, 1999). Saratoga's racetrack draws attention in Edward Hotaling, *They're Off: Horse Racing at Saratoga* (Syracuse: Syracuse Univ. Press, 1995), and Landon Manning, *The Noble Animals: Tales of Saratoga Turf* (Saratoga Springs, 1973).

Several studies detailing the transformation of sports in the nineteenth century are relevant to resorts, especially Steven Riess, *City Games: The Evolution of American Urban Society and the Rise of Sports* (Urbana: Univ. of Illinois Press, 1991), and Melvin Adelman, *A Sporting Time: New York City and the Rise of Modern Athletics, 1820–1870* (Urbana: Univ. of Illinois Press, 1990). Newport's role as a pioneer of the active life is covered in Donald Mrozek, *Sport and American Mentality, 1880–1910* (Knoxville: Univ. of Tennessee Press, 1983). Norbert Elias and Eric Dunning analyze the modern desire for "safe thrills" in *Quest for Excitement: Sport and Leisure in the Civilizing Process* (Oxford: Blackwell, 1986). A useful bibliography is *The Leisure Literature: A Guide to Sources in Leisure Studies, Fitness, Sports, and Travel,* edited by Nancy Herron (Englewood, Colo.: Libraries Unlimited, 1992).

Like the rise of the middle class and the expansion of capitalism, the emergence of consumer society keeps getting pushed to an earlier date in American history. A free market, acquisitiveness, and a rising standard of living all seem to be widespread in both *Of Consuming Interests: The Style of Life in the Eighteenth Century,* edited by Cary Carson et al. (Charlottesville: Univ. Press of Virginia, 1994), and Richard Bushman's *The Refinement of America: Persons, Houses, Cities* (New York: Knopf, 1992). The middle volumes in the Everyday Life in America series—Jack Larkin, *The Reshaping of Everyday Life, 1790–1840* (New York: HarperCollins, 1988), and Thomas Schlereth, *Victorian America: Transformations in Everyday Life* (New York: HarperCollins, 1991)—are wonderful compendiums of social history. Scott Martin deals with the impact of the market economy on more rural patterns of entertainment, especially Fourth of July celebrations, in *Killing Time: Leisure and Culture in Southwestern Pennsylvania, 1800–1850* (Pittsburgh: Univ. of Pittsburgh Press, 1995). The usually forgotten urban South is examined in Patricia Click, *The Spirit of the Times: Amusements in Nineteenth-Century Baltimore, Norfolk, and Richmond* (Charlottesville: Univ. Press of Virginia, 1989). Provocative essays on roller-skating, German American culture, Christian watering places, and stereoscopes can be found in *Hard at Play: Leisure in America, 1840–1940,* edited by Kathryn Grover (Rochester: Strong Museum, 1992).

That the expansion of the market inspired vast cultural anxiety and helped create a distinctive middle-class culture is considered in Karen Halttunen's thought-provoking *Confidence Men and Painted Women: A Study of Middle-Class Culture in America, 1830–1870* (New Haven: Yale Univ. Press, 1982). T. Jackson Lears deals with the unease at the other end of the century in *No Place of Grace: Antimodernism and the Transformation of American Culture, 1880–1920* (New York: Pantheon, 1981). Lawrence Levine's *Highbrow/Lowbrow: The Emergence of Cultural Hierarchy in America* (Cambridge: Harvard Univ. Press, 1988) is a model of lucid historical scholarship and remains invaluable for its description of the creation of a class hierarchy in American culture. The impact of capitalist values on holidays and sex is covered (respectively) in Leigh Schmidt, *Consumer Rites: The Buying and Selling of American Holidays* (Princeton: Princeton Univ. Press, 1995), and Timothy Gilfoyle, *City of Eros: New York City, Prostitution, and the Commercialization of Sex, 1790–*

1920 (New York: Norton, 1992). Warren Susman, in *Culture as History: The Transformation of American Society in the Twentieth Century* (New York: Pantheon, 1984), traces the shift from the older republican, producer-capitalist culture, with its emphasis on "character," to the new twentieth-century consumer culture, which insisted on the dominance of "personality."

Advice and success manuals can be a fascinating source of American attitudes toward leisure; see John Kasson, *Rudeness and Civility: Manners in Nineteenth-Century America* (New York: Hill and Wang, 1990), and Judy Hilkey's examination of the gendered language in these works in *Character Is Capital: Success Manuals and Manhood in Gilded Age America* (Chapel Hill: Univ. of North Carolina, 1998). Daniel Horowitz stresses the ambiguity regarding the value of ambition and materialism in *The Morality of Spending: Attitudes toward the Consumer Society in America, 1875– 1940* (Baltimore: Johns Hopkins Univ. Press, 1985).

Confidence men have attracted considerable attention in these postmodern times; in addition to Karen Halttunen's work, they are analyzed in Gary Lindberg, *The Confidence Man in American Literature* (New York: Oxford Univ. Press, 1982). Kathleen de Grave tries hard to find confidence "women" in *Swindler, Spy Rebel: The Confidence Woman in Nineteenth-Century America* (Columbia: Univ. of Missouri Press, 1995). Neil Harris's classic, *Humbug: The Art of P. T. Barnum* (Chicago: Univ. of Chicago Press, 1973), suggests that the commercial dime-museum audience willingly participated in all the trickery. Andie Tucher discusses the sensationalist nature of the new penny press in *Froth and Scum: Truth, Beauty, Goodness, and the Ax Murder in America's First Mass Medium* (Chapel Hill: Univ. of North Carolina Press, 1994). Gordon Stein's *Encyclopedia of Hoaxes* (Detroit: Gale Research, 1993) is a useful reference tool.

In many studies since the 1970s, historians have conceived of leisure as a cultural battleground and emphasized the active agency of workers and immigrants in resisting repressive capitalist cultural hegemony. According to Roy Rosenzweig, in *Eight Hours for What We Will: Workers and Leisure in an Industrial Society, 1870–1930* (Cambridge: Cambridge Univ. Press, 1983), workers in Worcester, Massachusetts, rejected mobility, thrift, sobriety, and competition through the creation of an alternative culture that endorsed public modes of mutuality and conviviality. Their cousins in the metropolis shatter stuffy "Victorian" culture in Lewis Erenberg's *Steppin' Out: New York Nightlife and the Transformation of American Culture, 1890–1930* (Chicago: Univ. of Chicago Press, 1981). Gunther Barth enthusiastically promotes the egalitarian nature of department stores, baseball parks, and vaudeville houses in *City People: The Rise of Modern City Culture in Nineteenth-Century America* (New York: Oxford Univ. Press, 1980). In *The Voice of the City: Vaudeville and Popular Culture in New York* (New York: Oxford Univ. Press, 1989), Robert Snyder concludes that vaudeville deserves "two cheers" despite its commercialism, racism, and sexism. David Nasaw's darker *Going Out: The Rise and Fall of Public Amusements* (New York: Basic, 1993) relentlessly details the exclusion of African Americans in leisure activities ranging from baseball to amusement parks. The public realm as contested space between competing classes with diverse usage patterns (and perhaps different consciousness) is presented in Paul Boyer, *Urban Masses and Moral Order in America, 1820–1920* (Cambridge: Harvard Univ. Press, 1978), and Susan Davis, *Parades and Power: Street Theater in Nineteenth-Century Philadelphia* (Berkeley: Univ. of California Press, 1986). David Scobey singles out see-and-be-seen culture as affirming class and sexual hierarchies, in "Anatomy of the Promenade: The Politics of Bourgeois Sociability in Nineteenth-Century New York" (*Social History* 17 [May 1992]: 203–28). Essays by Richard Butsch and John Clarke in *For Fun and Profit: The Transformation of Leisure into Consumption,* edited by Richard Butsch (Philadelphia: Temple Univ. Press, 1990), help make sense of it all.

An extensive social science literature affords valuable theoretical perspectives on resorts and tourism. Dean MacCannell's *The Tourist: A New Theory of the Leisure Class* (New York: Schocken, 1976) has become the classic sociological study of modern tourism, although his emphasis on staged inauthenticity has limited applicability to many forms of domestic travel. Current assessments of social science research include Douglas Pearce, *Tourism Today: A Geographical Analysis* (New York: Wiley, 1987); Gareth Shaw and Allan Williams, *Critical Issues in Tourism: A Geographical Perspective* (Oxford: Blackwell, 1994); Donald Lundberg, *The Tourist Business* (6th ed., New York: Van Nostrand, 1990). Also useful in spots are Philip Pearce, *The Social Psychology of Tourist Behavior* (New York: Pergamon, 1982); Eric Leed, *The Mind of the Traveller: From Gilgamesh to Global Tourism* (New York: Basic, 1991); Geoffrey Hindley, *Tourists, Travellers, and Pilgrims* (London: Hutchinson, 1983); and Chris Rojek, *Ways of Escape: Modern Transformations in Leisure and Travel* (Lanham, Md.: Rowman and Littlefield, 1994). Rojek nicely summarizes the historiography of theoretical trends up to but not including postmodernism in *Capitalism and Leisure Theory* (London: Tavistock, 1985). Any issue of *Annals of Tourism Research* contains valuable perspectives and up-to-the-moment research.

Cross-cultural reference helps to place American resorts in perspective. The origins of tourism can be traced in Lynne Withey, *Grand Tours and Cook's Tours: A History of Leisure Travel, 1750–1915* (New York: Morrow, 1997); Swedish anthropologist Orvar Lofgren carries the story through the twentieth century in *On Holiday: A History of Vacationing* (Berkeley: Univ. of California Press, 1999). Excellent general studies of the British seaside and spa include John K. Walton, *The English Seaside Resort: A Social History* (New York: St. Martin's, 1983), and Phyllis Hembry, *The English Spa, 1560–1815: A Social History* (London: Athlone, 1990). The decline of the British seaside resort is covered in *The Rise and Fall of British Coastal Resorts: Cultural and Economic Perspectives,* edited by Gareth Shaw and Allan Williams (London: Mansell, 1997), and an excellent chapter in John Urry's *The Tourist Gaze: Leisure and Travel in Contemporary Societies* (London: Sage, 1990). Across the Channel, Charles Rearick's *Pleasures of the Belle Époque: Entertainment and Festivity in Turn-of-the-Century Paris* (New Haven: Yale Univ. Press, 1985) is useful on the creation of manufactured fetes in an urban environment. Douglas Mackaman, *Leisure Settings: Bourgeois Culture, Medicine, and the Spa in Modern France* (Chicago: Univ. of Chicago Press, 1998), concludes that French spas, in contrast with those of Saratoga, appealed to the middle classes by promoting the therapeutic vacation as a productive expenditure of time. These resorts are also examined in *Villes d'eaux en France*, edited by Lise Grenier (Paris: Institut Français d'Architecture, 1985). James Haug captures the ambivalent interrelationship between host and guest in *Leisure and Urbanism in Nineteenth-Century Nice* (Lawrence: Regents Press of Kansas, 1982).

Victor Turner, who popularized the concept of "ritual liminality" ("Liminal to Liminoid in Play, Flow, and Ritual: An Essay in Comparative Symbology," *Rice University Studies* 60 [Summer 1974]: 53–92), extends it to a wide range of modern ritual activities in *Celebration: Studies in Festivity and Ritual*, edited by Victor Turner (Washington, D.C.: Smithsonian Institution Press, 1982). In the controversial *Image and Pilgrimage in Christian Culture* (New York: Columbia Univ. Press, 1978), Victor and Edith Turner conclude that "a tourist is half a pilgrim, if a pilgrim is half a tourist. . . . Even when people bury themselves in anonymous crowds on beaches, they are seeking an almost sacred, often symbolic, mode of communitas" (20). This definition of tourism has enlivened both studies of pilgrimage and studies of tourism. A good summary of this position can be found in Nelson Graburn's essay, "Tourism: The Sacred Journey," in the pioneering work on the anthropology of tourism edited by Valene Smith, *Hosts and Guests: The Anthropology of Tourism* (2d ed., Philadelphia: Univ. of Pennsylvania Press, 1989). The distinction between pilgrims and tourists is not useful in examining Chinese pilgrimage sites, according to *Pilgrims and Sacred Sites in China*, edited by Susan Naquin and Chün-Fang Yü (Berkeley: Univ. of California Press, 1992), or in Tokugawa Japan, according to Constantine Vaporis's *Breaking Barriers: Travel and the State in Early Modern Japan* (Cambridge: Harvard Univ. Press, 1994). American usage of the idea of tourism as a secular pilgrimage can be found in Alexander Moore, "Walt Disney World: Bounded Ritual Space and the Playful Pilgrimage Center" (*Anthropological Quarterly* 53 [October 1980]: 207–18), and Patrick McGreevy, "Niagara as Jerusalem" (*Landscape* 28 [1985]: 26–32). On the other hand, Erik Cohen ("Pilgrimage and Tourism: Convergence and Divergence," in *Sacred Journeys: The Anthropology of Pilgrimage*, edited by Alan Morinis [Westport, Conn.: Greenwood, 1992], 50–61) feels that the analogy can be pushed too far. Editors John Eade and Michael Sallow take issue with other aspects of the Turners' theory in *Contesting the Sacred: The Anthropology of Christian Pilgrims* (London: Routledge, 1991).

The classic work on the space created when ordinary people emerged from their homes to engage in conversation and display is Jürgen Habermas, *The Structural Transformation of the Public Sphere: An Inquiry into a Category of Bourgeois Society* (trans. Thomas Burger [1962; Cambridge: MIT Press, 1989]). Erving Goffman's provocative microstudies of interpersonal behavior make fascinating reading; the most famous is *The Presentation of Self in Everyday Life* (1959; Woodstock, N.Y.:

Overlook, 1973), in which he discusses front and back regions. For public space, I have also used Richard Sennett's masterful *The Fall of Public Man: On the Social Psychology of Capitalism* (New York: Vintage, 1974). The American city is depicted as a place of disorder and possible sexual danger in Amy Srebnick, *The Mysterious Death of Mary Rogers: Sex and Culture in Nineteenth-Century New York* (New York: Oxford Univ. Press, 1995), and Patricia Cline Cohen, *The Murder of Helen Jewett: The Life and Death of a Prostitute in Nineteenth-Century New York* (New York: Knopf, 1998). Mary Ryan chronicles the ritual ceremonial performance of antebellum urban crowds, and the subsequent privatization and degeneration of public space, in *Civic Wars: Democracy and Public Life in the American City during the Nineteenth Century* (Berkeley: Univ. of California Press, 1997). Kenneth Jackson discusses the American fetish for security and privacy in *Crabgrass Frontier: The Suburbanization of the United States* (New York: Oxford Univ. Press, 1985).

Finally, some intriguing older works still retain their ability to inspire new insights. These include Sebastian De Grazia's elegant *Of Time, Work, and Leisure* (New York: Twentieth Century Fund, 1962) and Mircea Eliade's *The Sacred and the Profane: The Nature of Religion* (trans. Willard Trask [New York: Harcourt, Brace, Jovanovich, 1957]). Johann Huizinga's penetrating *Homo Ludens: A Study of the Play Element in Culture* (1944; Boston: Beacon, 1950) first turned me to the study of the pursuit of pleasure many years ago, and it has borne up exceedingly well over many rereadings.

Index

Brooklyn Jockey Club (Coney Island), 232

Brooks, Charles, 197

brothels, 236, 238–240

Bryant, William Cullen, 106

Buckingham, James, 114, 115

Burgwyn, Anna Greenough, 45

Burr, Aaron, 21, 207

Butler, William, 138

Calhoun, John, 21, 44

Calvert, George, 53, 103

camera obscura, 105

camp meetings, 69, 298n. 49

Canfield, Richard, 155–156, 181, 219, 273

Cape May, N.J., 26, 109, 192; and railroads, 18; on resort circuit, 64; as seaside resort, 57, 60, 77

carnival. See festival

carousel, 97–98, 174, 248–249, 262

carriage parade, 34, 53, 60, 62–63, 199

Casanova de Seingalt, Giovanni, 132–133

Catskill Mountains (N.Y.): Catskill Mountain House, 17, 264; Charles Baldwin at, 133; cottage system at, 166; Jews visit, 106, 108; on resort circuit, 194

celebrity, concept of, 181

Central Park (N.Y.), 99

Chadwick, John, 196–197

Channing, Ann, 44

Channing, George, 46–47

Channing, William Ellery, 55, 59

Chapin, Alfred, 83

character, American, 140

chattel mortgages, at Saratoga, 15–16

Chevalier, Michel, 30

Child, Lydia Maria, 131, 226

Chopin, Kate, 110

Churchill, Randolph, 222

circular railway, 34, 35, 60

Circular Street (Saratoga Springs), 12

Clarke, John, 11–13, 18, 176

Clay, Henry, 21, 79

Cleveland, Grover, 236

Cliff Walk (Newport), 54–55, 62, 192, 200

Clinton, Maria Franklin, 143–144

clothing, at Saratoga, 138, 179

Club House, Saratoga (see also Saratoga Casino), 3, 149–155, 151, 275

Cobden, Richard, 134

Cohen, Jacob, 12

Cohoone, Sarah, 61

Cole, Thomas, 17, 68

Coles, Mrs. Oscar, 136

Comfort, Lucy, 127

commercialization (see also commodification): benefits of, 270–271; at Coney Island, 242–250, 258–259, 262; consumerism, 3, 160, 243; at European resorts, 57; and market economy, 147; at Newport, 330n. 31; at resorts, 2, 5, 267–271, 276–277; at Saratoga, 146–181

commodification (see also commercialization): defined, 178; landscape painting, 62; leisure, 30, 267, 272; mineral water, 11–14, 31, 176–177; panoramas, 35; at Saratoga, 168–169, 175–177; of travel, 242; of visitors, 24, 30, 168–169, 218

Comstock, Anthony, 154–155, 234–235

conductors, celebrity, 246

Coney Island (N.Y.), 75–111, 229–262, 274–275

Coney Island Jockey Club (CIJC), 3, 230–231, 231, 233, 241

Coney Island Point, 79–80, 98, 240

confidence men, 80, 129–131, 153, 267

Congress Hall (Saratoga Springs): and African Americans, 168; on Broadway,

Grosvenor, Eleanor, 20, 24

Grund, Francis, 19, 38

guidebooks: promote Coney Island, 78, 180, 246; promote mineral waters, 12, 177; promote Newport, 47, 61–62; promote resorts, 17, *59;* promote Saratoga, 17–20, 26, 162, 170, 172; relationship to pilgrimage, 67, 70; as souvenirs, 170, 172

Gunther, Charles, 81, 235

Gut, The (Coney Island), 234, 258

Habersham, Robert, 44, 133

Hale, Sarah Joseph, 17, 103, 144

half-holiday, 99–100

Hall, Basil, 16

Hall, Francis, 20

Hall, William, 122

Halleck, Fitz-Greene, 64, 79

Hamilton, Alexander (doctor), 41

Harrison, Benjamin, 174, 236

Harrison, James, 47

Harte, Bret, 107, 153, 197

Hathorn, Henry, 21

Hawthorne, Nathaniel, 17, 57, 67, 139

Hazard, John, 186, 188

health: associated with pilgrimage, 7–8, 68; and Coney Island, 77, 80, 237; and mineral water, 8, 176–177; and Newport, 22, 41; rationalization for travel, 9–10, 57; and Saratoga, 8–9, 11, 22, 24, 176–177

hegemony, 336n. 2, 346n. 18, 347n. 19

Herbert, Victor, *171,* 246

heterosocial leisure (*see also* flirtation): at Coney Island, 108–110, 250–252, *252;* expands capitalism, 271; at Newport, 60–61, 199; resorts as pioneer of, 4, 110, 133–137; at Saratoga, 31, *32, 35, 149*

Higginson, Thomas Wentworth, 197, 213

High Rock Spring (Saratoga Springs), 9, 15, 70–71, 176, 177

Hilliard, Robert, 179

Hilton, Henry, 106, 108, 207

hoaxing, 128–130

Hodgson, Adam, 40

Holley, Marietta, 172, 268

Holmes, Oliver Wendell, Sr., 197

Homer, Winslow, *56, 149*

Hone, Philip, 19, 21, 78, 122, 140

Hooper, Johnson, 130–131

horse racing: commercialization of, 230–233, 337n. 6; at Coney Island, 230–233, *231, 232,* 237; at Saratoga, 3, 146–153, *149*

hot dogs, 239

hotel keepers, 24–25, 54

hotel registers: at Coney Island, 79; at resorts, 132; at Saratoga, 27, 36, 146

hotels: "colonization" of guests, 12, 22; crucial at resorts, 1, 4, 113–121; decline of, 214, 268–273; discomfort at, 115–116; great size, 21–22, 112–121, 157–159; increasing privacy at, 163–166, 177–178; invention of, 112–114; as liminal places, 116, 121–126, 131–132, 145, 265–266; loss of liminality, 163–166, 181–185, 191–193, 197–198, 268–272; as public spaces, 88, 112–121, 162–163, 198, 265–266; rental of space to stores, *157,* 161–162; as tourist attractions, *89,* 113–114, 162; ubiquity of, 78, 93

hotels, at Coney Island (*see also* Brighton Beach Hotel; Manhattan Beach Hotel; Oriental Hotel): "Cables," 82; Coney Island House, 76–79, 132; Coney Island Pavilion, 79–80; Elephant, 95, *97,* 229, 241, 243, 270; expansion of, 78, 87–93; Ocean Hotel, 93; Ocean Pavilion, 239, 249; Pavilion Hotel, 80; Sea Beach Palace,